Samuel Stearns, Robert Hodge, Samuel Campbell

The American Oracle

Samuel Stearns, Robert Hodge, Samuel Campbell

The American Oracle

ISBN/EAN: 9783337375577

Printed in Europe, USA, Canada, Australia, Japan

Cover: Foto ©Thomas Meinert / pixelio.de

More available books at **www.hansebooks.com**

THE
AMERICAN ORACLE.

COMPREHENDING

A N

ACCOUNT OF RECENT DISCOVERIES

IN THE ARTS AND SCIENCES,

WITH

A VARIETY OF RELIGIOUS, POLITICAL, PHYSICAL,
AND PHILOSOPHICAL SUBJECTS,

Neceffary to be known in all *Families*, for the Promotion of their
prefent *Felicity* and future *Happinefs*.

———————

BY THE HONOURABLE
SAMUEL STEARNS, L.L.D.

*And Doctor of Phyfic ; Aftronomer to the Provinces of Quebec and
New-Brunfwick ; alfo to the Commonwealth of Maffachufetts,
and the State of Vermont, in America.*

———————

*Quam ampla funt Opera tua, O Jehova! Quam en
Omnia fapienter fecifti!*

———————

NEW-YORK:

Printed for, and Sold by HODGE and CAMPBELL, BERRY
and ROGERS, and T. ALLEN.
M.DCC.XCI.

[Price two DOLLARS in BOARDS.]

PREFACE.

KIND READER,

THE author in the courfe of his travels in nine of the American governments, and in England, Scotland, Ireland, and France, hath written the Mifcellaneous Work, contained in the fubfequent pages which are now prefented to the public, for the purpofe of fpreading ufeful knowledge amongft the human race.

It was not his defign to have made thofe things public at fo early a period: but to gratify a number of his private friends, who efteemed his productions in a light, perhaps beyond their intrinfic value, and who requefted they might be immediately publifhed for the benefit of mankind, he has been induced to abandon his original intention, and thus publifh them to the world.

Some things in profe are extracted from various authors; but the poetry with the exception of a few lines was compofed by himfelf; and feveral pieces are added which he publifhed in fundry fmall pamphlets in time paft. As the fubjects are numerous, brevity has neceffarily been attended to, and every endeavour ufed to comprehend *multum in parvo*, and alfo to preferve accuracy and correctnefs: But as errors may have efcaped his obfervation, fhould any be difcovered by his readers, he will thankfully receive their communications of the fame, and carefully endeavour to attend to their correction in a future edition.

Philofophy, and the liberal arts and fciences, which have been nurtured by its progrefs and improvements, and has fhone out with fuch remarkable fplendor in thefe modern ages, have been the objects of his early and unremitting ftudy. The practice of phyfic, and the making of aftronomical calculations engaged his attention for upwards of twenty years; he has had a familiar acquaintance with the lateft and moft approved authors upon the liberal and mechanical arts and fciences; has attended lectures upon phyfiology, chymiftry, magnetifm, electricity, optics, aftronomy, and other branches of natural and experimental philofophy, all of which have contributed to furnifh him with the knowledge that is communicated to the public through the medium of this work, and has enabled him to complete it in fuch a manner, that he hopes it may be productive of the good purpofe for which it is intended; and, although it is called the *American Oracle*, yet, by reafon of the variety of fubjects which it comprehends, it will be found to be the *Oracle of the World*, becaufe it contains a general account of the univerfe.

As the work is calculated to diffufe ufeful knowledge amongft mankind, to induce them to fhun vice, and to ftimulate them to acts of goodnefs and virtue, in order to promote their prefent felicity and future happinefs ; fhould it eventually prove conducive to thofe great and important objects, it will be an ample reward for the labour that has attended its profecution, and afford lively fenfations of joy and pleafure, to the reader's and the public's moft

Obedient,

Humble

Servant,

THE AUTHOR.

New-York, Sept. 12, 1791.

E R R A T A:

Page 3, line 25, for 411, read 511.

—— 31 —— 11 for Sept. read Oct. 19.

—— 32 —— 11 for Oct. 6, Peace proclaimed in 1782,
read 1783.

—— 33 —— 9 read Peace proclaimed between Great-
Britain, Holland and America.

—— 60 —— 31 for proceſſion, read preceſſion.

—— 93 —— — for 39 read 93.

——176——10 for colume, read column.

——187—— 7 for twenty millions, read fifty.

——232—— 7 for live wou'd, read live I wou'd.

—— 269 ——24 for are inclined, read is inclined.

——398——18 for inimentum, read Linimentum.

—— 486 —— 1 for 6, read page 486.

—— 602 —— 1 for at, read as.

—— ——— ——15 eraſe out " clean animals that had."

——609—— 12 for a thing is, read a thing which is.

——618——25 for 1789, read 1790.

The author was informed in England, that the Legiſlatures in the United American ſtates, north of Maryland, had ſet all the negroes free; but has been informed ſince his arrival in New-York, that they are
not yet wholly freed in ſome of thoſe governments.
Vid. page, 252. And he has not found any Swedenborghers in this city. Vid. p. 558.

Direction to the book-binder.

Let the figure of the ſolar ſyſtem face the 90th page.

By a late publication in the New-York Daily Advertiſer, it appears that the number of the inhabitants of the United States are by eſtimation as follows: and alſo that they have a right to ſend the annexed number of members to Congreſs.

	Inhabitants.	Members.
*Vermont, - -	85,000	2
New-Hampſhire, - -	141,885	4
Maſſachuſetts, - -	475,327	15
Rhode-Iſland, - -	68,825	2
Connecticut, - -	237,946	7
New-York, - -	340,120	11
New-Jerſey, - -	184,139	5
Pennſylvania, - -	434,373	14
Delaware, - -	59,094	1
Maryland, - -	319,728	9
Virginia, - -	821,287	23
North-Carolina, - -	393,751	11
*South-Carolina, - -	240,000	6
Georgia, - -	82,548	2
*South-weſtern territory, -	30,000	1
*North-weſtern-territory, -	5,000	0
Total, - - -	3,919,023	113

The ſtates marked thus * have their numbers mentioned only by conjecture: The inhabitants of the others have been lately computed. 96,540, of thoſe in Maſſachuſetts belong to the province of Main: and 73,677, of thoſe in Virginia, to Kentuckey.

It appears by this account, that the inhabitants of the ſtates have been much augmented of late, as their numbers are much larger than they were a few years ago. Vid. p. 70.

AMERICAN ORACLE.

C H A P T E R I.

Of CHRONOLOGY—*with Tables of remarkable Æras
and Events, from the Creation to the Year* 1790.

A S *astronomers* begin their computations at certain fixed points in the heavens, called æpo-
chas, or radical places; so *historians* begin their
reckonings from certain fixed points of time, called
æras, or radixes of time; as that of the Creation,
Noah's Flood, &c. as in the subsequent Tables.

	Anno Mundi
The creation of the world	0
Noah's flood	1656
The birth of Abraham	1948
Sodom and Gomorrah destroyed	2107
The departure of the Israelites out of Egypt	2452
Their entrance into Canaan	2492
Saul, the first King of Israel, began to reign	2909
Solomon's temple began	2932
The destruction of Samaria	3226
An angel destroys 184,000 of the Assyrians	3294
Babylonish captivity	3349

B   Solomon's

Anno Mundi

Solomon's temple deſtroyed - -	3360
The beginning of Daniel's 70 weeks	3492
Death of Alexander the Great -	3626
Reſtoration of the Jews - -	3784
Correction of the Calendar by Julius Cæſar	3905
Herod began to reign in Judea -	3949

Anno Domini

The reputed æra of the birth of Chriſt	0
He diſputes with the doctors in the temple	12
Is baptiſed by John in the Wilderneſs -	27
And crucified by the Jews - -	33
Stephen is ſtoned to death - -	34
St. Paul is converted - -	36
St. Matthew writes his Goſpel -	39
The followers of Chriſt firſt called Chriſtians	40
Claudius Cæſar's expedition into Britain	43
St. Mark writes his Goſpel - -	44
London founded by the Romans -	49
The council of the apoſtles at Jeruſalem	52
St. Luke writes his Goſpel - -	55
St. Paul ſent in bonds to Rome, preacheth, and	
writes his epiſtles - -	62
The acts of the apoſtles written -	63
The Chriſtians perſecuted at Rome -	64
St. Peter and St. Paul put to death -	67
Titus takes Jeruſalem; 1,100,000 Jews periſh;	
97,000 taken priſoners - -	70
A plague kills 10,000 perſons at Rome	78
The Philoſophers expelled Rome by Domitian	83
St. John, the evangeliſt, wrote his Revelation	96
Writes his Goſpel - -	97
The Jews murder 200,000 Greeks and Ro-	
mans - - -	115

The

Anno Domini

The Jews all baniſhed out of Judea ; 580,000
    deſtroyed by the Romans   -   135
Juſtin writes his firſt Apology for the Chriſtians 139
Ptolomicus Geographus lived   -   140
Galenicus Medicus lived   -   -   143
Arrianus Hiſtoricus lived   -   -   145
Antoninus Philoſophus lived   -   161
Oppianus Poeta   -   -   -   217
Purgatory invented   -   -   -   250
Silk firſt brought from India to Europe   274
Conſtantine the Great began to reign   306
Cardinals firſt began   -   -   308
The Chriſtian Religion tolerated by Conſtan-
    tine   -   -   -   -   313
The firſt general council at Nice   -   325
St. Martin lived   -   -   -   363
Bells invented by Biſhop Paulinus, of Campag-
    nia   -   -   -   -   400
Rome taken by Alcrie, king of the Viſi-Goths 410
The Romans evacuate Britain   -   -   426
Socrates, an hiſtorian, lived   -   -   -   435
Chriſtianity introduced into Britain by the
    Romans   -   -   -   477
The Chriſtian Religion introduced in France 496
The doctrine of purgatory introduced   411
Dionyſius, a monk, introduces the computing
    of time by the Chriſtian æra   -   516
The manufacturing of ſilk introduced in Eu-
    rope   -   -   -   551
A terrible plague continues near 50 years all
    over Europe, Aſia, and Africa   -   557
Latin ceaſes to be ſpoke in Italy   -   580
Auguſtin, a monk (with 40 more) comes into
    England   -   -   -   596

Anno Domini

The power of the popes begin   -   606

Mahomet dies, aged 64   -   -   634

Jerufalem is taken by the Saracens   -   637

Alexandria in Egypt taken by ditto, and the
    grand library burnt   -   -   640

Glafs invented in England, by Benalt, a monk 664

The Saracens conquer Spain   -   713

The computing of years from the birth of
    Chrift firft ufed in hiftory   -   748

A plague deftroys 34,000 perfons in England 772

Charlemagne, K. of France, gave the prefent
    names to the winds and months   800

Alfred the Great divides England into coun-
    ties, compofes a body of laws, erects county
    courts, and founds the univerfity at Oxford 896

The univerfity at Cambridge founded   915

A plague deftroys 40,000 people in Scotland 954

The coronation oath firft ufed in England,
    and juries firft inftituted   -   979

Figures in arithmetic brought into Europe
    from Arabia, letters having been ufed in
    their room   -   -   991

Paper, made of cotton rags, ufed   -   1000

The Turks take Jerufalem from the Saracens 1065

Mufical notes invented   -   -   1070

Juftices of the peace firft appointed in Eng-
    land   -   -   -   1076

The tower of London built   -   -   1080

The order of Knight Templars inftituted   1118

The canon law collected by Gratian, a
    monk of Bologna   -   -   1151

London bridge firft built of ftone   -   1160

Paper

Anno Domini

Paper firſt made of linen rags -	1170
Glaſs windows began to be uſed in private houſes in England - -	1180
Conjunction of the ſun, moon, and all the planets, in Libra. Sept. -	1186
Dieu et Mon-droit firſt uſed as a motto ,	1194
Chimnies firſt made, and ſirnames firſt uſed, in England - -	1200
Aſtronomy firſt ſtudied by the Moors	1201
London firſt incorporated into a city, with a Mayor, &c. - -	1208
Magna Charta ſigned by King John; and the Court of Common Pleas eſtabliſhed	1215
Aſtronomical tables conſtructed by Alonſo, King of Caſtile - -	1253
Commons firſt ſummoned to Parliament in England - - -	1264
Mariners' compaſs invented, or improved, by Givia of Naples - -	1302
Gold firſt coined in Chriſtendom -	1320
The firſt comet whoſe courſe is deſcribed with exactneſs - - -	1337
The French loſe 400 veſſels, and 30,000 ſeamen, in a ſea-fight with the Engliſh	1340
Gun-powder and guns invented, oil-painting firſt uſed, and the Herald's College inſtituted - - -	1348
Ninety-thouſand people die of a plague in Germany - -	1348
Knights of the Garter inſtituted in England; and a plague deſtroys near nine-tenths of the people in Britain	1349

B 3

Coals

Anno Domini

Coals firft brought to London -	1357
A fhower of hail kills 1000 men, and 6000 horfes, in England - -	1359
A dreadful plague in England -	1361
57,374 people die of a plague in England	1362
Windfor Caftle built - -	1386
A terrible plague and famine in England; and cards invented in France for the King's amufement - -	1391
Weftminfter Abbey re-built -	1399
Guild-hall, in London, built -	1410
The univerfity of St. Andrews, in Scotland, founded - -	1411
Pumps firft invented - -	1425
Printing invented in Holland - -	1440
100,000 people deftroyed by an inundation in Holland - -	1446
The univerfity at Glafgow, in Scotland, founded - - -	1454
Engraving and etching on copper invented	1460
The univerfity of Aberdeen, in Scotland, founded - -	1477
Firft ftanding army in England eftablifhed	1483
Maps and fea-charts firft brought into England - -	1489
The ftudy of the Greek language introduced in England - -	1491
The Spanifh inquifition;—15,000 Jews driven out of Spain - -	1492
America difcovered by Columbus	1492
Algebra firft known in Europe -	1494

South

Anno Domini

South America difcovered by Americus Vefpufius - -	1497
North America difcovered by Sebaftian Cabot, about - -	1498
Thirty thoufand perfons die of a plague in London - - -	1499
Shillings firft coined in England -	1505
Columbus died, aged 59 -	1506
Gardening introduced into England, from the Netherlands; and half of the people die of a plague in Britain	1509
Martin Luther began the Reformation	1517
The Pope gives the title of Defender of the Faith to the King of England	1520
Cannon began to be ufed in fhips -	1539
Pins firft ufed in England, in the room of fkewers; and filk ftockings firft worn by the King of France -	1543
Council of Trent begins -	1545
Firft law in England eftablifhing the intereft of money - -	1546
Books of aftronomy and geography deftroyed, as infected with magic, in England - -	1552
The Reformation compleated in Scotland by John Knox; and filk ftockings firft worn in England by Q. Elizabeth	1561
Knives firft made in England -	1563
The Royal Exchange in London built	1569
Thirty thoufand necromancers in France; and a great maffacre of the Proteftants at Paris - -	1572

B 4

The

Anno Domini

The Dutch in Holland revolt from the Spanifh government   -   -   1579
Eaft India company incorporated   1579
Sir Francis Drake, the firft Englifh circum-
navigator, returns from his voyage
round the world   -   -   1580
New Style introduced in Italy by Pope Gre-
gory.   -   -   -   1582
Tobacco firft brought from Virginia into
England; and Newfoundland fettled by
the Englifh   -   -   1583
Q. Elizabeth beheads Mary Q. of Scots,
after 18 years imprifonment   -   1587
Coaches introduced into England   1589
A band of penfioners inftituted in England 1590
Trinity College, in Dublin, founded   1591
Watches firft brought into England from
Germany   -   -   1597
Theory of the Tides firft given by Keplar   1598
Decimal arithmetic invented at Burges   1602
England and Scotland unite under the name
of Great Britain   -   -   1603
30,578 perfons died of the plague in London 1604
Powder plot difcovered at Weftminfter   1605
Oaths of allegiance firft adminiftered in
England; and Canada fettled by the
French   -   -   1606
Virginia fettled   -   -   1607
New York, the Jerfies, and Pennfylvania,
fettled by the Dutch and Swedes; and
Galileo difcovers four of the fatellites
of Saturn   -   .   -   1608

Six

Anno Domini

Six hundred wizards condemned, and moſt
of them burnt, in France - 1609
Jupiter's moons firſt diſcovered by Galileo 1610
Baronets firſt created in England; and
200,000 perſons die of the plague in
Conſtantinople - - 1611
Logarithms invented by Napier, a Scotch-
man; and Sir Hugh Middleton brings
the New River to London, from Ware 1614
Harvey confirms the circulation of the blood 1619
The broad ſilk manufacture from raw ſilk,
introduced into England; and negroes
firſt imported into Virginia 1620
Nova Scotia ſettled by the Scotch; and
New Plymouth, in New England, ſet-
tled by Puritans - - 1621
Firſt neat cattle imported to America 1624
The iſland of Barbadoes ſettled by the Eng-
liſh; and 35,417 people die of the
plague in London - - 1625
Maſſachuſetts ſettled - - - 1628
New Hampſhire ſettled - - 1629
Boſton built - - - 1630
Maryland ſettled - - 1631
Died of a plague at Lions in France, 60,000
people; and Maryland given to Lord
Baltimore - - 1632
Huygens diſcovers Saturn's ring; and Pro-
vidence, in Rhode Iſland, built 1634.
Connecticut ſettled; and regular poſts eſta-
bliſhed from London to Scotland, Ire-
land, &c. • • - 1635

Rhode

Anno Domini

Rhode Island settled - - -	1638
Newport built - - -	1639
Forty thousand English Protestants massacred by the Irish - -	1640
Sir Isaac Newton born - -	1643
Electricity, the first idea of it, given by Ottoguericke - -	1647
K. Charles I. beheaded, aged 49 -	1649
Cromwell assumes the protectorship	1654
Huygens discovers the fifth moon of Saturn; and Admiral Penn takes Jamaica from the Spaniards -	1655
Cromwell dies - - -	1658
K. Charles II. restored - -	1660
The Royal Society established at London	1662
Carolinas planted - - -	1663
The Dutch and Swedish settlements in North America conquered by the English	1664
68,000 persons die of a plague in London	1665
Great fire in London; and tea first used in England - -	1666
Peace of Breda - -	1667
Peace of Aix-la-Chapelle -	1668
Peace of Ninceguen; and Habeas Corpus act passed - - -	1672
49,487 people die of a plague in Vienna	1679
A great comet appeared from Nov. 3, to March 9; and the true orbits of comets demonstrated by Doetsel -	1680
Philadelphia founded - -	1682

Bayonets

Anno Domini

Bayonets firſt uſed by the French—Bank
   of England eſtabliſhed—and, the firſt
   public lottery drawn   -   -   1693
Stamp duties inſtituted in England   1694
Peace of Ryſwick   -   -   -   1696
Darien, in America, ſettled by the Scotch   1699
Pruſſia erected into a kingdom; and, Soci-
   ety eſtabliſhed for the propagation of
   the goſpel in foreign parts   -   1701
Gibraltar taken from the Spaniards; and
   Court of the Exchequer inſtituted in
   England   -   -   -   1704
Dr. Benj. Franklin born Feb.; and a treaty
   of union between England and Scotland   1706
A new mountain riſes out of the ſea in Tur-
   key, in Europe called *Thera*; and the
   firſt Britiſh parliament   -   1707
Minorca taken from the Spaniards; and
   Sardinia erected into a kingdom   1708
St. Paul's church re-built by Sir Chriſtoph.
   Wren, in 37 years   -   -   1710
The peace of Utrecht, whereby Newfound-
   land, Nova Scotia, New Britain, and
   Hudſon's Bay, were yielded to Great
   Britain, and Gibraltar and Minorca
   were alſo confirmed to the Britiſh crown   1713
Aurora Borealis firſt ſeen   -   1715
A rebellion in Scotland in favour of the
   Pretender   -   -   1715
An act paſſed for ſeptennial parliaments   1716
Lombes, at Darby, erects a ſilk throwing
   machine, containing 26,586 wheels, all
                     of

Anno Domini

of which take up one-eighth of a mile, and are moved by one water wheel : In 24 hours it works 318,504,960 yards of Organzine filk thread   -   1719

Died of a plague, at Marfeilles, 18,000 perfons   -   -   1720

Inoculation firft tried on criminals, with fuccefs ; and Sir Ifaac Newton dies, aged 84 nearly   -   -   1727

Georgia, in North America, fettled ; and Gen. Wafhington born Feb. 11.   1732

Died of a plague at Meffina, in Sicily, 50,000 perfons   -   -   1743

Commod. Anfon returns from his voyage round the world   -   -   1744

A rebellion in Scotland, projected by the French ; and 6000 Americans, with affiftance from England, take Cape Breton from the French   -   1745

Electric fhock difcovered at Leyden, by Cuneus   -   -   -   1746

The peace of Aix-la-Chapelle   -   1748

Weftminfter bridge, after 12 years labour, finifhed : (it coft 389,000l.)   -   1750

The Antiquarian Society at London incorporated   -   -   1751

Sea water made frefh by experiment   1752

Old ftyle ceafes, Sep. 3.   -   -   1752

The Britifh Mufeum erected ; and a Society of Arts, Manufactures, and Commerce, inftituted in London   -   -   1753

A. D. 1754.

A. D. 1754.

The British colonies in North America being almost surrounded by French, Spaniards, and Savages; and the French having augmented their armies, and made encroachments upon the British settlements, by erecting forts on the banks of the river Ohio, to which place Col. Washington, at the head of 4000 men, marches; builds a fort, which, on being demanded by a small party of French, they are taken prisoners. The Governor of Canada attacks the fort; and Washington, on being overpowered with numbers, capitulates, surrenders, and marches towards Virginia. Many of the English are plundered and murdered by the Indians. From hence a war broke out between England and France.

1755.

The English take from the French two ships, 600 soldiers, with their officers, and 5000 crowns, off the banks of Newfoundland.

Two thousand men from New England take Nova Scotia, and disarm 15,000 neutral French and Indians.

Gen. Braddock defeated by the French and Indians, near Fort du Quesne

Gen. Johnson defeats the French at Fort Edward, and takes their commander, Baron de Dieskau, prisoner

Gen. Johnson is created a Baronet, and the parliment gives him 5000l. for his good services.

Gerith, near Bombay, taken by the English.

A. D. 1756.

A. D. 1756.

The French land 18,000 troops on the island of Minorca. Admiral Byng's cowardice. Fort St. Philip, and Fort St. Ofwego, taken by the French. Marine Society established in London. Parliament resolves to augment the land army from 35,000 to 49,749 effective men; and the seamen to 55,000, including 11,419 marines; and to raise 8,350,325l. to defray the charges of the war, &c.

That the electric fluid would emit sparks, discovered

1757.

Admiral Byng shot. The Duke of Cumberland goes to Hanover; has sundry battles with the French: Resigns, and Prince Ferdinand succeeds him—who obtains several victories over the Gallic troops, and recovers a number of places that had been in their possession. The Isle of Aix taken from the French. The French take and demolish Fort William Henry. Bufbudgia, in Bengal, with sundry other places, are taken by the English. The Nabob's army is defeated: he is imprisoned, and put to death.

Admiral Watson dies. Parliament settles the supplies, which amount to 10,486,452l.

1758.

Several French vessels are taken by the English near Carthagena. The Prince George, of 80 guns, commanded by Rear-Admiral Broderick, on a passage to the Mediterranean, accidentally takes fire, and burns till she sinks: The admiral, with about 300 men, make their escape

A. D. 1758.

escape to land; and 500 perish. Lord Anson
and Sir Edward Hawke sail to St. Malo. The
British troops, under the command of the Duke
of Marlborough, take possession, and burn a
French fleet, consisting of 2 men of war, 33
privateers, and above 70 sail of merchant
ships.

The English fleet and army leave St. Malo, and
take possession of Cherburgh, where they destroy the famous bason, harbour and sluice, in
that place. They leave Cherburgh, go to St.
Briac, near St. Malo, and destroy about 15
small vessels. On re-embarking, the French
fall on them, and kill and take about 1000
men. Gen. Drury and Sir John Armitage
were among the slain.

Fort Louis and the town of Senegal taken by the
English. Goree taken from the French by
Commodore Keppel.

Fifty thousand English troops in America. Gen.
Amherst and Admiral Boscawen take Cape
Breton. The Island of St. John, in the Gulph
of St. Lawrence, taken from the French by the
English, under the command of Lieutenant-
Colonel Lord Rollo. Gen. Abercrombie re-
pulsed at Ticonderoga—where Lord Howe is
slain.

Fort Frontinac taken from the French and Indians,
by Col. Bradstreet: He destroys nine armed
vessels belonging to the enemy.

Brigadier-General Forbes takes Fort du Quesne
from the French.

The

A. D. 1758.

The Englifh demolifh a fort in Grand Ana Bay, in
Martinico, and take four privateers from the
French.

Prince Ferdinand, with the allied army, obtains
great victories over the French in the Hanove-
rian dominions.

The Duke of Marlborough dies. Parliament grants
12,761,310l. 19s. 5d. to fupport the war.

1759.

The French and the Pretender meditate to invade
England.

Admiral Rodney bombards Havre, and burns the
ftores intended for the invafion. The French
abandon the town.

Admiral Bofcawen cannonades the French at Tou-
lon. Afterwards he takes two French men of
war, and deftroys two more, near Gibraltar.

Sir Edward Hawke blocks up the French fleet in
the harbour of Breft, but is driven from thence
by a ftorm. The French purfue, and are defeated by having a number of their fhips deftroyed by Sir Edward, which renders their
intention of invading England abortive.

Guadaloupe taken by the Englifh, commanded by
Gen. Hopfon and Barrington, with the iflands
Defeada, Los Santos, and Marigalante, in the
Weft Indies. The French in Canada induce
the favages to commit the moft horrid barbari-
ties upon the fubjects of New England. The
Englifh make peace with fifteen Indian nations.
Gen. Amherft takes Ticonderago and Crown
Point.

A. D. 1759.

Point. Sir William Johnſon takes Niagara.
Gen. Wolfe killed, Sept. 12. Quebec taken,
Sept. 18. Col. Ford obtained a complete victory over the French near Maſulipatam. Col.
Maitland takes the town and caſtle of Suart.
Vice-Admiral Pocock fights with a French
fleet, and becomes maſter of the Indian coaſt.
A Dutch Commodore refuſing to let Captain
Wilſon paſs, the Captain reinforces Col. Coote
on the coaſt of Coromandel, defeats the French,
and takes four of the Commodore's ſhips ; and
alſo took Fort Wandewaſh. Theſe victories
were in the Eaſt Indies.

Minden, in Hanover, taken from the French by
Prince Ferdinand.

Munſter taken by Gen. Imhoff. Many more ſkir-
miſhes happened in that country that year, in
which the Engliſh and allied armies were vic-
torious.

Parliament raiſes 16,130,561l. 9s. 8d. for de-
fraying the charges of the war.

1760.

The French take Carrickfergus in Ireland, which
they leave ſuddenly : are overtaken near the
Iſle of Man, by Capt. Elliot, Capt. Logie, and
Capt. Clement. A ſmart engagement enſues,
in which the French ſquadron are taken, and
their Commander, M. de Thurot, is ſlain.

The Cherokee Indians on the back of North Carolina (inſtigated by the French) break the peace,
and plunder and maſſacre many of the Britiſh
ſubjects.

C   The

The Governor of North Carolina makes peace with
them; but as foon as he had returned home,
they attempted to furprife Fort George, killed all the Englifh traders in their country,
and maffacred forty of the defencelefs inhabitants.

Gen. Amherft fends Col. Montgomery with 1200
men, who chaftifed the Cherokees by deftroying every village and houfe in the lower nation,
putting great numbers to death, and bringing
40 women and children as prifoners to Fort
George.   Afterwards they made another ex-
curfion in the middle fettlements, deftroying
all before them with fire and fword.   The Indians, in revenge, attacked Fort London; and,
after granting a capitulation, maffacred the
greateft part of the garrifon.

M. de Levis, with 12,000 men, befieges Quebec.
And Gen. Murray, with 3000 men, (Ap. 28.)
marched out near three miles from the city,
loft 1000 men in killed and wounded, and was
obliged to retreat back to the city.   On the
arrival of an Englifh fleet from Halifax, under
the command of Lord Colville, the fiege was
raifed, and the French fled to Montreal—where
three Englifh armies met afterwards; and Vau-
dreuil, the French Governor, finding himfelf
entirely inclofed by the three armies, furrendered the garrifon, with all Canada, Sept. 8,
on condition that the French fhould enjoy their
religion and effects; and that thofe of the
French

A. D. 1760.

French that chofe to return to France, fhould be tranfported thither.

In the courfe of the fummer, Captain Byron, with three fhips, deftroyed the French fettlements in the Bay of Chaleur, where he took 3 frigates and 19 fmaller veffels.

This year the walls of Cape Breton were demolifh-ed, and the implements of war, artillery and ammunition carried to Halifax, by order of his Britannic Majefty.

Arcot, Parmacoil, Alumparva, Carical, and Pon-dicherry, in the Eaft Indies, taken by the Eng-lifh.

The French army in Germany confifted of near 130,000 men, and the Englifh of 25,000: the allied fell very fhort of the French army in numbers, but they exceeded in the quality of the troops. Many heavy battles were fought, and many victories obtained over the enemy.

King George II. dies, and King George III. begins to reign. The Commons grant upwards of 19,000,000l. for the fervice of the current year.

A. D. 1761.

Prince Ferdinand, with the allied army, obtains a victory over the French, who lofe 5000 men in battle.

In another battle Prince Henry, brother to the hereditary Prince, is mortally wounded. Many fkirmifhes enfue.

Major Hector Monro takes Mahie, in the Eaft In-dies.

C 2

Shah

A. D. 1761.

Shah Zadda, a prince of the Mogul empire, joins
the French in the East Indies, but is routed by
the English troops, who take all their artillery,
part of their baggage, and a number of French
officers.

Lord Rollo, and Sir James Douglas, take the island
of Dominique from the French in the West Indies.

Numbers of vessels are taken from the French this
year, in different parts of the world.

The island of Belleisle taken from the French by
Admiral Keppel, and Major-General Hodgson,
June 7th.

The Commons settle the supplies, which amounted
to 18,229,135l. 18s. 11½d.

The Spaniards declare war against Great Britain.

1762.

England declares war against Spain.

Peter III. Emperor of Russia, is deposed, imprisoned, and murdered.

American Philosophical Society established at Philadelphia.

The English take Martinico, with all the Caribbee
islands in the West Indies, from the French.

Havannah taken from the Spaniards by the English.

Manilla, in the East Indies, taken by the English
from the Spaniards.

Sundry victories obtained over the French in Germany, by the English and the allied armies.

1763.

Peace established between Great Britain, France,
Spain, and Portugal; and Canada, Nova Scotia,

A. D. 1763.

tia, Eaſt and Weſt Florida, part of Louiſiana, Granada, St. Vincent, Dominica, and Tobago, are confirmed to the Britiſh empire.

1764.

Parliament grants 10,000l. to Mr. Harriſon for his diſcovery of longitude by his time piece.

1765.

A Society of Artiſts incorporated in England.

Stamp act paſſed. The Americans oppoſe it. The merchants enter into a non-importation agreement.

Society of Arts, Manufactures and Commerce, inſtituted at New York, March 18.

Stamp act repealed.

April 21. A ſpot, or macula of the ſun, more than thrice as big as this earth, paſſes over the centre of his body.

1768.

Academy of Painting eſtabliſhed in London.

War declared between the Ruſſians and Turks.

Great diſturbances in America concerning duties laid by Parliament on glaſs, ſalt, &c.

The merchants agree, not to import ſuperfluities from England. The Boſtonians demoliſh the houſes of the cuſtom-houſe officers. Two regiments ſent from Ireland, to ſupport the civil power at Boſton.

The King acquaints the Parliament with the conduct of the Americans.

96 public edifices, 4048 houſes, and 1000 perſons, deſtroyed by a hurricane at the Havannah.

C 3 A. D. 1769,

A. D. 1769.

The Boftonians petition Parliament, praying that the revenue acts may be repealed.

The prayer of the petition not granted. Mention is made of the riots and tumults in Bofton, &c. and Parliament refolves, that all acts made in the Colonies, which tended towards the throwing off the fovereignty of the Britifh Parliament, were illegal and unconftitutional, and derogatory to the crown and dignity of his Majefty, &c.

A comet appears, with a very long tail.

1770.

The King acquaints the Parliament with the diftracted condition of America.

Some of the merchants in England petition Parliament, praying that the duties might be taken off of fundry articles imported to America: their prayer is in part granted.

Mar. 5. Capt. Prefton, of the 29th regiment, with a number of his men, being furrounded and abufed by a mob, the mob is fired upon, and five are killed; which action was afterwards called by the Americans, *the Bofton maffacre.*

The King acquaints the Parliament with the condition of the Colonies in general, and the conduct of the Boftonians in particular.

250,000 people die of the plague in Poland.

1771.

Dr. Solander, Mr. Banks, and Lieut. Cooke, return to England from a voyage round the world,

A. D. 1771.

world, having made feveral important difcoveries in the South Seas.

1772.

The King of Sweden changes the conftitution from ariftocracy to a limited monarchy.

The Emperor of Germany, Emprefs of Ruffia, and King of Pruffia, ftrip the King of Poland of a great part of his dominions, which they divide among themfelves, in violation of the moft folemn treaties.

1773.

Capt. Phipps fent to explore the north pole; but is ftopped by the ice at lat. 81 deg. N.

The Jefuits expelled the Pope's dominions.

The Eaft India Company fends their cargoes of tea to confignees in America, Parliament having lowered the duty from 12 to 3d. per pound.

Dec. 16. A mob at Bofton deftroys 342 chefts, by throwing it into the fea.

Died of a plague at Baffora, in Perfia, 80,000 perfons.

1774.

Peace proclaimed between the Ruffians and Turks.

The Americans deny that the Britifh Parliament had a right to tax them.

Parliament paffes an act for fhutting up the port of Bofton, till fatisfaction fhould be made to the Eaft India Company, &c.; and alfo another act, for regulating the government of the Maffachufetts Bay, and for fending criminals to England to be tried, if juftice could not be had in

C 4 the

the Colonies. Alſo, an act was paſſed for the future government of Quebec, in which the Romiſh clergy were allowed the free exerciſe of their religion.

Gen. Gage arrives at Boſton with a fleet and army.

The port is ſhut up.

The Boſtonians enter into a ſolemn league and covenant, not to export or import any commodities to or from Great Britain, nor to have connection or trade with any one ſo doing, till all their rights and charters ſhould be reſtored to them.

Sept. 5. A Continental Congreſs meets at Philadelphia. The people in the Maſſachuſetts mob the King's counſellors and other friends of Government, who flee to his Majeſty's army for protection.

Committees of correſpondence are choſen; the courts of juſtice are ſtopped; and many of the military officers reſign their commiſſions in the Maſſachuſetts.

Gen. Gage ſeizes the provincial ſtores in the Maſſachuſetts, and fortifies the town of Boſton, in conſequence of the preparations for war in the colonies by the Americans.

The Repreſentatives, without the advice and conſent of the Governor and Council, proclaim a faſt. And,

Some of the clergy, refuſing to obey the proclamation, are treated as enemies to the country.

The millers not allowed to grind any grain for the friends of Government, nor the merchants and
mechanics

A. D. 1774.

mechanics to have any correspondence with them. The printers were forbid to print for the tories; and the people were not allowed to drink tea, nor the clergy to pray for the King.

The people conſtrained to ſign leagues and covenants; ſpend much time in making implements of war, and in running to trainings, town and committee meetings, county conventions, &c.

A proclamation iſſued in England to prevent the exportation of arms and ammunition to America.

The people in Rhode Iſland and New Hampſhire ſeize and carry off the cannon and other property belonging to the crown, which was depoſited in thoſe governments.

Minute-men, or men to be ready at a minute's warning to fight againſt the King's troops, choſen in the Maſſachuſetts.

A falſe report is ſpread, *viz.* that the King's troops had been from Boſton to Cambridge, and had, without any provocation, killed ſix innocent people there. Whereupon the militia was raiſed in the Maſſachuſetts, Connecticut, &c. and marched, in great multitudes, to take Boſton; but, on finding they had been miſinformed, returned back to their habitations.

1775.

April 19. The battle of Lexington.

May 10. Ticonderago taken from the Britiſh by Col. Ethan Allen.

May 14. Crown Point taken from the King's troops.

May 25.

A. D. 1775.

May 25. Gen. Howe, Clinton, and Burgoyne, arrive at Boſton.

June 17. Battle at Bunker's Hill: Charleſtown
burnt: Gen. Warren ſlain.

Aug. 23. The King iſſues a proclamation for the
ſuppreſſion of ſedition and rebellion.

Oct. 18. The Britiſh fleet burns the town of Fal-
mouth.

Dec. 10. Battle at Grave's Iſland in Virginia.

31. Gen. Montgomery ſlain at Quebec.

1776.

March 17. Boſton evacuated by the Britiſh.

May 6. The ſiege of Quebec is raiſed.

June 28. Battle at Sullivan's Iſland.

July 4. Independency declared by Congreſs at Philadelphia.

July 11. The battle at Gwin's Iſland.

Aug. 27. Long Iſland taken by the Britiſh.

Sept. 15. New-York taken by the Engliſh.

Nov. 18. Fort Lee abandoned by the Americans.

20. Fort Waſhington taken by the Britiſh and
Germans.

Dec. 26. Heſſians taken at Trenton by the Americans.

1777.

Jan. 2. Battle at Princetown, in the Jerſies.

March 23. Stores deſtroyed at Peek's-kills by the
Britiſh.

April 27. Danbury, in Connecticut, burnt by the
Engliſh.

April 29. Gen. Wooſter killed.

I   July 6.

A. D. 1777.

July 6. Ticonderago taken by the Britifh.

18. Gen. Prefcott taken at Rhode Ifland by the Americans.

Aug. 16. Englifh defeated at Bennington, in Vermont.

Aug. 28. Gen. Howe landed at the head of the Elk.

Sept. 11. Battle at Brandywine.

27. Philadelphia taken by Gen. Howe.

Oct. 4. Battle at German Town.

7. Battle at Stillwater.

9. Fort Montgomery taken by Sir Hen. Clinton.

15. Efopus burnt by the Britifh.

17. Gen. Burgoyne furrendered at Saratoga.

21. Red Bank, in Pennfylvania, attacked.

Nov. 15. Mud Ifland taken.

1778.

Feb. 6. An alliance made between France and the United States of America.

April 13. The Earl of Carlifle, W. Eden, Efq. and Geo. Johnfton, Efq. appointed Commiffioners to reftore peace to the Colonies: They arrive at Philadelphia—and Congrefs refufes to treat with them, &c.

June 18. Philadelphia evacuated by the King's troops.

June 28. St. Pierre and Miquelon taken from the French by Admiral Montague.

—. Battle at Monmouth, in the Jerfies.

July 27. Sea-fight off Breft, between Admiral Keppel and the French fleet.

July 27.

A. D. 1778.

July 27. Count d'Eftaing arrived at Rhode Ifland.

Aug. 29. Battle at Rhode Ifland.

Sept. 7. Dominica taken from the Englifh by the French.

Oct. 3. The Commiffioners iffue a manifefto and proclamation for reftoring peace in America.

Oct. 17. Pondicherry, in the Eaft Indies, furrenders to the Englifh.

Dec. 28. St. Lucia taken from the French by the Englifh.

1779.

Jan. 4. Georgia furrendered to the Britifh troops.

—. St. Vincents taken by the French.

July 3. Grenada taken by the French.

6. Adm. Byron and Count d'Eftaing fight.

—. D'Eftaing and Gen. Lincoln repulfed at Savannah in Georgia; and New Haven, in Connecticut, plundered by the Britifh.

July 9. Fairfield, in Connecticut, burnt by the Englifh.

July 12. Norfolk, in Connecticut, burnt by the King's troops.

July 16. Stony Point taken from the Britifh by the Americans.

Aug. 14. Penobfcott taken by the Britifh from the Americans.

Aug. 18. Paulus Hook taken from the Britifh.

Oct. 10. Count d'Eftaing repulfed at Georgia.

24. Omoa taken from the Spaniards.

25. New Port evacuated by the Britifh.

A. D. 1780.

A. D. 1780.

Jan. 8. Admiral Rodney takes two fail of Spanish ships.

Jan. 16. He takes and deftroys feven Spanish ships of the line.

March 14. Mobille taken by the Spaniards.

April. Admiral Rodney fights in the Weft Indies.

9. Weft Florida furrenders to the King of Spain.

May 12. Sir Henry Clinton takes Charleftown in South Carolina.

May 17. Admiral Rodney fights with the French fleet.

——. A great riot in London. The rioters demolish fome Romifh chapels, Newgate, the King's Bench and Fleet prifons, alfo fundry private houfes and other edifices in London and Southwark. The rioters were at length fuppreffed by the military, and many of them tried and executed for felony.

May 19. A remarkable dark day in New England.

Aug. 8. Five Eaft Indiamen and 50 merchant ships taken from the Englifh by the combined fleets of France and Spain.

Aug. 16. Earl Cornwallis obtains a victory over Gen. Gates near Camden, South Carolina.

——. General Sumpter defeated by Col. Tarleton

Sept. 3. Henry Laurens, Efq. who had been a prefident of Congrefs, taken by the Englifh near Newfoundland.

Sept. 23.

A. D. 1780.

Sept. 23. Major André taken by the Americans as a fpy.

Sept. 24. Gen. Arnold deferts, and goes to New-York, where he is made a Brigadier-General in the royal fervice.

Oct. 2. Major André hanged as a fpy at Tappan.

    4. Mr. Laurens committed to the Tower in London, on a charge of high treafon.

   10. Dreadful hurricanes in the Weft Indies.

Dec. 20. Declaration of hoftilities againft Holland.

   —. Tarleton and Morgan fight.

1781.

Jan. 6. The French repulfed at the ifland of Jerfey.

   11. Admiral Hughes takes Trincomale on the ifland of Ceylon.

Feb. 3. St. Euftatia taken by the Englifh from the Dutch.

   —. St. Martin's, Saba, St. Bartholomew, taken from the French by the Englifh.

   —. Demerary and Effequibo, on the Spanifh main, taken from the Dutch by the Englifh.

March 13. Dr. Herfchel difcovers a new planet, called *Georgium Sidus*, or *Herfchel*.

March 15. Earl Cornwallis obtains a victory over Gen. Green, at Guildford-court-houfe, North Carolina.

Camden burnt by the Britifh in South Carolina.

Norfolk, in Virginia, burnt by Gen. Arnold.

May 12. Negapatam taken.

June 2.

A. D. 1781.

June 2. Tobago taken by the French from the English.

Aug. 5. Admiral Parker fights with a Dutch fleet.

Sept. 6. New London, in Connecticut, burnt by Gen. Arnold.

—. Lieut. Colonel Tarleton defeated Sieur de Choife.

Sept. 7. French and English fight off Chefapeak Bay.

Sept. 19. Lord Cornwallis furrenders to the French and Americans.

1782.

Sir Eyre Coote obtains a victory over Hyder Ally.

Jan. 14. Nevis taken by the French.

Feb. 13. St. Chriftopher's taken from the English by the French.

Feb. 25. Minorca taken from the English by the Spaniards.

March 1. The Houfe of Commons addrefs the King againft any further profecution of the war in America; and refolve, that all thofe who fhould advife, or by any means attempt the further profecution thereof, fhould be confidered as enemies to his Majefty and the Britifh nation.

March 28. Holland acknowledges the independence of America.

April 12. Admiral Rodney obtains a victory over the French fleet commanded by C. de Graffe, in the Weft Indies.

April 13. Admiral Hughes had a fevere engagement with the French fleet near the ifland of Ceylon,

A. D. 1782.

Ceylon, in which a great number of men were loft on both fides.

May 8. The ifland of Bahama taken by the Spaniards from the Englifh.

Aug. 29. The Royal George, of 110 guns, is overfet, and funk in the Englifh Channel, and about 900 people perifh.

Sept. 13. Gen. Elliot defeats the combined fleets of France and Spain at Gibraltar.

Oct. 6. Peace proclaimed between Great Britain, France, and Spain.

Nov. 30. Provifional articles of peace figned at Paris between Great Britain and the United States of America.

Dec. 20. Dr. STEARNS, having made calculations, publifhes the firft *Nautical Almanack* that ever was printed in America.

1783.

Jan. 20. Preliminary articles of peace between his Britannic Majefty and the Kings of France and Spain figned at Verfailles.

April. An ifland rifes out of the fea, near Iceland, iffuing great quantities of fire from two of its eminences, like burning vulcanoes.

Sept. 3. The definitive treaty of peace between Great Britain, France, Spain, and the United States of America, ratified.

The Britifh Fifhing Society incorporated.

A. D. 1784.

Jan. 14. Congrefs ratifies the definitive treaty of peace between Great Britain and America.

Jan. 16.

A. D. 1784.

Jan. 16. Congrefs iffues a proclamation, recommending and ftrictly enjoining the citizens of the United States, to carry into effect every fentence and claufe of the definitive treaty.

March. A comet appears.

May 20. The definitive treaty of peace between Great Britain and Holland figned at Paris.

July. Peace proclaimed in Great Britian between Holland and America.

Sept. 15. Lunardi afcends in an Air Balloon, the firft attempt of the kind in England.

1786.

Auguft 2. Margaret Nicholfon, a lunatic, attempts to ftab the King of England with a knife, in confequence of which fhe is fent to Bethlehem Hofpital.

Sept. 19. A plan fet forth in Great Britain for eftablifhing a Colony in Botany Bay, in New Holland. A commercial treaty is figned at Verfailles between England and France. An infurrection in the Maffachufetts—The fitting of many of the courts of juftice is ftopped by the infurgents.

Congrefs recommends to the Legiflative Affemblies of the United States, to repeal their laws, which had been fuffered to exift and operate, that were repugnant to the definitive treaty of peace between Great Britain and America.

1787.

Jan. The infurgents under the command of Gen. Shays, ftill continue to impede the fitting of the courts of juftice. The Legiflative Affem-

D   bly

bly raifes an army, which was put under the command of Gen. Lincoln. Several fkirmifhes enfue, and fome are killed on both fides. The infurgents defert Gen. Shays. He flees with his Head Officers to Canada. Many of the infurgents are afterwards tried for their lives. Some receive fentence of death; but are all, with their General, afterwards pardoned.

The Maffachufetts, with fundry other States, repeal their laws that were repugnant to the articles of the peace.

Some difturbances in Holland, the male-contents defire to abridge the Stadtholder's power. The public tranquillity is reftored. The Legiflative Affemblies in the United States of America fend a Convention to Philadelphia, in order to amend the articles of confederation and perpetual union between the States. The Convention frames a new conftitution, which they call the Federal Conftitution. This makes a great difturbance amongft the citizens.

1788.

Jan. 17. Lord George Gordon having been found guilty of publifhing two libels, one againft the Queen of France, and the other againft the criminal jurifprudence of England, is fentenced to be imprifoned in Newgate three years, then to pay a fine of £500, and find fecurity for his good behaviour for fourteen years.

26. Dr. STEARNS formed a new *Hypothefis* upon the caufe of the *Aurora Borealis.*

Jan. 31.

A. D. 1788.

Jan. 31. Died at Rome, Prince Charles Lewis Caffimir Stuart, called the Pretender, aged 67 years and 2 months.

June 13. A provincial treaty of defenfive alliance is figned by the minifters plenipotentiary of their Majefties the Kings of Great Britain and Pruffia.

1789.

April 23. His Britannic Majefty, having been indifpofed from Oct. 1788 till March 1789, appoints a thankfgiving, and vifits St. Paul's.

24. General illumination on the King's recovery. Dr. Herfchel difcovers the 6th and 7th moons of Saturn. Great infurrections in Paris, occafioned by the people's paying enormous taxes, from which the nobility and clergy were exempt. The people carry their point in fubjecting thofe claffes to taxation, and contend for a right of reprefentation, as forming one of the three eftates, according to the conftitution of Great Britain. They meet with oppofition, but carry their point at laft.

1790.

Jan. 26. Dr. STEARNS receives a letter from Dr. HERSCHEL, informing that Mrs. HERSCHEL, fifter to the Doctor, difcovered a comet on the 7th inftant.

April 6. A violent fhock of an earthquake at Oczakow, which deftroyed a church, and did other damages.

May 27. London Bridge ftruck with lightning.

April

A. D. 1790.

April 20. Doctor Benjamin Franklin died, aged 84 years and 3 months.

July 14. Democratical *Conſtitution eſtabliſhed in France.*

Dec. 23. A terrible ſtorm of thunder, lightning, wind, hail, and rain; which did much damage in London and elſewhere, by overturning chimneys, houſes, trees, &c.

Chronologiſts frequently contradict one another—hence their works are not always to be depended on. The Author has taken much pains to collect the beſt accounts that could poſſibly be obtained; and therefore flatters himſelf, that the preceding Tables are the moſt accurate of any that have hitherto been publiſhed.

C H A P.

CHAP. II.

A Description of the AUTHOR'S *Philosophical Con-
templations, Astronomical, and other Labours.*

IN profound studies I take much delight,
  At high noon day, and in the silent night;
Of wond'rous things I aim to find the cause,
By diving into Nature's secret laws.
Sometimes I sit, and with myself converse,
And contemplate upon the universe;
Sometimes, when on my downy bed I lie,
My wand'ring thoughts to distant objects fly:
Sometimes they're fixed on the splendid sun,
To see the planets round his body run,
In that position there to stand and gaze,
Whilst rambling comets in the system blaze.
Then, from the sun, my thoughts do take a flight
To globes extended far beyond our sight:
There I survey the works that DEUS made,
When He the basis of great heaven laid;
When He rais'd up the arches of the sky,
And fram'd a num'rous train of worlds on high,
Where suns, no doubt, do shine with splendid light,
And planets roll, adorn'd with day and night,
Where beings do perhaps their voices raise,
In celebrating their Creator's praise!

  When I've thus view'd the systems to and fro,
My wand'ring thoughts descend to objects low:
From upper worlds most rapidly they fall,
To view God's works upon this earthly ball.

D 3

Here

Here I gaze at the lands, the rocks, the seas,
The num'rous plants, and diff'rent kinds of trees ;
The birds, the beasts, the fishes—all that be
In air, in earth, and the extensive sea.
I view the people all, both great and small,
In kingdoms, towns, and cities large and tall ;
See their religion, customs, and their laws,
Their times of peace, and times of bloody wars.
The elements I view of ev'ry kind,
And all their qualities do try to find.
And whilst I'm thinking of great Nature's laws,
I ask myself, what truly is the cause
Why clouds arise ? Why storms of rain and snow ?
Why fogs appear, and boist'rous winds do blow ?
Why tides spring up, and billows roar aloud ?
And the grum thunder rumbles thro' the cloud ?
Why flaming lightning often zigzag flies ?
And the mock suns appear within the skies ?
The meteors why ? and why the northern light ?
And rainbow comes so frequent in our sight ?
Why other things so often do appear
Within the earth's extensive atmosphere ?
Why inundations do so oft arise,
And drown the people in a great surprise ?
Why mountains burn ? and why the hills do shake ?
What thing it is that causes an earthquake ?
Why cities sink ? and other places fall
So low that they cannot be seen at all ?
Why islands rise, that ne'er were seen before ?
And hills spring up upon the rocky shore ?
Why stones fall downwards ? Why the smokes arise
Towards the regions of the upper skies ?
Why the hot flame the fuel doth consume,
And where its gone when turned into fume ?
What makes the springs, in diff'rent kinds of soil,
With a great heat from day to day to boil ?
Why water-spouts and whirlwinds do arise,
And raise things up towards the azure skies ?
Why the broad sea, with a fine brilliant light,
Doth look so fiery in the darkest night ?

                                        Why

Why the bright fun upon an axis turns,
And, unconfum'd, his body ever burns?
Why the ALMIGHTY gives its heat fuch force,
Orders its motion, and directs its courfe?
Why planets do in wond'rous order run,
From age to age, around the fplendid fun?
Why this great globe, with unfelt motion, rolls
Upon an axis pointing to the poles?
What makes the cold, and what doth make the heat?
And the proud waves againft the mountains beat?
What brings the fpring, the fummer, and the fall,
And winter time, upon this earthly ball?
What makes the day? and what doth make the night?
And what divides the darknefs from the light?
What makes the compafs vary from the poles?
And why the variation weftward rolls?
Why northern lights weren't feen upon the ftage,
Until men liv'd within the prefent age?

When in the morn I'm weary of my bed,
I rife and write what came into my head,
What I upon great Nature's laws had thought,
What in the night had to my mind been brought:
But ftill I find my thoughts, without controul,
Upon a number of great objects roll.
I go to work, and, with a fteady mind,
The planets places in their orbits find.
For times not come I find their longitude,
And compute their diurnal latitude;
Their right afcenfions, declinations too;
Their rifings, fettings —all point out I do.
Eclipfes, tranfits, occultations, I
Foretel how foon they will be drawing nigh,
In obfcurations of the fhining fun,
I find the courfe that the dark moon will run;
Where her penumbra firft will ftrike the globe,
And bring thereon a doleful mourning robe!
How far her fhadow really will expand,
And obumbrate the fea and folid land.
I always aim to be exceeding fure
To tell how long eclipfes will endure:

When

When they'll begin, likewife how large they'll be;
And when their end the gazing world may fee!

In the defections of the rambling moon,
(Which happens oft, at ev'ning, morn, and noon)
I find the magnitude of the earth's fhade,
And how therein the Lunar globe will wade:
Whether one part, or whether there'll be all
The rays of Sol hid from the Lunar ball:
From thefe things only 'tis that I conclude,
What will be the eclipfe's magnitude.
The beft of rules obferve I always do,
In occultations and in tranfits too.

Whilft at my ftudies I am fitting ftill,
I'm often call'd to vifit perfons ill:
Then I hafte where malignant ills do rage,
And againft them with all my fkill engage.
Sometimes I bleed, fometimes I puke and purge:
I ufe fuch things as Nature feems to urge.
I am not fond of getting worldly pelf,
But ufe the poor juft as I do myfelf.
The beft of med'cines any one can choofe,
I to my patients orders give to ufe;
And to the fick cannot for confcience' fake,
Give things myfelf would not incline to take.
Unlefs I know of what a pill is made,
To give or take it always I'm afraid.
The ufe of *noftrums* therefore I defpife,
With the whole train of quackifh villanies.
I've often thought, that people, when they're ill,
Do take fuch things till they themfelves do kill.
A man well fkilled in the medic art,
Can have no need to act a knavifh part:
Out of good fimples, compounds he can make,
Fit for his patients and himfelf to take:
If he his med'cines doth incorporate,
He'll know their ftrength, and how they'll operate.
He'll eafe the pained, and he'll give relief
To men and women overwhelm'd with grief;
As all of them may ftand a chance to find
Themfelves reliev'd according to their mind;

To

To get quite freed from all their racking pain,
Have health reſtor'd, and ſtrength return'd again.
But if he knows not what he gives, I'm ſure,
He nor his patients can't expect a cure.
Let all therefore who to phyſicians run,
The knaviſh quacks and all their *noſtrums* ſhun ;
Leſt they, like fools, do ſpend their caſh in vain,
Take the *ſlow poiſon,* and at laſt be ſlain.

  Theſe are the ways that I, by night and day,
Do exerciſe as time rolls faſt away.
The field I find, in which I did engage,
Is large enough for mortals on the ſtage ;
Who being weak, and very ſhort in ſight,
Know not ſome things hid by the GOD *of Might !*

Compoſed, A. D. 1790.

C H A P.   III.

A Definition of ASTRONOMY—*Where it is suppofed it was firft ftudied—The Names and Ages of fome eminent Aftronomers — Obfervations on thofe of Great Britain, France, and America—The great Utility of the Science—Qualifications neceffary for thofe who calculate the Motions of the Celeftial Luminaries.*

ASTRONOMY is a fcience that teaches the diftances, magnitudes, orders and motions of the heavenly bodies; and was a myftery hidden from ages and generations, until it was made known in thefe modern centuries, by the ftudies, obfervations, and improvements of ingenious men. —It has been faid, that the Moors firft ftudied the fcience, and that it was brought into Europe in 1201. — Some have alfo fuppofed, that the true theory of Aftronomy took its rife in Egypt or Babylon, and that it was firft taught by Pythagoras in Greece, who died 497 years before Chrift.

After a long and dark night of oblivion, the Pythagorian Syftem was revived by Copernicus of Thorn in Pruffia, who died A. D. 1543, aged 70.—John Kepler, born at Wittenberg in Upper Saxony, in Germany, made a great progrefs in

Aftronomy;

Aftronomy; he died 1630, aged 59.—Afterwards
the celebrated Sir Ifaac Newton, who was knighted
by Queen Ann when he was about 62 years of age,
brought the knowledge of this fcience to a high
degree of perfection; he died 1727, aged 84.—
We have alfo had feveral other eminent Aftronomers in Great Britain befides Sir Ifaac ; as Mr.
Flamftead, who died 1718, aged 73.—Dr. Halley,
who died 1742, aged 86.—Mr. Whifton, who
died 1752, aged 85.—Dr. Bradly, who died
1762.—Mr. Mayor, famous for conftructing Aftronomical Tables, who died 1762.—A Mr. Robert
Heath, who has been dead upwards of 20 years,
if I miftake not ; and a Mr. Ferguffon, who died
1776.—At prefent there is the Rev. Dr. Mafkelyne,
Aftronomer Royal, and the celebrated Dr. Herfchel, who has made great difcoveries and improvements in the divine fcience, as he has difcovered
one primary planet, *viz.* Georgium Sidus, and
four fecondary fatellites, which had not been feen
before. Two of thefe fatellites revolve round
Georgium Sidus, and the other two round Saturn.
—The Doctor has alfo difcovered, that the ring
of Saturn has a rotation in about ten hours, as
he informed me.

Dr. Herfchel difcovered the Georgium planet
with a telefcope about fix feet in length ; and
he has lately conftructed another, which is
about 40 feet long, and 4 feet 9 inches in
diameter. This is the largeft I ever faw, and I
believe of any in the world. It has enabled him
to make the other difcoveries.

I perceived

I perceived in July 1790, when I was at the Royal Obfervatory in Paris, that the French Aftronomers are very accurate in taking obfervations.

I have not learnt that the American Aftronomers have ever made any great difcoveries or improvements in taking aftronomical obfervations; but they have fome eminent Calculators, as the celebrated Mr. Weft, Profeffor of Mathematics and Aftronomy in the Univerfity in Rhode-Ifland Government—Dr. Low, and a Mr. George, of the Maffachufetts—Mr. Strong, Dr. Perry, and Mr. Dabol, of Connecticut: but I am not acquainted with the Calculators in the Southern States.— I obferved at Philadelphia, in 1783, that a number of Almanacks were publifhed from one calculation, under fictitious names, as Father Abraham, Poor Will, Poor Richard, &c.; but could not learn who was the author. The fame calculation was alfo publifhed in the Jerfies, under fome other name.

At New-York, an Almanack was publifhed under the name of a Mr. Hutchens, who had been dead fome years.

An Almanack was publifhed in French, in Canada, when I was there, fuppofed to be calculated by a Mathematician in the Seminary in Quebec; but it was very deficient, as neither the Moon's place, rifing, fouthing, or fetting, was given.

I have made and publifhed Aftronomical Calculations for feveral Governments in America,

for

for upwards of twenty years, annually calculated for fix meridians and latitudes; and have not heard of any Aftronomer that ever attempted to calculate and publifh a Nautical Almanack, in that quarter, but myfelf; and I only undertook the tafk once. The greatnefs of the work, and the commotions that exifted on account of the war, obliged me to difcontinue it.

There are two gentlemen in America, who are faid to be very accurate in the conftruction of Orreries, *viz.* a Mr. Rittenhoufe of Philadelphia, and a Mr. Pope of Bofton:---The former conftructed one that exceeded every thing of the like kind in the world; and fince that, the latter conftructed another, that exceeds the former : He made a prefent of it to the Prefident, Profeffors, &c. of the Univerfity at Cambridge, in the Common-wealth of Maffachufetts; and the General Affembly of that Republic gave him three hundred guineas (as he informed me, when I faw him in London) in confequence of his performance, and donation.

No fcience can be of greater utility to the human race than Aftronomy; for, by it, we not only point out the longitudes and latitudes of the planets, with their rifings, fouthings, fettings, eclipfes, tranfits, and occultations—but determine many important things in chronology, navigation, and furveying. Hence, if we had no knowledge in this fcience, we fhould not be able to find the limits of kingdoms and ftates, nor to fteer a veffel over the great oceans to the remote parts of the globe, which would hinder our growing rich by trade and commerce, and prevent our receiving many of thofe foreign productions that

are

are neceffary for the prefervation of life; fuch as clothing, food, phyfic, &c.

There are but a few Aftronomers on the globe, owing no doubt to the deepnefs of the myftery, and the extenfivenefs of the labour in attaining the knowledge neceffary for a Profeffor of the divine fcience.

An Aftronomer muft be well fkilled in every branch of the mathematics, *viz.* arithmetic, algebra, geometry, trigonometry, navigation, furveying, &c.; and if he undertakes to make calculations for one year only, he will find that he enters into a large field of bufinefs, and into a puzzling, perplexing, and intricate work, that will be attended with the expence of much time and hard ftudy. A calculation that is made for one year, never will anfwer for another, by reafon of the unfteadinefs of the motions of the luminaries.

There are three kinds of Aftronomers, if I may be allowed to ufe the expreffion, *viz.* One that marks the places of the ftars, planets, and comets, by taking aftronomical obfervations—One that points out their places for times to come, by aftronomical calculations — And another that reprefents their motions, by making mathematical machines, as orreries, artificial globes, and planetariums.

C H A P. IV.

Of the Motions of the Primary and Secondary Planets
—Caufes of the Eclipfes, Tranfits, and Occultations
—The Signs of the Zodiac, and the Number of the
Northern and Southern Conftellations—Aftronomical
Characters—Superftition of the Ancients.

WE may reafonably fuppofe, that there are innumerable fyftems of worlds in the boundlefs expanfion of the univerfe; and that the great fixed ftars are funs to fyftems of planets and comets. But be this as it may, it has been demon-ftrated by aftronomical obfervations,

I. That the fun is placed nearly in the centre of our fyftem, and that it has no circular motion, only a rotation upon its axis.

II. That feven primary, and fourteen fecondary planets, complete their revolutions round the fun, in their determinate or appointed times.

III. That the primaries are moved with an an-nual and a diurnal motion.

IV. That the fecondaries revolve around their primaries, as the primaries do round the fun; and both are moved round the fun together, as the pri-maries complete their revolutions.

V. That fome primaries have fecondaries, and others have none.

VI. That our earth is a primary planet, and completes her revolution round the fun between the orbits of Mars and Venus.

VII. That Mars, Venus, and Mercury, have no moons or fecondary planets; and that the earth has

one,

one, Jupiter four, Saturn feven, and Georgium Sidus two.

VIII. That the orbits of the planets are not circular, but elliptical, and have different degrees of excentricity.

IX. That they are moved by a projectile force in their orbits, and a central force towards the fun.

X. That their motions are regular and uniform, and the areas they defcribe around the fun are proportionate to the times of their periods.

XI. That the fquares of the times which the planets fpend in revolving round the fun, are always proportionable to the cubes of their greateft diftance from him. Hence the longer their orbits are, the longer will their revolutions be.

XII. That they all revolve through the twelve figns of the zodiac, which is a zone that is 18 deg. and 30 min. in breadth, in the middle of which is the ecliptic, or fun's path. Hence they make an angle with the ecliptic of 9 deg. and 15. min. called their north and fouth latitude.

XIII. That they revolve according to the order of the figns of the zodiac, but appear at different times to be direct, ftationary, and retrograde; which phænomena arife from their various fituations, and the velocity of the motion of the earth.

XIV. That when a primary planet is in that part of its orbit that is neareft to the fun, it is at its perihelion; but when it is moft remote, it is at its aphelion.

XV. That when a fecondary planet is in that part of its orbit that is neareft to its primary, it is at its perigeon; but when it is moft remote, it is at its apogeon.

XVI. That

XVI. That the annual motion of the earth caufes the fpring, fummer, autumn, and winter; but the diurnal caufes the day and the night.

XVII. That an eclipfe of the fun is caufed by the moon's coming between the fun and the earth at the time of her change; and that of the moon by her falling into the earth's fhadow at the time of her full, occafioned by the earth's coming between the fun and the moon.

XVIII. That the fun and moon cannot be eclipfed, only on the full and change days; and not always then, becaufe fhe makes an angle with the ecliptic of 5 deg. and 18 min. and therefore often paffes to the north or fouth of the fun at the time of her change, and to the north or fouth of the earth's fhadow at the time of her full, without caufing any eclipfe.

XIX. That there cannot be more than feven, nor lefs than two eclipfes in a year; but more happens of the fun than of the moon, by reafon of his being greater than the earth's fhadow.

XX. That the points where the moon's orbit interfects the ecliptic, are called her nodes; but they run retrograde, or contrary to the orders of the figns of the zodiac. Her menftrual motion, however, is always direct, or from weft to eaft: and when fhe is three figns to the eaftward of the fun, fhe is at her firft quarter; when fix figns, at her full; and when three figns weft of the fun, at her laft quarter.

XXI. That the moon is very unfteady in her motion, as her velocity is fometimes fwift, and fometimes flow; the figure of her orbit being neither a circle, nor an ellipfis, nor a parabola.

E   XXII. That

XXII. That she always moves with the same face towards the earth, and her diurnal motion is equal to her menstrual motion, *viz.* 27 days and 8 hours. She has no light of her own, but shines with a borrowed light reflected from the sun. Hence she appears horned, halved, gibbous and round, according to her position in her orbit, and distance from the sun.

XXIII. That no planet, in all our system, is half so difficult to trace as the moon, and a calculation made for one year will not answer for another.— Hence Astronomers are obliged to make new calculations, as they do for the other planets, every year.

XXIV. Sometimes Venus and Mercury pass betwixt us and the sun, and appear like a dark spot on his disk. These eclipses are called transits, and there are more of Mercury than of Venus.

XXV. That the satellites of Georgium Sidus, Saturn and Jupiter, are easy to trace ; and the quantities, durations, rest and affections of their eclipses (called occultations) are easily found by reason of the steadiness of their motions.

XXVI. That Mercury is situated the nearest to the sun of any planet in our system, and revolves between the sun and Venus. Venus revolves between the orbit of Mercury and that of the earth ; the earth between Venus and Mars ; Mars between the earth and Jupiter ; Jupiter between Mars and Saturn ; Saturn between Jupiter and Georgium Sidus ; and Georgium Sidus between Saturn and the sphere of the fixed stars, which are placed at an

immense

immenfe diftance from our fyftem. *Vide* the figure of the folar fyftem.

XXVII. That the figns of the zodiac are called conftellations, each of which contains 30 degrees, each degree 60 minutes, and each minute 60 feconds, &c.

XXVIII. That north of the zodiac there are 36 conftellations, and fouth of it 32; which numbers being added to thofe of the zodiac, make 80, and includes the whole canopy of the heavens.

XXIX. That the concave furface of the ftarry heavens, with the different conftellations, are marked on the convex furface of an artificial celeftial globe; and they are reprefented by the forms of various animals, whofe names and figures are printed on the paper that covers the globe.

XXX. That the names of the northern conftellations are,

LATIN NAMES.	ENGLISH NAMES.
Andromeda	Andromeda
Aquila cum Antineo	The eagle with Antionus
Anfer cum Vulpecula	The goofe with the fox
Auriga	The waggoner
Bootes	Bootes
Caffiopeia	The lady in her chair
Camelopardus	The cameleopard
Cepheus	Cephus
Coma Berenices	Berenices hair
Corona Septen.	The northern crown
Cygnus Gallina	The fwan hen
Delphinus	The dolphin
Draco	The dragon

Equuleus

LATIN NAMES.	ENGLISH NAMES.
Equuleus Equifectio	The horfe's head
Hercules	Hercules kneeling
Leo minor	The leffer lion
Lacerta	The lizard
Lynx	The lynx
Lyra	The harp
Perfeus, C. M.	The Perfeus
Pegafus Equus	The flying horfe
Sagitta	The arrow
Serpens Ophiuchi	Serpentarius
Scutum	The fhield
Serpentarius, or Ophiu-chus	The ferpent
Triangulum	The triangle
Urfa major	The great bear
Urfa minor	The little bear
Canes Vanatici	The dog greyhound.

XXXI. The characters and names of the con-ftellations of the zodiac are,

	LATIN NAMES.	ENGLISH NAMES.	
♈	Aries	The ram	Head
♉	Taurus	The bull	Neck
♊	Gemini	The twins	Arms
♋	Cancer	The crab	Breaft
♌	Leo	The lion	Heart
♍	Virgo	The virgin	Belly
♎	Libra	The balance	Reins
♏	Scorpio	The fcorpion	Secrets
♐	Sagittarius	The archer	Thighs
♑	Capricornus	The goat	Knees
♒	Aquarius	The water-bearer	Legs
♓	Pifces	The fifhes	Feet

XXXII. That

XXXII. That the fouthern conftellations are,

LATIN NAMES.	ENGLISH NAMES.
Ara cum thuribulo	The altar with a cenfer
Argo vel navis	The fhip
Apus	The bird of paradife
Canis major	The greater dog
Canis minor	The leffer dog
Cetus	The whale
Centaurus cum lupe	The centaur with the wolf
Chameliontis	A chameleon
Columba Noahi	Noah's dove
Corona Auftralis	The fouthern crown
Corvus	The crow
Crater	The cup
Eridanus fluvius	The river
Grus	The crane
Hydrus	The water-adder
Lepus	The hare
Mufca	The fly
Monofceres	The unicorn
Orion	Orion
Pavo	The peacock
Phœnix	The phenix
Pifcis volans	The flying fifh
Robur Carolinæ	The royal oak
Sextans	The fextant
Toncan	The American goofe
Triangulum Auftr.	The fouthern triangle
Dorado Xiphias	The fword fifh

XXXIII. That various accounts have been given by different Aftronomers, of thenumber of the fixed ftars.

E 3

ftars. Mr. Flamſtead, in the year 1689, ſuppoſed
their number to be 3001, *viz.* 1511 in the northern hemiſphere, 943 in the zodiac, and 547 in
the ſouthern hemiſphere; and diſtinguiſhed them
by ſeven degrees of magnitude. But ſcarce 1000
can be diſcerned in Great Britain by the naked eye
in a clear night. The ſtars, however, are ſo numerous, that no man on earth can number them; for
by looking into Dr. Herſchel's teleſcope, thouſands
and tens of thouſands appear beyond thoſe mentioned by Mr. Flamſtead.

XXXIV. That beſides the aſtronomical characters annexed to the names of the ſigns of the zodiac, there are others which repreſent the ſtars,
planets, and aſpects:

LATIN NAMES.	ENGLISH.	GENDERS.
✳ Stella	A ſtar	Feminine
☉ Sol	The ſun	Maſculine
☿ Mercurius	Mercury	Maſculine
♀ Venus	Venus	Feminine
⊖ Terra	The earth	Feminine
♂ Mars	Mars	Maſculine
♃ Jovis	Jupiter	Maſculine
♄ Saturnus	Saturn	Maſculine
G Georgium Sidus	George's ſtar	Maſculine
☽ Luna	The moon	Feminine
7 ✳'s Pleiades	The ſeven ſtars	

XXXV. That when a planet is moving northward, it is in its aſcending node, called the dragon's
head, and marked ☊ : and when it is moving
ſouthward, it is in its deſcending node, called the
dragon's

dragon's tail, and is marked ☋. But when it intersects the ecliptic, it is in the node itself.

XXXVI. That the following characters represent the aspects, as when two planets are in the same degree, they are in conjunction, marked ☌

When 30 degrees apart,	Semisextile	SS
—— 60 —— ——	Sextile	✳
—— 54 —— ——	Quintile	Q
—— 90 —— ——	Quartile	□
—— 120 —— ——	Trine	△
—— 144 —— ——	Biquintile	Bq
—— 150 —— ——	Quincunx	Vc
—— 180 —— ——.	Opposition	☍

XXXVII. That the Ancients supposed the moon had a great influence upon the human body, as she passed through the signs of the zodiac; that when she was in *Aries*, she governed the head; when in *Taurus*, the neck, &c.; and that it was unsafe to let blood in the head, or any other part, whilst she remained in that sign which governed the part. But I have found by my own experience and observation, in bleeding patients, that this hypothesis was founded altogether upon superstition.

This opinion was undoubtedly instilled into the Ancients by the Astrologers, who formerly imposed upon the ignorant world, by pretending that they could foretel future events by the motions of the heavenly bodies. But we still retain the ancient custom of representing the moon's place in the signs of the zodiac, by saying in our almanacks, *head, neck, arms,* &c.

CHAP.

CHAP. V.

A Description of the Ecliptic, Poles, Equinoctial, Zenith, Nadir, Spheres, Latitude, Longitudes, Horizon, Hemispheres, Meridians, Amplitude, Right Ascension, Equinoxes, Azimuths, Cycles, Parallaxes, Tropics, Polar Circles, Solstices, Cardinal Points, Seasons of the Year, Zones, Semi-diurnal Arcs, Length of the Days, Square Miles on the Surface of the Globe, Number of Inhabitants, &c.

THE ecliptic is the path in the heavens which the sun appears to describe as the earth passes through the twelve signs of the zodiac. Aries, Taurus, Gemini, Cancer, Leo, and Virgo, are northern signs; Libra, Scorpio, Sagittarius, Capricornus, Aquarius, and Pisces, are southern.

2. The poles of the world are two fixed points in the heavens, diametrically opposite to each other, and a right line supposed to be drawn from each, is called the axis of the earth, about which the diurnal motion is performed.

3. The equinoctial line is a great circle, that surrounds the globe, at right angles, with the axis of the earth : it is 90 degrees from each pole, and intersects the ecliptic at the beginning of Aries and Libra. The length of the equinoctial is equal to the circumference of the globe, which is 360 degrees, or 21,600 geographic miles.

A de-

A degree of the equator, and one of the ecliptic, and other great circles of the fphere, is fuppofed to be equal, though the latter is much longer than the former. The equator is divided into 24 equal parts, each containing 15 degrees, which are equal to an hour of time, as each degree is equal to four minutes.

4. The diameter of the earth from pole to pole is not quite fo large as it is through the equinoctial, which is evident by her fhadow in an eclipfe of the moon; but the difference of the polar and equatorial diameters, arifes, it is probable, from the expanfion of the globe by the heat of the fun in the torrid zone, and the condenfation of the fame by the cold in the polar regions.

5. The zenith is the point directly over our heads; the nadir is the point directly under our feet; and when the fun, the moon, or a ftar is in the zenith, it is verticle.

6. There are three fpheres, *viz.* a right, oblique, and parallel; as,

Firft, When a fpectator is on the equator, he is in a right fphere; the poles of the world are in the horizon, and the equinoctial paffes through the zenith and nadir. The equator, with its parallels, *viz.* the tropics and polar circles, make right angles with the horizon. The days and nights are equal as the fun, moon, and ftars; are twelve hours above, and twelve below the horizon, at the times of the equinoxes.

Secondly,

Secondly, When a fpectator is between the equator and the poles, he is in an oblique fphere.   One
pole is elevated lefs than 90 degrees above the horizon, and the other is depreffed as many below.——
The luminaries afcend and defcend obliquely, tho'
fome of them that are fituated near the poles never
afcend at all.   The days and nights are of different
lengths, according to the different degrees of latitude, and the feafons of the year.   The diurnal and
nocturnal arcs of the fun vary in all parallels of
latitude.

Thirdly, When a fpectator is at either of the
poles, he is in a parallel fphere.   One pole is in the
zenith, and the other is in the nadir.   The equinoctial is parallel to the horizon; and all the parallels of the equator, *viz.* the tropics and polar circles, are alfo parallel to the horizon.   The fun is
half the year above, and half the year under the
horizon, and the days and nights are fix months in
length.   When our fummer folftice happens, the
fun at the north pole is 23 deg. 28 min. above the
horizon; when the equinoxes happen, he is in the
horizon; and when he is declined 18 degrees to
the fouth, the twilight ends at the north pole,
which remains in utter darknefs till the fun returns
within 18 degrees of the equator again, unlefs it
is illuminated by the moon, the Aurora Borealis,
&c.

7. The latitude of a place is its diftance north
or fouth of the equinoctial, and is always equal to
the height of the pole above the horizon: hence,
if a fpectator is 20 degrees from the equator, that

will

will be the elevation of the pole, and, of courfe, the latitude of the place.

8. The longitude of a place is its diftance from fome firft meridian, eaft or weft, as that of the Royal Obfervatory at Greenwich; and every ftep we move, north or fouth, brings us into another latitude; and every ftep we travel, eaft or weft, brings us into another longitude, and alfo into another meridian.

9. The horizon is a great circle of the fphere which divides the upper hemifphere, or half compafs of the heavens, which is vifible from the lower, which is invifible.

10. There are two horizons, *viz.* the fenfible and the rational. The fenfible is that which appears to a fpectator placed on the furface of the globe; and the rational, that which would appear to him, if he was placed at, and could fee from the centre. This horizon would divide the firmament into two equal parts, called the real and true horizon.

11. The hemifphere is that part of the heavens which is above the horizon; it is alfo one half of the globe, and likewife all the firmament that is below the horizon.

12. A meridian is a great circle paffing through the poles of the world, and the zenith and nadir croffing the equinoctial at right angles, dividing the hemifphere into two equal parts, called the eaftern and weftern hemifpheres; and when the fun comes to the meridian, it is noon.

13. The

13. The meridian altitude of the fun, moon, or ftar, is its height above the horizon when it is on the meridian.

14. The femi-diurnal arc of the fun, moon, or ftar, is half the time it is above the horizon; and the femi-nocturnal arc is half of the time that it is below the fame.

15. The amplitude of the fun, moon, or ftar, is an arch of the horizon between their rifing or fetting, and the eaftern or weftern points thereof.

16. The afcenfional difference of the fun, moon, or ftar, is the difference between the right and oblique afcenfion and defcenfion, or the time they rife and fet before and after fix o'clock.

17. The longitude of the fun, planet, or ftar, is its diftance from the vernal equinox, which is moveable about 50 feconds *per annum*, or its diftance from the firft ftar of Aries, which is immoveable.

18. The latitude of a planet is its diftance from the ecliptic, as was before obferved.

19. The heliocentric longitude of a planet is its place as feen from the fun, and the geocentric as feen from the earth. The fame is to be obferved with regard to the heliocentric and geocentric latitude.

20. The right afcenfion of the fun, moon, or ftar, are the degrees of the equinoctial, reckoned from the beginning of Aries, coming to the meridian with a ftar or planet, or to any hour circle at right angles with the equinoctial.

21. The proceffion of the equinoxes are the going back of the equinoctial points 50 feconds in a year,

year, caufed by the earth's fpheroidal figure in its diurnal motion; it will complete a revolution in about 25,920 years. This revolution is called the Platonic Year, at the period of which the Ancients fuppofed that every thing will come round in the fame order they then were.

22. When a ftar rifes as the fun fets, it rifes achronically; when it fets with the fun, it fets achronically. When it rifes with the fun, it rifes cofmically; when it fets as the fun rifes, it fets cofmically. When a ftar emerges from the fun's light weftward, fo as to be feen in the morning before the fun rifes, it rifes heliacally; when a planet emerges eaftward from the rays of the fun, fo as to be vifible in the evening, it fets heliacally.

23. The anomaly of a planet is its angular diftance from its aphelion.

24. Azimuth circles are verticle circles paffing through the zenith and nadir.

25. The cycle of the fun is a revolution of 28 years, and that of the moon a revolution of 19 years.

26. The elongation of a planet is its angular diftance from the fun as feen from the earth. The greateft elongation of Mercury is 28 deg. 21 min. 8 fec. and that of Venus 47 deg. 38 min. 35 fec. —Venus and Mercury are called inferior planets; Georgium Sidus, Saturn, Jupiter, &c. fuperior.

27. The parallax of a planet is the difference between its true place, as feen from the earth's centre, and its apparent place as feen from the earth's furface.

28. The

28. The parallax of the annual orb is the angle the earth would appear under to the eye, at each planet, to be elongated from the fun ; being greateft and leaft at the extreme pofitions.

29. There are two fpheres befides thofe already mentioned, *viz.* the celeftial fphere and the terreftrial. The terreftrial circles and poles of the earth are fuppofed to be extended to the heavens. Hence, if two ftars fhould be found in thofe points, they would be called pole ftars ; but as there are not any vifible ftars in thefe points, the neareft to them are called by that name.

30. The ecliptic hath poles and circles ; thefe poles make an angle with thofe of the earth of 23 deg. 28 min. The circles of the ecliptic are called the circles of the celeftial longitude ; and thofe parallel to the ecliptic, circles of the celeftial latitude.

31. If the axis of the earth was perpendicular to the plane of the ecliptic, there would be no declination from the equinoctial points ; the equator, the tropics, polar circles, and the poles, upon that fide of the globe next the fun, would always be illuminated, and the days and nights equal. But the axis being inclined 23 deg. 28 min. to the plane of the ecliptic, and keeping obliquely and in a parallel pofition to itfelf through each revolution, produces the fpring, fummer, autumn and winter, and the inequality of the days and nights.

32. The angle that the equinoctial makes with the ecliptic, is called the fun's declination, and is equal to 23 deg. 28 min. It is half the year north, and half the year fouth of the equinox. From the

2cth

20th of March to the 23d of September, his declination is north ; and from thence to the 20th of
March, it is fouth. When the fun enters Aries,
the vernal equinox happens ; when he enters Cancer, the fummer folftice happens ; when he enters
Libra, the autumnal equinox happens ; and when
he enters Capricorn, the winter folftice happens.
The equinoxes and folftices are called the four
cardinal points. The fummer folftice happens
about the 21ft of June; then the days are the longeft
in the northern latitudes, but fhorteft in the fouthern. The winter folftice happens Dec. 21. then
the days are the fhorteft in the northern, but
longeft in the fouthern latitudes : but the days and
nights are of an equal length at the times of the
equinoxes. The fummer half-year is about nine
days longer than the winter half-year, owing to
the earth's being nearer to the fun in the winter
than fhe is in the fummer, which quickens the
rapidity of her motion ; for the nearer a planet or
comet is to the fun, the fwifter will their motions
be : therefore the earth paffes quicker through the
fouthern than the northern figns ; for it is about
nine days longer in going from the vernal equinox
to the autumnal, than it is in going from the latter
to the former. Let us compute —

SUMMER

SUMMER HALF-YEAR.		WINTER HALF-YEAR.	
Days.		*Days.*	
March	11	Sept.	7
April	30	Oct.	31
May	31	Nov.	30
June	30	Dec.	31
July	31	Jan.	31
Aug.	31	Feb.	28
Sept.	23	March	20
	187		178
Subtract	178		

Difference　9 days.　*Quod erat demonstran-
dum.*

33. The terraqueous globe is divided into five
parts called zones, *viz.* one torrid, two temperate,
and two frigid zones. The torrid is 46 deg. 56
min. in breadth, and limits the sun's greatest declination north and south. It is bounded northerly
on the tropic of Cancer, and southerly on the
tropic of Capricorn. In this zone the heat is very
extreme, and the sun rises and sets 46 deg. 56 min.
farther to the south at the time of the winter sol-
stice, than it doth at the time of the summer sol-
stice. The moon rises and sets 57 deg. 32 min.
and the other planets 65 deg. 26 min. further to
the south at some times, than they do when they
are at their greatest declination northerly. And
as the declination of the moon and planets is
often greater than that of the sun, by reason of
their latitude from the ecliptic, their semi-diurnal
and

and femi-nocturnal arcs are frequently longer than thofe of the fun. The fun is always verticle in fome part of the torrid zone, and he is always rifing and always fetting in fome parts of the globe.

The temperate zones are fituated between the torrid and the frigid zones, and each of them are 43 deg. 4 min. in breadth.

The northern temperate zone is bounded by the arctic circle on the north, and by the tropic of Cancer on the fouth. The fouthern temperate zone is bounded northerly by the tropic of Capricorn, and foutherly by the antarctic circle. In thefe zones the heat is not fo extreme as it is in the torrid, nor the cold as it is in the frigid zones.

The frigid zones are each of them 23 deg. 28 min. broad. The northerly one is bounded north by the north pole, and foutherly by the arctic circle. The foutherly frigid zone is bounded north by the antarctic circle, and foutherly by the fouth pole.— The cold is very extreme in thefe zones.

34. When the fun's declination is the greateft northerly, his femi-diurnal arc at Philadelphia, or in the latitude 40 deg. north, is $7h.\ 29m.$

When the moon's is the greateft north, her femi-nocturnal arc is   -   7— 53—

When the other planets are the greateft north, &c.   -   -   8— 13—

The moon's femi-nocturnal arc is longer than the fun's, by   -   -   0— 24—

Planets longer than, &c.   -   0— 44—

The

	Deg.	Min.
The fun's greateft declination is	23	28
The moon's greateft declination is	28	46
Jupiter's greateft declination is	32	43

The moon's declination greater than the
fun's   -   -   -   5   18

The planets declination is greater than
the fun's, by   -   -   -   9   15

35. There is a confiderable variation in the
length of the days in the capital towns and cities
in North America. At Quebec, at the time of the
fummer folftice, the days are   15*h.* 50*m.* long

At Bofton -	15— 14—·...
At New-York -	15— 2—·...
At Philadelphia ■	14— 58—·...
At Charleftown -	14— 16—·...

Longer at Quebec than Bofton   0— 36—·...
———— at ditto than New-York   0— 48—·...
———— at ditto than Philadelphia   0— 52—·...
———— at ditto than Charleftown   1— 34—·...

Deduct the length of the day from
24 hours, and the remainder will be
the length of the night :

Thus—   -   -   24— 0—·...
Length at Quebec   -   15— 50—·:··

Length of the night   -   8— 10—·...

Aftronomers do not agree about the lengths of
the days at the above places; but I have conftructed
this

this calculation according to the direction given by a celebrated Royal Aſtronomer.

36. The terraqueous globe is compoſed of land and water, and near three quarters of its ſurface is ſuppoſed to be overwhelmed with the watery element.

There are four great continents, *viz.* Europe, Africa, Aſia, and America; and alſo the continents near the poles: the northern is called Terra Arctica, and the ſouthern Terra Antarctica.

There are five great oceans, *viz.* the Northern, the Pacific, Southern, Indian, and Atlantic.

The Northern Ocean flows along between the arctic continent and the northern parts of Europe, Aſia, and America.

The Pacific, which is about 11,000 miles from north to ſouth, and 10,000 from eaſt to weſt, waſhes the weſtern and north-weſtern ſhores of America, and the eaſtern and north-eaſtern ſhores of Aſia.

The Southern Ocean lies ſouthward of America and Africa, joins the Pacific Ocean to the ſouthward, and reaches ſome parts of the antarctic continent. Its extent is not yet known.

The Indian Ocean is bounded by Aſia on the north, extends to the Pacific on the eaſt, and to part of the ſouthern antarctic continent. It is between ſeven and eight thouſand miles from north to ſouth, and four thouſand from eaſt to weſt.

The Atlantic divides Europe and Africa from America, bounds on the Indian and Southern Oceans, and is about ſix thouſand miles from north to fouth, and three and four thoufand from eaft to weft.

Befides oceans, there are feas, bays, gulphs, ftraits, lakes, ponds, rivers, &c. on the furface of the globe ; and befides continents, there are iflands, peninfulas, ifthmuses, promontories, capes or head-lands, &c. though fome of thefe join to the *terra firma.*

The

The Superficial Contents of the GLOBE *are estimated as follows :*

	Square miles.	ISLANDS.	Sq.miles.	ISLANDS.	Sq. m.
The Globe	199,512,595	Hifpaniola	36,000	Skye	900
Seas and unknown Parts	160,522,026	Newfoundland	35,500	Lewi	880
The Habitable World	38,990,569	Ceylon	27,730	Funen	768
Europe	4,456,065	Ireland	27,457	Yvica	625
Afia	10,768,823	Formofa	17,000	Minorca	520
Africa	9,654,807	Anian	11,900	Rhodes	480
America	14,110,874	Gilolo	10,400	Cephalonia	420
Perfian Empire under Darius	1,650,000	Sicily	10,400	Amboyna	400
Roman Empire, in its utmoft height	1,610,000	Timor	9,400	Orkney Pomona	324
Ruffian	3,303,485	Sardinia	7,800	Scio	300
Chinefe	1,749,000	Cyprus	6,600	Martinico	260
Great Mogul	1,116,000	Jamaica	6,300	Lemnos	220
Turkifh	960,057	Flores	6,000	Corfu	194
Prefent Perfian	800,000	Ceram	6,000	Providence	168
ISLANDS.		Breton	5,400	Man	160
Borneo	228,000	Scotora	4,000	Bornholm	160
Madagafcar	168,000	Candia	3,600	Wight	150
Sumatra	129,000	Porto Rico	3,220	Malta	150
Japan	118,000	Corfica	3,200	Barbadoes	140
Great Britain	72,926	Zealand	1,520	Zant	120
Celebes	68,400	Majorca	1,935	Antigua	100
Manilla	58,500	St. Jago	1,400	St. Chriftopher's	80
Iceland	46,000	Negropont	1,400	St. Helena	80
Terra del fuego	42,075	Teneriff	1,500	Guernfey	50
Mindinao	39,200	Gotland	1,272	Jerfey	43
Cuba	38,400	Madeira	1,000	Bermudas	40
Juva	38,250	St. Michael	950	Rhode	36

The

The number of inhabitants in the known world, according to the beft computations, are eftimated at 953 millions : Of which Europe contains 153 ; Afia, 500; Africa, 150; and America, 150 millions.

The inhabitants of the United American States, according to an account publifhed in the Maffachufett's Regifter for the prefent year, 1790, are as follows : Viz.

States.	Chief Towns.	Inhabitants.
1. New Hampfhire	Portfmouth	102,000
2. Maffachufetts	Bofton	360,000
3. Connecticut	Hartford	202,000
4. Rhode-Ifland	New-Port	58,000
5. New-York	New-York	238,000
6. New-Jerfey	Trenton	138,000
7. Pennfylvania	Philadelphia	360,000
8. Delaware	Wilmington	37,000
9. Maryland	Baltimore	218,000
10. Virginia	Richmond	420,000
11. North Carolina	Newburn	200,000
12. South Carolina	Charleftown	150,000
13. Georgia	Savannah	90,000
14. Vermont	Bennington	200,000
Total - - -		2,773,000

The inhabitants of Vermont were not mentioned in the Regifter. I received the account by a news-paper.

Prefidents

Prefidents that have been chofen in the Continental Congrefs.

1.	Peyton Randolph, Efq.	Of Virginia
2.	John Hancock, Efq.	— Maffachufetts
3.	Henry Laurens, Efq.	— So. Carolina
4.	John Jay, Efq.	— New-York
5.	Samuel Huntington, Efq.	— Connecticut
6.	John Hanfon, Efq.	— Maryland
7.	Elias Boudinot, Efq.	— New-Jerfey
8.	Thomas Mifflin, Efq.	— Pennfylvania
9.	Richard Henry Lee, Efq.	— Virginia
10.	Arthur St. Clair, Efq.	— Pennfylvania
11.	Cyrus Griffen, Efq.	— Virginia
12.	George Wafhington, Efq.	— Virginia

CLIMATES.

37. There are 30 climates between the equator and each of the poles. In the firft 24, the days increafe by half-hours; but in the remaining fix, between the polar circles and the poles, the days increafe by months.

The following Table exhibits the northern and fouthern boundaries of each climate, with their breadth, and the length of the days.

Clim.	Latitude. °	Latitude. '	Breadth. °	Breadth. '	Longest Day. H.	Longest Day. M.
1	8	25	8	25	12	30
2	16	25	8	0	13	0
3	23	50	7	25	13	30
4	30	25	6	30	14	0
5	36	28	6	8	14	30
6	41	22	4	54	15	0
7	45	29	4	7	15	30
8	49	1	3	32	16	0
9	52	0	2	57	16	30
10	54	27	2	29	17	0
11	56	37	2	10	17	30
12	58	29	1	52	18	0
13	59	58	1	29	18	30
14	61	18	1	20	19	0
15	62	25	1	7	19	30
16	63	22		57	20	0
17	64	6		44	20	30
18	64	49		43	21	0
19	65	21		32	21	30
20	65	47		22	22	0
21	66	6		19	22	30
22	66	20		14	23	0
23	66	28		8	23	30
24	66	31		3	24	0
25	67	21		1	Month	
26	69	48		2	Months	
27	73	37		3	Months	
28	78	30		4	Months	
29	84	5		5	Months	
30	90	0		6	Months	

Countries in the different Climates North of the Equinoctial Line.

I. Within the first climate, lie the gold and silver coast in Africa; Malacca, in the East Indies; Cayenne and Surinam, in Terra Firma, South America.

II. Here lie Abyssinia, in Africa; Siam, Madras, and Pondicherry, in the East Indies; Straits of Darien,

Darien, between North and South America; Tobago, the Grenades, St. Vincent, and Barbadoes,
in the Weſt Indies.

III. Mecca, in Arabia; Bombay, part of Bengal,
in the Eaſt Indies; Canton, in China; Mexico, Bay
of Campeachy, in North America; Jamaica, Hiſ-
paniola ; St. Chriſtopher's, Antigua, Martinico,
and Guadaloupe, in the Weſt Indies.

IV. Egypt, and the Canary iſlands, in Africa;
Delly, capital of Mogul empire, in Aſia ; Gulph
of Mexico, and Eaſt Florida, in North America;
the Havannah, in the Weſt Indies.

V. Gibraltar, in Spain ; part of the Mediterranean Sea; the Barbary coaſt, in Africa ; Jeruſalem,
Iſpahan, capital of Perſia ; Nankin, in China ; California, New Mexico ; Weſt Florida, Georgia, and
the Carolinas, in North America.

VI. Liſbon, in Portugal ; Madrid, in Spain;
Minorca, Sardinia, and part of Greece, in the Me-
diterranean ; Aſia Minor ; Part of the Caſpian
Sea ; Samarcand, in Great Tartary ; Pekin, in
China ; Corea and Japan ; Williamſburg, in Vir-
ginia ; Maryland and Philadelphia.

VII. Northern provinces of Spain ; ſouthern
provinces of France ; Turin, Genoa, and Rome, in
Italy ; Conſtantinople, and the Black Sea, in Turkey; the Caſpian Sea, and part of Tartary ; New-
York, and Boſton, in New England.

VIII. Paris, Vienna, capital of Germany; New-
Scotland, Newfoundland, and Canada.

IX. London,

IX. London, Flanders, Prague, Drefden; Cracow, in Poland; fouthern provinces of Ruffia, part of Tartary; north part of Newfoundland.

X. Dublin, York, Holland, Hanover, and Tartary; Warfaw, in Poland; Labrador, and New South Wales, in North America.

XI. Edinburgh, Copenhagen, Mofcow, Cape of Ruffia.

XII. South part of Sweden; Tobolfki, Cape of Siberia.

XIII. Orkney Ifles, Stockholm, capital of Sweden.

XIV. Bergen, in Norway; Peterfburgh, in Ruffia.

XV. Hudfon's Straits, North America.

XVI. Siberia, and the South-weft part of Greenland.

XVII. Drontheim, in Norway.

XVIII. Part of Finland, in Ruffia.

XIX. Archangel, on the White Sea, Ruffia.

XX. Hecla, in Iceland.

XXI. Northern parts of Ruffia and Siberia.

XXII. New North Wales, in North America.

XXIII. Davis's Straits, in ditto.

XXIV. Samoieda.

XXV. South part of Lapland.

XXVI. Weft Greenland.

XXVII. Zembla Auftralis.

XXVIII. Zembla Borealis.

XXIX. Spitzbergen, or Eaft Greenland.

XXX. Unknown.

A degree

A degree of latitude is 60 geographic miles, which is equal to about 69¼ miles Britiſh meaſure ;— and a degree of longitude is of the ſame length on the equator : But the degrees decreaſe in all parallels of latitude between the equinoĉtial and the poles, and at thoſe places they come to a point. The ſubſequent TABLE exhibits the variation, or decreaſe, in geographic miles, and hundredths of miles, in all the intermediate degrees of latitude.

Deg. Lat.	Long Miles	100th part of a mile.	Deg. Lat.	Long Miles	100th part of a mile	Deg. Lat.	Long Miles	100th part of a mile
1	59	96	31	51	43	61	29	4
2	59	94	32	50	88	62	28	17
3	59	92	33	50	32	63	27	24
4	59	86	34	49	74	64	26	30
5	59	77	35	49	15	65	25	36
6	59	67	36	48	54	66	24	41
7	59	56	37	47	92	67	23	45
8	59	40	38	47	28	68	22	48
9	59	20	39	46	62	69	21	51
10	59	8	40	46	0	70	20	52
11	58	89	41	45	28	71	19	54
12	58	68	42	44	95	72	18	55
13	58	46	43	43	88	73	17	54
14	58	22	44	43	16	74	16	53
15	58	0	45	42	43	75	15	52
16	57	60	46	41	68	76	14	51
17	57	30	47	41	0	77	13	50
18	57	4	48	40	15	78	12	48
19	56	73	49	39	36	79	11	45
20	56	38	50	38	57	80	10	42
21	56	0	51	37	73	81	9	38
22	55	63	52	37	0	82	8	35
23	55	23	53	36	18	83	7	32
24	54	81	54	35	26	84	6	28
25	54	38	55	34	41	85	5	23
26	54	0	56	33	55	86	4	18
27	53	44	57	32	67	87	3	14
28	53	0	58	31	79	88	2	9
29	52	48	59	30	90	89	1	5
30	51	96	60	30	0	90	0	0

CHAP.

C H A P. VI.

Of the Circumference and Diameter of the Earth's Orbit, and her Diurnal Motion—Why the Style was, and ought to be altered—Of the Division of Time—When different Nations begin their Days— Of the Birth and Crucifixion of CHRIST *—The reputed Æra not the true Æra of his Birth, which is demonstrated by Astronomical Calculations —Of the Clock Equations—How to regulate a Clock, &c.*

THE mean distance of the earth from the sun is about 81 millions of geographic miles, and the circumference of her orb is 509; millions, and she travels about 1,394,520 miles in twenty-four hours—a motion much more rapid than that of a cannon-ball. Her diurnal motion is 21,600 miles in a day.

Her revolution round the sun is completed in 365 days 5 hours 48 minutes and 57 seconds of time; and by reason of those odd hours, minutes and seconds, we are obliged to add one day to the month of February, every fourth year, to make the years agree as near as possible to the earth's revolutions; but as there are 11 minutes and 3 seconds wanting in each year to make 6 hours, the time is

carried

carried forward 44 minutes and 12 feconds in the
fpace of four years. At this rate, it advances 18
hours and 25 minutes every century, and 1 whole
day, or 24 hours, in fomething more than 130
years and three months and an half. From hence
arifes the neceffity of altering the ftyle; for if it
was not altered, the feafon of the year that now
happens in the middle of July, would fall in the
middle of January, in about 23,725 years. The
ftyle was altered or brought back eleven days in
1752; and fince that period, the time has run forward 6 hours 59 minutes and 54 feconds; and in
1882, it will be time to bring it back a whole day,
or alter the ftyle again.

Time is divided by us into centuries, years,
months, weeks, days, hours, minutes, feconds, &c.
A century is a revolution of 100 years. A year is
one revolution of the earth through the figns of the
zodiac. A month is the quantity of time that the
earth fpends in paffing through one fign, called a
yearly or a calendar month. A week is 7 days;
24 hours is a day; 60 minutes is an hour, and 60
feconds a minute. Four weeks is called a weekly
month.

Common or civil years are of different lengths,
according to the cuftom of different nations.——
Some reckon their year by folar, and fome by lunar
motion.

The civil year contains 365 days for three years,
which are called common years; and every fourth
year contains 366 days, called Biffextile, or Leap
Year. The civil years are alfo called Julian Years,
becaufe

becaufe Julius Cæfar was the firft perfon who added one day to every fourth year.

The civil, or common lunar year, contains 12 lunations, or 354 days; which is 11 days fhorter than the folar. Therefore, to fupply this defect, and make the lunar correfpond with the folar time, the Jews added 30 days to every third year: but that was not enough by about 30 days and ·18 hours, to make thofe reckonings agree. Twelve lunations was called the *complete*, and the addition of the 30 days the *vacant* or *embolimic* year. The firft Romans ufed the Jewifh mode of reckoning; and afterwards Julius Cæfar introduced his mode of computation: but as his mode was deficient, and the time had advanced too forward, Pope Gregory, in 1582, ordered that ten days fhould be added to the 5th of October—which brought the feafons back to their proper places—and the 5th of this month was called the 15th.

Aftronomers begin their day at noon—the Jews began their days at the fetting of the fun; (hence it is faid in the Scripture, that the evening and the morning was the firft day:)—the Chriftians begin their days at midnight; and the ancient Babylonians, Perfians, Syrians, and modern Greeks, begin their days at the rifing of the fun.

There are two kinds of hours—an equal, and an unequal. An equal hour is one 24th of a mean day, meafured by a regulated clock. An unequal, is one-twelfth part of the time that the fun is above the horizon; and the longer the days are, the longer will the hours be. ——The Jews made
their

their hours in this manner, and reckoned time by saying, the firſt, ſecond, third, &c. hour of the day, or the firſt, ſecond, third, &c. hour of the night.

The ſun riſes and ſets at Boſton, in America, about ſeven hours later than it does at Jeruſalem, and about four hours and forty minutes later than it doth at London.

The common æra of Chriſt is four years later than the true æra : hence what we call 1790, ought to be called 1794; for he was born before the death of Herod the Great, who ſought to kill him as ſoon as he heard of his birth. And, according to the teſtimony of Joſephus, (b. xv. ç. 8.) there was an eclipſe of the moon in the time of Herod's laſt ſickneſs, a little before his death;—which eclipſe ſome aſtronomical tables ſhew to have happened in the 4710th year of the Julian period, March 13*th*, 3*h*. 21*m*. after midnight, at Jeruſalem. Now Chriſt muſt have been born ſome months before Herod's death; becauſe, in the interval between his birth and Herod's death, he was carrièd into Egypt for the preſervation of his life.—His birth therefore muſt be about four years before the reputed æra.

Chriſt died in the 4746th year of the Julian period, on Friday the third of April, in the 33d year of his age, according to the reputed æra—or 37th, according to the true æra, diſcovered by the eclipſe of the moon already mentioned. He was put on the croſs about noon, and expired at about three in the evening, the whole neighbourhood of Jeruſalem being overſpread with a miraculous

darkneſs

darkneſs during the time of his ſuffering.   A heathen writer, *viz.* Phlegon, the Trallian, for want of
knowledge in Aſtronomy, imputed the cauſe of
this darkneſs to an eclipſe of the ſun ; but as the
moon was near her full, there could not be any
eclipſe of the ſun by her interpoſition at that time.

There are but four days in a year, in which a
clock, or watch, that meaſures time even, will agree
with the ſun, *viz.* April 15, June 16, Auguſt 31,
and December 24.   At all other times, he will be
too faſt or too ſlow.   From Dec. 24, to April 15,
he will be too ſlow ; from thence, to June 15, too
faſt : from thence to Auguſt 31, ſlower ; and from
thence to Dec. 24, too faſt.   This variation is called
the equation of time.

The greateſt equations are as follow, *viz.*

Feb. 10.			14 m. 41 s.	too ſlow
May 14.	the ſun will vary		4 m. 2 s.	too faſt
July 25.			5 m. 58 s.	too ſlow
Nov. 1.			16 m. 11 s.	too faſt

Theſe variations ariſe from the inequalities of the
earth's motion, which performs her diurnal rotations ſooner at one time than ſhe doth at another.
When the ſun agrees with the clock that meaſures
time even, the rotation is performed exactly in 24
hours ; but when he is too faſt of the clock, the
rotation is performed in leſs than 24 hours ; and
when it is too ſlow, it is performed in more, &c.

One apparent revolution of the ſun to the meridian, will be loſt by a planet moving round him—in
the ſame manner that a traveller would loſe a day
going

going round the earth the fame way with the apparent motion of the fun, who would reckon one day lefs at his return than the inhabitants remaining at the place of his fetting out, whatever number of days he had fpent in going round the globe.

Hence we have two years, *viz.* the folar and the fidereal. The former contains fomething more than 365 revolutions of the fun to the meridian, and the latter upwards of 366 revolutions of a fixed ftar to the fame meridian.—Hence alfo we have two kinds of days, *viz.* a folar and a fidereal. The folar is that quantity of time that the fun fpends in going from a meridian till he returns to it again; the fidereal is the time that a fixed ftar fpends in departing from a meridian till it returns again. A mean folar day is equal to 24 hours; a mean fidereal, to 23 hours 56 minutes 4 feconds.

How to regulate a Clock or Watch.

Obferve through a fmall hole in a window-fhutter the time any fixed ftar difappears behind a chimney, or any other object at a fmall diftance; and if on the fucceeding night it comes to the meridian 3 minutes 56 feconds fooner by the clock or watch, and on the next night 7 minutes 52 feconds fooner, the next night 11 minutes 48 feconds fooner, and fo on for every night fooner in that proportion, your watch, &c. is right. In one month the variation from the firft obfervation will be two hours, in three months fix hours, in fix months twelve

G   hours,

hours, in nine months eighteen hours, and in twelve months twenty-four hours.

A TABLE of the Annual Revolutions, Diurnal Motions, and Diſtances of the Primary Planets from the Sun, &c.

	Annual Revolutions.				Diurnal Rotations.			
	D.	H.	M.	S.	D.	H.	M.	S.
☉	Has no revolution.				25	12	0	0
☿	87	23	14	34	Unknown.			
♀	224	16	41	31	0	23	20	0
⊖	365	5	48	57	0	23	56	4
♂	686	22	18	19	1	0	40	0
♃	4330	8	35	4	0	9	56	0
♄	10750	13	14	4	Unknown.			
G	82 ½ years.				Unknown.			

The Diameters of the Primary Planets, with their Diſtances from the Sun.

	Diameters in Engliſh miles	Diſtances in Engliſh miles.
☉	890,000	
☿	3,000	42,000,000
♀	7,900	49,000,000
⊖	7,970	100,000,000
♂	5,400	167,000,000
♃	90,000	570,000,000
♄	70,000	949,000,000
G	797,000	1898,000,000

The ☽'s diameter is 2180 miles.

The

The Revolutions of the Secondary Planets.

	D.	H.	M.	S.	Dift. from the Primary. Miles.
1. Of the Earth's moon	27	7	43	0	240,000
2. Of Jupiter's firft moon	1	18	28	36	363,600
3. Of his fecond ditto	3	13	18	52	580,000
4. Of his third ditto	7	3	59	40	925,000
5. Of his fourth ditto	16	18	5	6	1,630,000
6. Of Saturn's firft moon	0	22	40	46	
7. Of his fecond ditto	1	8	53	9	
8. Of his third ditto	1	21	19	0	202,800
9. Of his fourth ditto	2	17	40	0	257,900
10. Of his fifth ditto	4	12	27	0	362,900
11. Of his fixth ditto	15	22	41	0	841,000
12. Of his feventh ditto	79	22	0	0	2,463,000
13. Of Georgium's firft moon	13	11	5	1	
14. Of his fecond ditto	18	17	1	19	

C H A P.   VII.

A fhort Hiftory of Comets—Of the Laws by which they are governed—Their Utility in the Univerfe.

COMETARY Aftronomy is but in its infant ftate; for, their motions are fo very irregular that it is very difficult to determine their revolutions with exactnefs, by aftronomical obfervations.

I fhall, in the firft place, give a fhort hiftory of Comets:

Secondly, Mention the laws by which they are governed; and,

Thirdly, Shew their utility in the univerfe.

I. *Of*

I. *Of the History of Comets.*

COMETS, called Blazing Stars, are durable bodies, compofed of matter capable of undergoing prodigious degrees of heat and cold, as will hereafter be demonftrated. They have undoubtedly appeared in every age fince the creation; for the ancient Egyptians and Chaldeans had fome knowledge of them: But it is evident that the Ancients knew but little concerning the nature of Comets, for they were not able to trace their motions. The celebrated Sir Ifaac Newton was the firft mathematician that difcovered the nature, philofophy, and aftronomy of thofe luminaries.

Ariftotle, and the Learned among the Greeks, were of opinion, that Comets were nothing but fublunary vapours, or airy meteors; and from hence they neglected to trace them through their intricate paths.

The Ancients fuppofed that the appearance of Comets were ominous of fome future judgments, fuch as terrible thunders, lightnings, earthquakes, inundations, wars, famines, peftilences, &c.; and fome among the Moderns retain that opinion to this day: However, it is exploded by the Learned.

The Comets are fo very numerous, that fome have fuppofed that more than four hundred belong to our fyftem: But it is not really known how great their number is; and it is probable that fome centuries muft roll off before their number is known. Dr. Herfchel informed me in October 1790, that four had made their appearance within

that

that year; but none of them had been vifible to
the naked eye. But though the number of Comets
are fo great, I have not learnt that the periods of
more than three have been determined by aftronomical obfervations. The firft appeared in 1661,
the fecond in 1680, and the third in 1757. The
period of the firft is 129 years, that of the fecond
575, and that of the third 75 only. It has been
expected that the firft would have been vifible this
year : but I have not heard of its appearing. Dr.
Herfchel does not fuppofe that either of thofe
difcovered by his telefcope, was the one we have
been looking for.

II. Of the Laws by which Comets are governed.

1. THE comets perform their revolutions round
the fun in certain determinate or appointed times,
like Saturn, Jupiter, Mars, &c.

2. They are moved by a projectile force in their
orbits, and a central force towards the fun, like
the planets : hence their motions, in fome meafure, are regular and uniform ; and the areas they
defcribe round the fun, are proportioned to the
times of their periods.

3. Their orbits are not right lines, nor circular,
but elliptical or parabolic, much like thofe of the
planets, only they have greater degrees of excentricity.

4. Some of their excentricities are fo very extenfive, that the fides of their elliptic or parabolic
orbits are almoft converted into right lines.

5. Thofe comets that have the greateft excentricities, approach the neareft to the fun at the

times

times of their perihelions; and thofe that have the leaft, are *vice verfa*.

6. The comets and planets are governed by one and the fame law: hence the fquares of the times they fpend in revolving round the fun, are always proportionate to the cubes of their greateft diftance from him: hence alfo, the longer their orbits are, the longer will their revolutions be.

7. The motions of fome comets are direct, according to the order of the figns of the zodiac; but others run retrograde, or contrary to that order.

8. The planes of the orbits of fome comets have not three degrees of elevation above the plane of the ecliptic, whilft others have almoft ninety.

9. Some comets have extreme degrees of light and heat, when they are at their perihelions; and fuch degrees of cold and darknefs, when they are at their aphelions.

10. When they are near the fun, their motions are very fwift; but when they are at their greateft diftance from him, their motions are remarkably flow.

11. The comets, like the moon, fhine with a light reflected from the fun: they are environed and compreffed by a large atmofphere, confifting of fine matter replete with clouds and vapours.

12. The head of a comet is the atmofphere itfelf, in which is a large internal body called the *Nucleus;* it fhines with the borrowed light that I have but juft mentioned.

13. The

13. The tail of a comet generally arifes from the *Nucleus*, and is an exhalation in the form of a fiery beam.

14. The length of the tails of fome comets have been feventy or eighty millions of miles; and their breadth or thicknefs, thirty or forty millions more. Their tails are always turned to the parts that are oppofite to the fun, becaufe it is natural for fumes to fly from the heat, like the fmoke from the fire.

15. The magnitude of fome comets have been fuppofed to be equal to that of the earth; and the diameters of their atmofpheres, near twelve times greater than that which furrounds our globe.

16. The extremities of the tails of fome comets are fo thin and tranfparent, that the fixed ftars may be feen through them; but no fuch thing can be difcovered through thofe parts of their tails that are near the heads of the comets, by reafon of the denfity of their parts.

17. The comets are fo very numerous, that they make the greateft part of our folar fyftem: they may be properly called a fort of planets, becaufe they revolve round the fun.

18. As the path of a comet appears much like a great circle of the fphere, it may eafily be delineated upon the furface of a celeftial globe.

19. The velocity of a comet will feem to be lefs than it really is, if the earth moves the fame way; but if it moves contrary, it will appear greater.

20. The tails of fome comets, when they are in the afcending or defcending nodes, may ftrike acrofs the orbit of the earth, and involve this

globe

globe in them. The dreadful comet of 1680 was, on the 11th of November, found to be not more than the femi-diameter of the fun to the northward of this orbit.

21. The comets have an annual parallax, but not any of a diurnal kind.

22. They are capable of undergoing prodigious degrees of heat. Sir Ifaac Newton demonftrated, when the comet I have but juft mentioned arrived at its perihelion, which happened December 11, 1680, it was as much nearer to the centre of the fun than the earth was to the fame, as 6 is to 1000; and that the fun's heat on the comet, was 2000 times greater than a red-hot iron. Hence it is evident, that the comet muft retain its heat a long time afterwards: for it has been proved, that a red-hot globe, of the magnitude of our earth, would fcarcely lofe all its heat in 50,000 years. It is therefore probable, that the comets carry a part of their heat to their aphelions, or greateft diftances from the fun.

23. The tails of comets are generated by the heat of the fun, for they have no tails at all until they come within a certain diftance of that luminary; then the exhalations begin to appear, and they grow longer and longer until the comets have juft paffed their perihelions: afterwards, the tails grow fhorter and fhorter as the heat decreafes, and at laft they wholly difappear:—hence it is manifeft, that the nearer they approach to the fun, the longer will their tails be.

24. It is probable, that in the atmofpheres of the comets, there may be violent tornados, and

terrible

A Figure of the SOLAR SYSTEM,

Engraved for the AMERICAN ORACLE.

by I. Robinson. London.

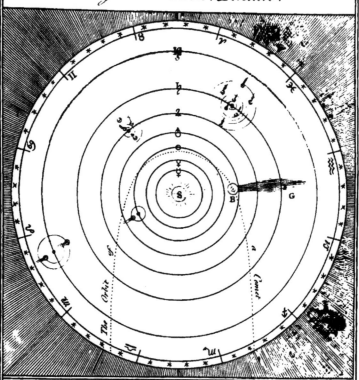

EXPLANATION.

S In the Centre represents the Sun: The other Characters the Orbits of the Primary Planets. The smaller Circles the Orbits of the Moons, of Georgium Sidus, Saturn, Jupiter, & the Earth. But the Orbits of the Primaries, and Secondaries, are not drawn at proper distances for the want of room: however, they will serve to give the Reader an Idea of the System. The outermost Circle represents the Sphere of the fixed Stars, & the twelve signs of the Zodiac. B. the Body, G. the tail of the Comet.

terrible ftorms of thunder, rain, hail, fnow, &c. :
but what damage our earth might receive by being
ftruck by the tail of a comet, is unknown; only,
as their motions are very fwift, it is reafonable to
fuppofe that this globe and the comet would both
receive a very great fhock.

III. *Of the Utility of Comets.*

AS to the utility of comets, we may reafonably
fuppofe, that the *Supreme Creator* made them not
in vain, and that they are ferviceable in rectifying
and reftoring the gradual decays of other heavenly
bodies : for, as the comets pafs through our fyftem,
their atmofpheres are fo greatly rarified and expanded by the heat of the fun, that they are fcat-
tered through all the planetary regions ; and being
thus difperfed, muft be, by the power of gravitation,
attracted into the atmofphere of our earth and the
other planets; which undoubtedly enriches the
circumambient air, repairs the decays of thofe
globes, and promotes the generation and nutrition
of the vegetable and animal productions; laying
a foundation for the prefervation of the health,
and prolongation of the lives, not only of the
human race, but of the birds, beafts, and fifhes.
Eminent philofophers have fuppofed, that the
moft fubtile and active particles of our air, upon
which the life of things chiefly depends, is derived
to us, and fupplied by comets.

It has been obferved, that the dark fpots in the
fun are only parts that have been burnt out; and
that they are nothing but a dead calx, left without
fire;

fire; and as thofe fpots have fhined out again with great fplendour, it has been fuppofed, that, by the central force of the comets, they are brought nearer and nearer to the fun in each revolution; that fome have already fallen into him, and fupplied that immenfe body of fire with new fuel; that from his being thus renewed and recruited, he has fhined out again with a greater luftre; and that the fpots that had appeared for a long time before, have thus fuddenly become invifible*.

The great fixed ftars are undoubtedly funs to other fyftems of planets and comets; and it has been fuppofed, that thofe funs do frequently lofe their brightnefs by the emiffion of light and vapours; and that they are rekindled at certain times, by comets falling upon them: that by their being thus renewed, they fuddenly fhine again with remarkable fplendour; that from hence they have been taken for new ftars, as fuch ftars have often feemed to appear, and others grow dim and difappear.

---

* A fpot more than thrice the bignefs of this earth, paffed over the fun's centre, April 21, 1766, which I fuppofe was a Comet.

I fhall

I shall conclude with the following:

THE Mighty God hath all the systems made
Of worlds, and hath a solid basis laid
On which the universal fabric stands,
Obeying of his great and good commands.
I have attempted truly to describe,
How all the planets and the comets slide
In wond'rous order, as they all do run,
As they revolve around the splendid sun.
The comets' use likewise I did relate,
How their expanded air doth circulate
Through all the system; how that they may fall,
And be like fuel on Sol's burning ball.
As time rolls off, the stars shall fade away,
And the glad face of sun and moon decay:
If not renew'd,—we don't pretend to doubt,
The light in all such globes will soon go out.
Heart can't conceive, nor mortal tongue express,
Whilst we abide in this world's wilderness,
What wondrous works the Great Supreme hath laid
Within the vast expanse which he hath made.
Thus I've the works of the Great God *of Might*
In part describ'd, whose power is infinite!
Who, from this globe, will all his saints convey
To the bright regions of immortal day!

CHAP.

C H A P. VIII.

A Definition of ASTROLOGY—*Where it is supposed it was first studied—How Astrologers pretend to tell future Events, and where stolen Goods are conveyed—Of Conjurers, Witches, Wizards, Sorcerers, Necromancers, Dreams, Visions and Apparitions— Whether the Devil knows future Events.*

ASTROLOGY is an art whereby its professors pretend to tell things past, present, and to come, by the influence of the stars, their motions, and aspects to one another.

It is supposed that this art was first studied in Egypt or Babylon, and that from those countries it has been spread over the face of the globe.

This art consists of two branches, *viz.* the astronomical and the astrological. The former is the art of erecting a figure of the firmament, representing the situations of the planets for any given time, with the aspects they bear to each other ; and the latter is the art of judging of the events of things by the figure erected, as that of the telling of fortunes, where stolen goods are conveyed to, &c. But as I acquainted myself with every branch of the art when I was young, and found by my own experience and observation that it is only a

deception

deception as to the telling of future events, I fhall explode it as an impofition contrived by impoftors to delude the ignorant, and get away their money for nothing. It is true, indeed, that an Aftrologer may chance to guefs right fometimes; but I am perfuaded that he cannot tell when any perfon will be married, how long he will live, nor where things are fecreted that have been carried off by thieves.

I therefore advife all Aftrologers who follow the practice of impofing upon the ignorant world, to defift from their evil conduct, and all rational people not to wafte their time and money in running after fuch impoftors.

As to conjurers, witches, wizards, forcerers, and necromancers, it is faid that they ufe magic or the black art, deal with familiar fpirits, ufe enchantments, and have their affiftance from the devil. It is alfo faid, that the necromancers tell future events, by calling up dead men's ghofts, or the devil; and that the witch of Endor raifed up Samuel in this manner. Many fuppofe that there are no witches in thefe times: but be that as it may, it is evident by the Scriptures that there were witches in old times; for it is faid in the Mofaical Law, " Thou fhalt not fuffer a witch to live;" and in the New Teftament, witchcraft is mentioned in the catalogue of capital abominations.

As I never acquainted myfelf with magic, I cannot tell how far the mafters of the art can go in telling future events; but one author told me, that he did not believe that there is any devil in the

the univerfe : For he faid, he had been alone in a wildernefs feven days and feven nights, and had fpoke to no being during that time; only he fum-moned the devil to make his appearance—and as he did not appear, he concluded that there is no fuch fpirit. But, by the fame rule, the author might have concluded that there is no Supreme Being in the univerfe, if he had been fummoned, and had not appeared.

A dream is the action of our imaginations when we are afleep; and there are fome that are good, and others that are bad. The good confift in the revelation of the will of the Almighty, and the bad in divers vanities. Vid. *Ecclef.* v. 7.

A vifion is an apparition, phantafm, or ghoft, which is the fpirit of a perfon deceafed, and alfo a divine revelation, by a dream, or an outward voice.

An apparition is the appearing of a fpirit, ghoft, or vifion. Hence an angel may be called an appa-rition; for the Almighty maketh his angels fpirits, and his minifters a flame of fire. Vid. *Heb.* i. 7.

That there were dreams, vifions and apparitions in ancient times, cannot be doubted by thofe who believe the facred Scriptures; for the Almighty revealed his mind and will to his patriarchs, pro-phets and apoftles, by fending his angels or fpirits to them, who fometimes made a vifible appearance, and delivered their meffages by outward voices, dreams, &c.

The angels that gave Lot warning concerning the deftruction of Sodom and Gomorrah, made an

outward

outward appearance, and delivered their meffage by an outward voice. Vid. *Gen.* xix. And the angel that warned Jofeph to depart into Egypt, appeared to him in a dream, faying, " Arife! take the young child and his mother, and flee into Egypt, &c." Vid. *Matt.* ii. 13.

We have alfo an account in the Scriptures, of the appearance of feveral perfons after they had been dead hundreds of years; for when Chrift was transfigured on the top of a high mountain, when his face did fhine as the fun, and his raiment became as white as the light, Peter, James and John being prefent, there appeared unto them Mofes and Elias talking with him. Vid. *Matt.* xvii. 1, 2, 3. When the angel of the Lord had liberated Peter from confinement, he went to the houfe of Mary, where thofe that were within, not believing it was Peter, faid, It is his angel. Vid. *Acts* xii. Hence it is manifeft that ghofts or fpirits appeared in thofe times, or they would not have expreffed themfelves in fuch a manner.

Moreover, we have alfo an account in the Scriptures, of the appearance of evil fpirits; for when Micaiah related his vifion concerning the deftruction of Ahab, he faw a lying fpirit, which was the devil, for he is the father of lies. Read the twenty-fecond chapter of the Firft of Kings. In the book of Job it is faid, that there was a day when the fons of God came to prefent them before the Lord, and Satan came alfo amongft them; and in the fourth chapter of Matthew, we have an account of the Devil's coming to tempt CHRIST.

From

From hence it is manifeſt, that both good and bad ſpirits have appeared in old times; and as the power of the Holy One of Iſrael is not limited, as he is the ſame yeſterday, to-day, and for ever, and doth of his ſovereign will and pleaſure in the armies of heaven above, and amongſt the inhabitants of this lower world, he can ſend his angels, the ſpirits of his ſaints, or thoſe in the infernal regions, to any part of the univerſe, and cauſe them to appear to whomſoever he pleaſes; for all the material and immaterial beings are at his command, and all are obliged to obey his ſovereign orders.

Many ſuppoſe that neither the angelical nor the diabolical ſpirits, nor the ghoſts of perſons deceaſed, are ſuffered to appear in the preſent age. However, it is evident by the teſtimonies of perſons of the beſt credit and reputation, that apparitions have been ſeen of late. Of this there have been a number of recent proofs, two of which I will juſt mention.

A young man who had left his father in the North of England, and was off many leagues at ſea, being at cards in the cabin, ſtopped playing all at once, and gazed with aſtoniſhment. The company aſked, what he was gazing at? and he ſaid that his father appeared to him. After his arrival in Great Britain, he found that his father died at the inſtant that he made his appearance. This I had from a lady of undoubted veracity, who was a near neighbour to the father and the ſon.

A woman with whom I was well acquainted, being on her death-bed, expreſſed a great deſire,

juſt

juſt before ſhe expired, of ſeeing her only ſon, who was then at ſea, and of delivering to him a meſſage. She mentioned to the by-ſtanders what ſhe wanted to ſay to her ſon, and died immediately. She was in New-England, and her ſon near the Weſt-Indies; and about the time that ſhe died, ſhe appeared to him ſtanding on the ſhrowds of the veſſel, delivered her meſſage, walked over ſeveral barrels on the deck, then went down the ſide of the veſſel, and appeared to be floating on, the water ſome time, and then ſunk. The young man ſet down the day and the hour that ſhe appeared, and alſo the words ſhe had ſpoken. He ſuppoſed that what he had ſeen was a token of his mother's death; and, on his arrival home, found that ſhe died at the time ſhe appeared to him, and that the words that he had written correſponded exactly with thoſe delivered to the by-ſtanders. He went to ſea afterwards, and was drowned. Perhaps her appearing to him in that manner, was a forerunner, not only of her own, but of his death.

Apparitions may be ſeen by ſome, and not by others, which is evident by the company's not ſeeing the man that appeared to his ſon in the cabin; but though every one is not permitted to ſee them, it is no proof that they do not appear at all. Many that have retained the opinion for a long time that there are no ſuch appearances, have afterwards been convinced of their error by ſeeing ſuch things themſelves.

Thoſe that deny that the ſpirits of the inviſible world have ſometimes made their appearance, muſt affirm that the writings of the holy patriarchs,

H   prophets

prophets and apoftles,. and the teftimonics of many good men and women, are all falfehoods, and that the Almighty is an imperfect being, that it is not in his power to caufe fuch appearances ; but fuch an opinion muft be very abfurd and ridiculous.

Befides the appearance of good angels, the fpirits of fome that have been dead, and Satan himfelf, we have an account in the Scriptures, of the appearance of the Almighty ; for he appeared to Adam and Eve, to Cain, to Noah, and to others in the antediluvian world, and to Mofes and others fince the flood.

Although I am far from being timorous or fuperftitious, and believe people are often affrighted and think they fee apparitions when they do not, yet I am convinced that they do fometimes appear, not only from the writings of the Scriptures, and the teftimonies of perfons of good repute, but from my own experience and obfervation, having feen not lefs than five in the day-time, and when I was not thinking of any fuch things, nor the leaft affrighted till they all vanifhed ; excepting one, which I knew to be an apparition as foon as I faw it, becaufe it was in the form of a coffin, and proved ominous of the death of a near relation : three of the others were in the forms of men, and the other in the form of a woman. I have alfo heard noifes, which, together with the apparitions, I efteemed to be forerunners of the deaths of certain perfons.

I have often been afked, whether I believed that the Devil knows future events? and my anfwer has been, that it is probable that he does ; for when he tempted Adam and Eve in Paradife, he faid,

" For

" For God doth know, that, in the day ye eat
thereof, then your eyes fhall be opened, and ye
fhall be as gods, knowing good and evil." Vid.
Gen. iii. 5.; which proved true according to the
Almighty's own words, viz. " And the Lord
God faid, Behold! the man is become as one of
us, to know good and evil." Gen. iii. 22.

When the witch of Endor had raifed up
Samuel, or the Devil in his fhape, a true account
was given of the things that happened afterwards.
From hence we may conclude, that the Devil
knows future events, though perhaps not every
thing that is to happen.

To conclude, I do not fee any thing in natural
philofophy that is repugnant to my hypothefis
concerning apparitions ; and I believe it is in the
power of the Great Governor of the Univerfe, to
caufe them to appear to the fons and daughters of
men, and to reveal his mind and will to his children by his own Spirit, or by the fpirits of his
faints or angels.

CHAP. IX.

A Definition of ATHEISM, SUPERSTITION, *and*
IDOLATRY—*Of the four Religions—The Chris-*
tians divided into different Sectaries—Partiality
reigns too much among them—The Articles of the
Mahometan Religion—When the Pagan commenced
—The Heathen Gods and Goddesses.

ATHEISM is the denying or disbelieving
the Being of a God.

Superstition is an introduction of needless ceremonies into the modes of worship; the adding of
things not required by the *Great Governor* of the
Universe; a false and mistaken devotion.

Idolatry is the worshipping of the sun, moon,
and stars; the birds, beasts and fishes; and images
made by the hands of men, &c.

Some have supposed that there are no Atheists
in the world; others say, that Atheism rather
prevails in some parts: But be this as it may,
there is a plenty of Superstition and Idolatry in
many places, and I am sorry that Superstition
reigns too much in Christendom.

There are but four Religions in the world, the
Jewish, Christian, Mahometan, and Pagan.

The Jews adhere to the Mosaical law: The
Christians, to the doctrine of Christ and his apostles:

The

The Mahometans, to the tenets of Mahomet; and the Pagans worſhip different kinds of idols.

The Chriſtians are divided into a great number of Sectaries, as Roman Catholics, Lutherans, Preſbyterians, Baptiſts, Quakers, Methodiſts, Moravians, Sandemanians, Arians, Socinians, Arminians, Univerſaliſts, &c. many of which are too uncharitable to thoſe not of their own perſuaſion. I was even taught myſelf, when I was young, that if I aſſembled with any ſect to perform religious worſhip beſides the one I was brought up with, I went on to the devil's ground. However, I ſoon forſook that ſuperſtitious notion, when I came to conſider that the earth is the Lord's, the fulneſs thereof, the world, and they that dwell therein; and that the poor Devil has not one foot of land on the globe, although he offered to give all the kingdoms of the world to Chriſt, if he would fall down and worſhip him.

The Mahometan religion commenced about 622 years after the birth of Chriſt.

The articles of the religion are:

1. That there is but one God.
2. That Mahomet was ſent by God.
3. The obſervation of purifications.
4. The praying at appointed times.
5. The giving of alms.
6. The faſting in the month Ramezan.
7. The going once in pilgrimage to Mecca.
8. The abſtaining from ſpirituous liquor and gaming.
9. A man may marry four wives, and may keep concubines.

H 3

10. Every

10. Every male flave who profeffes this religion fhall have his freedom : But as it is fuppofed that the women have no fouls, it is immaterial what perfuafion they are of.

According to Chronology, the Pagan religion was firft introduced by Ninus king of Affyria, 2084 years before Chrift. The gods of the Heathenifh nations have been very numerous; and fome were called mafculine, and fome feminine, as will appear by the following catalogue, *viz.*

Abeona, the goddefs of voyages; Adraftea, goddeffes of Nemefis and Fortuna; Ægeria, a beautiful nymph worfhipped by the Romans, and much by their ladies; Æolus, the god of the winds; Æfculanus, god of riches, worfhipped by the Romans; Æfculapius, god of phyfic; Agenoria, the goddefs of induftry; Anatis, the goddefs of proftitution among the Arminians; Angerona, the goddefs of filence; Anteverta, the goddefs of women in labour; Apollo, the god of mufic, poetry, and the fciences; Argentinus, the god of wealth; Ate, the goddefs of revenge; Averruncus, a god of the Romans, fuppofed to keep off and remove evils and misfortunes; Aurora, goddefs of the morning, and mother of the ftars and winds; Autumnus, the god of fruits.—Baal, an Affyrian god; Bacchus, the god of wine; Bapta, the goddefs of fhame; Bellona, the goddefs of war; Britomartis, a Cretan goddefs; Bubona, the goddefs of oxen.—Cabrus, a god to whom falt fifh was offered in facrifice; Camæna and Carna, goddeffes of infants; Canopus, an Egyptian god; Cardu, an houfehold goddefs; Cardua, a

Romifh

Romiſh goddeſs, ſuppoſed to preſide over the vital parts of mankind ; Catius, a tutelar god to grown perſons ; Ceres, the goddeſs of agriculture ; Cerus, the god of opportunity ; Cœlum, the moſt ancient of the heathen gods ; Collina, the goddeſs of the hills ; Comus, the goddeſs of laughter and jollity ; Concordia, the goddeſs of peace among the Romans ; Cunia, a goddeſs of new-born infants ; Cupid, the ſon of Mars and Venus, and god of love, ſmiles, &c.—Dagon, a god worſhipped in Canaan ; Dercete, a goddeſs ; Deverra, a goddeſs of breeding women ; Diana Lucina, a goddeſs of women in labour ; Diſcordia, the goddeſs of contention ; Domiducus and Domitius, two nupᵗial gods ; Dryades, nymphs or gods of the woods. —Educa, a goddeſs of new-born infants ; Egeria, a goddeſs.—Fabula, the goddeſs of lies ; Fabulinus, a god of infants ; Fama, the goddeſs of report ; Februa, a goddeſs of purification ; Felicitas, the goddeſs of happineſs ; Feronia, the goddeſs of the woods ; Feſſonia, a goddeſs of wearied perſons ; Fidius, a goddeſs of treaties ; Flora, the goddeſs of flowers and of corn ; Fluviales or Potamides, goddeſſes of rivers ; Fornax, a goddeſs of corn and bakers ; Fortuna, the goddeſs of happineſs and miſery, ſaid to be blind.—Gelaſinus, the god of myrth and ſmiles.—Harpocrates, the god of ſilence ; Hebe, goddeſs of youth ; Hippona, the goddeſs of horſes and ſtables ; Hoſtilina, a goddeſs of corn ; Hyale, a beautiful goddeſs of the woods, and one of Diana's conſtant attendants ; Hygia, a goddeſs of health ; Hymen, the god of marriage. —Janus, a god of new-born infants ; Intercidona,

H 4

a goddeſs

a goddefs of breeding women; Jugatinus and
Jupiter, perfectus, nuptial gods; Juno, the
daughter of Saturn and Ops, fifter and wife of
Jupiter, great queen of heaven, and goddefs of
marriages and births; Jupiter, the fon of Saturn
and Ops, and fupreme deity of the Pagan world;
Juventa, a goddefs of youths.—Lactura or Lactu-
cina, a goddefs of corn; Lares, the fons of Mercury and Lara, worfhipped as houfehold gods;
Lateranus, a houfehold god; Laverna, a goddefs
of thieves; Lemoniades, goddeffes of meadows;
Levana, a goddefs of new-born infants; Libitina,
the goddefs of funerals; Limnades, goddefs of lakes
and ponds; Lubentia, the goddefs of pleafure.——
Manageneta, a goddefs of women in labour; Man-
tura, a goddefs of corn; Manturna, Matuta, and
Mena, nuptial goddeffes; Mars, the god of war;
Meditrina, a goddefs of grown perfons; Melicerta,
a fea god; Mellona, the goddefs of honey; Mercury,
the fon of Jupiter and Maia, meffenger of the gods,
inventor of letters, the god of eloquence, merchandize, and robbers; Minerva, the goddefs of wifdom,
arts, and war, &c.; Mnemofyne, the goddefs of
the memory; Momus, god of raillery; Morpheus,
the god of dreams; Mors, the daughter of night
and fleep, and goddefs of death; Muatta, or Muta,
the goddefs of filence.—Nænia, the goddefs of
funeral fongs; Naiades, goddeffes of rivers and
fountains; Napæ'æ, goddeffes of groves and vallies;
Natio and Nudina, goddeffes of infants; Neæra,
a goddefs loved by Apollo; Nemefis, or Adraftæa,
the goddefs of revenge; Neptune, the god of

the

the fea; Nereides, fea-goddeffes; Nox, the moft ancient of all the Heathen gods; Numeria, a goddefs of grown perfons; Nyctimene, a goddefs of Theffaly.—Occator, a god of harrowing; Oceanus, a very old fea god; Orbona, a goddefs of grown perfons; Orcades, the nymphs of mountains; Ofiris, an idol worfhipped by the Egyptians, under the form of an ox.—Pales, the goddefs of fhepherds; Pan, a god of the fhepherds; Partunda, a nuptial god; Patelina, a goddefs of corn; Paventia and Polina, goddeffes of infants; Pellonia, a goddefs of grown perfons; Penates, fmall ftatues, or houfehold gods; Phæcafiani, ancient gods of Greece; Phorcus, a fea god, who could take any form; Picumnus, a rural god; Pilumnus, a god of corn and breeding women; Pitho, a goddefs of eloquence; Pluto, the god of Hell; Plutus, god of riches, the blind, lame, and timorous; Pomona, the goddefs of fruits and autumn; Priapus, god of gardens and debauchery; Propætides, goddeffes in Cyprus; Profa or Porrima, a goddefs of women in labour; Pfyche, the goddefs of pleafure.—Quies, the goddefs of grown perfons.—Robigus, a god of corn; Rumina, a goddefs of new born infants; Runcina, the goddefs of weeding; Rucina, a rural deity.—Salus, the goddefs of health; Sancus, a god of the Sabines; Sator and Sarritor, rural gods; Seia and Segetia, goddeffes of corn; Senta, a goddefs of married women; Somnus, the god of fleep; Stata, a goddefs of grown perfons; Statanus and Sentia, deities of infants; Stercutus, or Sterquilinus, the god of dung; Stimula and Strenua, goddeffes

of

of grown perfons; Suada, a nuptial goddefs; Sylvanus, a god of woods and forefts; Syrinx, a nymph of Arcadia.—Tacita, a goddefs of filence; Tantalus, nymph of Plota; Tereus, the nymph Biftonis; Terminus, the god of boundaries; Terror, the god of dread and fear; Themis, the daughter of heaven and earth, and goddefs of juftice; Thetis, the goddefs of the fea; Tutelina, a goddefs of corn.—Vacuna, the goddefs of idle perfons; Vagitanus, a god of little infants; Vallonia, a goddefs of vallies; Venus, the goddefs of love, beauty, and marriage; Vertumnus, god of the fpring; Vefta, a goddefs of fire; Viales, deities of highways; Vibilia, a goddefs of wanderers; Virginenfis and Viriplaca, nuptial goddeffes; Vitula, the goddefs of mirth; Volumna, Volumnus, and Volupia, deities of grown perfons; Volufia, a goddefs of corn; Vulcan, the god of fubterraneous fires.

Thus numerous were the idols of the Heathens; and befides thofe I have mentioned, fome worfhipped the Thunder and Lightning, with many other things too numerous to mention.

C H A P. X.

*The Works of the Visible Creation demonstrate the
Existence of a SUPREME BEING—From whence
Superstition and Idolatry sprang—Atheistical,
Superstitious, and Idolatrous People exhorted to
study Philosophy.*

THAT there is a *Supreme Being* of *infinite
wisdom* and *power*, that created, upholds,
preserves and governs the universe, is evident
by the systems of worlds, the revolutions and
rotations of the heavenly bodies, and the contents
of our terraqueous globe ; for all demonstrate his
existence, omnipotence, omniscience, and omni-
presence ; who is justly named the King Eternal,
Immortal, and Invisible, as he is King of kings,
and Lord of lords, rules over all, is from everlasting to everlasting, the same yesterday, to-day,
and for ever.

This infinite and incomprehensible Fountain of
life and motion is an Invisible Spirit : hence the
idolatrous nations have become so vain in their
imaginations, that they have taken the Works of
the Creator, for the Creator himself ; have paid
adoration to the sun, moon and stars ; birds,
beasts, and fishes ; and to dumb idols, made of
gold, silver, wood, and stone, which can neither
hear,

hear, fee, feel, nor walk, as they are void of
fenfe, life, and motion. Thus have the Heathens
changed the truth of God into a lie, and worfhipped and ferved the creature more than the *Creator*,
who is bleffed for ever. Amen !

Befides this vanity of worfhipping the works of
the Almighty inftead of himfelf, another has prevailed in places where the knowledge of the true
God has in fome meafure been made known. It
is an introduction of a great mafs of formality,
fuperftition, ceremonies and orders into the modes
of worfhip, which are entirely needlefs. This has
been a great burden to the people, has tended to
keep them in vaffalage and flavery, and to make
them have erroneous notions concerning God and
the things of Religion. Thefe impofitions were
undoubtedly contrived by defigning men, to
aggrandize themfelves with worldly honours and
profits.

I befeech all that are or may be of an atheiftical,
fuperftitious, or an idolatrous principle, to ftudy
Philofophy, which is the mother of all good arts,
as it will teach them that there is a Creator, make
them happy in this prefent life, and ripen them for
glory in a future ftate. Acquaint yourfelves, therefore, with this divine fcience. Survey the heavens
and earth ; contemplate upon the wonderful works
of the vifible creation ; trace their phænomena, and
inveftigate their laws; and you will undoubtedly be
convinced, that there is a *Supreme Being* of infinite
wifdom and power, that created, upholds, and
governs the univerfe. View the fyftems of worlds;
and confider of the diftances, magnitudes, orders,
and

and motions of the heavenly bodies:—the periods
of comets; the revolutions and rotations of the
primary 'and fecondary planets; their directions,
ftations, retrogradations, nodes, excentricities,
aphelions, perihelions, heliocentric and geocentric
longitudes and latitudes; right afcenfions, declinations, amplitudes, altitudes, femi-diurnal and
femi-nocturnal arcs; rifings, fouthings, fettings,
afpects, conjunctions, oppofitions, quadratures;
eclipfes, tranfits, and occultations:—the quantities,
durations, reft and affections of the folar and
lunar obfervations; the magnitudes of the apparent diameters of the luminaries:—the courfe of
the penumbras; the obumbration of the terreftrial
difc, and of the lunar rays; the rotation of the
fun upon its axis:—the annual revolution and
diurnal motion of the earth; its journey through
the figns of the zodiac: the equinoxes and folftices:
fpring, fummer, autumn, winter, day and night:
—the diverfities of colours, velocity of the rays of
light, expulfion of darknefs, generation of heat,
difperfion of cold:—the moon's attraction upon
the waters, at the times of her apogeon and
perigeon:—the fpring and the neap tides; the
ebbing and flowing of the fea, &c.

View the wonderful formation and contents of
the terraqueous globe; its compofition of earth,
air, fire and water; its rocks, mines and minerals; vegetable and animal productions of trees,
plants and herbs; birds, beafts and fifhes; men,
women and children; kingdoms, towns and
cities; and the different complexions, languages,
religions,

religions, cuftoms, manners, forms of government, and fyftems of laws among the nations.

Behold the wondrous atmofphere, that environs and compreffes the globe!—Confider of its
elaftic powers and mutations; of its expanfion and
elevation by heat, and condenfation and depreffion
by cold:—its different currents and motions; as
hurricanes, tornados, trade winds, monfoons, gales,
breezes, whirlwinds, &c.—how replete it is with
clouds and vapours, from which are generated the
rain, hail, fnow, froft, dew, mift, fog, &c.—of
the caufe of the rainbow, mock funs, meteors,
northern-lights, and other phænomena:—of the
roaring of the winds, raging of the feas, and eruptions of burning volcanos:—of the various prodi-
gies and judgments that are frequent in the world;
fuch as, thunders, lightnings, earthquakes, inundations, wars, famines, peftilences, &c.

When you have taken an accurate furvey, and
ferioufly contemplated upon thefe objects, you muft
be convinced, that thofe things could not be formed,
put in motion, and conducted in fuch a regular
order and manner, without *a primary caufe*, or *a
Divine Artificer*, endowed with infinite power,
wifdom and fkill. " For the invifible things of
him from the creation of the world are clearly
feen, being underftood by the things that are
made, even his eternal power and godhead. The
heavens declare the glory of God, and the firmament fheweth his handiwork."

Befides the great benefits you will receive from
the ftudy of Philofophy, in being led into the knowledge

ledge of the *Creator;* it will teach you the nature and utility of the liberal and mechanical arts and fciences, *viz.* grammar, rhetoric, logic, mufic, arithmetic, algebra, geometry, trigonometry, aftronomy, navigation, furveying, agriculture, trade, commerce, mechanics, architecture, manufactures, magnetifm, botany, chymiftry, pharmacy, anatomy, phyfic, furgery, hydroftatics, pneumatics, optics, electricity, &c. All the difcoveries and improvements in thefe things owe their origin to Philofophy, which is the very bafis of your happinefs, eafe and comfort. Without this knowledge, the world would be filled with violence, and its inhabitants brought into a deplorable condition.

Wherever this excellent fcience has fhone out in its meridian fplendour, the clouds of darknefs and ignorance, that overfpread the minds of many, have been difpelled. Hence atheifm, fuperftition, and idolatry, have been deftroyed : the craft of falfe priefts, witches, wizards, necromancers, conjurers, aftrologers, and all thofe kinds of locufts difcovered, and the deluded people freed from the burden of their impofitions. The knowledge of the true God has thus been made known ; the idols of the Heathen deftroyed, the true religion difcovered, proper modes of worfhip eftablifhed, and the way to heaven and happinefs made plain. In a word, Philofophy is not only the fource and foundation of abundant ufefulnefs, but of abundant profit and pleafure. It is the nobleft fcience in which the human mind can poffibly be engaged ; a delightful ftudy, attended with the moft beneficial

ficial confequences to the inhabitants of the world. It teaches us to fear the Lord, which is the beginning of wifdom; and to depart away from iniquity, which is a good underftanding.

By the cultivation of this divine fcience, the Aftronomer is enabled to meafure the diftances, determine the magnitudes, calculate the motions, and point out the places of the heavenly bodies: the Geometrician, to determine the boundaries of continents, empires, kingdoms and ftates: the Navigator, to conduct his veffel, and meafure his voyage to the remote parts of the globe: the Phyfician, to prefcribe proper remedies, and cure difeafes: the Apothecary, to prepare and compound natural and artificial fubftances for medicinal purpofes: the Divine, to preach orthodox fermons; and the Lawyer, to conduct, according to the direction of the ftatutes, laws and ordinances of the country or place in which he refides. In fine, it enables every one, let his profeffion be liberal or mechanical, to tranfact bufinefs in the moft accurate, eafy, and advantageous manner.

Furthermore, I befeech you to take a further furvey of the works of the *Divine Artificer*, that appear in the vifible creation. Confider of the generation, formation, nutrition, growth and prefervation of all the different kinds of vegetables and animals:—of the wondrous conftruction of the human frame; which is compounded of folids and fluids, confifting of bones, cartilages, ligaments, fibres, membranes, mufcles, glands, tendons, arteries, veins, nerves, teguments, teeth, nails, &c.

—of

—of the chyle, blood, bile, faliva, tears, perfpiration, pancreatic juice, mucous milk, fabaceous
humour, cerum, gummi occuli, amygdalæ, gaf-
tric fluid, lympha, phlegm, fpiritus animalis, &c.—
of the vital, natural, and animal functions : the
action of the heart, lungs, and arteries ; and of the
folids and fluids upon each other : the manducation of food, and the deglutition and digeftion
thereof, for the nourifhment of the body : its
mufcular motions and voluntary actions, which
conftitute the fenfe of feeing, hearing, feeling,
fmelling, tafting, perceiving, reafoning, imagining,
remembering, and judging ; with all the affections
of the mind. Confider, I fay, ferioufly upon all
thefe things, and you will undoubtedly be convinced that they did not come by chance : you will
know that you are fearfully and wonderfully made ;
that there is a *primary caufe*, a *Divine Architect*,
who is the Former of your bodies, the Father of
your fpirits, the God in whom you live, move, and
have your being :—you will no longer be like the
fool, that hath faid in his heart, there is no God,
nor like thofe that follow fuperftition and idolatry ;
but be fenfible that there is an infinite and an
incomprehenfible Fountain of *life* and *motion*, by
whom all things were created, both in heaven and
earth, whether they be vifible or invifible to us
in this mortal ftate ; who requires no worfhip, but
that which is performed in fpirit and truth :—your
minds will be exalted, your faculties enlarged,
your ideas raifed, your underftandings illuminated;
and you will join with the faints in celebrating

I   the

the praifes of *Him,* who is the only proper *objeƐt* of religious *adoration* and *worſhip*; faying, " Great and marvellous are thy works, *Lord God Almighty!* juft and true are thy ways, thou *King of Saints!* Who ſhall not fear thee, *O Lord!* and glorify thy name ?"

CHAP.

C H A P. XI.

*A Definition of Oppreſſion, Tyranny, Sedition, Trea-
ſon, Rebellion, and Perſecution.—The evil Effects
of thoſe Abominations.*

OPPRESSION is the laying of ſuch heavy
burthens upon the people, that they are
unable to bear; and the cruſhing of them, by
authority and violence. Thus Pharaoh oppreſſed
the children of Iſrael, by putting them under taſk-
maſters, and requiring brick without ſtraw.

Tyranny conſiſts in a cruel, violent, and unjuſt
government. It is the abuſe of royal power, by
depriving the people of their religious and civil
rights, by cruelty and injuſtice.

Sedition is the exciting of mutinies, ſtrifes,
contentions, diviſions, animoſities, inſurrections,
mobs and riots.

Treaſon conſiſts in attempting to kill a king,
queen, or a prince; a levying of war againſt them,
adhering to their enemies; the coining of bad
money, and the counterfeiting of a king's great
privy-ſeal. Theſe things are called High Treaſon.

Petty Treaſon conſiſts in a ſervant's killing
his maſter; a woman, her huſband; a ſecular or
religious man, his prelate or ſuperior, to whom
he owes faith and obedience.

I 2   Rebellion

Rebellion is a wilful breaking of the laws, by difobeying the commands of the Almighty, or the good and wholefome laws of the land; a revolting from the government of a king, and the rifing up in arms againft a fovereign.

Perfecution is an unjuft or violent depriving of people of their civil and religious liberties, by fcourging, fines, imprifonments, banifhment, the confifcation of property, death, &c.

All thefe abominations ought to be fuppreffed, wherever they do or may exift; becaufe they tend to deftroy the felicity of mankind, and make them miferable. Wherever oppreffion and tyranny reigns, the progrefs of the cultivation and improvement of the arts and fciences is impeded, the kingdom or ftate is weakened, and poverty and diftrefs muft inevitably enfue. Sedition, treafon, rebellion and perfecution, are all productive of the fame calamities, for they involve the people in vaffalage and flavery.

A rebel muft be a horrid monfter, for he muft break his oath of allegiance, and expofe himfelf to a variety of perils and dangers : he has no reft day nor night, for he is continually afraid of being detected and brought to condign punifh-ment; but if he fucceeds in his attempts to de-throne a king or a prince, or to run off with the government of an empire, or a part of it, then thofe that adhere to him fall a facrifice to his tyrannic laws; and thofe that have been in oppofition to his evil conduct, are perfecuted, becaufe they could not in confcience follow the multitude to do evil. Has not rebellion been the

caufe

caufe of all the calamities that have happened in the univerfe?—Was it not a rebellion that caft the fallen angels out of Heaven, and caufed them to be referved in chains under darknefs, until the dreadful coming of the great day?—Was it not a rebellion that caft Adam and Eve out of Paradife, and expofed them to all the miferies of this life, and that which is to come?—Was it not a rebellion that made Cain a fugitive and a vagabond in the earth?—Was it not a rebellion that caufed the antideluvian world to be filled with violence, and brought the deluge which fwept off all excepting Noah and his family, who were loyal fubjeéts?— Was it not a rebellion that brought that fhower of fire and brimftone upon Sodom and Gomorrah, which deftroyed thofe cities? and in a word, has not rebellion been the caufe of all the calamities that have befel the human race fince the creation of man?

A rebel is a tranfgreffor of the laws: therefore, all oppreffors, all tyrants, all evil feducers, all traitors, and all perfecutors, are rebels; becaufe their conduét is repugnant to the commands of the Great Governor of the univerfe.

The conduét of a rebel is not like a rational creature, but like a roaring lion, tearing tiger, devouring wolf, and a raging bear; violence and oppreffion, carnage and defolation, poverty and diftrefs, vaffalage and flavery, are the things which he promotes. He carries on his abominations under a cloak of religion and liberty, difturbs people in their bufinefs, robs them of their property, and takes away the lives of the innocent.

I 3   He

He is a curfe upon earth, a judgment to the human race, and a child of the devil. Hence indignation and wrath, tribulation and anguifh, will be the reward of fuch workers of iniquity.

Let all rational people remember, that rebellion is an abominable fin; that it is pregnant with every evil work, and that it is like the fin of witchcraft; that it brings a train of judgments upon the human race, deftroys the public tranquillity, and makes mankind miferable. Let them have no correfpondence with thofe difturbers of the peace; but labour to fupprefs rebellion in all its various forms, wherever it may fpring up. Let them fear GOD, honour the King, and thofe in authority; and live peaceable and quiet lives, in all godlinefs and honefty; for the wrath of the Lord is againft them that do evil.

CHAP.

CHAP. XII.

Definition of LIBERTY—*All have a right to it, but some deprive themselves of that right by their own conduct, and some by the conduct of others—Of the Duty of Nations—The evil Effects of bad Constitutions—Of the French Revolution—The happy Condition of the British Empire.*

AS Liberty confifts in the free exercife of our religion, the enjoyment of our rights, and the profits of our labour, with the protection of our perfons and properties, it is a privilege of an immenfe value: and as it is the natural right of every man, it is our indifpenfible duty to feek after it, whenever we are deprived of its benefits. But we find that many deprive themfelves of liberty by their own evil conduct—by breaking the good and wholefome laws of the land, by doing things difhonourable to the Creator, and injurious to mankind. Thus thieves, robbers, murderers, &c. deftroy their own freedom by their vicious behaviour; and expofe themfelves, not only to confinement, but to more fevere punifhments.

We alfo find, that many are deprived of liberty by the inhuman conduct of tyrants, who opprefs and perfecute thofe over whom they have ufurped dominion and power, by taking from them the liberty of confcience, and loading them with burthens which they are unable to bear.

It

It is the duty of every nation to guard against all these evils; and from hence arises the necessity of having a good constitution and system of laws in every kingdom or state, binding upon all ranks, orders and degrees of men. Hence also arises the necessity of having kings, counsellors, governors, magistrates, and other officers appointed, for the administration of justice, and the preservation of public tranquillity.

Various constitutions and systems of laws have been framed and established amongst different nations; and where ignorance and superstition have reigned triumphant, the constitution and laws have been very deficient, so that things have been established and practised that were repugnant to the principles of justice and humanity. What numerous multitudes have been massacred for a difference of opinion in matters of religion and modes of worship! And how many thousands have worn out their days in vassalage and slavery, because laws have been made contrary to the requisitions of the great law of Reason! But whenever the minds of the people are illuminated, and the clouds of darkness, ignorance and superstition, are dispelled, the spirit of Liberty breaks forth like the sun in its meridian splendour; the constitutions are altered, oppressive laws abolished, the bands of tyranny and oppression are broken asunder, distressed objects are discharged from confinement, the liberal and mechanical arts and sciences thrive and flourish, and all enjoy those liberties which are the natural right of every man.

The

The illumination of the minds of the people in France, has been productive of the great and glorious Revolution; of the forming of a new constitution, the enacting of new laws, and the abolishing of those things that were repugnant to the interest and prosperity of the kingdom. How pleasing must it be to see both the King and the National Assembly unite together in establishing the new constitution, and in promoting whatever may conduce to the good of the nation, and benefit of mankind in general! May the flame of Liberty, like the refulgent beams of the sun, be extended over the face of the whole globe; and may all nations partake of the great and glorious blessings of natural freedom!

And with pleasure we recollect, that once in the *British Empire*, the inhabitants, fired with the love of Liberty, drove ignorance, darkness, and superstition before them; made a glorious stand for their rights, and were thereby brought into a happy situation. We are now blest with a good King, with good rulers, and with a good constitution and system of laws: here a man enjoys a free toleration of religion: here he is rewarded for his labour: here he is protected in his person and property: here agriculture, navigation, trade, commerce, architecture, and the manufactories, thrive and flourish; and the nation has arrived to an inconceivable pitch of grandeur and affluence. Our constitution, being pregnant with a variety of privileges, is admired by distant nations: foreigners come from afar, and find shelter and protection, liberty and freedom, under our government.

CHAP.

CHAP. XIII.

The Great CONSTITUTION *of* LIBERTY, *founded upon the Principles of Juſtice, and the Laws of Humanity.*

EVERY conſtitution and ſyſtem of laws ought to be conſtructed upon the principles of juſtice and humanity, which will enſure the rights of a King, and the peace, liberty, and happineſs of his ſubjects. I ſhall therefore beg leave to obſerve,

1. That every man has a legal right to perform religious worſhip according to the dictates of his conſcience, at ſuch times and places as ſhall be moſt agreeable to himſelf; providing he doth not injure others in their perſons, characters, or properties.

2. That it is unlawful to perſecute any of the human race, for a difference of opinion in matters of religion or modes of worſhip.

3. That public teachers are needful to inſtruct people in the principles of religion and morality.

4. That good rulers, both in church and ſtate, ought to be reaſonably rewarded for their ſervices out of the public funds, and empowered to remove officers for male-conduct; and, by and with the
advice

advice and confent of the body corporate, to expel members for vicious practices.

5. That the freedom of fpeech, and the liberty of the prefs, are the natural rights of every man, providing he doth not injure himfelf nor others by his converfation or publications.

6. That legiflative and executive officers, confifting of kings, counfellors, governors, judges, magiftrates, reprefentatives, and other rulers, are neceffary to make and execute laws for the prefervation of the public tranquillity in empires, kingdoms, and ftates.

7. That it is unlawful for rulers to make and execute laws repugnant to thofe of the Great *Governor* of the univerfe, or deftructive to the peace and profperity of the community at large.

8. That the people have a right to chufe and fend delegates to reprefent their ftate and condition in a legiflative affembly.

9. That a legiflative body ought to confift of a mixture of monarchical, ariftocratical, and democratical governments; and be divided into three branches, as that of a King, Lords, and Commons.

10. That each branch ought to have a negative voice on the other branches ; and no bill ought to be paffed into a law without the advice and confent of, at leaft, two thirds of the members of two of the branches of the legiflature.

11. The legiflators ought to meet once in a year, and as much oftner as the circumftances of the nation may require, at fuch times and places as may be moft convenient.

12. That

12. That the people have a right to petition the legiflature for a redrefs of grievances.

13. That every branch of an empire ought to be fubject to the fupreme legiflative head of a nation: to render all proper honour and obedience to the King, and to all in authority, and to be fubordinate to the good and wholefome laws of the land.

14. That a King ought to be confidered as the firft fupreme legiflative and executive officer in a kingdom, and to be empowered to grant pardons to criminals whenever it may be needful. He has a right to a free liberty of confcience; to protection in his perfon, character, and property; to rule and govern his people according to the conftitution, ftatutes, laws and ordinances of his realm; to that honour and obedience that is due to perfonages in fuch an exalted ftation; and to fuch a revenue as his circumftances may require, and his fubjects be able to raife.

15. That no man ought to be chofen into office, unlefs he is endowed with wifdom and knowledge, and can be well recommended for good works and pious actions.

16. That it is lawful to confer titles of honour upon, and to give rewards to fuch perfons as may merit them by their vigorous exertions and good conduct.

17. That legiflators ought to be exempted from being arrefted for debt, whilft they are paffing to, remain at, and are returning from the legiflative affemblies, becaufe an arreftment would impede the public fervice.

18. That

18. That courts of juſtice ought to be eſtabliſhed, and juſtice adminiſtered to all without reſpect of perſons.

19. That every man ought to be allowed a trial by jury.

20. That thoſe under confinement ought to know what they are confined for ; who their accuſers are ; not be compelled to bear witneſs againſt themſelves ; be allowed to bring evidence, with the benefit of counſel ; and ſhould not be condemned, unleſs found guilty by the teſtimony of two or three credible witneſſes.

21. That exceſſive bail ought never to be demanded, exceſſive fines required, nor exceſſive puniſhments inflicted.

22. That criminals under confinement ought to have no puniſhment laid upon them, but that which is requiſite for the ſecuring of their bodies ; unleſs, after they have been found guilty, it is ordered by the judges, agreeable to the laws of the land.

23. That no man ought to be impriſoned for debt, providing he gives up his property to his creditors, and has not waſted his time in idleneſs, nor his eſtate by intemperance, gaming, or any other vicious practice.

24. That perſons falſely impriſoned, ought to be immediately liberated, and to have ample ſatiſfaction for the injuries they have received ; and thoſe guilty of the abomination of confining the innocent, ought to be ſeverely puniſhed for their atrocious conduct.

25. That

25. That every one who is a fubject of taxation, ought to be allowed to vote for a reprefentative, providing he is twenty-one years of age.

26. That every man ought to be taxed in proportion to his abilities.

27. That the power of levying and collecting taxes, duties, imposts, &c. with that of coining money, emitting bills of credit, borrowing money for the public ufe, entering into treaties and alliances with foreign powers, appointing, commiffioning, and fending of ambaffadors, minifters, confuls, meffengers, &c. belongs to the legiflature.

28. That fuch treaties ought to be efteemed as a part of the law of the land; kept inviolate; and whenever they are broken, reftitution ought to be made to the party injured.

29. That as money is a defence as well as wifdom, a circulating medium ought to be eftablifhed, confifting of gold, filver, copper, and bills of exchange. Its credit fhould be kept up, and but one currency eftablifhed in a kingdom.

30. That churches ought to be built for the accommodation of the people when they perform religious worfhip; public fchools, colleges, academies, and univerfities erected, for the promotion of literature; hofpitals founded, for the reception of the fick; work-houfes for the employment of idle perfons; and prifons for the fecuring of thieves, robbers, murderers, and other felons;— and focieties inftituted, for the purpofe of making further difcoveries and improvements in the liberal and mechanical arts and fciences.

31. That

31. That cuftom-houfes, poft-offices, and poft-roads, ought to be eftablifhed in every kingdom and ftate.

32. That weights and meafures ought to be alike in every part of an empire, if not through the world.

33. That all foreigners ought to be treated with hofpitality, and protected by the laws of the land.

34. That the heirs of an eftate ought not to be difinherited by reafon of the ill conduct of their parents; nor thrown out of their pofts of honour and profit, in confequence of the unlawful behaviour of their relations.

35. That every author ought to have the benefit of his own productions, whether they be upon theological, mathematical, philofophical, phyfical, mechanical, or any other fubject.

36. That all officers, whether ecclefiaftical, civil, or military, with every other perfon, ought to guard againft fedition, treafon, rebellion, and every thing that may tend to fow difcord amongft brethren, deftroy the public tranquillity, and make mankind unhappy.

Thus have I framed a CONSTITUTION, which appears to me to be according to the law of reafon, and the dictates of found policy. Perhaps fome things have efcaped my obfervation, that might juftly be added. However, I believe, that one calculated and eftablifhed upon thefe principles, would fecure the rights of kings, and thofe of their fubjects, which is all that any rational perfon can defire.

CHAP.

C H A P. XIV.

Of the Impoſſibility of framing a Conſtitution that will
pleaſe every-body—Anecdote of two Iriſhmen—
The Rights of Kings, and Liberties of their Sub-
jeĉts, ought to be ſecured by a good Conſtitution and
Syſtem of Laws.—Story of the Parſon's Wig—
Thoughts on the Mode of chuſing Repreſentatives—
The Happineſs of the People ought to be promoted.

I CANNOT expeĉt my political ſentiments will
pleaſe every body, let them be ever ſo well
founded on reaſon; for there are ſuch a number
of diſcontented mortals in the world who luſt
after dominion and power, and ſuch multitudes
that do not wiſh to be under any government at
all, that ſhould the *Angel Gabriel* frame and ſend
a *Conſtitution* from *Heaven*, ſome would be found
to murmur at it.

Many are of ſuch a craving temper and diſpoſi-
tion, that they would engroſs the whole world to
themſelves, and rule and govern it, were it in
their power. The ambition of ſome men is almoſt
boundleſs.—This brings to my mind an anecdote
of two Iriſhmen, who being intoxicated with liquor
at an inn, began to think that they were maſters
of the whole globe, and agreed to divide it equally
between themſelves: but as the intoxication in-
creaſed,

creafed, one of them, who was of a very craving difpofition, concluded that he had the beft right to the world, and fwore that he would have it all to himfelf; whilft the other contended, that he was juftly entitled to one half of it, and wanted no more than his right. At laft they fettled the matter by a number of heavy blows; but whether the world was to be equally divided, or whether one was to have it all, and the other no part of it, I have forgot, although I had my information from a gentleman who was witnefs to this very fingular conteft, and knew fomething of our *wife* combatants.

The fame temper and difpofition amongft others, has prevailed too much in the world; and has fometimes broke out into fuch acts of violence, that kings and nobles have been deprived of their rights, and oftentimes the people at large of theirs. A monarch may crave the eftates, and all the profits of the labours of his fubjects: and, on the contrary, the people may crave thofe things that legally belong to their king; and, by acts of violence and injuftice, both may lofe their rights. —But, thefe extremes ought to be carefully guarded againft; and the rights of kings, and thofe of their fubjects, fecured by a *good Conftitution* and fyftem of laws. Is it not ftrange that mortal men, who can abide but a very fhort time in this troublefome world, fhould be fo craving as to luft after more riches, honours and profits, than they can enjoy, or that can poffibly do them any good?

" Why doth the mifer all his cares employ,
" To gain thofe riches that he can't enjoy ?"

K   When

When the powers of legiſlation are lodged altogether in one man, and the nobles and other inhabitants of a country are ſhut out from having any voice in the making of laws; or when the powers are in the nobles, or in the people only, it will naturally generate ·a ſpirit of diſcontent amongſt thoſe who have not a ſhare in that power. Will not a king feel very uneaſy, if he has no part of the legiſlative power? Will not the nobles be diſcontented, if they have no part of it? And, will not the people murmur, if they have no ſhare in the ſame? Therefore, to prevent uneaſineſs, and promote a ſpirit of union and harmony in empires, kingdoms and ſtates, it is beſt, in my opinion, to have a mixture of monarchy, ariſto-cracy and democracy in every legiſlative body, like the parliament of Great-Britain.

The things of this world are ſo mutable, that we cannot foretel what conſtitutions may be eſta-bliſhed hereafter. And although an aſtronomer can determine the revolutions and rotations of the rambling planets, and point out the directions, ſtations, and retrogradations of the luminaries of heaven, for thouſands of years to come; yet he cannot foretel what will be done hereafter, even in his own country, or in any other part of the globe, in regard to the overturning, altering, framing, and eſtabliſhing of conſtitutions, king-doms, or ſtates. It is probable that there may be alterations in theſe things; and perhaps the fu-ture generations may have a greater knowledge in politics than the preſent, and be able to frame better modes of government than the nations are in this

age :

age: for, if the knowledge of philofophy increafes in the world, and the glorious fun-fhine of liberty and freedom breaks forth, the clouds of darknefs and ignorance will be difpelled ; atheifm, fuperfti-tion and idolatry will wear away ; and the people be freed from thofe burthens and impofitions that involve many, in the dark and benighted corners of the globe, in vaffalage and flavery ! It is probable they will difcover that fome conftitutions have been deficient, and be able to correct and amend what-ever has been amifs.

But many are of fuch a changeable temper and difpofition in the prefent age, that they would be for ever altering a conftitution that is conftructed in the beft manner, and continue their alterations 'till it is wholly ruined, like the *Minifter's wig ;* an account of which I will juft relate as I re-ceived it.

A *Reverend Divine* having loft his hair in his old age, bought a large white wig to cover his naked head : But it difpleafed his auditors to that degree, that they had a church-meeting on the fub-ject, and concluded that the wearing of fuch a large wig was idolatry ; and accordingly fent a committee to their *Reverend Paftor*, to acquaint him that his congregation was much difpleafed, &c. He told them, that he did not wifh to have any uneafinefs about the wig ; and if they thought it was too large, they might make it fmaller ; and delivered it to the committee, who laid it before the congre-gation, to have it altered ; when one cut off a lock of hair in one place, and another in another, &c.

K 2 till

till the wig was utterly fpoiled. At length they agreed that it was fit to be feen in the pulpit; whereupon it was returned to the owner, who faid, it could not now be *idolatry* to wear the wig, for it had not the *likenefs* of any thing in *Heaven* or *Earth*.—Juft fo it is with a conftitution that is conftructed in the beft manner: it will not fuit every one; and if it is clipped by every difcontented mortal, it will be wholly ruined, *like the Reverend Divine's wig.*

There is a vanity that I have feen under the fun, and have often wondered that it has not been fuppreffed in this enlightened age—I mean the unjuftifiable mode of chufing legiflators in fome parts of the globe.

When the people are called upon to chufe their reprefentatives, a number will put up in fome public place, when perhaps not more than one is to be chofen. There fcaffolds muft be erected, publications fent forth, mobs convened day after day, harangues delivered, and many thoufands fpent to induce the freeholders to chufe their delegates—when the whole of the work might be completed in half a day, by the people's affembling at the places appointed for the performance of religious worfhip, and carrying in their votes, in writing, to the clerk of every parifh, who might eafily fend them to fome perfon that might be authorifed in the county to receive and count the fame, and to promulgate who has the greateft number, or who the people have chofen for their legiflators. Would not this mode take

up

up lefs time, be much eafier to the people, and much more commendable, and beneficial to the community, than to have the freeholders fatigue themfelves by coming a great diftance, wafting their time by being kept from their employments day after day, quarrelling and wrangling about the choice of a reprefentative? or, than to have the candidates for fuch places wafte their eftates by keeping open houfes, giving away victuals, drink, ribbands, cockades, &c. till they have ruined themfelves, families, and creditors?

As it is our indifpenfible duty to promote the happinefs of mankind, I have mentioned things in the preceding chapters, which I hope will be inftrumental in promoting their peace and profperity.

In fome parts of America, the people have chofen their reprefentatives in the way that I have dif-approved; and in others, in the way that I have recommended. Candidates often merit the atten-tion of the public by their good conduct, and by publications fpread abroad by their friends; and are frequently chofen into office that way, without being put to the expence of keeping open houfes, and of troubling the people to affemble day after day.

K 3   CHAP.

C H A P. XV.

The Epiſtle of the AUTHOR—*A Deſcription of the Road to Liberty.*

TO all people, nations, and languages, that dwell in all the world.

2. Grace, mercy, and peace be multiplied unto you.

3. It hath ſeemed good unto me to promulgate this *Epiſtle,* and to make known thereby the genuine deſcription of the road which leads to that liberty which is deſtitute of licentiouſneſs.

4. To mention thoſe things that will make you comfortable in this life, and conduct you in the way to everlaſting felicity in the realms of immortal bliſs and happineſs.

5. I beſeech you, therefore, to remember, that atheiſm, ſuperſtition, idolatry, ſedition, treaſon, rebellion, covetouſneſs, theft, robbery, murder, intemperance, debauchery, bad language, gaming, idleneſs, and all kinds of vice, will carry you out of the road that leads to liberty, and involve you in deſtruction and miſery.

6. Shun, therefore, all kinds of vice and immorality, and walk in the pleaſant paths of piety and virtue, which will eſtabliſh your freedom on a permanent baſis.

7. Let

7. Let thofe who doubt the exiftence of a *Supreme Being;* and thofe who worfhip the fun, moon, or ftars—the birds, beafts, or fifhes—or idols made by the hands of men, contemplate upon the works of the vifible creation; which will naturally convince them of their error, and excite them to pay homage and adoration to HIM, who created, upholds, and governs the univerfe, and is the only proper object of religious worfhip.

8. Avoid contentions, divifions, and animofities, which too frequently terminate in bloodfhed and devaftation.

9. Follow peace with all men; break not your oaths of allegiance, fulfil your obligations; fear GOD, honour the King, and thofe in authority; and be fubordinate to the good and wholefome laws of the kingdom or ftate in which you refide.

10. Walk honeftly; render to all their dues; pay your debts, and your proportion of the public taxes.

11. Be kind to the poor and needy, relieve the oppreffed, vifit the fick, bury the dead, feed the hungry, clothe the naked; and fhew acts of kindnefs, charity, and humanity to ftrangers, captives, and prifoners.

12. Love yourfelves, your families, and your neighbours; do good to your enemies; avenge not yourfelves.

13. Be not high minded in profperity, but patient in adverfity.

14. Cultivate and improve the liberal and mechanical arts and fciences, and promote every thing that may tend to make mankind happy.

K 4 15. Be

15. Be careful of your credit, your time, and your money; fhun bad company, ufe not bad language, be not idle, wafte not your eftate in fuperfluities, be temperate and exemplary in your lives and converfations.

16. Shun the pollutions that are in the world, fupprefs that which is evil; do as you would be done by, and continually follow that which is good: then will ye be in the road that leads to liberty.

17. Grace, mercy, and peace be multiplied unto you all.   *Amen.*

This EPISTLE of the AUTHOR, was written from *Anglia*, to the inhabitants of the world.

CHAP. XVI.

A Definition of ELECTRICITY—*Who made Discoveries in the Science—How Buildings, Vessels, &c. ought to be furnished with Rods to carry off the Electrical Fluid—Of the Electrical Kite—Whether it is dangerous to wear Hair-pins, &c. in a Thunder Storm—The wonderful Effects of Lightning—Communication of Mr. Woodward—Of Animals killed by Lightning—Where it is safest to be in a Thunder Storm—The Sea an Electric Machine—What Diseases may be cured by Electricity.*

ELECTRICITY is said to be an attraction without magnetism. It is the attracting and repelling of very light bodies, when the attracting body is rubbed or chafed.

The first idea of Electricity was given by Otto-guericke, A. D. 1647; and the electrical shock was first discovered at Leyden, in 1746, by Cuneus; and in 1756, it was found that it would set spirits on fire.

The electrical fluid seems to be in all bodies in a greater or a less degree. Some things will attract and conduct it, but others repel its force. Glass, hair, silk, and gums, are called electrics, or non-conductors; but metals, water, green wood,
and

and moſt animal and vegetable ſubſtances, are non-electrics, or conductors.

Dr. Benjamin Franklin, of Philadelphia, made diſcoveries and improvements in Electricity. He found that an electrical kite, and pointed rods, would attract and conduct the electrical fluid. On making his diſcoveries known, he was made a Fellow of the Royal Society, and was afterwards honoured with a diploma from the univerſity of Oxford in England, conſtituting him a Doctor of Laws.

Dr. Prieſtley, it is ſaid, has alſo made great improvements in Electricity; and ſome ſuppoſe, that they are equal to thoſe made by Doctor Franklin.

Great advantages have already been derived from thoſe diſcoveries and improvements, on account of the preſervation of buildings, and many people in thunder-ſtorms. All towers, ſteeples, other buildings, and ſhips, ought to be well furniſhed with pointed rods, to attract and con-duct the electrical fluid; though ſome are ſo ſuper-ſtitious as to ſuppoſe it is not lawful to try to defend thoſe things againſt the violence of the lightning: but they may as well ſuppoſe that it is unlawful to brace a houſe, and defend it that way againſt the violence of the wind; for the wind and the lightning are both ſent by the *Almighty*.

Small iron or ſteel rods, with ſharp points, are ſaid to be the beſt conductors. The electrical fluid will make its way to thoſe that are the neareſt, and it chuſes thoſe that are of the beſt kind. The

rods

rods fhould be placed in fuch directions as to convey the lightning into the ground from the buildings, or into the water from veffels.

A kite fent up into a thunder cloud by a wire, having a key tied to its end, and held by a filk ribband, will attract the electric fluid from the clouds, and conduct it to the ground in a beautiful and furprizing manner.

Some fuppofe it is dangerous to wear hair-pins, jewels, necklaces, buckles, &c. in a thunder-ftorm, becaufe thofe metals attract the electric fluid; but I have feen it demonftrated, where lectures have been delivered upon Experimental Philofophy, that hair-pins and other metalics may, if placed in proper directions, preferve the lives of people, by conveying the lightning from their bodies and limbs. I have been credibly informed, that a man in America had his fhoe-buckles melted on his feet by a flafh of lightning, and that he received no other damage.

The lightning has ftrange effects upon minerals, vegetables, and animals: fometimes it will melt metals, at others it will not; fometimes it fets trees, buildings, &c. on fire, at others it will not; fometimes it burns animals, at others it will not; fometimes it tears things to atoms, at others it leaves them whole; fometimes it breaks every bone in an animal to fine pieces, leaving the flefh and fkin whole; at others it has no fuch effect: fometimes it tears their flefh to atoms, and leaves their bones found; fometimes they are killed, and no figns of a bruife can be found in their bodies

or

or limbs. When they are killed in this manner, it is fuppofed that their breath is taken away by the force of the lightning, as it is fometimes from others by the force of a cannon-ball, when the body appears to be unhurt.

The lightning flies in all directions : fometimes it will run in a horizontal courfe, cutting down large trees, &c. It often falls perpendicular, oblique, zigzag, &c. I have known it ftrike the ground, and then run upwards, tearing all before it. When it ftrikes a ftick of hewed timber, it will follow the grains to where they have been cut off; then it will leave the ftick, and pafs on to where they have been cut off in another place ; there it will enter, and tear the timber to the heart, if the grains lead to it. Of fuch things I have been an eye-witnefs.

The Hon. Bazalel Woodward, Efq. vice-prefident, and profeffor of the mathematics and natural philofophy at Dartmouth College, in the State of New Hampfhire, gave me an account of a very remarkable phænomenon which happened juft by his houfe.—Two large pine-trees, which I viewed myfelf, were both ftruck at the fame inftant with the lightning, at about eleven in the evening. They ftood near 66 yards from each other. One of them was a dry, and the other a green tree. The lightning ran from their tops to their roots, and tore out near a quarter part of each tree, which was fpread round in fine fplinters. Mr. Woodward ran immediately from his bed to the other fide of the room, to comfort one of his children

that

that cried on being furprized at the noife of the thunder; and feeing a light fhine through the window, fuppofed his barn was on fire. He therefore ran to the window, and, behold, the dry tree appeared to be on fire from the top to the bottom! and it emitted fparks in different directions, fome horizontal, fome oblique, others perpendicular; fome arofe to a great height above the tree, when all at once the light difappeared; and that which is very remarkable, is, that the tree was not burnt in the leaft in any place. He afked my opinion upon this phænomenon; and I fuppofed, that the tree was highly charged with electrical fluid, and that it burft through the bands of its confinement, and emitted thofe corufcations till the fluid was exhaufted and difperfed in the atmofphere without fetting the tree on fire.

Animals killed with lightning fwell to an enormous fize. An ox killed that way, was found ftanding on his legs the next day, much fwelled. A man was killed in one church, and a woman in another, fitting in an erect pofture, and remained fo after they were dead. I have had the care of three patients that lived at a great diftance from each other, who were ftruck with the lightning. The firft was thrown into hyfteric fits, the fecond confiderably burnt, and the third was ftruck with numbnefs: but they all recovered. Thus rapid is the force, wondrous the operation, and dreadful the effects of this fubtile electric fluid.

It is fuppofed to be fafer to fit in the middle of a large room during a thunder-ftorm, than it is to
be

be near the fides, or in a fmall apartment, becaufe the lightning frequently runs on the fides of a building. The windows aught to be fhut; for, a perfon ftanding with his cloaths dry, in the open air, in a room, under a fhed or a tree, will be in great danger of attracting the electrical fluid: but he is not in fo much danger if his cloaths are wet, becaufe the water is a conductor.

The earth and waters are full of the electric matter, as well as the atmofphere; and it is fuppofed that there is enough in the fea to confume it, were it put in motion. As water is a conductor, and falt a non-conductor, the fea may be called a huge electrical machine; for when it is agitated by the wind, it collects fire on its furface from beneath: hence it appears in the night as though it was on fire. A cloud, therefore, raifed from a rough fea, contains more electric fire than one raifed from the land or a calm fea. Hence, if two fuch clouds meet, that which is the higheft charged will difcharge itfelf into the other by a flafh of lightning, which will reftore the equilibrium. This fire clearing the air, the adjoining air will rufh in with a report called thunder. If a cloud highly charged, is attracted by a mountain, tower, fteeple, houfe, or tree charged in a lefs degree, it will difcharge its contents, tearing whatever obftructs its force: hence appears the need of wires to attract and convey the fluid.

I have neither time nor room to give any long hiftory of Electricity, nor even a defcription of the electrical machines and experiments that I h ve

feen

feen where I have attended lectures upon Experimental Philofophy; fhall therefore only obferve, that a fpectator would be furprized, were he to attend fuch lectures, at the wonderful difcoveries and improvements that have been made in this fcience in the prefent age.

Electricity is faid to be beneficial in agues, St. Anthony's fire, lofs of fight from a *gutta ferena* and other caufes, extravafated blood, bronchocele, chlorofis, coldnefs of the feet, confumptions, contractions of the limbs, cramp, deafnefs, dropfy, epilepfy, *fiftula lachrymalis*, ganglions, gout, gravel, headach, hyfterics, inflammations, king's evil, leprofy, mortifications, palfy, peripneumony, pleurify, rheumatifms, ringworms, fcalds, *fciatica*, fhingles, fprains, furfeits, toothach, tumours, and St. Vitus's dance.

But it is hurtful when the pulfe run high, and alfo to pregnant and fuckling women, and to unborn children. It is very prejudicial in all venereal cafes, becaufe it increafes the *momentum* of the blood.

In intermitting cafes, the patient fhould be electrified when the pulfe are at the lowest ; and none ought to apply this remedy without the advice of a fkilful phyfician, becaufe it may convey a diforder to every part of the human body, and do much damage thereby.

When the pulfe are higher than in a ftate of perfect health, electricity muft be entirely omitted : but when the body is in a proper condition, difeafes may be cured by the electrical fluid, when other remedies fail.

CHAP.

CHAP. XVII.

Of the Cause of THUNDER, LIGHTNING, EARTH-
QUAKES, *and* INUNDATIONS—*A Table of remarkable Earthquakes, and the Places and People
that have been swallowed up.*

AS Thunder is only the report of the Lightning, it is needless to say much upon that
subject : What we have to do, is to point out the
cause of the Lightning.

In the preceding chapter we mentioned, that
" when two clouds meet, that which is the most
highly charged with the electrical fluid, will discharge itself into the other by a flash of lightning,
which restores an equilibrium. This clearing the
air, the adjoining air rushes in with a report called
Thunder." Let us now observe, that the Lightning is produced by sulphureous steams exhaled
by the heat of the sun, and the nitrous acids or
salts floating in the air, which, combining together, generate heat by fermentation ; and the
violent action and great rapidity of the motion of
the different currents of air upon the combustible
composition, makes it take fire, and cause those
dreadful explosions we call thunder-claps.

Hence,

Hence, then, the heat or fire muft proceed from the antiperiftafis which exift between the particles, and their friction, or rubbing againft one another. We find, that *Aqua Fortis*, and the filings of copper, will generate heat; that the oil of caraway-feed, poured on the compound fpirits of nitre, will kindle immediately into a flame, and caufe a prodigious explofion; and that the flowers of fulphur, mixed with an equal quantity of the filings of iron, will produce a blaft. Hence, if twenty pounds of each are mixed into a firm pafte with a little water, and the compofition is buried four or five feet under ground, in fix or feven hours the earth will tremble, crack, fmoke, open her mouth, and vomit flames of fire. A large quantity of fuch matter would make a burning volcano; if it fhould burft under the fea, it would produce a water-fpout; if in the clouds, thunder and lightning. This is called an Artificial Earthquake, &c.

I have heard thirteen Earthquakes in America, and have obferved, that the found of fome refembled the noife of thunder; fome, the roaring of wind; fome, the running of water; and fome, the burning of fire. Hence I concluded, that there are different kinds of Earthquakes, produced from various caufes. Thofe that I have felt, all happened in fair weather, and when the wind did not blow: excepting one, which made a noife like heavy thunder at a diftance; the fhock was violent, and the weather very windy and rainy.

They commonly happen in calm, warm, dry, fultry, or frofty feafons, and are felt both at land

L and

and fea. Some are confined to narrow limits; others are extended to many countries. Some are gentle in their motions; others are violent, laying all in ruins. A hollow rumbling noife rolling in the air, like the roaring of a cannon, precedes the fhock. They are felt more in high places than in thofe that are low, and have a greater effect upon ftone and other folid buildings than thofe of flighter materials. Great towns and cities, fituated on feas, bays, rivers, or burning mountains, are the moft fubject to Earthquakes. They caufe the water in wells to become foul; and fometimes they fhut up fome fprings, and open others. Sometimes they fwallow up mountains, iflands, towns and cities; affrighten and deftroy the birds, beafts, and fifhes; men, women, and children. Sometimes the fea roars, and rifes into billows; and the earth opens her mouth, and vomits flames of fire, with great quantities of water, fand, ftones, fulphur, &c. The atmofphere is turned red: new mountains and iflands are thrown up: the rocks are fplit to pieces; fome canals of water are filled with earth, whilft new ones are opened. Sometimes the bells in churches ring; the tops of fteeples and chimneys are fhaken down; the beafts of the field, and the fowls of the air, cry out; whilft the inhabitants of the earth are filled with lamentation. Thefe are the works of the Almighty! He looketh on the earth, and it trembleth; He toucheth the hills, and they fmoke.

It is faid, that Earthquakes have produced pains in the head, back and joints, rheumatifms, vertigos, hyfteric complaints, and other nervous diforders,

ders, arising perhaps from sulphureous and other disagreeable effluvia that issues out of the earth, and the frightful appearance of things.

Philosophers have accounted various ways for the causes of these dreadful phænomena ; as,

1. From subterraneous cavities, vaults and canals in the bowels of the earth, some of which are filled with wind, some with water, and some with liquid fires.

2. From sulphur, bitumen, salts, amber, minerals, &c. deposited in the globe ; which, being of an inflammable nature, generate exhalations by fermentation or other causes.

3. The motion of the wind and water in the subterraneous caverns and canals, may drive the rocks, mines and minerals together with such a rapidity as to cause them to emit sparks that may set fire to the sulphureous, nitrous, and other inflammable steams that are of a combustible nature, which, wanting vent, produces eruptions, and all the violent and dreadful effects that are frequent in Earthquakes.

4. From subterraneous clouds bursting out into lightning.

5. The falling-in of arches weakened by continual subterraneous fires.

6. The bursting out of rarefied steams of water.

7. The ignition of inflammable exhalations.

8. The violence of the electrical fluid.

In some places, the combustible matter may find vent without producing any direful effects ; but when the ground is tightly condensed, the inflam-

mable

mable matter will burſt open the gates of its confinement, the ſides of the ſubterraneous caverns
will fall together, and down will go mountains,
iſlands, towns and cities, if they are ſituated upon
ſuch places ; and where there are waters contained
in ſuch ſubterraneous apartments, they will aſcend,
and overwhelm the parts where the mountains,
&c. have been ſwallowed up. Hence, new lakes,
new rivers, new ponds, &c. are made on the
ſurface of the globe.

When new mountains and iſlands are thrown up
by the combuſtible matter, a ſufficient quantity of
earth and water ruſhes under them, to ſupport
them from ſinking, otherwiſe they would naturally ſubſide.

About the year 1749, Dr. Stukeley invented a
new hypotheſis concerning the cauſe of Earthquakes, which is what is already mentioned, *viz.*
the violence of the electrical fluid. He ſuppoſed
that the earth is ſometimes ſo overcharged with
it, that it breaks out into the atmoſphere, and
cauſes all the dreadful phænomena ; that when
the earth is highly charged, the touch of a non-
electric body, ſuch as a cloud not charged with the
electrical fluid, will produce an earthquake ; and
alſo, that one may be produced from a cloud
more highly charged than the earth, if it empties
its contents on the globe.

Let us therefore obſerve, that when the electrical
fluid in the earth and atmoſphere is in a perfect
equilibrium, there can be no earthquake, if this
fluid is the cauſe of thoſe commotions ; that when
ſuch

such convulfions happen, as foon as the terreftrial and atmofpherical electric fluid is equally difperfed, the Earthquakes ceafe, and all things are at reft.

It is my opinion, that Earthquakes are produced from various caufes; but that they moft frequently happen from the generation of heat, by the fermentation of beds of fulphur combined with divers kinds of minerals; that the heat increafes until the combuftible matter takes fire, and produces thofe dreadful explofions, which are fometimes fo violent as to caufe the earth to open her mouth, vomit flames of fire, torrents of water, wind, fand, rocks, &c. and to fwallow up mountains, iflands, towns, and cities.

" In deepeft caves are beds of fulphur made,
And in a fecret fearful ambufh laid;
When God's avenging hand fhall touch the train,
Some warn'd devoted city quick is flain.
The earth 's convuls'd, her jaws are open'd wide;
Churches with all their lofty fpires fubfide;
To Nature's womb they fink with dreadful throes,
And on poor fcreaming fouls the chafms clofe!"

I fhall conclude this Chapter by the addition of the fubfequent Table of Remarkable Earthquakes and Inundations:

EARTHQUAKES.

	A. D.
TWELVE cities overturned in Afia	17
Nicomedia, and feveral neighbouring cities, fwallowed up	120
One hundred and fifty cities fwallowed up in Macedonia	357
Fifty thoufand perfons deftroyed by an earthquake and an inundation in Alexandria	365

L 3   Several

A. D.

Several cities fwallowed up in Europe	394
Several cities fwallowed up near Cybyra	417
Several cities fwallowed up in Paleftine	419
The walls of Conftantinople and 17 towers overthrown - - -	446
The city of Antioch almoft deftroyed -	458
One at Conftantinople, that lafted 40 days, and overturned feveral edifices -	480
Several cities deftroyed near Antioch -	526
Four thoufand eight hundred people fwallowed up at Antioch -	528
One at Conftantinople -	552
Many houfes overthrown at Rome and Conftantinople - - -	557
France, Germany and Italy fhaken, and St. Paul's thrown down at Rome -	801
One through all England -	1090
One at Shropfhire -	1110
One at ditto - , -	1116
One at ditto - -	1120
One at ditto, when flames of fire iffued out of the earth - -	1134
The city of Catania, and above 15,000 people, fwallowed up -	1137
One that overthrew a church at Lincoln, and fome others -	1185
A dreadful one in - -	1228
One in Shropfhire - -	1249
One at St. Albans -	1250
A general one, that threw down St. Michael's near Glaftonbury -	1274
The greateft in England -	1328

Several

	A. D.
Several churches thrown down -	1382
A very dreadful one -	1426
Another - -	1661
Fifty-four towns and cities, with 60,000 people, fwallowed up in Sicily	1691
Port-Royal in Jamaica fwallowed up	1693
Sixty thoufand perfons deftroyed in Sicily	1693
Near 400,000 people deftroyed in China	1699
Peru laid wafte by an earthquake, 300 leagues in length, and 90 in breadth	1700
An earthquake at Rome -	1703
One at China -	1718
The kingdom of Chili deftroyed -	1730
Four provinces deftroyed in China -	1731
One at Naples -	1732
Two thoufand fouls, 100 houfes, and five churches, deftroyed in Ireland	1734
Lima and Callao, with about 3,000 people, fwallowed up in Peru -	1746
Two in London - -	1750
Four thoufand perfons deftroyed at Philipoli in Romania - -	1750
Two hundred mofques, and a great part of the city of Alexandria, deftroyed	1752
Many villages fwallowed up in Morea	1754
Forty thoufand people deftroyed at Conftantinople and Grand Cairo -	1754
Two thoufand houfes deftroyed in the Ifland of Metylene - -	1755
Quito in Peru deftroyed -	1755
Lifbon, and 70,000 inhabitants, deftroyed	1755
Four earthquakes in North-America	1755

One

A. D.

One at Azores - - 1757
One at Tripoli - - - 1759
A terrible one in Syria - 1760
Eight hundred and eighty perfons buried in
    an earthquake at Conftantinople 1766
One thoufand fix hundred people deftroyed
    at Martinico - - 1767
One at Altdorf in Switzerland - 1774
The city of Gualtimala, and 8,000 families,
    fwallowed up - 1774
A dreadful one at Smyrna - 1778
Thirty thoufand people, and the city of Mef-
    fina, fwallowed up - 1783
Two earthquakes in North-America 1783
Part of Oran in Africa deftroyed - 1790
Two earthquakes at Cherburg, on the coaft
    of France, which deftroyed many houfes
    and people - - 1791

The Author is forry he is not able to give a
fuller account of the numerous Earthquakes that
have happened in America: though he has heard
thirteen, he has forgot the particular times when
fome of them happened. As he is now in London, and at a great diftance from America, where
his records are, he is incapable of giving a further
account at prefent: however, he expects to be
able to do it in fome future edition of the *American
Oracle.* Jan. 17, 1791.

Of

Of the Caufe of INUNDATIONS.

INUNDATIONS are fometimes caufed by Earthquakes, and fometimes by violent ftorms, which makes the fea rife fo high as to overwhelm the land. When ftorms are the caufe, the water rifes higher at the times of the fpring-tides, than it does at other times. We have no account of a general deluge, excepting that of Noah's flood.

Inundations are frequent in low lands in America, fituated near the fea; but I have not heard that many lives have been loft, neither have I underftood that many have been loft in Great-Britain, Ireland, or France: Though at Newcaftle upon the Tyne, about 120 perfons loft their lives by an inundation, in 1446—100,000 people were drowned at Dort, in Holland, 1568—72 villages were overflowed in Zealand, and above 20,000 people perifhed, in 1717—1300 were drowned in the fame country, and there was a dreadful inundation at Peterfburgh, in 1777.

Since I wrote the preceding, I have received the following account, *viz.*—That a terrible Earthquake began on the 5th of February 1663, and raged through all Canada till July following, almoft every day or night, for a quarter or half an hour at a time. Its effects were horrible; as the mountains clafhed together, and fome tumbled partly into the river St. Lawrence, and were partly removed to vaft diftances, with their trees ftanding upon them.

CHAP.

C H A P.   XVIII.

Of the Number and Caufe of Burning Mountains—
Their terrible Eruptions—What makes Hot Springs.

IN Europe, there are three noted Volcano's, *viz.*
Mount Ætna in Sicily, Hecla in Iceland, and
Vefuvius near Naples in Italy.

In Afia, there are Mount Albours ; one on the
Ifland of Ternale, fome among the Molucca Iflands,
one on one of the Mauritian Iflands, one on the
Ifland of Sorca, feveral in Japan, and a number
more in the neighbouring Ifles ;—there are alfo
feveral in the Philippine Iflands ;—one in the
Ifland of Juva, Mount Gounapi in the Ifland of
Barida ;—and there are others in the Indies, as in
Sumatra, and the Northern parts of Afia.

In Africa, there is Mount Beni-guazeval, near
Fez ;—Mount Fugo, on one of the Cape de Verd
Iflands ;—and 'the Pike of Teneriffe, in the
Canaries.

In America, there are a great number of burning
mountains. In Peru, there is Mount Arequipa,
Mount Carapa, Mount Malahallo, and many
more.

In Mexico, Mount Popochampeche, and Mount
Popocatepax. There are alfo fome in the Weft-
India Iflands. It is faid, that there are upwards
of

of fixty burning mountains in the world; but thofe whofe names I have mentioned, are the moft remarkable ; and their eruptions frequently caufe earthquakes.

Burning Mountains are caufed by beds of fulphur, bitumen, minerals, pyrites, &c. depofited in the bowels of the earth, which are capable of generating heat by fermentation. Thefe taking fire, produce explofions in proportion to the quantity of inflammable fubftances. Sometimes they are more violent than thofe of gunpowder or thunder; have aftonifhed, terrified, and deftroyed mankind, and defolated the earth around them. A Volcano may be called a terreftrial cannon, whofe mouth is often more than a mile and an half in circumference, out of which is vomited torrents of fmoke and flames, rivers of fulphur, bitumen, melted metal, clouds of afhes and ftones, enormous maffes of rocks and calcined vitrified fubftances, which bury towns and forefts, cover the country a hundred or two hundred feet deep, and form new hills and mountains. The action of the fire is fo vehement, and the force of the explofion fo powerful, as to fhake the earth,' agitate the fea, overthrow mountains, and deftroy cities, at a very confiderable diftance.

Some have fuppofed, that thefe torrents of liquid fires proceed from the very centre of the globe, and that they come from Hell. The inhabitants of Iceland have believed, that the roaring of their Volcano was the cries of the damned in the infernal regions, and that its eruptions proceeded from the fury and defpair of thofe confined

in

in that horrible pit. Their aftonifhment begets
fear, and their fear generates fuperftition. Some
fuppofe that thofe fires do not reach many miles
below the furface of the globe: however, it is
probable that fome of them run very deep, or
they could not vomit fuch vaft quantities of
matter. Some mountains that have been on fire
are gone out, according to the accounts given of
them by hiftorians: it is probable that all the
fuel that was in them has been confumed.

New Volcanos have burft out; perhaps fome
have been fet on fire by fermentation, and fome by
lightning from the clouds,

It is not known when Mount Ætna firft took
fire; but by digging 68 feet into the ground,
marble pavements, and other ruins of an ancient
city, have been found. The fmoke and flames of
this Volcano have been feen at the diftance of 60
leagues. In 1650 and 1659, new fiery mouths
did burft out through this mountain, and they have
alfo burft out at other times. An eruption in
1537, caufed an earthquake through all Sicily,
that continued 12 days, and overthrew a great
number of houfes and edifices. The earthquake
ceafed on the opening of a new mouth, which
vomited a torrent of fire, that burnt up every thing
within five leagues of the mountain. Great quantities of afhes were thrown out, fome of which
were carried to Italy; and fhips at a great diftance
from the Sicilian fhore, were incommoded with
them. Stones have been thrown out of this
mountain, to the diftance of 60,000 paces. One
of

of the eruptions, in 1693, deſtroyed upwards of 60,000 people, as we obſerved before.

Mount Hecla vomits its fires through ice, ſnow, and a frozen ſoil, with as great a violence as Mount Ætna. It throws out vaſt quantities of aſhes, pumice ſtones, and ſometimes boiling water. There is no living within ſix leagues of this Volcano.

Mount Veſuvius buried the city of Heraclea 60 feet deep under the matter thrown out in one of the eruptions. In 1737, there was ſuch a dreadful eruption, that a large torrent of red-hot melted metalline ſubſtance was vomited through ſeveral mouths, which overſpread the country, and ran to the ſea, which was ſix or ſeven miles from its ſource. The breadth of this torrent was about 50 or 60 paces, and its depth about 6 or 7 feet.

In 1693, a burning mountain on the iſland of Sorca in Aſia, vomited bitumen, and other inflammable ſubſtances, in ſo great a quantity as to form a burning lake, which extended till it covered the whole iſland. There have alſo been terrible eruptions in other parts of Aſia, where the burning mountains are ſituated.

The Volcano in the top of Teneriffe in Africa, frequently cauſes earthquakes. In 1704, an eruption of ſulphur and melted ore ran down like a river, deſtroyed ſeveral towns, and converted the richeſt land in the iſland into a barren deſert. Other burning mountains in Africa have their eruptions, and cauſe earthquakes, and ſo do thoſe in America.

I ſhall conclude this Chapter by juſt mentioning the cauſe of *Hot Springs*.

As

As there are fubterraneous veins of liquid fires in the bowels of the earth, fome of the waters in thofe fprings may be heated that way ; and others may be heated by paffing over beds of minerals, that generate heat by fermentation : — but more of this, when I come to treat of the virtues of the mineral waters.

CHAP.

C H A P. XIX.

How the AUTHOR *came to form a new Hypothesis concerning the Cause of the* AURORA BOREALIS— *What his opinion is—Why those Lights did not appear in former Ages—His Hypothesis versified.*

IN the evening of the 26th of January 1788, as I was fitting in a large room in the State of Vermont, the weather being very fevere, a cat jumped into my lap, whofe hairs were ftiffened with the cold ; and, as I ftroked them, I obferved that they emitted corufcations, and began to conclude that they were the electrical fluid. In a few minutes I turned my attention to the caufe of the Northern Lights. Said I, why may not the atmofphere emit corufcations as well as the hairs of the cat, if it is properly ftiffened with the cold, and agitated by the different currents of air ? I therefore formed a new *hypothesis* concerning the caufe of the *Aurora Borealis;* and fuppofed, that thofe phænomena are generated by aqueous, nitrous, fulphureous, bitumenous, and other exhalations from the fumes of various kinds of waters, earths, minerals, vegetables, animals, fires, burning volcanos, &c. ; which being charged with a fufficient quantity of the electrical fluid, and rarefied by the heat of the

fun,

fun, become lighter than the furrounding atmofphere : that from hence they afcend, until they are elevated to the upper regions of the air ; and being driven by the wind from the equatorial and temperate to the polar regions, meet with the cold, combine and ftiffen to a proper confiftence by reafon of their humidity ; and, being afterwards agitated by different currents of air, crackle and fparkle, like the hairs of cats and other animals when ftiffened with the cold ; which corufcation in the temperate and frigid zones, appears in the horizon, zenith, or elfewhere, according to the pofitions of the fpectators, and the elevated exhalations : that the diverfities of the colours arife from the difference of the qualities of the combined particles, as thofe which are of the moft inflammable nature fhine with the greateft luftre.

That the Northern Lights did not appear in ancient times, becaufe the air was not impregnated with proper materials to generate thofe phænomena ; that the confuming of great quantities of fuel in America in thefe latter ages, the breaking out of burning mountains, and the vifitation of our . fyftem by blazing ftars, whofe atmofpheres have been fo greatly expanded by the heat of the fun ; that a part of them have fell into the atmofphere of our earth, and charged it with new matter ; that from this, and the other fumigations, the air has undergone fuch a change, that whenever it is brought into a proper confiftence, the *Aurora Borealis* makes its appearance, unlefs it becomes invifible by the rays of the fun or moon.

That

That the rays of the Northern Lights rife much higher than the combined particles from whence the lights proceed ; which is manifeft by the rays of a candle being extended to the fides of a room, the light of a fire to the clouds, and that of the fun to this globe.

Sometimes I have heard the combined particles crackle, when they have been agitated by the wind : their noife refembled, in fome meafure, that of a loofe fail flapped in a gale of wind.

The hemifphere is often illuminated till it is as light as bright moon-fhine ; the particles move in different directions, and appear in different forms : they frequently fend forth ftreamers, which dance like lucid pillars ; and about two or three times I have feen them appear like armies fighting againft each other.

The hemifphere is fometimes as red as a fiery oven; but in general thefe phænomena are more brilliant, and the lights are more bright and frequent, in the temperate and frigid zones, than they are in the torrid.

Thefe lights do not go out immediately, like a flafh of lightning, but often continue fome hours. This appears myfterious : but the humidity of the particles undoubtedly caufes them to combine immediately after they are agitated by the wind; but when the humidity is deftroyed, the combination ceafes, and of courfe the phænomena.

Some have imputed the caufe of the *Aurora Borealis* to the electrical fluid, and I am confident that it is that fluid that produces thofe lights ; but the queftion is, What puts it in motion, and

M   makes

makes it break through the bands of its confinement, if it is not the frictions produced by the wind?

Thus have I mentioned the hypothesis I formed:—It has been published through America; and since my arrival in England, it has been promulgated here. I have not heard that any person ever wrote against it: and if I am in the dark, I shall rejoice in being enlightened; as it is the truth I aim to find, and publish to the world for the benefit of mankind.

I shall conclude this chapter with the following lines, *viz.*

IN seventeen hundred eighty-eight, I sat
In a large room, with a good natur'd *Cat*:
She soon jump'd up, and stood upon my knees;
I strok'd her back, which did her not displease.
As she purr'd round, and grew exceeding bold,
I found her hairs were stiff'ned with the cold:
When I strok'd them—behold, the sparks did fly!
Like flaming lightning through the azure sky.
From what, said I, from what can this proceed?
Must not this be electric heat indeed?
Is it not strange, that it doth break its bands!
When the cat's hairs are stroked by my hands?
Whilst in my studies I did thus proceed,
I form'd a new *hypothesis* indeed!
I turn'd my thoughts upon that gloomy night,
Unto the cause of the great northern light:
May not, said I, the vapours here and there
Emit such coruscations in the air,
When they into a proper state are roll'd,
Condens'd and stiff'ned by the freezing cold,
And agitated by the lofty sails
Of breezy currents, or of gentle gales?

Sol's

Sol's heat, faid I, moſt rapidly exhales
Fumes from the mountains and the deepeſt vales ;
From earths and waters, mines and fulphurs all,
From plants and herbs, from trees both low and tall ;
From creeping things of diff'rent kinds of names,
From burning hills, and all the fiery flames ;
From nitrous falts, and other things that be
Found on the land and the great wat'ry fea.
By the Sun's heat, thefe fumes are much enlarg'd ;
And, being with electric matter charg'd,
Become more light, it cannot be deny'd,
Than the furrounding air on ev'ry fide.
Hence they afcend, and elevated are
Unto the regions of the upper air ;
And being driven by the wind that rolls
From the equator onward to the polls,
Meet with the cold—their humid parts from thence
Combine with others, and become more denfe.
The compofition, fhaken by the means
Of windy currents called airy ftreams,
Emit fine fparks, as I've already told,
Like the cat's hairs, when ſtiff'ned by the cold ;
Which corufcations in the zones appear
Sometimes to draw towards us very near :
Sometimes they're high, and then again they're found
Defcending gently to the folid ground ;
Illuminating, in the filent night,
The hemifphere with a refulgent light !
    Thefe northern lights, as I have oft been told,
Were never known within the days of old ;
But now, behold ! they're often feen to dance
In Britain, Holland, Germany, and France !
Nay to and fro they by the winds are hurl'd,
'Till they appear in moſt parts of the world.
In divers forms within the changing year,
Thofe floating exhalations oft appear :
Sometimes they do like lofty pillars rife,
And fhoot their ftreams towards the higher fkies ;
Sometimes they dance about like fiery fails,
Sometimes they look like clouds—like comets tails ;

Sometimes

Sometimes like armies fighting in the air !
But this phænomenon is something rare !
Sometimes they're red, and then again they're white ;
Sometimes they shine with a refulgent light !
Sometimes they crack, and rapidly the sound
Extends itself down to the solid ground :
Sometimes their motion, ev'ry one doth know,
Is very swift, and then again 'tis slow.
May we not now with reason here suppose,
That these diversities of colours rose
From particles which in the air exist,
And do of diff'rent qualities consist ?
That those which were of the most flaming kind,
Have always with the greatest lustre shin'd ?

In later times, a change without all doubt
Within the atmosphere was brought about ;
Which is the reason why the light appears
To us so frequent in these modern years,
And why it did not in the former age
Appear to those that then were on the stage.
Perhaps the earth some time hath drawn a share
Of rambling comets' atmospheric air :
For, as they pass in their elliptic course
Through this great system with a rapid force,
Sol's burning heat their atmospheres expand,
'Till part of them into the earth's do land ;
Her great attraction causing them to fall,
And change the air that doth surround her ball.

Some burning mountains, too, without all doubt,
Have on this globe in modern times burst out ;
Whose fumes have charg'd the circumambient air
With new expanded matter every-where.

The air also might change in some degrees,
By the consumption of the num'rous trees,
And other fuel, in these modern times,
Burnt by the people in the western climes.
The air thus chang'd, its particles combine,
And wond'rous lights now frequently do shine ;
Some red, some white, some crimson, pale, and blue ;
Some shining bright, some with a greyish hue :

But

But oft they're hid by Sol's refulgent light,
And the Moon's rays within the filent night.

The northern lights afcend more high, indeed,
Than the great mafs from whence they do proceed;
Illuminating, as they do arife,
The hemifphere, towards the upper fkies.

To tell the truth, it is my candid mind,
That the electric matter lies confin'd
Within the vapours ftiff'ned in the air,
Until an agitation makes them rare:
Then the electric fluid breaks its bands,
As from ftiff hairs when ftroked by our hands;
Through its confinement truly it doth burft,
Something like lightning in a thunder guft.
If you fhou'd afk, what makes this fiery train
In the wide hemifphere fo long remain?
Why in an inftant it doth not go out,
Like flaming lightnings hurling round about?
I fhou'd the myftery thus to you unfold:
The particles keep ftiff'ned with the cold;
Although expanded by a gentle breeze,
Yet in an inftant they again do freeze.
Thus they go on from time to time to fhine;
At laft they're broke fo that they can't combine:
Then in the air, behold, they take a flight!
And the phænomenon goes out of fight.

Thus I've attempted to relate, indeed,
The caufe from whence the northern lights proceed:
If I am wrong, with pleafure and delight
I'll thank the perfon that may fet me right;
As 'tis the truth—the truth I aim to trace,
And fpread the fame amongft the human race.

London, Jan. 27, 1791.

CHAP.

CHAP. XX.

Of the CAUSE *of the Rain-bow, Meteors, Sun-dogs, Jack-with-a-lanthorn, Hurricanes, Trade-winds, Monfoons, Whirlwinds, Water-fpouts, Clouds, Rain, Hail, Snow, Froft, Mift, Fog, and Dew— The Rifing and Falling of the Tides, with an American Tide-Table.*

THE Rain-bow is a meteor of divers colours, occafioned by the refraction and reflection of the light of the Sun falling on the furface of the drops of rain.

There are two Bows, the internal, and external. The former is produced by two refractions and one reflection. The firft refraction is of incident rays proceeding to one common point, from which they are reflected to another, and from thence refracted a fecond time to another, which produces the various colours of the bow; as, the red, orange, yellow, green, blue, indigo, and violet.

The external bow is produced by the reflection of the interior bow. The internal is the brighteft, and the external the lefs brilliant.

The higher the fun is above the horizon, the lower will the bow be; but the lower the fun is, the

the more will the bow be elevated. Rain-bows often appear where great rivers fall down fteep places with fuch rapidity as to raife a mift in the air.

A Meteor is an imperfect mixed body, confifting of vapours drawn up into the middle regions of the air: they appear in divers forms. Some meteors are very large, and make a tremendous noife like a clap of thunder, and even caufe the earth to tremble. We have had feveral in Ameririca, fince my remembrance, that have made dreadful explofions: they were undoubtedly generated by fuch combuftibles as produce the thunder and lightning; but, in general, they fly through the hemifphere without any remarkable report.

Sun-dogs, called Mock Suns, becaufe they refemble the fun, are two fpots that frequently appear in a cloud when the fun fhines through it, and when he is about 15 or 20 degrees above the horizon. We often fee them in America, and they commonly precede a ftorm. Their colour is much like that of the rain-bow, and their magnitude equal to that of the apparent folar difc. One is fituated on the north, and the other on the fouth fide of the fun. The refraction and reflection of the rays of light are the caufe of thefe phænomena.

We have alfo circles round the fun and moon frequently in America, which appear fomething like the rain-bow, but of a paler colour. Thefe are occafioned by the refraction and reflection of the folar and lunar rays, and are figns of rain or fnow.

M 4   A Jack

A Jack with a Lanthorn, called *Ignis Fatuus*, or Will with a Wisp, is a fiery meteor, consisting of a viscous substance, or fat exhalation; which being kindled in the air, reflects a kind of thin flame, without any sensible heat. They commonly appear in low lands, in foggy nights; and dance up and down according to the motion of the air. People that attempt to follow them, often wander out of their way, and sometimes run into hedges and ditches. I have seen three of these meteors in my travels.

A Hurricane is a violent storm of wind; and a wind is a current or stream of air, as a river is a current or stream of water. The blowing of the Wind arises principally from two causes, *viz.* from the rarefaction and elevation of the atmosphere by the heat of the sun, and the condensation and depression of the same by the cold. Hence the air, where the sun is verticle, becomes the most heated and rarefied; and being thereby made lighter, rises upwards, and the cold air on either side rushes in to restore an equilibrium. Some suppose that the diurnal motion of the earth is the cause of the blowing of some easterly winds; but when particles are exhaled by the heat of the sun, they must necessarily subside as they become condensed with the cold, and are thereby made heavier than the particles that are underneath: hence they fall, and cause the air which is under them to be driven away; but when they are all subsided, an equilibrium is restored, and the atmosphere is at rest.

Hurricanes

Hurricanes are fometimes fo violent, that they tear trees up by the roots; overthrow houfes, churches, and fteeples; fweep off vegetables and animals, and defolate countries. They deftroy veffels on the fea, and throw the watery element into fuch raging waves and billows that they produce inundations.

The Trade-winds blow from north-eaft on the north fide of the equinoctial, and from the fouth-eaft on the fouth fide, and almoft due eaft at and near the equator; but at two or three degrees on each fide the winds vary, and it is fometimes calm weather for a month together.

The Monfoons are periodical winds, which blow about fix months in one direction, and the other fix months directly oppofite. Thefe winds fhift at the times of the equinoxes, and produce terrible ftorms of wind, thunder, lightning, and rain. The monfoons are chiefly in the Indian feas, and do not extend above two hundred leagues from the land.

Sea and Land-breezes are alfo periodical winds, which blow from the land from midnight till about noon; and from the fea, from about noon till midnight. They do not extend more than three leagues from fhore.

Beyond the latitude of 30 deg. north and fouth, the winds blow from all the different points of the compafs.

A Whirlwind is caufed by three or more winds meeting in one point, which makes them fly upwards; and that which is the ftrongeft, drives the other before it.

A Water-

A Water-fpout is a mafs of water collected between a cloud and the furface of the fea, in fhape
of a pillar of water. Thefe fpouts are frequent in the Weft-Indies; and fhips that are near
them are in great danger, unlefs the fpouts are
broken and difperfed by a fhot from the cannon.
Some have fuppofed that water-fpouts are caufed
by fulphureous explofions burfting out under the
fea; and perhaps that may be the caufe fometimes.
I do not remember that I ever faw above one water-
fpout, and that was extended to the clouds: I
fuppofed it was occafioned by a whirlwind. It
doth not appear to me, that fuch explofions are the
caufe of water-fpouts in general; becaufe they
would fend the water up in an inftant, and then
it would immediately fubfide, unlefs a ftream of
fiery matter fhould continue to iffue from under
the fea. Again, if a fiery explofion was the caufe,
I fhould think they would not travel from place
to place, as the one did which I faw.

Clouds are a collection of vapours exhaled from
the earth and waters into the middle regions of
the air; but the more they are rarefied, the higher
they rife, and, being lighter than the air that buoys
them up, float in the atmofphere until they are
condenfed by the cold:—hence the upper parts
fall on the lower, till a thick mafs is formed.

The Rain is caufed by the aqueous particles
condenfing till they become heavier than the air
which is under them:—hence they fall in drops
called *rain*.

Hail is occafioned by the watery particles meeting with fuch degrees of cold as to make them
freeze after they have been formed into drops.

The

The Snow is produced by the vapours freezing before they get formed into drops.

Froſt is cauſed by the freezing of thoſe moiſt particles which we call dew.

The Miſt is occaſioned by the vapours being ſo condenſed with the cold, that they cannot riſe high above the earth ;—hence they hover about upon and near its ſurface.

A Fog is cauſed juſt like a miſt; only the particles are not quite ſo much condenſed with the cold.

A Dew is produced by the condenſation and ſubſiding of the inviſible vapours which have been exhaled in the day-time by the coolneſs of the evening, when the weather is not cold enough to make them freeze.

The Riſing and Falling of the Tides are occaſioned by the attraction of the ſun and moon upon the waters ; and the nearer thoſe luminaries are, the higher will the tides be. When the moon is at her perigeon, or in that part of her orbit that is the neareſt to the earth, and there happens to be a conjunction or an oppoſition, the tides will aſcend very high : But tides are not only raiſed every day upon the waters, but upon the land ; for the atmoſphere riſes and falls like the ſea, and the higher the one riſes, the more will the other be elevated.

There are two kinds of tides, *viz.* the ſpring, and the neap. The former begins three days before, and continues three days after the full and change of the moon; and the latter happens about the times of her firſt and laſt quarters. The
ſpring

spring tides are the higheft, and the neap the loweft.

As the tides follow the courfe of the moon, it is not high water twice in twenty-four hours, but twice in twenty-five nearly, which is called a lunar day; for, as fhe moves every day in her men-ftrual courfe to the eaftward, and as her motion is very unfteady, it is fometimes a little more, and fometimes a little lefs than twenty-five hours from the time of her leaving the meridian till fhe returns there again.

At the time of the new and full moon, the fun and moon attract together, which makes the tides rife higher than at other times; but when fhe is in her quadratures, thofe attractions are in oppo-fition to each other :—hence, when the fun raifes the water, the moon depreffes it.

The tides do not rife fo high in the torrid zone, as they do in the temperate and frigid : hence they are not fo high in the Weft-Indies, as they are at New-York, Bofton, Halifax, &c.

In the Bay of Funday, it is faid, they frequently rife feventy feet, owing to the rapidity of the Gulf-ftream, which meets the waters that come from the rivers in that part of the world, and throws them up in billows. The tides often rife twenty-five feet at Quebec, although it is fituated about three hundred and twenty miles up the river St. Lawrence.

At fome places, it is high-water when the moon is on the meridian; at others, fome hours before that time; and at others again, fome hours after fhe has paffed it. Thefe inequalities arife from the

waters

waters being obſtructed by lands, gulphs, and other ſtreams. The general motion of the tides in the great oceans, are from eaſt to weſt, according to the apparent courſe of the moon.

When the wind blows the fame way with the coming in of the tide at any place, it will be high water ſooner than the time mentioned in a tide-table; and when it blows againſt the tide, it will be full ſea later. The higher the tides riſe, the lower they fall, as one extreme follows another.

Some have ſuppoſed that our terraqueous globe is a living animal, and that it has not only life, but breath, as well as motion; and that its inſpiration and reſpiration is the cauſe of the riſing and falling of the tides:—but this is a matter I ſhall not undertake to determine at preſent.

Beſides the earth, air and water, the moon hath an effect upon the vegetable and animal creation, and attracts their fluids in proportion to her various ſituations from the ſun, and her different diſtances from our globe.

I ſhall conclude this chapter by adding the following Tide-table, which I have taken much pains to conſtruct from the beſt authorities I have been able to collect. It may be of great ſervice to mariners failing on the North-American coaſt, if they ſhall be pleaſed to buy, and keep by them, the AMERICAN ORACLE.

A TIDE.

A TIDE-TABLE, exhibiting the Time of HIGH WATER at a great Number of Places in NORTH AMERICA. Constructed and Published at New-York, in 1783.

A	B	C	D	E	F	G	H	I	J	K	L	M	N	O	P	Q	R
0 15	9 0	2 3	3 15	5 54	6 40	7 35	7 48	8 0	8 17	8 30	9 15	9 30	10 0	11 15	11 45	12 0	0 30
1 16	9 48	2 51	4 3	6 42	7 28	8 23	8 36	8 48	9 5	9 18	10 3	10 18	10 48	12 3	12 33	12 48	1 18
2 17	10 36	3 39	4 51	7 30	8 16	9 11	9 24	9 36	9 53	10 6	10 51	11 6	11 36	12 51	1 21	1 36	2 6
3 18	11 24	4 27	5 39	8 18	9 4	9 59	10 12	10 24	10 41	10 54	11 39	11 54	12 24	1 39	2 9	2 24	2 54
4 19	12 12	5 15	6 27	9 6	9 52	10 47	11 0	11 12	11 29	11 42	12 27	12 42	1 12	2 27	2 57	3 12	3 42
5 20	1 0	6 3	7 15	9 54	10 40	11 35	11 48	12 0	12 17	12 30	1 15	1 30	2 0	3 15	3 45	4 0	4 30
6 21	1 48	6 51	8 3	10 42	11 28	12 23	12 36	12 48	1 5	1 18	2 3	2 18	2 48	4 3	4 33	4 48	5 18
7 22	2 36	7 39	8 51	11 30	12 16	1 11	1 24	1 36	1 53	2 6	2 51	3 6	3 36	4 51	5 21	5 36	6 6
8 23	3 24	8 27	9 39	12 18	1 4	1 59	2 12	2 24	2 41	2 54	3 39	3 54	4 24	5 39	6 9	6 24	6 54
9 24	4 12	9 15	10 27	1 6	1 52	2 47	3 0	3 12	3 29	3 42	4 27	4 42	5 12	6 27	6 57	7 12	7 42
10 25	5 0	10 3	11 15	1 54	2 40	3 35	3 48	4 0	4 17	4 30	5 15	5 30	6 0	7 15	7 45	8 0	8 30
11 26	5 48	10 51	12 3	2 42	3 28	4 23	4 36	4 48	5 5	5 18	6 3	6 18	6 48	8 3	8 33	8 48	9 18
12 27	6 36	11 39	12 51	3 30	4 16	5 11	5 24	5 36	5 53	6 6	6 51	7 6	7 36	8 51	9 21	9 36	10 6
13 28	7 24	12 27	1 39	4 18	5 4	5 59	6 12	6 24	6 41	6 54	7 39	7 54	8 24	9 39	10 9	10 24	10 54
14 29	8 12	1 15	2 27	5 6	5 52	6 47	7 0	7 12	7 29	7 42	8 27	8 42	9 12	10 27	10 57	11 12	11 42

An EXPLANATION of the above TABLE.

A In the first column denotes the Moon's Age, in Days.
B the time of H. W. at N. York, C. Henlop, Eliza, Town Point, N. London, Cockspur in Georgia, Brunswick, North-Carolina.
C Philadelphia.
D Mobile Po. Kingston, Esopus.

E Albany.
F San. H. Geo. T. Bar, Charl. Bar.
G Newp. St. Aug. Bar, N. Prov.
H Savannah, Bedford in Dartm.
I Cape Fear.
J Amboy, Providence.
K Port-Royal Bar.
L Tybee Bar.

M Sunbury in Georgia, Hell Gate.
N Tarpaulin Cove, Newtown La.
O Boston, Reedy If. Falm. Casco-Bay, Say Brook. B. Wilm. N. C.
P White Stone.
Q N. Har. Hack. and Pollepel's If.
R Guildford and Nantucket.

N. B. If you deduct 7 hours and 57 minutes from the time of high water at New-York, it will give the time of high water at Philadelphia.

Deduct 5h. 45m. and it gives high water at
        Mobile Point, Kingston, and Esopus.

Deduct 3h. 6m.	Albany.
Deduct 2h. 20m.	Sandy-Hook, George-town Bar, and Charlestown-Bar.
Deduct 1h. 25m.	Newport, Saint Augustine Bar, and New-Providence.
Deduct 1h. 12m.	Savannah and Bedford in Dartmouth.
Deduct 1h. 0m.	Cape Fear.
Deduct 0h. 43m.	Amboy and Providence.
Deduct 0h. 30m.	Port-Royal Bar.
Add 0h. 15m.	Tybee Bar.
Add 0h. 30m.	Sunbury in Georgia, and Hell-Gate.
Add 1h. 0m.	Tarpaulin Cove, and New-town Landing.
Add 2h. 15m.	Boston, Reedy-Island, Falmouth, Casco Bay, Saybrook Bar, Wilmington, North-Carolina.
Add 2h. 45m.	White-Stone.
Add 3h. 0m.	New-Haven, Hackinsack, Pollepel's Island.
Add 3h. 30m.	Guildford and Nantucket.

If you would find the time of high water at any place mentioned in the above Table, proceed thus, *viz.*

1. Find how many days old the moon is, and apply it to this Table.

2. Take

2. Take out the hours and minutes which ſtand in the column for the place you mean to find the time of high water for, which ſtands againſt the day of the moon's age.

EXAMPLE.

Suppoſe you would find the time of high water at New-York, the moon being eight days old :

With the number Eight enter the Table, and againſt Eight under A, you will find in the ſecond colume, under B, 3h. 24m. the time required, &c.

CHAP.

C H A P. XXI.

What may properly be called MONEY—*Silver a Circulating Medium in Abraham's time—When Metals
were first coined according to Chronology—Of Bills
of Exchange and Public Banks—Of the good and
bad Effects of Paper Money in America—The
New Currency ordered to be coined by Congress—
The Disadvantages of Bills upon Interest, and of
a Sinking Fund—What Currency might be most
beneficial to the Nations—Weights and Measures
ought to be alike through the World—The Credit
of Money rises and falls in proportion to the
Demand there is for it—The great Advantages
of a Circulating Medium, and the Calamities that
follow where People are destitute of one—Why
some Countries are drained of Cash—How to get
Money, and grow rich.*

MONEY is a piece of metal stamped with the
effigies of a Prince, or arms of a State,
which makes it current and authentic to pass at a
common rate for a medium of trade.

Gold, silver, and copper, are the principal metals
used in the coining of money; and nothing but
metals coined can properly be called money, although paper, parchment, leather, &c. have been

N   made

made ufe of for a circulating medium, and called money in divers countries.

It appears by Sacred Writ, that filver was in circulation in Abraham's time; for he bought a piece of ground for a burying-place, for which he gave four hundred fhekels of filver, which was about fifty pounds fterling, or but half that fum if the fhekels were of the fmalleft kind : for the Jews had two kinds of fhekels; one was equal to two fhillings and fixpence, and the other to one and threepence. How long money was in ufe before Abraham's days, we have no account: but, according to chronology, it was firft coined by Phydon, a tyrant of Argos, 894 years before Chrift; and firft ufed in England 25 years before the Chriftian æra, but coined at Rome 269 years before the faid æra commenced.

	A. D.
Sterling money firft coined in England -	1216
Gold in ditto - - - - - - - -	1257
Shillings in ditto - - - - - - -	1505
Copper in ditto - - - - - - -	1672
Sovereign coin was valued at 20 fhillings in	1532
at 24 ditto in -	1550
at 30 ditto in -	1552
Guineas went for - - 30 ditto in -	1688
But were reduced to - 21 ditto in -	1717

It was ordered that gold fhould pafs by weight, and that which was too light fhould be recoined - - - - - - - June 4, 1774

Hence it appears, that the facred and profane hiftories do not agree concerning the firft coining

of

of money, for Abraham lived a long time before
Phydon.

	A. D.
Bills of exchange were invented in England	1160
And an act was paffed to prevent the fending of any other money out of the kingdom, in	1381
And alfo another for regulating their payment, in - - - - - - - - -	1698
The firft public bank was eftablifhed at Venice, in - - - - - - - - -	1550
And that of England, in - - . - -	1693

Bills of exchange, bank-notes, and-emiffions of
paper-money, have been of very great utility in the
carrying on of trade and commerce, wherever their
credit has been kept up : but where they have loft
their credit, they have been very injurious to individuals, and the community at large.

The circulating medium in North America, has
confifted of gold, filver, copper, and paper.

There has been a number of emiffions of paper-
money in that quarter, fome of which have been
very advantageous in the payment of public taxes
and other debts, and in the carrying on of trade
and commerce : but others, by lofing their credit,
have done much damage, not only to the people
of that country, but to foreigners.

About the year 1745, paper-money was emitted
in New England, for the purpofe of carrying on
a war againft the French, when Cape Breton was
taken. This currency depreciated in the Maffachufetts, till forty-five fhillings were not worth
more than a dollar, or four fhillings and fixpence

fterling;

sterling; and their paper-money in Rhode-Island, till eight pounds were equal to a dollar only.

In 1750, Great-Britain sent one hundred and eighty-three thousand pounds sterling to the Massachusetts, as a remittance to reimburse the expence that province had been at in taking Cape Breton; and their depreciated paper-money was called in, and paid off at the rate of one dollar for forty-five shillings, and the bills were burnt. Hence, the use of paper-money was totally prohibited in the Massachusetts, till the war commenced between Great-Britain and her Colonies; and as their imports overbalanced their exports, the province was drained of its money, till it became very scarce: hence they were obliged to carry on much of their trade and commerce by barter.

I am sorry I am not able to tell how their paper-money in Rhode-Island was redeemed, or what became of it; but the depreciation continued till 1759. They had paper-money in circulation in Connecticut just before the commencement of hostilities between the mother-country and her colonies, and its credit was nearly equal to that of gold and silver.

In New-York, the Jersies, and Pennsylvania, they were destitute of a paper-currency for a long time; and as those provinces were drained of their hard money. by reason of their imports overbalancing their exports, the inhabitants, to bring hard money from foreign countries, offered to give more for guineas, crowns, dollars, &c. than their nominal value: hence, eight shillings at New-York,

the

the north part of the Jerfies, and feven fhillings
and fixpence in the fouth part, and in Pennfylvania, was given for a dollar. But this fcheme
had not the defired effect; for, although it brought
a little money into thofe Governments at firft, yet
the merchants ftopped its progrefs, by raifing the
price of their commodities in proportion to the
elevated price of the coin : the people were therefore obliged to carry on their trade chiefly by barter;
a very dull way of doing bufinefs :—their trade
became fo ftagnated, and their commerce was
brought to fuch a ftand, that they were obliged
at laft to emit paper-money for a circulating medium. This gave new life and vigour to navigation, trade, commerce, architecture, agriculture, and the fettlement of new lands. The inhabitants were greatly benefited by their various
emiffions, and, to the honour of thofe provinces,
they kept up the credit of their bills equal to that
of gold and filver ; and they anfwered for a medium of trade, and the payment of debts both at
home and abroad.

The people at Delaware and Maryland had
paper-money, which preferved its value equal to
gold and filver. In Virginia and the Carolinas
they alfo had paper-money ; but I have not learnt
that they ever emitted any in Georgia, before the
commencement of the hoftilities between Great-
Britain and her Colonies.

The paper-money depreciated in South Carolina, till thirty-two fhillings and fixpence was
efteemed to be equal to no more than a Spanifh
milled dollar ; but its credit was raifed by taxa-

N 3   tion,

tion, and remained equal to hard money, till the Province revolted from the Britifh Government.

I have been informed, that the firft emiffion of paper-money in this province, was at the rate of four fhillings and fixpence for a dollar; but how their emiffions were iffued afterwards, I know not; nor how much their paper-currency depreciated in Virginia and North-Carolina, I have not learnt.

It has been faid, that the French in Canada and Nova-Scotia had paper-money in circulation when thofe provinces were taken by the Englifh, and that they loft their bills in confequence of their coming under the Britifh Government. The circulating medium of thofe Governments at prefent, is gold, filver, and copper; and their currency is different from that of Great-Britain.

The fubfequent Table exhibits the different currencies that have been eftablifhed in the North American Governments:

	Value of a Guinea.			Value of a Dollar.		
	£.	s.	d.	£.	s.	d.
Canada and Nova-Scotia	1	2	6	0	5	0
New-England - -	1	8	0	0	6	0
New-York, and North Jerfey	1	17	4	0	8	0
South Jerfey - -	1	15	0	0	7	6
Pennfylvania - -	1	15	0	0	7	6
Delaware - - -	1	15	0	0	7	6
Maryland - - -	1	15	0	0	7	6
Virginia - - -	1	8	0	0	6	0
North-Carolina - -	1	17	4	0	8	0
South-Carolina - -	1	1	0	0	4	8
Georgia - - -	1	1	0	0	4	8

In South Carolina and Georgia, the guinea ought to be 21s. 9¾d. according to the elevated price of the dollar above 4s. 6d.

Thefe

Thefe have been the eftablifhed currencies; but in fome of the Governments fouth of Canada, their currencies have gone backwards and forwards, and efpecially in the Maffachufetts, Rhode-Ifland, and South Carolina.

The currencies of the Weft-India Iflands have alfo varied from that of Great Britain, as follows:

	£.	
At Jamaica -	140	
Barbadoes -	135	
Nevis and Montferrat	175	} equal to 100 Sterl.
Antigua and Saint		
Chriftophers	165	

The reafons why the currencies were fo changeable and different from one another in the colonies, are as follow:

1. Thofe Governments, in their infant ftate, had but little trade, and of courfe but little money.

2. They were involved in debt for goods imported from Great Britain.

3. They had not many commodities for exportation, and were therefore obliged to export their gold and filver, which was as much a merchandize as any thing they dealt in.

4. The want of a circulating medium obliged them to emit bills of credit.

5. Their bills falling into difcredit, by merchants giving more for gold and filver than the nominal value of the paper-currency; as that of giving forty-five fhillings for a dollar in the Maffachufetts; eight pounds, in Rhode Ifland; eight fhil-

lings,

lings, at New-York, &c. Hence the credit of the
paper-money always depreciated in proportion to
the elevated price of the folid coin.

Let us, in the next place, fay fomething concerning the depreciation of the paper-money emitted
in America after the commencement of hoftilities
between Great Britain and her colonies.

The Legiflative Affemblies in various Governments emitted paper-money for the purpofe of carrying on the war; and afterwards the Continental
Congrefs followed the fame example *. The credit
of thofe emiffions were equal to that of gold and filver
for fome time; and many who had hard money,
exchanged it for thofe bills at an equal par: but
injured themfelves greatly thereby; for, in procefs
of time, the credit of the bills depreciated to that
degree, that a hundred paper dollars were fcarcely
worth one of filver.

Various methods were taken to keep up the
credit of the paper-currency: in fome places, the
prices of the neceffaries of life were ftated; but
all proved abortive, for the credit fell till Congrefs
refolved that the paper-money fhould be called in
by a tax, which was accordingly done; and the
paper-currency being loft, the people were greatly
diftreffed for a circulating medium, as law-fuits
were multiplied, and many imprifoned for taxes
and other debts.

It has been faid, that the great fcarcity of money
was the caufe of thofe emiffions paffing equal to

* Two hundred millions of paper dollars were in circulation
about the year 1781.

filver

filver and gold at firft, and that they depreciated in confequence of the following occurrences, *viz.*

1. From the rife of the neceffaries of life, by reafon of the war.

2. By the Loyalifts refufing to take the money emitted by the revolted colonies, as they fuppofed the provinces would be conquered, and that the credit of the paper-money would fall to the ground.

3. From the Quakers refufing to take the money, becaufe they fuppofed it was emitted for the purpofe of promoting the effufion of blood.

4. From counterfeit emiffions being put into circulation.

5. From the conduct of fharpers, who monopolized both the foreign and domeftic productions, and fold them for extravagant prices.

6. From their having no public funds to redeem thofe emiffions, by exchanging them for gold and filver.

After the commencement of the peace between Great Britain and America, the Legiflative Affemblies of Rhode-Ifland, Vermont, New-York, the Jerfies, Pennfylvania, North Carolina, South Carolina, and Georgia, emitted paper-money, which was a great relief to the inhabitants of thofe Governments: but their bills depreciated very much in Rhode-Ifland, and fome in Vermont; but not a great deal in the middle Governments, tho' confiderably in the Southern. The inhabitants of thofe States where paper-money has not been emitted fince the peace, have been greatly harraffed with law-fuits, imprifonments, &c. for the want of a circulating medium.

But,

But, according to the prefent conftitution of the American States, no money but gold and filver is to be made a legal tender in the payment of debts : hence paper will not be made a legal tender, as it was formerly. The Britifh merchants have fuffered greatly in times paft, by being obliged to take the paper-money when it was depreciated ; but now that inconveniency will be removed, for the Congrefs have paffed an Act for the coining of certain pieces of money, under the following names, *viz.*

An Eagle			10 dollars
Half Eagle			5 ditto
A Dime	equal to		$\frac{1}{10}$th ditto
A Cent			$\frac{1}{100}$th ditto
A Mille			$\frac{1}{1000}$th ditto.

This is to be the currency of the United States, and I underftand that all the other currencies are to be abolifhed : which is a very laudable act of the Congrefs ; for, whilft fo many different currencies were fuffered to pafs through the States, they were productive of many injuries to navigators, traders and travellers, becaufe the bills emitted in one State would not pafs in another, which was very detrimental to the tranfaction of bufinefs.

How much money would be fufficient for a circulating medium in the United States, is uncertain : But I fhould think, that ten millions of pounds fterling would not be too much, according to the number of people ; for it is faid, that their

inhabitants

inhabitants confift of about two millions and upwards of feven hundred thoufand fouls; and according to a late publication, their national debt amounts to about fixty-five millions of dollars.

How large the circulating medium of Great Britain is, is unknown to me; but fome have fuppofed it is near twenty millions, befides bank-notes and bills of exchange. According to the news-papers, the national debt is two hundred and fixty-three millions; but fome fuppofe it is but about two hundred and forty millions.

The number of the inhabitants of France are computed at about twenty-five millions; their circulating medium at 91,666,666l. 13s. 4d. and their national debt at 141,666,666l. 13s. 4d. fterling. Therefore, I cannot fuppofe that ten millions would be too large a circulating medium for the United States of America.

Bills have fometimes been emitted upon intereft in the American States, and have paffed as a medium of trade. But this kind of currency has been injurious to the people: For,

1. They were a great hindrance to the tranfacting of bufinefs with expedition, at fairs, markets, fhops, &c.; for, whilft the people were counting their money, they had to caft up the intereft of their bills before they could tell what they were worth; and thus, much time has been wafted through the inconveniency of fuch a medium.

2. They were a great damage to people in diftrefs, who wanted to borrow money; for, if the owners of the bills were able to keep them, they would hoard them up in their chefts, inftead of lending

ing them, becaufe they were fure of their intereft whilft they had the principal in their own hands.

3. They diminifhed the circulating medium greatly, by being hoarded up.—Therefore I cannot recommend bills upon intereft for a medium of trade.

Some have fuppofed, that a finking fund is the beft for a circulating medium, where people are obliged to have a paper-currency in circulation: But of this I difapprove, though it would tend to make the money circulate brifkly; for people would be very careful how they kept fuch money hoarded up in their chefts, becaufe its nominal value would be continually finking; but when they attempt to pay a debt, they muft be put to the trouble of computing, before they can know what their money is worth. Hence, if a twenty-fhilling bill was to run down in as many years, and the poffeffor was to put it off after it had been emitted eleven years and two months, he muft ftand to compute before he could know what it was worth, which, at that inftant, would be but eight fhillings and ten-pence; and if he had owned the bill but fix months, he muft lofe fixpence of its nominal value: and befides all this, when the credit of fuch bills are wholly run down, the circulating medium is totally deftroyed. Therefore, the people would be obliged to emit new bills, or live without money, if no other currency could be obtained.

This erroneous opinion concerning a finking fund, hath arifen from fome who have fuppofed

that

that a nation is in debt for the money the people emit themfelves ; but they will be convinced of their error, when they confider that the nation did not borrow it, that it is their own manu-factory, and that they owe nobody for it.

Different nations have different currencies ; but, in my opinion, that of pounds, fhillings, pence, and farthings, is the moft convenient : and if fuch a currency was to be eftablifhed through the world, it might be very beneficial to the nations. It might alfo be very beneficial to have all the different pieces of coin correfpond with the pounds, fhillings, pence, and farthings, agreeable to the following Table, *viz.*

	£.	s.	d.	q.
A Guinea	1	0	0	0
Half Guinea	0	10	0	0
Crown	0	5	0	0
Half Crown	0	2	6	0
Shilling	0	1	0	0
Sixpence	0	0	6	0
Penny	0	0	1	0
Halfpenny	0	0	0	2
Farthing	0	0	0	1

equal to

Likewife Bills of Exchange

Of	2	0	0	0
	5	0	0	0
	10	0	0	0
	20	0	0	0
	30	0	0	0, &c.

Hence the currencies might be alike through all the parts of the known world, if the nations would

would agree to it; and a guinea made in Great Britain, might be equal in weight and value to one made in France; and one coined in France, might be equal to one coined in America, &c. This would be a great advantage in the carrying on of trade and commerce both at home and abroad, as it would 'fave the trouble and expence of reducing the value of one currency to that of another.

This currency would be much eafier reckoned than that of dollars and other forts of coin, for once reckoning might anfwer: but we have to reckon or count our money twice when we take or put off dollars, &c. for we are obliged to count our dollars firft, and afterwards reduce them into pounds, and juft fo it is with guineas; whereas if they were equal to twenty fhillings each, once counting would be fufficient.

And although the guineas and other pieces of money might be made of equal weight and value through the world; yet, the money coined in each kingdom might be diftinguifhed by having the effigies of each King, and the arms of each State, enftamped on it. It is my opinion, that if all the different currencies, with weights and mea-fures, were reduced to one ftandard through the world, it would be a great benefit to mankind.

A paper-currency is the beft, if the credit of it is kept up; for it is lighter to carry from place to place, and may be more eafily fecreted from thieves and robbers, than gold and filver: but if the credit of paper-money is fuffered to depreciate,

it

it proves an engine of fraud and oppreſſion, be-cauſe it reduces people to beggary and want.

The credit of a currency will fall in time of war, in proportion to the advanced price of the neceſſaries of life. Hence, when Samaria was be-ſieged by Benhadad the king of Syria, the peo-ple in that city were ſo greatly diſtreſſed for the want of proviſions, that an aſs's head was ſold for fourſcore pieces of ſilver, which was equal to eighty pounds ſterling, and the fourth part of a cab of doves dung for five pieces. *Vid.* 2 Kings, vi. 25.

When people are pinched and ſtraitened, they will ſometimes give all their ſubſtance for relief. Hence, Satan ſpake the truth, though he is a liar, when he ſaid, Skin for ſkin, yea, all that a man hath will he give for his life. *Vid.* Job, ii. 4.

It has been ſaid, that the people of Montreal in Canada were ſo greatly pinched for ſalt, juſt before that place was taken by the Engliſh troops, that they gave fifty dollars a buſhel for that com-modity.

I have already mentioned, that the bills emitted by the Continental Congreſs, depreciated, in the time of the war, at the rate of a hundred for one. At New-York, the credit of the gold and ſilver was judged to be depreciated as much as ten for one, whilſt that place was in the poſſeſſion of the Britiſh troops, as proviſions were ten times as dear as they were before the war commenced; but ſince the war is over, it is ſaid that the credit of the money is as high as ever it was before the troubles began.

From

From hence we may infer, that the credit of a circulating medium rises and falls in proportion to the demand there is for it, and the elevated price of the neceffaries of life: But money ought by no means to be undervalued, becaufe its credit rifes and falls; neither ought the people to be deprived of a circulating medium, becaufe its credit has been reduced in a time of public calamity.

There is no intrinfic value in bills of credit or paper-money, as there is in gold and filver; although in reality it is of very great utility in the tranfaction of bufinefs, wherever its credit is kept up, as was before obferved. Hence it is neceffary to have public funds of hard money, to exchange for that of paper.

A Kingdom or State may have too much, juft enough, and not enough money for a circulating medium; for if the Almighty fhould rain down a fhower of guineas upon a kingdom or country, and make money as plenty as the fands upon the fea-fhore, it would foon be of little value amongft the people; and its credit would fall, till a ton of gold would not fetch more, if fo much, as an ounce will now. It is therefore requifite that every nation fhould not be overftocked with money, but only have juft enough for a medium of trade, and to defray foreign and domeftic debts: And it is alfo requifite, that the people fhould have a fufficient quantity of fpecie for thefe purpofes: for, wherever they are deftitute, the wheels run heavy; the progrefs of navigation, trade, and commerce, is impeded; agriculture, architecture,

ture, and the manufactures, do not thrive and
flourish: the people are oppressed with heavy
taxes, hampered and harrassed with law-suits, and
frequently imprisoned for debt. Hence, that people
that is destitute of a circulation medium, must be
in a deplorable condition.

Surely oppression will make a wise man mad;
and where people have heavy burthens laid upon
them, which they are unable to bear. When
they are in debt, straitened and pinched for
money, they run mad; quarrel and contend
with one another; commence needless law-suits;
take away goods, lands, provisions, and other
property; strip poor women and children almost
naked, and reduce them to poverty and distress:
The honest and industrious husband must go to
prison, have his constitution injured by confinement, must be kept from following his lawful
occupation; whilst his wife and children are lan-
guishing for the necessaries of life. These things
are not only hurtful to individuals, but to the
community at large:

Vanitas vanissima! ista omnia sunt vanitas!

The want of money also hinders people from
travelling abroad, to do business of importance;
for if a man is obliged to take a long journey, and
is destitute of cash, unless he can carry provisions
enough upon his back, or on his horse, to support himself, he must perish on the road, without
he turns beggar, which would expose him to the
mock and ridicule of the populace; and let
him be at home or abroad, he will be teased in his
mind, disturbed of his rest, and hindered from

O   performing

performing his duty in fome lawful employment. If he has money due to him, he will be obliged to fpend much time in running after it;—and all to no purpofe: his debtors cannot pay him; neither can he fatisfy the lawful demands of his creditors. All thefe, and many more calamities, naturally refult from the want of a circulating medium.

The Wife Man faid, that *money is a defence*, as well as wifdom. This was a very good obfervation; for, it defends us againft hunger and nakednefs, relieves us in ficknefs and health, prevents our being imprifoned, and having our families ruined by poverty and diftrefs. It gives life and vigour to the cultivation and improvement of the liberal and mechanical arts and fciences, and no nation can be happy without it. *Pecunia obediunt omnia.*

The advantages of a circulating medium are fo great, that no nation can be happy without one; and where people are deftitute of this auxiliary engine, one ought to be immediately made; and if gold and filver cannot be obtained, fomething elfe ought to be fubftituted. A paper-currency may have all the defired effects, if things are conducted with wifdom and prudence.

Some countries have been drained of their cafh, by neglecting to carry on their manufactures, and fuffering their imports to overbalance their exports; but fuch evils ought to be prevented by induftry.

I come, in the next place, to fhow how people may get money, and grow rich. I fhall therefore recommend the following, *viz.*

1. Induftry,

1. Induſtry, becauſe the diligent hand maketh *rich*.

2. The abſtaining from intemperance, idleneſs, playing, gaming, and the keeping of bad company.

3. The uſe of ſuperfluities in apparel and every other thing.

4. The not ſuffering of our expences to over-balance our incomes.

5. The laying up of ſomething againſt a rainy day.

If theſe directions are ſtrictly adhered to, people in general will grow rich ; though ſome may be prevented by unavoidable misfortunes, ſuch as ſickneſs, loſſes at ſea, fire, &c.

We cannot live without labour ; for the farms and gardens muſt be cultivated, or we muſt ſtarve ; and the arts and manufactures muſt be carried on, or we ſhall go naked, let us have ever ſo much money. Therefore, Tom and Dick and Harry, and Jenny and Sally and Nancy, muſt all follow ſome lawful employment for a livelihood.

There are two kinds of poor in the world, which are called by ſome, the Lord's poor, and the devil's. The former are thoſe who are made poor by un-avoidable misfortunes ; and the latter by ſloth, idleneſs, intemperance, &c. The firſt are objects of charity ; but the latter ought to be treated with neglect and contempt.

Some are born poor, and remain ſo by reaſon of oppreſſion, which keeps them in vaſſalage and ſlavery all their days : This is the hard fate of many of the poor Africans in ſome parts of the world.

O 2   A TABLE

A TABLE *of the Weight and Value of Coins.*

GOLD.	dwt.	gr.	SILVER.	dwt.	gr.
English Guinea	5	8	Crown	19	8
Half Guinea	2	16	Half Crown	9	16
Quarter Guinea	1	8	Shilling	3	20
Johannes	18	0	Sixpence	1	22
Moidore	6	18	Dollar	17	8
Dubloon	16	12	Half Dollar	8	16
Pistole	4	3	Quarter Dollar	4	8
Eagle	11	10	Piastereen	3	11 $\frac{1}{5}$
Half Eagle	5	17	Dime	1	17 $\frac{6}{10}$

	Sterling.				New England			New York.			
	£.	s.	d.	q.	£.	s.	d.	£.	s.	d.	q.
An Ounce of Gold is worth	3	17	10	2	5	6	8	7	2	2	2
A Penny-weight	0	3	10	3	0	5	4	0	7	1	1
— Grain	0	0	2	0	0	0	2$\frac{2}{3}$	0	0	3	1
— Guinea	1	1	0	0	1	8	0	1	17	4	0
— Johannes	3	12	0	0	4	16	0	6	8	0	0
— Moidore	1	7	0	0	1	16	0	2	8	0	0
— Dubloon	3	6	0	0	4	8	0	1	9	4	0
— Pistole	0	16	6	0	1	2	0	1	9	4	0
— Eagle	2	5	0	0	3	0	0	4	0	0	0
— Crown	0	5	0	0	0	6	8	0	0	9	0
— Dollar	0	4	6	0	0	6	0	0	0	8	0
— Piastereen	0	0	10	3$\frac{1}{5}$	0	1	2$\frac{2}{5}$	0	1	7	0
— Dime	0	0	5	$\frac{4}{10}$	0	0	7$\frac{2}{10}$	0	0	9	$\frac{6}{10}$

INTEREST

SIX PER CENT.

£	1 Month				2 Months				3 Months				6 Months				1 Year			
	£	s.	d.	q.	£	s.	d.	q.	£	s.	d.	q.	£	s.	d.	q.	£	s.	d.	q.
1			1	0			2	1			3	2			7	0		1	2	1
2			2	1			4	3			7	0		1	2	1		2	4	3
3			3	2			7	0			10	2		1	9	2		3	7	0
4			4	3			9	2		1	2	1		2	4	3		4	9	2
5			6	0		1	0	0		1	6	0		3	0	0		6	0	0
6			7	0		1	2	1		1	9	2		3	7	0		7	2	0
7			8	1		1	4	3		2	1	0		4	2	1		8	4	3
8			9	2		1	7	0		2	4	3		4	9	2		9	7	0
9			10	3		1	9	2		2	8	1		5	4	3		10	9	2
10		1	0	0		2	0	0		3	0	0		6	0	0		12	0	0
20		2	0	0		4	0	0		6	0	0		12	0	0	1	4	0	0
30		3	0	0		6	0	0		9	0	0		18	0	0	1	16	0	0
40		4	0	0		8	0	0		12	0	0	1	4	0	0	2	8	0	0
50		5	0	0		10	0	0		15	0	0	1	10	0	0	3	0	0	0
60		6	0	0		12	0	0		18	0	0	1	16	0	0	3	12	0	0
70		7	0	0		14	0	0	1	1	0	0	2	2	0	0	4	4	0	0
80		8	0	0		16	0	0	1	4	0	0	2	8	0	0	4	16	0	0
90		9	0	0		18	0	0	1	7	0	0	2	14	0	0	5	8	0	0
100		10	0	0	1	0	0	0	1	10	0	0	3	0	0	0	6	0	0	0
1000	5	0	0	0	10	0	0	0	15	0	0	0	30	0	0	0	60	0	0	0

SEVEN PER CENT.

£	1 Month				2 Months				3 Months				6 Months				1 Year			
	£	s.	d.	q.	£	s.	d.	q.	£	s.	d.	q.	£	s.	d.	q.	£	s.	d.	q.
1			1	1			2	3			4	0			8	1		1	4	2
2			2	3			5	2			8	1		1	4	3		2	9	2
3			4	0			8	1		1	0	2		2	1	0		4	2	1
4			5	2			11	0		1	4	3		2	9	2		5	7	0
5			7	0		1	2	0		1	9	0		3	6	0		7	0	0
6			8	1		1	4	3		2	1	0		4	2	1		8	4	3
7			9	0		1	7	2		2	5	1		4	10	3		9	9	2
8			11	0		1	10	1		2	9	2		5	7	0		11	2	1
9		1	0	2		2	1	0		3	1	3		6	3	2		12	7	0
10		1	2	0		2	4	0		3	6	0		7	0	0		14	0	0
20		2	4	0		4	8	0		7	0	0		14	0	0	1	8	0	0
30		3	6	0		7	0	0		10	6	0	1	1	0	0	2	2	0	0
40		4	8	0		9	4	0		14	0	0	1	8	0	0	2	16	0	0
50		5	10	0		11	8	0		17	6	0	1	15	0	0	3	10	0	0
60		7	0	0		14	0	0	1	1	0	0	2	2	0	0	4	4	0	0
70		8	2	0		16	4	0	1	4	6	0	2	9	0	0	4	18	0	0
80		9	4	0		18	8	0	1	8	0	0	2	16	0	0	5	12	6	0
90		10	6	0	1	1	0	0	1	11	6	0	3	3	0	0	6	6	0	0
100		11	8	0	1	3	4	0	1	15	0	0	3	10	0	0	7	0	0	0
1000	15	16	8	0	11	13	4	0	17	10	0	0	35	0	0	0	70	0	0	0

O 3

A TABLE

A TABLE of the RATES at which DOLLARS pass in the American States.

Dollars.	Vermont, New Hampshire, Massachusetts, Connecticut, Rhode Island, and Virginia.			New York, and North Carolina.			New Jersey, Pennsylvania, Maryland, and Delaware.			South Carolina, and Georgia.		
	£.	s.	d.	£.	s.	d.	£.	s.	d.	£.	s.	d.
1	0	6	0	0	8	0	0	7	6	0	4	8
2	0	12	0	0	16	0	0	15	0	0	9	4
3	0	18	0	1	4	0	1	2	6	0	14	0
4	1	4	0	1	12	0	1	10	0	0	18	8
5	1	10	0	2	0	0	1	17	6	1	3	4
6	1	16	0	2	8	0	2	5	0	1	8	0
7	2	2	0	2	16	0	2	12	6	1	12	8
8	2	8	0	3	4	0	3	0	0	1	17	4
9	2	14	0	3	12	0	3	7	6	2	2	0
10	3	0	0	4	0	0	3	15	0	2	6	8
20	6	0	0	8	0	0	7	10	0	4	13	4
30	9	0	0	12	0	0	11	5	0	7	0	0
40	12	0	0	16	0	0	15	0	0	9	6	8
50	15	0	0	20	0	0	18	15	0	11	13	4
100	30	0	0	40	0	0	37	10	0	23	6	8
200	60	0	0	80	0	0	75	0	0	46	13	4
300	90	0	0	120	0	0	112	10	0	70	0	0
400	120	0	0	160	0	0	150	0	0	93	6	8
500	150	0	0	200	0	0	187	10	0	116	13	4
1000	300	0	0	400	0	0	375	0	0	233	6	8

CHAP.

CHAP. XXII.

Concerning the Variation of the MARINER'S COMPASS.
*The Cause of it is supposed to arise from a Magne-
tical Effluvia, gradually circulating in the Bowels
of the Earth.*

THE Mariner's Compass was first invented in
the year 1229—exhibited in 1260—improved in 1300—and the variation discovered in
1538, by Sebastion Cabbot.

It appears that the attraction of the load-stone
was first discovered by Magnus, a shepherd, who
observed its sticking to the iron in his sandals,
which were a kind of a shoe open at the top,
and fastened with latchets; and that from him the
stone had its name, *viz.* Magnes.

This stone is an iron ore, of different colours
and solidities; the most solid is the best, and that
which is not very heavy. The medical virtues of this
stone were known in France before the year 1180.
It is somewhat astringent; but is not used in
medicine in the present age, though some have
lately attempted to cure distempers by the magnetical effluvia which arises from them.

The attraction of the load-stone is at two opposite points, called poles; and if the stone is

O 4

broke

broke into a thousand pieces, each piece will retain its attracting poles; and those that are small, will attract more in proportion to their magnitude, than the larger. The bodies they attract are, iron, steel, and other magnets; but they attract no other metals, unless they are combined with these things. Hence it is supposed, that Animal Magnetism is of some utility in the curing of distempers, because our blood is impregnated with ferruginous particles; and that the magnetical effluvia, that issues from a load-stone by attraction, repulsion, or some other way, operates upon the animal fluids, puts them in motion, and assists nature in throwing off diseases.

The attractive power of the Magnet is the strongest in contact, and it decreases by a proportion not yet found out: but that point which attracts one end of a touched needle, will repel the other.

Fluvius Gio, of Naples, about the year 1440, was the first that discovered, that steel rubbed with a load-stone, and then suspended, would point to the poles of the world; and therefore applied it to navigation.

About ninety-eight years afterwards, Sebastion Cabbot found that the needle varied in Great-Britain, about eleven degrees to the eastward of the north pole. The variation continued easterly near one degree in seven years, till it formed an angle with the meridian of London, of thirty degrees. The variation then shifted westward, and moved with the same velocity; and about the
year

year 1600, the line of non-variation paffed over
England, and the needle pointed directly to the
north and fouth poles.   Since that time, the variation has travelled weftward, and now makes an
angle with the meridian of London, of about 23
degrees.   Perhaps it may continue weftward till
the variation fhall be as great that way as it was
to the eaftward, and then return eaftward again.
If the occidental variation fhall happen to be as
great as the oriental, *viz.* 30 degrees, and it fhall
continue to move about one degree in feven years,
the line of non-variation will return again to London in about 315 years from this prefent year,
1791 ; and at that rate, a revolution of the magnetical variation will be completed in about 992
years, as it will be that time in removing. from
the eaftern extremity till it returns to the fame
again.   I have been informed, that the line of non-
variation has lately paffed fouthward near Ma-
dagafcar : that it doubled at the Cape of Good
Hope, floped acrofs the Atlantic, touching Brazil ;
and that it paffed from thence, in a ferpentine
courfe, through Canada, over the Weftern Lakes ;
and terminated at the north magnetical pole,
fituated about twelve degrees from that of the
earth, in the meridian of California : That from
thence the line of non-variation paffed over the
earth's north pole, inclining eafterly, over Siberia,
Tartary, China, the Landrone Iflands, and New
Holland, to the other magnetic pole, fituated
near lat. 56 deg. fouth, and long. 80 deg. weft
from London. But the lines of non-variation, and
the

the magnetical poles, all move weftward at prefent. I was informed, when I was in Canada, in the year 1788, that the variation in Quebec was 12 deg. weft, and 11 at Montreal: thofe cities are about 170 miles from each other. Hence, the further we go weftward from London, the lefs will the variation be, till we come where there is none; for the variation is greater at London than it is at Quebec, and at Quebec than it is at Montreal.

The whole globe is fuppofed to be a magnet; and where there are beds of minerals of a ferruginous kind, the power of attraction is very great upon magnetical needles; and furveyors meet with much difficulty in running their lines, by reafon of the variation of the Compafs.

Some have fuppofed, that Electricity and Magnetifm have a great affinity to each other; becaufe fteel, when ftruck with the lightning, or a ftrong fhock of electricity, immediately receives polarity and magnetic attraction.

I have often been requefted to make known my hypothefis concerning the caufe of the variation of the Compafs—Shall therefore juft give my opinion upon the fubject; but muft obferve, that Dr. Halley, a celebrated Britifh Aftronomer, fuppofed that the diurnal motion of the earth was the caufe of this variation. However, I believe he was miftaken; becaufe the diurnal motion is always from weft to eaft, but the variation is fometimes one way and fometimes the other. If the motion of the earth was fometimes from eaft to weft, and fometimes to the contrary, and the needle followed it, then might we have juft reafon

to

to fuppofe that the Doctor was not miftaken; but fince the motion of the earth is but one way, and that of the compafs two ways, he was undoubtedly wrong in his judgment.

Some have imputed the caufe of the variation to high mountains and deep vallies on the furface of the land and fea, and have fuppofed that they have caufed the needles to vary; but I cannot be of that opinion.

In the bowels of the earth, there are beds of fulphur, iron ore, and other minerals; befides fubterraneous veins of liquid fires. Now, it feems probable to me, that a fubtile fluid, of a magnetical kind, is generated by the fermentation of thofe things; and that it moves gradually in the earth and waters from weft to eaft, and from eaft to weft, attracting the needle to and from the poles. But I may be miftaken; and it is fuppofed, that there is not one Philofopher on the globe that is able to determine the matter.

C H A P. XXIII.

A Definition of ANIMAL MAGNETISM, *invented in Germany, taught and exploded in France—but practised in England in a different manner from what it was when it was first applied in a Medical way—A New Discovery.*

ANIMAL Magnetifm is the art of curing of difeafes by a fubtile fluid arifing from magnetical bodies, as load-ftones, fteel and iron rods, &c. and alfo by a fubtile effluvia which arifes from human bodies : the former is now laid afide in the cure of diftempers ; but the latter is applied for that purpofe.

The effluvia that arifes from the human body, is combined with the electrical fluid ; and the compofition is fuppofed to be a mixture of fire, air, light, and fpirit, and fo very penetrating as to pafs through every part of the human machine : but I imagine there are other kinds of particles in the compofition.

This effluvia is of a magnetical kind, becaufe our blood is impregnated with ferruginous particles, which the load-ftone will attract. Hence, it may be proper to call the compofition and operations, Animal Magnetifm.

It

It is faid that Animal Magnetifm was firft invented in Germany, by a *M. Mefmer*, who afterwards taught it in France, where five learned men were chofen to fee whether it was beneficial or not in the cure of difeafes; who declared that it was only an imaginary piece of work, becaufe the experiments ufed to convince them of its reality produced contrary effects.

When this art was firft made ufe of in a medical way, its Profeffors employed an apparatus confifting of a large tube, which was partly filled with load-ftones; through the tube a number of iron rods were projected, for the purpofe of conveying the magnetical fluid to their patients.

The operations were performed by the patient's ftanding with his breaft againft the end of one of the rods, and taking hold of it, firft with one hand, and then with the other, and by drawing them towards his vital parts; which conveyed the magnetic fluid from the load-ftones into his body, as it was fuppofed. But I have not learnt that it ever produced any violent commotions in the human frame.

Since the invention of this apparatus, I underftand that our Britannic Profeffors have made new difcoveries, whereby they have found, that the magnetical effluvia which arifes from the human body, is vaftly more efficacious in the cure of difeafes, than that which arifes from other magnets. Hence, they have exploded the firft mode of magnetical practice, have wholly laid afide the apparatus, and make ufe of the new invention only, in the cure of diftempers.

The

The human body is now converted into an electric or magnetic machine : the arms are the conductors, and the fingers the pointers, for conveying the magnetical effluvia to patients labouring under bodily weaknefs and indifpofition.

In the new method of practice, we are directed to proceed as follows :

1. The operator muft place the patient in a chair before him, and fome direct that a prayer be made for fuccefs in the operation.

2. He muft fix all the energy of his foul on the relief of the patient :—His mind muft be abftracted from every other thought, and filled with affection, benevolence, kindnefs, pity, fympathy, conftant intention, attention, confidence, and compaffion towards the object prefented for relief.

3. He muft hold the fingers of both his hands towards the invalid's pericardium; and afterwards move them in different directions, as, horizontally, perpendicularly, obliquely, &c. for the moving of them up and down is faid to agitate the bile, and produce eructations, vomitings, purgings, &c. But once in a while they muft be thrown with great velocity almoft to the breaft of the patient, and he muft rub the part affected with pain or any other diforder.

Thefe operations are faid to excite the magnetical effluvia to flow in proportion as the bodily and mental faculties of the operator are engaged: And if the diforder of the patient requires it, a *commoto* will be produced ; but if a commoto is not needful, a crifis will follow ; or if a crifis is not required,

required, the effluvia will operate fome other way, till the patient is reftored to health; but the operations muft be repeated as occafions may require: and fome direct their patients to rub themfelves with a cloth.

The motion of the hands of the operator, is called, *treating* the patient. The *commoto* is a difturbance in the human frame, attended with tremors, eructations, vomitings, &c. without a lofs of the fenfes: But a crifis is a kind of a thunder ftorm raifed in the mortal body by the violence of the magnetical effluvia; it is attended with fpafms, convulfions, fainting, lofs of fenfe, profound fleep, &c.—But more of this hereafter.

Some of the Magnetical Profeffors have pretended to cure diftempers without the motion of their hands. Thefe operations are performed by an act of the mind, which, with all its powers and faculties, muft be fet on the patient; and the ftronger the mental powers are in the operator, the more effectual the remedy is faid to be. In this manner they have attempted to cure patients at a great diftance.

As each body is furrounded with an atmofphere, and charged in a greater or lefs degree with the electrical fluid, or magnetical effluvia; that which has the moft motion, is faid to produce Animal Electricity, and communicate the fluid through the cutaneous pores into the other body, until an equilibrium is reftored.

The incorporation of the atmofpheres is faid to produce a ftrange connection between the operator

rator and the patient: The former fometimes feels in his hands and fingers, heat, pain, prickling, numbnefs, &c. and often a pain in that part of his body or limbs which is affected, which is fuppofed to be produced by fympathy; and the latter, a kind of a warm glowing fenfation, though fometimes cold chills will follow.

I have feen a woman thrown into a crifis by the violence of the magnetical effluvia. She was greatly convulfed, her limbs were diftorted, and fhe had twitchings in her nerves and tendons, a ftrangulation of her *fauces*, rifing in her throat, difficulty of breathing, threatening a fuffocation, lofs of voice and fenfe, palenefs of face, with a fainting, which was followed by a profound fleep. At laft a diaphorifis came on; and fundry torrents of the effluvia being poured upon her, which made her ftart furprizingly, fhe awoke in perfect health, as fhe informed us.

Some who have paffed through thofe dreadful commotions, have pretended they could fee through folid bodies, and that human bodies have appeared tranfparent during the crifis; but thefe phænomena are very rare, as I have been informed.

The magnetical effluvia, like the motion of the fea, and the operation of other remedies, has different effects on different conftitutions; to fome it proves emetic, to fome cathartic, to fome both emetic and cathartic, to fome anodyne, to fome diaphoretic, to fome antiphlogiftic, &c. It contains a complete fyftem of the virtues of all the fimples and compounds that have been derived from the mineral,

vegetable,

vegetable and animal kingdoms, according to the imaginations of some persons.

Hence it is a specific for all kinds of diseases. We often hear, that it restores the blind to sight, causes the deaf to hear, the dumb to speak, and the lame to walk; but perhaps some extol it too high, whilst others may have too low an opinion of it.

Some have been so imprudent, that they have accused the Magnetic Doctors of curing distempers by the power and influence of evil spirits; but I am sensible they are mistaken, for I never knew that Satan was ever transformed into a physician, though it appears that he has been transformed into an angel of light, and into a minister of righteousness. Vid. 2 Cor. xi. 14, 15.

Although Animal Magnetism was exploded in France before the Britannic Magnetisers had made the late discoveries, yet it may be very beneficial to the human race, for ought we know; for there was a time when all the Philosophers were banished from Rome, notwithstanding they were the wisest and most useful men in the world; and in the year 1552, all the books that had been written upon Astronomy and Geography, those infallible and useful sciences, were destroyed in England, because it was supposed they were infected with magic. Therefore, we ought not to decry our new art, unless we find, upon a due investigation of the matter, that it is of no use in the cure of distempers. Perhaps it would not have been exploded in France, if those discoveries had been made there, which have been made in Great Britain.

P

I have

I have attended fome of the magnetical opera-tions; and it appears to me, by the beft obferva-tions that I have been able to make, that the cures are performed by the ftagnated fluids and compacted humours being put into circulation, by the motions of the hands of the operators, the action of the magnetical effluvia, and the powers of imagination in the patients.

Certain it is, that fome patients will go into a crifis, and that others will be greatly agitated by thofe operations, whilft others again are not affected at all; but the Profeffors that I have been acquainted with, have confeffed that they could not render a philofophical reafon for thofe things. I have therefore contemplated much upon the fub-ject, and it was a long time before I could deter-mine in my mind how thofe terrible commotions are produced: but on the 15th of February 1791, I came to the following conclufion, *viz.*

That the thunder-ftorm raifed in the human frame, called the crifis, with the other fymptoms, are produced much like the thunder-ftorms in the terreftrial atmofphere. Let us therefore obferve, that when a non-electric body or cloud comes near to, or joins one that is electric, or highly charged with electrical fluid, the latter will dif-charge itfelf into the former, and produce terrible commotions, 'till an equilibrium is reftored.

Hence, if by the motion of the hands, or by any other means, a Magnetic Operator becomes higher charged with the magnetical effluvia than the body of the patient he is treating, the effluvia
will

will difcharge itfelf from him into the patient until an equilibrium is reftored; but a crifis, or fome other commotions, will be produced by fuch difcharges.

Again, if the body of the patient is higher charged than the operator, the effluvia will be conveyed from the patient into the operator, and produce thofe fenfations of heat, pain, prickling, and numbnefs, as before mentioned.

Furthermore, if both bodies are charged alike, neither the patient nor the operator will be affeéted; becaufe the effluvia is in a ftate of perfeét equilibrium.

Thus have I at laft rendered a philofophical reafon for the caufe of the different operations and effeéts of the magnetical effluvia in the *corpus humanum.* The hypothefis is new, and entirely of my own invention : I did not receive it from any perfon ; neither have I mentioned it to any body. Yefterday was the time I made the difcovery : and I think I am not miftaken ; if I am, I hope I fhall be convinced of my error.

But the powers of imagination will fometimes have a furprifing effeét in the cure of diftempers; and, perhaps, it has been an affiftant in fome of our magnetical operations.

London, Feb. 16, 1791.

For further information concerning Animal Magnetifm, fee a Treatife, intitled, " The Myftery of Animal Magnetifm revealed to the World," publifhed by the *Author* of the *American Oracle.*

P 2 C H A P.

C H A P. XXIV.

Of the Effects of the PASSIONS *of the* MIND, *such as Anger, Surprize, Fear, Terror, Grief, Vehement Desire, Sadness, and Despair—Of the Powers of Imagination—A remarkable Account of Two Women that went into a Crisis, and of two others that went into Convulsions—How a Man was affrighted to death.*

THE Violent Passions of the Mind, such as anger, surprize, fear, terror, grief, vehement desire, sadness, and despair; often make great ravages in the constitution.

Anger increases the strength; quickens the motion of the heart, lungs, pulse, and breathing; throws the whole frame into a tumult, and sometimes proves fatal.

Surprize, fear, and terror, contract the vessels in the external parts of the body and limbs, force the blood to the heart and lungs, produce a coldness of the extremities, palpitation of the heart, trembling, congestions in the sanguinary vessels, convulsions, swooning, syncope, apoplexies, palsies, epilepsies, and sometimes sudden death.

Grief, vehement desire, sadness and despair, impair the tone and strength of the nervous system,

syſtem, weaken and retard the motion of the pulſe, deſtroy the appetite and digeſtion, and produce weakneſs, paleneſs of face, looſeneſs of the ſkin, difficulty of breathing, coldneſs of the extremities, frightful dreams, melancholy, madneſs, ſleepy diſeaſes, hemiplexy, palſy, gutta ſerena, faintings, concretions, palpitations of the heart, polypuſes, diarrhœas, hypochondriac and hyſteric complaints, flatulencies, cachexy, and the ſcurvy.

Theſe paſſions have different effects in different conſtitutions; but in every conſtitution they tend to deſtroy the vital, natural, and animal functions of the body and mind, as,

1. The action of the heart, lungs, and arteries.

2. The manducation of food, and the deglutition and digeſtion thereof.

3. The muſcular motions and voluntary actions.

4. The imagination, judgement, reaſon, and memory.

The power of fancy is often ſo great in pregnant women, as to occaſion moles, alſo marks, and other deformities in the bodies and limbs of their children; and it has been ſaid, that ſome have had the plague and ſmall-pox from a ſtrong imagination only.

Violent love, called love-ſickneſs, has produced a cachexy and the green ſickneſs in women.

Too much intenſe ſtudy, or profound and laborious meditations, conſumes the ſtrength, weakens the nerves, and inverts the regulation of the natural motions.

But although the paſſions of the mind often bring on mortal diſtempers, yet the powers of imagina-

P 3 tion

tion have a furprizing effect in the cure of difeafes. I have been acquainted with a phyfician, who faid he was once requefted to vifit a woman that was fuppofed to be very near her end, but imagined that he could relieve her; and as his circumftances would not admit of his vifiting her, and as he knew fhe was troubled with an hyfteric complaint, he fent her feveral pills, made of nothing but a piece of bread, with ftrict orders for her to take them, becaufe fuch pills had faved the lives of thoufands. She accordingly obeyed the orders, and recovered; but imagined the Doctor had wrought a miraculous cure.

Of late I have been informed, that a Magnetic Doctor agreed to magnetife his patients at fuch an hour, when he was about ten miles from them; but at the time appointed he fell into company, and totally forgot his obligation: two women, however, who were his patients, conceited that he was magnetifing them at the time he had fet, and went into a crifis.

At about eight of the clock one evening, when I was learning to be a phyfician, three women came running into the houfe, in a great furprize: two of them threw themfelves on a bed, and went into convulfions; and the other fat down in a great chair. I afked what was the matter? But none of them were able to fpeak for a confiderable time. At laft the one in the chair informed me, that as they were attempting to walk through a field, fomething rofe out of the grafs, that made a ftrange noife, and appeared like a perfon in a white fheet. A man who had imprudently wrap-

ped

ped himfelf in a fheet on purpofe to affrighten them, came into the houfe immediately, told what he had been about, and that it was not his defign to have affrighted them to that degree: But all he could fay or do was in vain; the convulfions continued all night, with fuch violence that it took three or four robuft men to hold the patients. This affright was attended with very bad confequences; for one of the women went into a confumption, and died in a fhort time; and the other frequently had convulfions afterwards.

Here we may obferve, that, by the power of imagination, the woman recovered that took the pills;—that, by the fame power, the women went into a crifis;—and alfo, that, by the fame power, thofe affrighted went into convulfions. It was nothing but imagination: they fuppofed they had feen the devil; but were miftaken—no body had touched them, or hurt them; it was only their fancies that made thofe terrible ravages in their conftitutions.

I will juft mention another ftriking inftance of the powers of imagination.

A man who was under fentence of death, was permitted to chufe that mode of execution which he thought would be the eafieft, and he chofe to bleed to death. At the time appointed for the execution, a Surgeon blindfolded the criminal, tied him to a tree, and hung a bladder of warm water privately to his back, which he opened with a launcet, and cried, the " blood is now running! " the poor man has but a fhort time to live!"

The

The criminal, on feeling the warm water run down his back, fuppofed he was bleeding, fainted away, and died immediately.

As frights are often productive of very bad confequences, this is to caution all perfons into whofe hands this may come, againft affrighting any of the human race, left murder fhall be committed when it is not thought of. The woman I have mentioned, loft her life by the imprudence of the man that appeared in the white fheet ; and he fincerely regretted that he was ever guilty of fuch a wicked tranfaction.

I have frequently thought, that monftrous ill-fhaped pictures are no-ways beneficial to mankind, and efpecially to the female fex : perhaps they are too often the caufe of thofe deformities that fome children are born with.

CHAP.

C H A P. XXV.

An Account of the SHAKING QUAKERS *in America.*

THIS new fect fprang up about the year 1779; and an old woman, called the *Elect Lady*, with twelve difciples, all of whom were faid to be Europeans, were the founders of a new mode of worfhip: they drew thoufands of people after them, and pretended they were vefted with power from on High, to work miracles, heal the fick, raife the dead, caft out devils, and fpeak in unknown languages.

This Lady refided in the north-wefterly part of the State of New-York, where fhe began to inftil her tenets into fome of the people there. Afterwards fhe rambled from place to place, promulgating her religion, gaining profelytes in New-England and elfewhere; and fhe engroffed the kingdom of Heaven entirely to herfelf and her followers, to the feclufion of all others.

She pretended, her miffion was immediately from Heaven; that fhe travelled in pain for her elect; could fpeak in feventy-two unknown languages, in which fhe converfed with thofe that had departed this life; that there had not been a true Church on earth fince the Apoftles' days, until her's was

erected;

erected; that both the living and the dead muſt be ſaved, in, by, and through her; muſt confeſs their ſins unto her, and procure her pardon, or they could not be ſaved; that ſhe gathered her Church both from earth and hell; as every perſon that had died ſince the Apoſtles' time, until her Church was ſet up, had been damned; and that they were continually making interceſſion to her for ſalvation, which was the occaſion of her talking in thoſe unknown tongues.

Thoſe that entered into her Church, were obliged to confeſs their ſins, and deliver up their jewels, rings, necklaces, buckles, watches, &c. to be diſpoſed of as ſhe thought fit.

It has been ſaid, that ſome of thoſe confeſſions proved beneficial; for ſome of the members of her Church confeſſed they had ſtolen divers things that had been laid to the charge of innocent perſons.

When theſe people carry on their worſhip, they pretend to praiſe the Lord by ſinging, dancing, jumping, turning round, falling down, tumbling, &c. In the mean time, ſome will be trembling, groaning, ſighing, and ſobbing; whilſt others are preaching, praying, exhorting, &c. Others will be clapping their hands, ſhouting, hallooing, ſcreaming, and making ſuch an hideous noiſe that it may be heard at a great diſtance, and frequently affrightens people.

They often dance three hours without intermiſſion; and when any of them are tired of praiſing the Lord that way, they are whipped up by others, to make the worſhip go on briſkly. They

dance

dance till they are very much emaciated; the women grow pale, appear like ghosts or apparitions, or almost like deserters from a church-yard, if I may be permitted to use the sailors phrase.

They are not allowed to wear superfluities in their apparel: their cloathing is plain, and of a lightish colour.

They make no use of the Eucharist, or of water baptism, in their churches, are averse to wars and fightings, and to swearing, use the plain language, and say yea and nay, instead of yes or no; but all their tenets are not approved of by the other Quakers.

At particular times they labour very hard at their respective occupations, and are very careful that no portion of their time is spent in idleness.

They pretend they hold a correspondence with the Saints and Angels, and that they frequently see and converse with the Spirits of their departed friends.

I have been informed, that the number of Shaking Quakers has consisted of no less than six thousand people; and that many of the men have refused to lie with their wives, because they supposed that they were part of the hundred and forty and four thousand mentioned in the Revelations, that were redeemed from the earth, and were not defiled with women.

They pretend that they have already been made partakers of the first resurrection, and that on them the second death will have no power.

They do not allow instrumental music in their churches, because they suppose that that was ceremonial,

monial, and is aboliſhed.   But they pretend, that
they carry on their worſhip by the immediate
power and influence of the Holy Ghoſt, and that
they have Scripture warrants for their practice,
as, " Sing unto God ;—Praiſe ye the Lord in the
" dance;—O clap your hands, all ye people!—
" ſhout unto God ;—make a joyful noiſe;—fall
" down before the Lord, &c."

It is ſaid, that the *Elect Lady*, with one of her
brothers, died in the Jerſies ſeveral years ago.

CHAP. XXVI.

An Account of the BIBLE, *and its different Transla-*
tions—A Short History of Dictionaries—and the
Epistles of Philadelphus.

ACCORDING to History, the Old Testament was first written in Hebrew, and
afterwards translated into Greek, about 275 years
before the birth of Christ, by seventy-two Jews,
and by order of Ptolomeus Philadelphus king of
Egypt, who had erected a magnificent Library at
Alexandria. The Apocrypha was also undoubtedly written in the Hebrew tongue; and it is
said, that the New Testament was first wrote in
Greek.

The Bible has been translated sundry times into
English.

A. D.

King Alfred translated a part of it.
Aldemus translated the Psalms into Saxon, in 709
Edfrid, or Ecbert, translated some other
    parts, in - - - - - 730
Bede translated the whole - - 731
Trevisa published the whole in English, in 1357
Tindal's translation brought higher, in - 1534

Tindal's

A. D.

Tindal's tranflation revifed and altered, in　1538
Publifhed with a preface of Cranmer, in　-　1549
Another tranflation publifhed　　-　　-　1551
The fame revifed by feveral bifhops, and
　　printed with alterations　　-　　-　1560
A new tranflation was publifhed by King
　　James's authority, in　　-　　-　　-　1607

The laft tranflation is the one in prefent ufe; but it is not every whit perfect. The want of knowledge in the languages, has been the caufe of fo many tranflations and alterations; and it is thought that the prefent tranflation might be corrected and amended.

In the *Old Teftament* there are		In the *Apocrypha* there are		In the *New Teftament* there are	
Books	39	Books	15	Books	27
Chapters	929	Chapters	183	Chapters	260
Verfes	23,214	Verfes	6,081	Verfes	7,959
Words	592,439	Words	152,185	Words	181,253
Letters	2,728,100			Letters	838,380

A. D.

The Bible was tranflated into French, before 1356
The Vulgate edition was printed　　-　1462
Englifh tranflation firft allowed in every
　　family　-　-　-　-　-　1539
Firft fuffered to be read in churches　-　1549
Firft tranflated into Welfh　-　-　1567
The prefent tranflation finifhed　-　-　1611
No Irifh tranflation 'till　-　-　-　1685
Permitted by the Pope to be tranflated into
　　any language　-　-　-　-　1759

3　　　　　　　　A SHORT

A

SHORT HISTORY of DICTIONARIES.

IT is faid, that there are no Dictionaries, or Lexicons, for either the Latin, Greek, or Hebrew languages, that are more then 380 years old. Hence we muft conclude, that they had none either in Mofes's, David's, or Solomon's time, nor in the days of Chrift and his Apoftles; but that they have been compiled in thefe modern ages.

The Dictionaries, like the Tranflations of the Bible, have gone through feveral alterations and refinements; and about 60 or 70 years ago, fome words in the Englifh language had different meanings put to them: and as time rolls on, it is probable that new explanations of fome words, not only in the Englifh, but in other languages, will be made.

It is difficult to tell which of the Englifh Dictionaries are the beft; becaufe fome are beft upon one thing, and fome upon another. Bailey's, Fenning's, Johnfon's, Entick's, &c. are all good; and there are excellent Dictionaries upon the Arts and Sciences. The like may be faid of the Latin, Greek, and Hebrew Lexicons.

CHAP.

THE

EPISTLES of PHILADELPHUS.

EPIST. I.

Admonitions against the Usage of bad Language.

TO all People, Nations, and Languages, that dwell in all the world:

2. Grace, mercy, and peace, be multiplied unto you.

3. It hath seemed good unto me, to send forth this Epistle, beseeching you to forsake vice, and to follow virtue:

4. That whilst great discoveries and improvements are making in the liberal and mechanical arts and sciences, there may be a reformation amongst those who use bad language:

5. That they would no longer take the Sacred Name in vain, by continuing the practice of profane cursing and swearing; as that of saying, " I swear by God! I swear by Jesus! I swear by the Holy Ghost! &c.—God damn your blood! God damn your eyes! God damn your soul to hell!" &c.

6. That they would entirely leave off the use of those unjustifiable and nonsensical expressions; as those of saying, " That is a damned good man, a damned good woman, a damned good horse," &c.

7. That

7. That they would no longer weary themselves by the usage of such profane oaths, such horrible imprecations, corrupt and abominable language; but that they would swear not at all, use blessing instead of cursing, and adorn their conversation at all times with decent language.

8. That they would consider, that for every idle word, which they have, or may speak, they must give an account on the Day of Judgment; and that by their words they will be justified, and by their words they will be condemned.

9. I beseech you again to forsake vice, and follow virtue.

10. Grace, mercy, and peace, be multiplied unto you all.   Amen!

The first Epistle of *Philadelphus* was written from *Anglia*, to the inhabitants of the world, by *Philanthropos*.

The SECOND EPISTLE of PHILADELPHUS.

CHAP. I.

PHILADELPHUS *exhorteth the People to remember what was written in his former Epistle.—6. The Tongue an unruly member.*

PHILADELPHUS, a lover of the brethren, and a servant of the Most High God:

Q   2. To

2. To all People, Nations, and Languages, that dwell in all the world:

3. Grace, mercy, and peace, be multiplied unto you!

4. It is my heart's defire and prayer to God, that ye may remember the things that I mentioned in my former epiftle:

5. That the word thus fpoken may have a fuitable impreffion upon your minds; that ye may lay it up in your hearts, and practife it in your lives and converfations; and that it may do you all good, in this your time of trial and probation.

6. Know ye not, that the tongue is an unruly member, full of deadly poifon; a world of iniquity, that defileth the whole body; and that if any among you pretend to be religious, and bridle not their tongues, their religion is vain?

CHAP II.

An Exhortation to the Practice of Moral Duties.

I BESEECH you, therefore, my beloved brethren and fifters, that ye abftain from the ufage of bad language:

2. That you who are heads of families will be pleafed to fet good examples before your children and fervants, by living holy and exemplary lives, adorned with a good converfation:

3. That ye give thofe under your care a good education, and bring them up in the nurture and admonition of the LORD.

4. Remember,

4

4. Remember, that if ye ufe profane curfing and fwearing, with other ungodly expreffions, before your children and fervants, that they will follow the fame evil example.

5. Be careful therefore of your conduct; and teach thofe committed to your charge, to fhun the pollutions that are in the world:

6. To abftain from bad language, bad company, intemperance, idlenefs, playing and gaming.

7. Frequently remind them of the mortality of their bodies, of the Judgment to come, and of the account they muft give at the *Dread Tribunal* for the deeds done in the body:

8. That their thoughts, words, and actions, are regiftred in the books of Heaven; and that they will be rewarded according to their works:

9. That if they do evil, they will be punifhed with indignation and wrath, tribulation and an-guifh; but if they do that which is good, Glory, honour, peace, immortality, and eternal life, will be their reward in the world to come.

10. Grace, mercy, and peace, be multiplied unto you all. Amen!

The fecond Epiftle of *Philadelphus* was written from *Anglia*, to the inhabitants of the world, by *Philanthropos*.

The

THE

THIRD EPISTLE of PHILADELPHIUS.

The People exhorted to worſhip the CREATOR—4. *ſuppreſs Vice*—5. *live peaceably*—7. *and to keep a Faſt, &c.*

TO all People, Nations, and Languages, that dwell in all the world :

2. Grace, mercy, and peace, be multiplied unto you!

3. It hath ſeemed good unto me to ſend forth this third epiſtle, beſeeching you to render all proper adoration and obedience to the great *Creator, upholder, preſerver,* and *governor* of the univerſe :

4. That ye ſuppreſs atheiſm, ſuperſtition, idolatry, ſedition, treaſon, rebellion, and every thing that may tend to diſhonour the Creator, and diſturb the public tranquillity :

5. That ye live peaceable and quiet lives, in all godlineſs and honeſty ; fearing GOD, honouring Kings, and thoſe that are or may be in authority in the kingdoms and countries where ye do or may reſide :

6. That ye be ſubordinate to every good and wholeſome law, and cultivate and improve thoſe things that may promote your own felicity, and the happineſs of mankind in general.

7. Keep

7. Keep fuch a faſt as the Lord hath chofen; break the bands of wickednefs, undo the heavy burdens, and let the oppreffed go free.

8. Deal your bread to the hungry, clothe the naked with a garment, and provide fhelter and entertainment for thofe who are or may be deſtitute of houfe and home.

9. Be kind to ſtrangers, to widows, and to the fatherlefs.

10. Honour the aged, obey your parents, ferve your maſters.

11. Abufe not yourfelves, nor your fellow-creatures, nor even the brutal creation.

12. Do good to all men as ye have opportunity, follow peace, walk honeſtly.

13. Remember the things that I have communicated unto you.

14. Grace, mercy, and peace, be multiplied unto you all.   Amen!

The third Epiſtle of *Philadelphus* was written from *Anglia*, to the inhabitants of the world, by *Philanthropos*.

C H A P. XXVII.

The PHILOSOPHER's *Religion deſcribed—The Place*
he would chuſe for his Abode, and how he would
conduct himſelf through Life, &c.—A new Song
on the Works of Righteouſneſs.

LEST any ſhould be in diſtreſs,
    To really know what I profeſs,
In things of a religious kind;
I therefore do relate my mind
To all enquirers, and make known
The principles which are my own.
    I worſhip the Great GOD of might,
Whoſe wond'rous ſtrength is infinite!
Truly reſiſting, at all times,
Whatever leads to vicious crimes:
By no means taking worldly pelf;
Loving my neighbour as myſelf:
Helping the poor that are in need;
To ſtrangers very kind indeed:
I ſtrive as much as e'er I can,
To get to be a perfect man;
By imitating of the bleſs'd,
In doing things that's for the beſt.
My principles are ſuch as theſe;
And men may call me what they pleaſe—
A Turk, a Chriſtian, or a Jew,
Or one of the Paganic crew.

        Compoſed in America,
            in July 1786.

                                THE

THE

PHILOSOPHER's CHOICE.

I.

IT is my choice to find a place,
   Upon this earthly globe,
Within fome healthy pleafant fpace,
   To fettle mine abode:

2.

Where I from tyrants cruel rage,
   And robbers, may be free;
Where evil men do not engage,
   To fpoil true liberty:

3.

Where neighbours are exceeding kind,
   And virtue doth increafe;
And I, with a contented mind,
   May daily live in peace:

4.

With a good wife, replete with fenfe,
   Whofe manners are refin'd;
Whofe temper's fweet as innocence,
   And all her actions kind.

Q 4   Too

5.

Too much eftate I never chofe:
　　Wou'd be fo rich indeed,
That I may help myfelf, and thofe
　　That often ftand in need.

6

Thus independent, live I would
　　In fome convenient place,
And fpend my time in doing good
　　Amongft the human race.

7.

My times of leifure I would fpend
　　In ftudies that are deep:
The benefit of what I penn'd,
　　I'd let the people reap.

8.

And when my days on earth fhall ceafe,
　　I'd chufe, among the bleft,
A crown of glory, honour, peace,
　　And everlafting reft.

Compofed at *Weftminfter*, in the Kingdom of *Great-Britain*,
　　April 27, 1789,

A NEW

A

NEW SONG,

ON THE WORKS OF RIGHTEOUSNESS.

WHERE dwells the man that dares fupprefs
  The Godly Works of Righteoufnefs?
The wretch that would attempt the thing,
Ought on a gallows high to fwing.
   The works of righteoufnefs,
    Wherever they've been wrought,
   In this world's wildernefs,
    Much happinefs have brought:
  They are of great and mighty weight
  To mankind in this mortal ftate.

 Ye noble friends, humane and wife!
We hardly know what profits rife,
How much doth fpring we fcarce can guefs,
From the blefs'd works of righteoufnefs.
   The works of righteoufnefs, &c.

 How pleafing to a righteous foul,
To do good deeds without controul,
To help the brethren in diftrefs,
By gen'rous acts of righteoufnefs!
   The works of righteoufnefs, &c.

        How

How galling to a pious mind,
To fee the fons of men unkind,
To fee them oft too much opprefs,
Inftéad of working righteoufnefs!
   The works of righteoufnefs, &c.

My worthy friends, we fhall be blefs'd
With glory, honour, peace, and reft,
If we at all times truly prefs
After the thing call'd righteoufnefs.
   The works of rightcoufncfs, &c.

O Righteoufnèfs! thou lovely thing!
Much profit thou doft always bring:
The boundlefs good I can't exprefs,
Obtain'd by thee, O Righteoufnefs!
   The works of righteoufnefs,
    Wherever the've been wrought,
   In this world's wildernefs,
    Much happinefs have brought:
  They are of great and mighty weight
  To mankind in this mortal ftate.

Compcfed at *London,* Feb. 3, 1791.

CHAP.

C H A P.   XXVIII.

Of the STATE *and* CONDITION *of the Human Body;
and of the Birds, Beafts, and Fifhes ; Trees,
Plants, and Herbs—All muft die—Whether the
Soul had an Exiftence before the Creation of Man
—The happy Condition of the Dead.*

THE Human Body is a compofition of the
four elements; that is, of the earth, air,
fire, and water. It is nourifhed and fupported
by the vegetable and animal productions, the circumambient air, and fundry liquids. It is conftantly flying off by infenfible perfpiration, and
other evacuations ; and is fo very mutable, that
it changes once in feven years, and becomes entirely new. The old body is difperfed among the
elements ; and the new body is generated out of
the materials appointed for nutrition.

The Divine Artificer hath breathed into this body
the breath of life ; hath implanted in it an immortal foul, which is endowed with rational powers
and faculties, and is made capable of worfhipping,
knowing, ferving, and enjoying the *Author* of its
being, *viz.* the *Great Incomprehenfible Fountain* of
life and *motion.*

This

This body meets with various degrees of pleafure and pain ; and being but a temporary building, continues but a fhort time in this mortal
ftate. It is expofed to an innumerable train of
accidents and difeafes ; and as it is appointed that
all men fhall once die, at laft the appointed deftruction comes. The body becomes a lifelefs
lump, and returns to the elements out of which it
was formed. The terreftrial part returns to the
earth, the aërial to the air, the igneous to the fire,
the aqueous to the water, and the fpirit to *him*
that gave it.

Thus have I defcribed the compofition of the
human body, with the ftate, condition and fate
of all mankind.—But not only the human race,
but the birds, beafts and fifhes, trees, plants and
herbs, are formed out of the four elements, and
undergo various changes whilft their lives continue ; but at laft they die, and their bodies are
difperfed among the elements.

Some animals, and fome vegetables, live a long
time ; but others are very fhort-lived. Infants
often die, that never faw light. But we only live
at the prefent time ; for the time we have lived
is paft and gone, and that which we have to live
is not yet come :—Hence, we only live at the
prefent moment ; and our lives are as a vapour,
that appeareth for a very little feafon, and then
fuddenly vanifheth away. Mankind are like the
grafs, that is flourifhing in the morning, but in
the evening it is cut down and withereth. The
time of our continuance in this mortal ftate
is fo very uncertain, that we cannot tell whether
we

we fhall live one moment, or a confiderable number of years; but when we become old, we know
that we muft die in a fhort time, according to the
courfe of nature.

I have frequently been afked, whether I thought
that the fouls of men had an exiftence before the
formation of their bodies? And my anfwer has
been, that it is probable they had; for when the
Almighty had formed the body of Adam out of
the duft of the ground, he breathed into his
noftrils the breath of life; and that breath undoubtedly had an exiftence before it entered into
the body formed for its reception, becaufe it proceeded from the Great Fountain of life and motion.

Again—When the Almighty converfed with
Job, he faid, " Where waft thou when I laid the
foundations of the earth?" Vid. Job, xxxviii. 4.
It is therefore apparent, that Job was fomewhere
in the univerfe when the world was created,
though his body was not formed, nor his fpirit
put into it.

The very materials with which our prefent
bodies are compofed, were undoubtedly created
when the world was, though they were not framed
into thefe earthy tabernacles. - Hence, we may in
that fenfe be called as old as the earth, or the
fun, moon and ftars, if the earth was created as
foon as thofe luminaries.

Death is only a change from this ftate to another,—as our bodies return again to the elements,
and our fpirits to him that gave them; and the
dead being at reft, are totally free from the cares,
troubles, and vexations of a mortal life. None
are

are afraid of lofing their lives or eftates, by thunders, lightnings, earthquakes, inundations, ftorms,
or tempefts; nor of being deftroyed by the war,
famine, or peftilence. Thefe fcenes of trouble,
thefe perils and dangers, are all over and gone.

SHORT is our paffage through this nether world;
For foon, by death, we from the ftage are hurl'd.
The tender infants, in their lovely bloom,
Are often hurry'd to the filent tomb!
Adults grown up, nay fome of ev'ry age,
By cruel *death*, are taken from the ftage!
The high, the low, the rich, the poor, the fmall,
By the great *king of terrors* foon muft fall!
The richeft man, (it cannot be deny'd)
Who with good things moft amply is fupply'd;
Whilft he does live, doth grief and trouble find,
Is oft in pain, and vexed in his mind:
At laft he's ftruck a fatal ftroke by death!
Down falls his body, and off flies his breath!
But where it goes, or how far it doth fly,
No mortal man can tell below the fky.
The elements that in the body are,
Return to thofe from whence they taken were.
Thus duft to duft, and air to air, we find,
And heat to heat, are foon again combin'd;
Water to water, alfo, foon doth flow,
And the whole mafs to diffolution go!
   Await, O man! thy doom; for 'tis the fate
Of every creature in this mortal ftate:
But when death comes, the fpirits rife on high,
Of godly ones who *in the* LORD *do die.*
Thus whilft their bodies are behind at reft,
Their pious fouls with happinefs are blefs'd.
   O happy ftate, in which the dead are caft!
Their pain is gone, and all their trouble's paft:
Need no phyfician to give them relief;
Are free from pain, from forrow, and from grief;

And

And from the rage of all the fons of ftrife,
And the vexations of a mortal life.
The fland'ring tongue, and the back-biting knave,
Cannot hurt thofe within the filent grave:
Nor can the thief, who robs by night and day,
Nor any murd'rer who kills on the way.
By no means can the tyrant them opprefs,
Nor any mortal lead them to diftrefs.
When roaring winds bring up the thick'ned cloud,
And the grum thunder rumbles out aloud;
When the earth quakes, and lofty cities fall;
When places fink, and can't be found at all;
When inundations o'er the land arife,
And burning mountains burft towards the fkies;
When famine and the peftilence doth rage,
And wicked nations in a war engage;
When blood and carnage greatly doth expand,
And defolation overfpreads the land,
And boift'rous tempefts rage upon the fea:
Then are the *dead* from danger wholly free.
They're not afraid of being hurt, or flain,
Like wretched mortals who alive remain.
Let not the living, then, at death repine,
Since it was made by God, an *act divine*,
To raife the juft,—the *hufband, child,* and *wife,*
From fcenes of trouble, to a better *life!*

CHAP.

C H A P.   XXIX.

The Ages of the PATRIARCHS—*Thoughts on the*
Wearing of Mourning, and on the Burying of the
Dead under Churches.

ACCORDING to the Scriptures, the people
lived much longer in the antideluvian
world than they have fince, as will appear by the
fubfequent Tables:

BEFORE THE FLOOD,

		Years
Adam	lived	930
Seth	——	912
Enos	——	905
Canaan	——	910
Mahaleel	——	895
Jared	——	962
Enoch	——	365
Methufelah	——	969
Lamech	——	777
Noah	——	950

SINCE THE FLOOD,

Shem	lived	600
Arphaxad	——	438
Salah	——	433
Eber		

						Years
Eber	-	-	-	-	lived	464
Peleg	-	-	-		———	239
Rue	-	-	-		———	239
Serug	-	-	-	-	———	230
Nahor	-	-	-	-	———	148
Terah	-	-	-	-	———	205
Abraham	-	-	-		———	175
Ifaac	-	-	-	-	———	180
Jacob	-	-	-	-	———	147
Jofeph	-	-	-	-	———	110
Aaron	-	-	-	-	———	123
Mofes	-	-	-	-	———	120
Jofhua	-	-	-	-	———	110

Hence it is evident, that the days of man have fhortened by degrees; for Adam lived 930 years, and Jofhua only 110. Some, in thefe modern times, have lived till they were upwards of 150, years old, though but a very few live till they are an hundred years of age.

It is very natural for people to mourn when they have loft their relations and friends; and I have obferved, that fome mourn till they greatly impair their health and fenfes.

The practice of mourning feems to be very ancient; for Abraham mourned for Sarah, vid. Gen. xxiii. 2.—And Jofeph mourned feven days for his father, with a great and very fore lamentation. Vid. Gen. l. 10.—Alfo, the children of Ifrael mourned thirty days for Mofes. Vid. Deut. xxxiv. 8, &c.

It has been said, that some people have hired mourners to weep and make a lamentable howling at funerals.

Some of the savage nations have cut themselves, and torn their flesh to pieces, in consequence of their losing their relations. And some of the American Indians lay their dead upon scaffolds, where they erect seats for the mourners, who go and sit by the corpse every day for a considerable time, and weep and howl for their departed friends; but if they cannot go themselves, they hire others to howl in their room.

In those parts of Christendom where I have been acquainted, the people in general have made use of black cloaths, ribbands, veils, weeds, buckles, &c. for mourning. But the Spaniards formerly wore white garments for that purpose; and it would do just as well as black in these times, if it was the fashion.

Many families in America have been injured in time past by running into debt for mourning; for it was once the custom for every one in a family to dress in black, when they lost their relations; and if they were not poor, to give a pair of gloves to every one that attended a funeral. This practice was sometimes not only injurious to those who lost their friends, but to those that sold mourning; for they often lost their property, by trusting people that were unable to make payment.

But these excesses have been restrained in some places by the acts of the legislative assemblies, who,

who, if I miftake not, have prudently ordered that nothing fhould be worn for mourning, but black gloves, a weed, or a ribband, &c. which expence was but trifling.

It was formerly cuftomary in New-England, for every perfon that had an inclination, to attend a funeral without being invited. The parfon of the parifh alfo attended, and prayed with the mourners at the houfe of the deceafed. After prayers, if the deceafed was an adult, not lefs than four, and often fix bearers were chofen to carry the corpfe to the grave.

The corpfe was then moved out of the houfe, and laid upon a bier placed on a table, where the coffin was opened, and the mourners and others viewed the dead body; which being afterwards nailed up, a pall was put over it. Upon the pall white gloves were laid for the bearers. Gloves were then given to the parfon and others that attended. The bearers put on their gloves, and walked with the bier, &c. on their fhoulders, to the burying-place; the mourners walking two deep, next to the bearers; and both men and women fell into the proceffion, and walked in a regular and decent manner. If the burying-ground was at a confiderable diftance, the bearers were relieved on the way by the people, who took turns in carrying the corpfe: but the bearers took their places again when they came near the place of interment; and when they had arrived, they laid down the corpfe, took off their hats, and put the body into the grave, which was filled by the by-ftanders, the mourners ftanding in the mean

time

time at the head of the grave. When the burial was over, the oldeſt male among the mourners returned thanks to the people, for their kindneſs in attending the funeral. No orations, nor prayers, were made at the grave by the parſon, as he had prayed before at the houſe of mourning.

Sometimes the people walked back with the mourners in proceſſion, and were refreſhed at their houſe with a ſupper, &c. But the Quakers did not wear mourning, nor allow their coffins to be painted black, nor was a black pall uſed: their coffins were of the natural colour of the boards they had been made of.

The funeral ceremonies were different in the various governments. In Canada, the people ſang as they went with a corpſe to the grave; and I have been informed, that they buried ſhoes, candles, money, &c. with the dead; and alſo, that that is the cuſtom in other Catholic countries.

In the State of New-York, the people are invited to attend funerals. They aſſemble at the time appointed. The corpſe is carried to the grave by ten or twelve bearers; and the men walk in proceſſion, but the women do not go to the grave.

The parſon that attends the funeral, and the phyſicians that attended the deceaſed, each of them receives a ſcarf, that is, linen enough for a ſhirt, which they wear to the grave over their right ſhoulders, tied in a large knot under their left arms. Theſe are not only worn at the funerals, but at church the next Sunday morning.

When

When the corpfe is interred, they return in proceffion to the houfe of mourning, where they find the tables fpread, and furnifhed with fpiced wine, pipes and tobacco. They fall to drinking and fmoaking: the converfation runs upon a variety of fubjects, fome of which are very unfuitable for fuch folemnities. But they often have a fupper, and the houfe of mourning is converted into a houfe of feafting. This, however, is not the practice at every funeral in that government.

At Philadelphia, the people are invited to attend funerals. The parfon walks before the bearers: and if the deceafed was a woman, the ladies walk in proceffion next to the mourners, and the gentlemen follow after; but if the deceafed was a man, the gentlemen walk before the ladies: and the parfon delivers an oration at the grave.

The people are invited to funerals at Charleftown in South-Carolina. At the houfe of mourning, they receive cakes, wine, punch, &c. and alfo a fprig of green rofemary wrapped in a piece of paper, which they carry to the burying-ground, and throw into the grave whilft the people are burying the corpfe. Here the parfon either delivers a fermon, or makes an oration, at the time of the interment.

But fometimes, when the fnow is deep in America, or when the travelling is bad, the corpfe is carried in a carriage to the grave.

The funeral ceremonies are different in Europe, as well as in America. At fome places in England, they fing a hymn, whilft they are burying

R 3   the

the dead. I underſtand that this method is practiſed by the Moravians, and by the Methodiſts.

In ſome places of America, they bury their dead
under churches; but it is not ſo much practiſed
there, as it is in ſome parts of Europe. This
cuſtom was firſt introduced in England in 750.

I have been aſked, whether I thought it is prudent to bury the dead under the churches? And
my anſwer has been in the negative; becauſe the
infectious effluvia of putrifying bodies may be ſo
very penetrating, as not only to impregnate the
ſurrounding earth with its poiſonous qualities, but
even to eſcape through the bounds of its confinement, infect the air, and ſpread contageous diftempers amongſt the living, which muſt lay a
foundation for augmenting the congregation of the
dead. But how far my hypotheſis may ſeem rational, I leave to the judgment of Philoſophers,
and the Gentlemen of the Faculty, to determine.

When people die of putrid diſorders, their
bodies ought to be buried ſoon, to prevent the
ſpreading of infectious diſtempers. But if they
die in a fit of the apoplexy, or very ſuddenly ſome
other way, it may be proper to keep them a few
days; becauſe ſome have come to life, that have
appeared to be dead.

In divers parts of America, the graves fall in,
and become level with the ground within a year
after a dead body has been buried; but in other
parts, they do not fall in perhaps in the courſe
of twenty years.—I have been aſked to give a reaſon for theſe things. My anſwer has been, that
the earth is impregnated in ſome places with
ſalineous,

falineous, nitrous, and other particles, which preferve bodies from confuming, and that from hence
fome graves do not fall in for a long time; and
alfo, that it is impregnated in other places with
copperas and other qualities which are capable of
diffolving bodies in a fhort time, and that from
hence it is that fome graves fall in, in lefs than a year
after a body has been buried; for I have been informed, that a piece of beef will be confumed in
a few days, if it is put down into the copper-
mines in Connecticut.

Moreover, I rendered another reafon, that is,
the rage of putrefaction in fome bodies, which
may caufe them to diffolve, with the coffins that
contain them, fooner than others; for one body
has a greater degree of putrefaction than another.
I knew four young women, who were twins, that
took the dyfentery, and were all dead and buried
in fix days. They were laid within about eighteen inches of each other, and where there did not
appear to be any difference in the qualities of the
earth. The grave of the one that had the greateft
degree of putrefaction, fell in in a fhort time;
but the others did not fall in for a confiderable
number of years. This I imputed to the violence
of the diforder in the putrifying body.

It is cuftomary in great towns and cities in
England, to bury the dead upon one another. A
gentleman informed me in 1790, that he faw a
grave dug juft by Weftminfter-Abbey, and that
he counted fifty-three fkulls that were thrown out
of it, befides other bones:—He alfo faid that the
fmell was fo very difagreeable, that he could but
juft endure to ftand and count the fkulls.

　　　　　　　　　　　Now,

Now, who can fuppofe that the earth is not greatly impregnated with a contagious infection, where fo many diftempered putrifying bodies have been buried in fo fmall a place as one grave? and, who can fuppofe that this fubtile effluvia does not creep through the earth, and impregnate the air in a greater or a leffer degree with its poifonous qualities?

To conclude, I cannot, for the reafons I have mentioned, think it is prudent to bury the dead under churches, nor very near to them; and as there is room enough in the world, they may be carried to a proper diftance, and buried, without being put one upon another. It is our duty to exert ourfelves in promoting whatever may tend to preferve our own lives and thofe of others, and to fupprefs every evil practice that may render ourfelves and our fellow-creatures miferable.

It is a manifeft abufe of the creation, to deck and adorn ourfelves with things entirely needlefs. —As to the wearing of mourning, it is certain that it can do the dead no good, nor the living any further than that of covering their nakednefs, and fcreening them from the inclemency of the weather. The burying of gold and filver with the dead, and other things that can do no good, is alfo an abufe of the creation;—and it is the duty of every rational creature to guard againft excefs in thefe things. If people have any thing that they can fpare, let them give it to the poor; inftead of burying it in the ground, or wafting it for fuperfluities.

CHAP,

CHAP. XXX.

Thoughts on the SLAVE TRADE—*The Thunder of the Law, the Thunder of the Gospel, and the Thunder of the Conscience, forbid this abominable Practice.*

ONE thing is practised in some parts of Christendom, which is an abomination to the Lord, and a disgrace to the human race. It is that of stealing our African brethren, carrying them from their country, selling them like horses, sheep, or swine; and the keeping of them in cruel bondage all their days, without the allowance of any freedom, or even leave to return to the place of their nativity, to visit their families and friends.

Many of those miserable objects who have the misfortune of being born of such stolen and enslaved parents, have but a gloomy prospect before them; because they are obliged to spend the whole of their days in vassalage and slavery, without enjoying that liberty which is the natural right of every man: And not only so, but they are liable to be sold from place to place, like animals belonging to the brute creation.

This

This abominable practice commenced in Portugal, in the year 1443; in England, in 1562: and at Virginia, in 1620:—But, to the honour of the British Parliament, the Negroes are not enslaved in Great-Britain at the present time.

Surely those that follow this illicit trade, must be as hard-hearted as old wicked Pharaoh, the tyrannic King of Egypt:—nay they are more wicked then he was; for he only oppressed those he had under his own government, within the limits of his kingdom, without being guilty of the horrid sin of going abroad to follow the practice of theft and robbery. Hence he was guilty of but one crime. But our tyrannical wretches are guilty of two: the first is that of man-stealing; and the second is that of bringing their fellow-mortals, with their posterity, into cruel bondage and slavery, as long as life continues.

If the Lord, on hearing the cry of the oppressed Israelites, came down and punished the Egyptians with a number of heavy judgments, when they were guilty of but one crime; of how much forer punishment must those be counted worthy, who are guilty of two abominable crimes? —But though such offenders may sometimes escape punishment in this life, yet, by their hardness and impenitence, they treasure up to themselves wrath against the day of wrath, and the revelation of the righteous judgment of God, who will render to every man according to the deeds done in the body.

Let

Let thofe that live in the practice of thefe abominations, liften,

1. To the thunder of the Law;
2. To the thunder of the Gofpel; and,
3. To the thunder of Confcience.

1. To the thunder of the *Law.*—The Law ex-
prefsly fays, " Thou fhalt not fteal ;" and again,
" He that ftealeth a man, and felleth him, fhall
furely be put to death." Hence, thofe that follow
the Slave Trade, ought to be executed.

2. To the Thunder of the *Gofpel.*—" Indignation and wrath, tribulation and anguifh, upon
every foul of man that doth evil : For the wrath
of God is revealed from Heaven, againft all un-
godlinefs and unrighteoufnefs of men."—" For
the Law was not made for a righteous man, but
for the ungodly and profane, for murderers of
fathers, for murderers of mothers, for perjured
perfons, for man-ftealers," &c.—It is therefore
evident, that thofe who fteal, fell, and enflave
their brethren, difobey the Gofpel, and make themfelves liable to the dreadful punifhments denoun-
ced againft fuch rebellious finners.

3. To the thunder of *Confcience.*—This tells
you, that all nations were made by the Almighty:
that they are all entitled to freedom, though
it hath pleafed the *Former* of their bodies to
make them of different colours and complexions: That man-ftealing, and the bringing of
your brethren into cruel bondage, is a tranfgreffion of the Law, and a difobedience of the
Gofpel:

Gofpel : That whatfoever ye would that men fhould do unto you, ye fhould do even fo unto them : that you do not do as you would be done by, when ye practife thefe abominations.

That fhould the Negroes follow your evil example ; fhould they come into your country, and fteal yourfelves, your fathers and mothers, your brothers and fifters, your wives and children ; and carry both you and them, bound, and almoft ftarved, into Africa ; there to be fold, put under tafk-mafters, and kept in cruel bondage all your days ; do you not think that fuch treatment would be very cruel and unjuft ? Surely the thunder of confcience muft fay, *yes.*—Why then do ye follow this infamous, this diabolical, difgraceful, and abominable practice ? Surely fuch offenders ought to be branded with infamy, fpurned from fociety, and treated with neglect and contempt, for difgracing Chriftendom with their atrocious conduct.

Is it not very ftrange that this difgraceful kind of theft, oppreffion, and tyranny, has not been fuppreffed by the Legiflators in thofe countries where fuch abominations are practifed ?—Why do they not follow the laudable example of the Britifh Parliament ? Why do they not follow that of the Legiflators in New-England, New-York, the Jerfies, and Pennfylvania, who have liberated the poor Africans from the fhackles of their bondage ?—It is faid, that this abomination is ftill practifed in the governments South of Pennfylvania, in the Weft-India iflands, and in the Spanifh dominions : But thofe that follow this evil practice, muft certainly

tainly incur the difpleafure of the *Moft High*, and expofe themfelves to his wrath and indignation.

Liften, therefore, O ye tranfgreffors! to the thunder of the Law, to the thunder of the Gofpel, and to the thunder of your own Confciences. Refrain from your evil conduct;—forfake the practice of man-ftealing;—break your bands of wickednefs;—undo heavy burthens;—and let the oppreffed Africans be releafed from the fhackles of their bondage, and the chains of their vaffalage and flavery, left ye debar yourfelves *from entering into that reft which remains for the People of God.*

London, March 5, 1791.

CHAP.

C H A P.   XXXI.

Who ought to be licenſed to keep PUBLIC-HOUSES—
*Of Drunkenneſs and Gluttony ; how Drunkards
ought to be managed—Of the Evils which attend
Gaming, Lying, and Stealing—A Caution againſt
the keeping of Bad Company.*

NO perſon ſhould be licenſed to ſell ſpiritous
liquors, unleſs he can be well recommended
for his ſobriety and good behaviour ; and he
ſhould be ſtrictly enjoined to beware of entertain-
ing bad company, that of drunkards in particular,
whoſe exceſs in this abominable vice not only
proves ruinous to themſelves and families, but
often an inlet to every ſpecies of wickedneſs, to
the hurt of mankind in general.

An inn-keeper ought to be well furniſhed with
every-thing neceſſary for the entertainment of travellers. He ought to allow no gaming in his
houſe ; becauſe it has a tendency to waſte both
time and money, and alſo to diſturb ſober people,
who may be inclined to take their reſt. He
ought alſo to decline giving his town-cuſtomers
liquor, when he obſerves they have got enough ;
and to clear his houſe of their company, when it
is time for them to go home to their wives

and

and families. If they infift upon having more liquor, his prefenting them with a little fmall-beer or water will perhaps fatisfy their thirfty cravings, and may be the means of their going home foberly.

Drunkards ought not to be allowed to haunt inns, taverns, or ale-houfes; as they not only do hurt to themfelves, families, and connections, but alfo to the houfes they frequent, by preventing decent people from entering them to do bufinefs, for which purpofe they are particularly intended, as well as for entertainment. Some go to the ale-houfes on Saturday evenings when they have received their wages, where they ftay till their money is fpent, while their families are perhaps in want of the neceffaries of life.

The abominable vice of drunkennefs, which prevails fo much under the fun, burns up beauty, haftens age, makes a man a beaft, a ftrong man weak, and a wife man a fool. It deftroys the credit, reputation, wealth, and health of millions; as many a good conftitution has been ruined by it. By the immoderate ufe of fpiritous liquors, gouts, dropfies, rheumatifms, confumptions, and many other diftempers, are generated, which cut down great multitudes, before they have lived half their days: Numbers of poor women and children, who once lived in affluence, are reduced to beggary and want, by the imprudent conduct of thofe that wafte their eftates by intemperance. Nay it is thought that intemperance kills more than the fword.

A drunkard

A drunkard is a plague to himfelf, a trouble to his family, a difgrace to his neighbours, and a peft to fociety. He is like a fhip without helm or ballaft, under full fail to deftruction. He is defpifed by all good people; they treat him with neglect, and fhun his company. When intoxicated, he is incapable of taking care of himfelf; in danger of falling into the fire, and water; of being killed by carts, coaches, waggons and horfes, when he attempts to walk abroad; of perifhing with the cold in fevere weather, and of being robbed and murdered in the ftreets and highways.

People who are apt to drink to excefs, fhould be watched and governed by their friends; for if they are not capable of taking care of themfelves, it ought to be done by others.

If any perfon intoxicated with liquor comes into an inn, he ought to be turned out, to prevent the company from being interrupted; or if the weather is ftormy, and he is in danger of perifhing with cold, he ought to be put into fome apartment by himfelf, and allowed only water till he becomes fober.

As many are much indifpofed after drinking too much, I will prefcribe a cure for that dangerous diftemper:

1. Let the drunkard's head be raifed.
2. Dip a fponge in vinegar, and hold it to his nofe.
3. Let him be blooded.
4. Give him water to drink.
5. Pour cold water on his head.

6. Give

6. Give him a cathartic, or inject a laxative *enema*.

7. Put his feet into warm water.

8. If he recovers, keep him from spiritous liquors.

Gluttony is another vice that prevails too much; and though it does not destroy the senses by intoxication, like spiritous liquors, yet it hurts the vital, natural, and animal functions, and generates dangerous distempers.—The wise man says, *The drunkard, and the glutton, shall come to poverty.* Prov. xxiii. 21.—Again, the Apostle Paul says, *Drunkards,* &c. *shall not inherit the kingdom of God.* 1 Cor. vi. 10.

Gaming ought by no means to be allowed in any kingdom or state; because it is injurious, not only to individuals, but to the community at large. It is attended with a train of evil consequences, such as loss of time, credit, and reputation. It leads people into intemperance, such as drunkenness, &c.; generates contentions, divisions and animosities amongst friends; occasions wranglings, quarrellings, bad language, and fightings—and sometimes the loss of lives.—Hence, people that are one day very rich, may the next day be very poor; and families in affluent circumstances to-day, may be reduced to poverty and distress to-morrow.

Both drunkards and gamesters, that persist in their evil courses; ought to be confined in workhouses, and kept in some lawful employment; by which means they may in time, upon reflection, become useful members of society.

S   If

If any man, woman, or child, fhall be inclined to undo themfelves, let them take to lying and ftealing, or either of them may anfwer alone for the purpofe: For, befides the danger of fines or imprifonments, the whip or the halter, the liar and the thief are expofed to the hatred of all good people, and even to that of one another. Liars cannot be believed, even when they fpeak the truth; and if any thing is ftole, it will be laid to a thief's charge, whether he is guilty of the crime or not. In fhort, liars will not believe one another, and thieves are jealous of each other when goods are ftolen.

Thefe miferable animals are always in a wretched condition; for wherever they are known, people are afraid to harbour them in their houfes.

Liars may do much damage in places where their characters are not known, by defaming the innocent; and if they are permitted to bear falfe witnefs, they may be guilty of the horrid crime of fhedding innocent blood.

People of the beft credit and reputation are therefore always in danger of being injured by liars and thieves. Hence fuch villians ought not to be fuffered to run at large; but ought to be confined in fome place from which they cannot efcape, and there kept to hard labour.

The Legiflature of the Maffachufetts have contrived a very laudable mode of punifhment for thieves, and other villains whofe crimes have not been fo heinous as to bring the offenders to the gallows.—They are fent to Caftle William, which is an ifland furrounded by water, and fituated

about

about three miles from Boston, from which they cannot easily make their escape. There they are kept to hard labour, the profits of which are converted to the good of the public. Some are confined for one year, some for two, three, &c. and some for life. Their punishments are in proportion to the magnitude of their crimes.

This laudable example ought to be followed by all nations; for it is much better for the community to have such vagabonds kept in lawful employment, than to have them confined in prisons at the expence of the public, or to allow them to strole from place to place, robbing and stealing for a livelihood.

Let all liars remember, that whilst they live in that wicked practice, they are the children of the devil, who is the father of lies. John viii. 44.—That the Lord is the hater of a false witness, that speaketh lies. Prov. vi. 17—19.—That all liars shall have their part in the lake that burneth with fire and brimstone, Rev. xxi. 8. except they repent and reform from their evil courses. Let him that stole, steal no more; but let him labour with his hands, to get something for his maintenance, and to make restitution to those he has injured by his atrocious conduct. Eph. iv. 28.

I.

IF you're at home, or on a route,
Beware of knaves that run about
To rob and steal;—of them be shy,
And guard yourself when they come nigh.

S 2   A cor-

2.

A correſpondence have you not
With any thief, or drunken ſot:
Haunt not the taverns, nor grog-ſhops,
With gaming beaus, and ſilly fops.

3.

To keep with them always refuſe,
Who frequently bad language uſe;
From ev'ry gang that is too rude,
And all thoſe wretches that are lewd.

4.

Left they, before you are aware,
Lead you into ſome dreadful ſnare,
Deſtroy your innocence and fame,
And bring upon you a bad name.

5.

Thus, if bad company you ſhun,
To vice you'll not be apt to run:
In good repute you may remain,
And ſhun much trouble, grief, and pain.

CHAP.

C H A P. XXXII.

Of WHOREDOM, *viz.* That of Idolatry, Adultery, and Fornication.

THERE are feveral kinds of Whoredom; fuch as,

1. The worfhipping of falfe gods.

2. Adultery, or an unlawful conneâion between married perfons.

3. Fornication, or an illegal correfpondence between thofe that are unmarried.

All thefe abominations are called whoredom.— Let us therefore obferve, That when the Ifraelites forfook the worfhip of the Moft High, and paid homage to idols, it is faid that they went a-whoring after their own inventions. Vid. Pfal. cvi. 39. —That when David had an unlawful correfpondence with the wife of Uriah, it was faid that he committed adultery. Vid. 2 Sam. xi. 4.—And Shechem committed fornication with Dinah. Vid. Gen. xxxiv. 2.

Whoredom of every kind is an abominable vice. It tends to deftroy our felicity in this life, and our happinefs hereafter; for befides the fin of not worfhipping the True God, whoredom raifes a fpirit of jealoufy between a man and his wife; pro-

S 3   duces

duces contentions, divisions and animosities; breaks up families, and blasts their reputation. It also hurts the credit and character of unmarried persons, and reduces them to beggary and want, which excites them on to commit other abominations, such as theft, robbery, murder, &c.—By means of a whorish woman, a man is brought to a piece of bread, says Solomon, Prov. vi. 26. So also, by the means of a whorish man, a woman is brought to a piece of bread, says the *Author* of the *American Oracle*.

How does the world swarm in this degenerate age, with a great multitude of miserable wretches, who, by reason of whoredom, are reduced to such poverty and distress, that they are destitute of house and home, of food, raiment, and other things necessary for their subsistence!

In this deplorable condition they remain till they are thrown upon the town, confined in work-houses, or cast into prison, for theft or some other crime; and the poor children of such degenerated parents must be maintained by the parish, or by the charity of some friends, otherwise they must perish with hunger.

Those that live in the practice of these vices, pass through much care, trouble, and vexation of spirit. The whoremonger is continually afraid of being seized by an officer, and either committed to prison, or of having his estate taken from him, to support those vicious, lewd, debauched creatures, with whom he has had a correspondence.—The whore is also afraid of the miseries she may bring upon herself by her evil conduct. In short, both

live

live in fear that their reputations will be deſtroyed, and their conſtitutions ruined, by the reception of a certain *virus*, which will be mentioned in the ſubſequent chapter.

Let all perſons who have any regard for the preſervation of their health, wealth, credit, reputation, and ſalvation, ſhun the company of lewd men and women. This may prevent that anxiety, poverty and diſtreſs, which will inevitably come upon thoſe who keep their company, and follow their evil practices.—Let whoremongers, adulterers, and fornicators, forſake their evil conduct, and live pious and virtuous lives for the future; and let them remember the words of the Apoſtle, *viz.* that marriage is honourable in all, &c. but that whoremongers and adulterers God will judge. Heb. xiii. 4.

Various puniſhments have been inflicted for idolatry, adultery, and fornication. Under the Moſaical law, idolatry and adultery were puniſhed with death, and fornication by a fine. The Babylonians, Arabians, Tartars, Indians, Javans, and Mexicans, made adultery and fornication a capital crime. The Turks drowned ſuch women, and put the men to great torture. The Hungarians executed thoſe guilty of ſuch crimes. In Great Britain, adulterers are fined, and fornicators are obliged by the law to pay a certain ſum of money for the ſupport and maintenance of their baſtard children.

In the Maſſachuſetts, adulterers are puniſhed by fines, impriſonments, ſetting on the gallows, ſtanding in the pillory, and by being whipped at

S 4   the

the poft.—Fornicators are fined; and if a married man and woman has a child within fix or feven months after they have been married, they are obliged to make a public confeflion before the church and congregation unto which they belong, or they are debarred from having their children chriftened.

Some of the clergy have made fuch unfortunate perfons acknowledge, that they had been guilty of a breach of the feventh commandment, *viz.* of committing adultery. Thus they have been induced to tell a lie before the *Lord*, the church, &c.; for adultery cannot be committed when both of the perfons are unmarried.—Some again have made them acknowledge, that they had been guilty of the fin of uncleannefs; and others, that they had been guilty of the fin of fornication.

To conclude, neither Chrift nor his Apoftles have impofed any fuch degrees of punifhment under the gofpel difpenfation; and reafon and common fenfe tells us, that fines, imprifonments, &c. cannot forgive fins. Therefore, let all thofe who have been guilty of fuch abominations, " go their way, and do fo no more, left a worfe thing fhould come upon them."

CHAP.

C H A P.   XXXIII.

Of the VENEREAL DISEASE—*Its terrible Effects on
the Human Body—How to cure the Distemper.*

THIS malady is called the plague of Venus,
the venereal peftilence, the French difeafe,
&c. It was not known in Europe till it was
brought from the Spanifh Weft-Indies into Spain,
by Chriftopher Columbus's men, in 1493.

In 1494, it was carried from Spain to Italy;
and in 1495, it was fpread in Naples and France;
and from thofe countries it was fpread over Europe. Not only Europe, but America, and all
parts of the habitable world where trade and commerce are carried on, have become infected in a
greater or leffer degree. It has lately found its way
among the innocent inhabitants of the iflands
newly difcovered in the Southern Ocean, who
being ignorant of the method of cure, have been
in a deplorable condition: and I have been informed, that it is endemic in Peru.

When it firft began in the Spanifh Weft-Indies,
or what it proceeded from, I believe no mortal
can tell; but it has been fuppofed that it originated from a vegetable or an animal poifon.
However,

However, it is but a fuppofition, without any fubftantial proof.

Perhaps this diforder has done more damage in Europe, than the difcovery of America has done good; for it has flain thoufands, and ruined the conftitutions of an innumerable multitude of people. Every one of the human race is liable to take this terrible malady. The high and the low, the rich and the poor, the young and the old, the honeft and the difhoneft, are continually expofed to it. An honeft hufband may take it of a difhoneft wife; and an honeft wife may take it of a difhoneft hufband.

. The *virus* may be communicated various ways; for, befides that of an impure contact and coition with an infected perfon, a nurfe may take it, by fuckling a child born with it, or otherways infected; and a child may take it, by fucking a woman labouring under that complaint. It may alfo be taken by kiffing a perfon whofe mouth is ulcerated, and by the reception of the poifon in any part where the fkin is off. I knew a phyfician that was afflicted with an univerfal taint, who affirmed to me that he took it by handling a venereal patient when he had a wound in his finger. In fhort, wherever the *virus* can get through the fkin, it will enter into the mafs of the fluids, and lay a foundation for a confirmed *lues*.

The ftronger the *virus* is, the fooner it will operate. I heard a patient fay, that he felt it immediately after he had taken the infection; that the poifon feemed to run like a wild-fire, and in

4

lefs

less than 24 hours produced a cordee, and other bad symptoms.

Sometimes it is very flow in its operation; but the symptoms generally appear in three or four days after the infection has been received. It operates different ways in different constitutions. It usually begins with a sensation of heat, and pricking pain in making water : then comes on a running of virulent matter, of a white, yellow, green, or bloody colour; followed with a stricture, a cordee, phimofis, paraphimofis, strangury, buboes, chancres, warts, cutaneous eruptions of a red, white, or blue colour; nocturnal pains, inflammations, swellings, excoriations, ulcers, fissures, opthalmies, loss of fight, deafness, carious bones, spinas, ventolas, nodes, tophs, ganglions, gummas, caruncles, gangrens, and mortifications.

Sometimes the *virus* runs to the nose, and eats it off.—When the running is stopped, or what is improperly called a *gonorrhœa sicca* comes on, then the *virus* enters into the mass of the blood, and the patient is in a dangerous situation.

Men, by reason of their different formation, have more complaints than the women ; and children born with the disorder, are worse to cure than either.

The ancient physicians were entirely unable to cure this terrible malady, till they discovered the virtues of the *argentum vivum*. This discovery was made about the year 1522, which was 29 years after the poison was first brought into Europe. This is an excellent specific, and the only

remedy

remedy I believe that will perform a *radical cure*, though it muft be fometimes combined with other medicines. But it has been faid, that the North American Indians can cure themfelves when half rotten, with a decoction of the *rad. lobelia;* but I never in all my travels could get any of it.

The methods of cure muft be according to the conftitution and circumftances of the patient. The venereal *virus* muft be deftroyed; the parts defended againft its acrimony; and the irritation which it caufes abated. Hence phlebotomy, a diluting antiphlogiftic regimen, joined with mer-curials, and fundry vegetable productions, muft be exhibited; and every thing avoided that tends to inflame the blood. I have often obferved, that mercurial frictions are very efficacious when the taint is univerfal; but they muft be ufed with caution. The warm bath and mercurials joined with opium, are alfo very beneficial.

Let thofe that may have this diforder, apply immediately to fome fkilful phyfician, inftead of tampering with medicines themfelves, or of apply-ing to quacks, who impofe upon the ignorant world with noftrums which will not perform a radical cure. It is a pity this *virus* cannot be expelled out of the world;—but how it can be done I know not; unlefs all the people were put under a courfe of phyfic at one time, and even then I believe it would be difficult.

C H A P. XXXIV.

How to chuse a good WIFE, *and a good* HUSBAND
*—How young Gentlemen and Ladies ought to con-
duct themselves if they intend to get married—
How Husbands and Wives ought to treat each
other, bring up their Children, and behave to
Servants—Of the Duties of Children and Servants
to their Parents and Masters.*

THE chusing of a good wife, and a good husband, are matters of very great importance;
because a disagreeable companion must make a
man, or a woman, very unhappy:—Therefore,
let those unmarried Gentlemen, who may intend
to enter into the bands of matrimony,

> Chuse one that has an honest mind,
> Who is to moral good inclin'd;
> Endow'd with decency and sense,
> A temper mild as innocence.

And let the Ladies, who may be inclined to
marry,

> Chuse one that's pleasing to their sight,
> Whose character is very bright;
> Whose temper's good, whose noble mind
> To pious actions are inclin'd.

Those

Thofe who have fuch excellent tempers and difpofitions, are the only proper perfons to enter into a married ftate; becaufe they will live in peace and harmony, and make good members of fociety.

If Harry pays his addreffes to Nancy, under the pretence of marriage, fhe ought to confider of the matter well, before fhe confents to enter into the folemn obligation.—Hence fhe ought to know,

1. Whether he has common fenfe.

2. Whether he is good-natured, humane and generous.

3. Whether he is honeft in his dealings.

4. Whether he ufes bad language.

5. Whether he is a drunkard.

6. Whether he waftes his time and money in gaming.

7. Whether he keeps good company.

8. Whether he has been obedient to his parents and mafters.

9. Whether he is induftrious, or addicted to idlenefs.

10. Whether he belongs to a creditable family; though none that behave well, ought to be defpifed for the ill conduct of their relations.

11. Whether he is a man of his word, and punctual in fulfilling his obligations.

12. Whether fhe likes his perfon, religion, converfation, and behaviour.

13. Whether it is probable he can fupport her in ficknefs and in health, &c.

Now

Now if fhe fhall find that Harry is poffeffed of but few of thefe properties, and addicted to many failings, or that fhe cannot love his perfon, religion, &c. fhe had better not marry; becaufe, if fhe does, fhe may be miferable afterwards.—And Harry, before he attempts to marry, ought to confider of all thefe things; and to find by appearances at leaft, that Nancy's perfon, fenfe, temper, and conduct, will be agreeable.

Many people rufh too fuddenly into a married ftate, without weighing thefe things well in their minds before-hand.—Hence, a foundation is laid for contention and difcord, as well as for much trouble and vexation.

Nancy may undo herfelf by marrying; for, if Harry is a drunkard, thief, liar, gamefter, fcold, &c. he may treat her ill, wafte her eftate, and bring difgrace upon himfelf and his family.

And perhaps if their profeffions of religion are different, they may quarrel about the doctrines of original fin, election, reprobation, infant baptifm, &c. and like different fectaries, be fo puffed up in their vain imaginations, that they will cenfure each other to the infernal regions, ufe indecent language before their children and fervants, and learn them to follow a bad example.

The Catholics may fuppofe that their principles are right, and that thofe who diffent from them are heretics:—The Lutherans may fuppofe that their opinion is beft: And the Calvinifts may fuppofe that they are God's elect; and that thofe that do not think and act as they do, will not go to Heaven. The like may be faid of fome other fects;

sects; who, if they are unequally joined in matrimony, may contend about their religious sentiments, and make themselves unhappy. But the philosophers are perfuaded, that, in every nation and fect, they that fear God, and work righteousness, will be faved; and they with that that uncharitableness which fo much prevails amongst the different denominations of Christians in the present age, may subside—with all the superstitious notions which they have imbibed from their cradles, concerning their own righteousness, and the unrighteousness of others; and also that charity, humanity, brotherly love, and pure religion, might overspread the globe, as the waters cover the seas.

I have been informed, that a young man, who is a Calvinist, lately visited a young woman called a Universalist, with a design of marrying her. After fome time, she found what principle he was of, and that if they married, they should not agree about religion; and for that reafon, she carefully warded off the impending danger, by refusing to let him visit her again upon the subject of matrimony.

But although a man and his wife's being of a different sentiment concerning religion, commonly generates strife, yet fometimes such perfons have lived happily together. If they are of easy tempers and dispofitions, and can confent to let each other enjoy a free liberty of confcience without moleftation, they may live in peace as long as life continues.

A young lady, or gentlaman, who inclines to get married, should be good-natured, go cleanly dreffed,

dreffed, refrain from intemperance, idlenefs, gaming, bad company, bad language, and all kinds of vice. They fhould be charitable, courteous, kind and humane, obedient to their parents and mafters, and, in a word, they ought to walk honeftly; for all vicious practices tend to bring them into difcredit, and to hinder matrimony.

Sometimes good men have been married to bad women, who have afterwards reformed, and made good wives. And good women have fometimes been married to bad men, who have grown better, and made good hufbands.—Sometimes both have appeared to be bad, yet have done well: Again, when both have appeared to be good, they have proved bad after marriage.

A hufband ought to be very exemplary in his life and converfation. He fhould be no liar, thief, or drunkard; not a ufer of bad language, nor contentious, or covetous; but very kind and humane to his wife, provide well for her in ficknefs and health, and always remember the words of the Apoftle, *that men ought to love their wives as their own bodies*, Eph. v. 28.

A wife ought to be very pious and virtuous, a chafte keeper at home, good and obedient to her own hufband. She ought to be no fcold, tattler, brawler, or back-biter; but a promoter of peace and harmony, in her family, and amongft her neighbours. She ought to be kind to her hufband and family, and to take good care of them both in ficknefs and health, and to remember the words of King Solomon, *that a virtuous woman is a crown to her hufband*, Prov. xii. 4; *And that*

T *it*

it is better for a man to dwell in the corner of a house-top, than with a brawling woman in a wide house. Prov. xxix. 9.

Parents ought to fet good examples before their children; and, according to the advice of the Apoftle, to bring them up in the nurture and admonition of the Lord. The fame ought to be done to fervants.

Both children and fervants ought to be kept in fome lawful employment, and out of bad company, left they learn the pollutions that are in the world. But if parents and mafters ufe profane curfing and fwearing, their children, &c. will follow the fame evil example; for, according to the vulgar faying, " As the old cocks crow, fo crow the young ones."

Parents are often to blame for fcolding at, and beating their children and fervants, when they are not to blame. Thofe brought up in this way, are the moft hard to govern ; for where parents and mafters are continually fretting, fcolding, and ftriking thofe under their care, without any apparent caufe, they are foon difcouraged, and become hardened, fo that they will not move when they are bid, without the violence of a blow.—Many of the poor infants have been ruined by being ftruck on their heads, which has fometimes caufed deafnefs, a lofs of fenfe and fight: therefore, this cruel practice ought to be fuppreffed.

Children and fervants may be fpoiled this way, juft as a cruel mafter may fpoil a horfe that has high life, and is full of good nature; for if he mounts fuch a horfe, and falls to whipping of him,

him, he may foon wear him out, bring down his
fpirits, and difcourage him fo that he will not go
at all unlefs he is beat.

The prejudice of education, and the influence
of tradition, has a furprifing effect upon children,
and even upon grown perfons; for the latter generally (though not always) retain the principles they
imbibed in their infancy to their dying day.
Hence, if you teach a child that the Heavens and
Earth were created by Mahomet, it will retain
that belief, unlefs the voice of Reafon fhall teach
it better—It is therefore neceffary, that children
fhould have good principles inftilled into them
when they are young; for if a child is brought up
in the way it fhould go, when it is old, it will not
be apt to depart therefrom.

There are feveral vanities which have prevailed
in fome places where I have been acquainted. As,

1. Some parents, who were able, would not
help their children when they have come of age.
Hence, they have been provoked to anger, and
brought into a ftate of difcouragement.

2. Some parents have given near all of their
eftate to one of their children only, and have
turned the reft out naked into the world. This
has generated a fpirit of envy amongft brethren,
and been the caufe of much contention and
difcord.

3. Some have given all their eftate to their
children, who have become fpendthrifts, and thus
turned themfelves, with their fathers and mothers,
out of houfe and home.

But

But all these extremes should be carefully guarded against. Parents ought to help their children when it is in their power, and to consider that all must be provided for and supported through life, and that one child is an heir to an estate as well as another; and to remember that he that giveth all his substance to one child, and nothing to the rest, sows discord amongst brethren, which is a thing that the Lord doth hate. Prov. vi. 19.

Again, parents ought to keep enough of their estate in their own hands, to support themselves with as long as life continues.

Children ought to obey their parents, and servants their masters: For it is said, *Honour thy father and mother, that thy days may be long upon the land,* &c. ; and, *Children obey your parents in all things, for this is well pleasing to the Lord ;* and, *Servants, obey your masters,* &c. He that cursed his father or his mother, was to be put to death under the Mosaical law; and the Apostle, under the Gospel dispensation, mentions the disobedience of parents as a capital crime. Rom. i. 30.

Where children are obedient to their parents, and servants to their masters, a spirit of union and harmony generally exists in families, providing the parents and masters are exemplary in their lives and conversations ; but where a disobedience prevails, contention and discord, poverty and distress, frequently ensue.

Children

Children ought to be very kind to their parents in their old age, as well as at all other times, and especially if they have become poor: For, *they that provide not for their own, and especially for those of their own household, have denied the Faith, and are worse than Infidels.*

T 3   C H A P.

CHAP. XXXV.

*What becomes of the Fuel when it is confumed, the
Water when it is boiled away, and the Fire when
it is gone out—What produces Fire—How to prevent the Bread from being burnt—The advantages of the Heat of the Sun—Of the Qualities
of the Earth, Air, Fire, and Water.*

WHEN the Fuel is confumed, it is all gone
off by fumigation into the atmofphere,
except the terreftrial parts, or afhes, which are left
behind: And the fame may be faid of the water
when it is boiled away; for it is all gone off by
evaporation, unlefs it was impregnated with earthy
particles; and they, like the afhes, are left behind.

As to the Fire, it is totally gone off into the
air, when the fuel is confumed; where it mixes
with the other elements, and thus becomes invifible, until it is put in motion by the violent
agitation of different bodies. Hence, the fmiting
of flint and fteel together, will produce vifible
fparks, which will kindle into a flame, if they have
fuel to feed them; and burn till the fuel is confumed,
unlefs it is put out by water, or pent up from
the furrounding air.

The fire all flies off into the atmofphere, when
it is put out by water; and if a pot of burning
brimftone

brimftone is covered with a lid, the fire will go out, for it cannot burn where there is a fixed air. About one quarter of the air we breathe in is moveable, and the other part is fixed: the moveable is what caufes the fire to burn, and it is alfo the caufe of animal life.

Let an oven be ever fo hot, it will not burn the bread, if it is immediately ftopped tight; but if the air has an ingrefs into the oven, the bread will be burnt. Perhaps this information may be ferviceable to bakers.

Of the Heat of the Sun.

BY obfervations it doth now appear,
The land and fea, with the whole atmofphere,
Whilft they in their diurnal courfes run,
Do all expand when heated by the Sun.
Hence, by the heat of our great Sol alone,
The earth fwells larger in the torrid zone,
Than at the centre of her fteady poles,
Through which her body on an axis rolls:
The heat expands the globe on ev'ry fide;
But cold condenfes, and makes things fubfide.
Hence mountains, iflands, towns, and cities be,
With other things upon the land and fea,
At noon more high than when the fun doth rife,
Or when he fets in yonder weftern fkies.
If great Sol's heat did not all things expand,
On the wide fea, and on the folid land,
No tides wou'd rife, no murm'ring winds wou'd
    roar:
No waves wou'd dafh againft the rocky fhore;

To

No thunder-ftorms, no rain, no hail, no fnow,
No mift, no dew, no mock funs, no rain-bow,
No northern lights, no vapours wou'd appear,
Nor clouds condenfe in all the hemifphere.
As there'd be nothing but a fixed air,
'Twou'd make the weather keep exceeding fair.
No flames wou'd rife, no wood at all wou'd burn,
Nor any metals into liquids turn.
All things wou'd die—If you will me believe,
No animal upon the globe cou'd breathe:
In folemn filence ev'ry thing wou'd be,
Upon the land and the extended fea;
All calm, all dead, not any move at all
Upon the furface of this earthly ball.

Of the Four Elements.

THE whole terraqueous globe is a compofition of earth, air, fire, and water; and all its productions are compofitions of the fame elements. I fhall treat of each of thefe elements in their order.

I. Of the Earth.

THERE is but one kind of earth, one of air, one of fire, and but one of water; however they may be impregnated by the different fubftances with which they are combined or mixed.—Hence the earth may be mixed with metallics, the air and fire with different fumigations, and the water with various kinds of particles.

Earth, in a chemical fenfe, confifts in that part which cannot be melted in the fire, nor extended

by

by a hammer. It is called *caput mortuum*, becaufe it cannot be raifed by diftillation, nor diffolved by folution; being a thick, dry matter, that is left in the bottom of a ftill or furnace, after vegetable, metallic, or other operations have been performed.—This kind of earth is not fo pure as the other elements.

There are five kinds of mineral earths, three of the vegetable, and as many of the animal.

The Mineral Earths are,

1. The *cryftalline*, as flints and cryftals; they are friable in a ftrong fire.

2. The *calcareous*;—a ftrong fire will convert it into an acrimonious calx.

3. *Argiliaceous*—the pureft of clays, boles, and ochres.

4. *Talky*—this is fcarcely alterable by a vehement fire.

5. *Gypfeous*, Englifh talc, gypfa. A gentle heat will reduce them to a fine powder.

The Vegetable Earths are,

1. That from the burning of foft fpongy and farinaceous plants.

2. That from the burning of harder and lefs fucculent plants.

3. That from the burning of wood.

Animal Earths are,

1. That from the burning of fhells.

2. That

2. That from the burning of bones, horns, and hoofs.

3. That from the burning of blood, flesh, and skins.

Oyster shells, crabs eyes and claws, red and white coral, pearls, bezoar, chalk, some marles, lime-stones, marbles, and spars, are called *insipid* earths, because they are capable of absorbing acids.

Gold, silver, iron, copper, brass, lead, tin, mercury, antimony, bismuth, zinc, sulphur, salts, rocks, diamonds, precious stones, with all the other mines and metals, are *terrestrial* substances.

Gold is the heaviest of all metals, and tin is the lightest. The former is above nineteen times, and the latter six times heavier than an equal bulk of water.

These earths have an absorbing quality.

II. *Of the Air.*

THE Air is a transparent fluid substance, which environs and compresses the globe on every side. It is subject to expansion by the heat, and to condensation by the cold: Hence, it rises higher in the torrid, than it doth in the frigid zones. Its height, at a medium, is from 45 to 50 miles. It may be compressed into a very small compass, and expanded to a great magnitude, being very elastic and ponderous. Vid. *The cause of the blowing of the winds*, p. 168, &c.

I

The

The preffure of the air is fo very great upon our bodies, that, to every fquare inch, we bear near 15 pound of avoirdupois weight: Hence, if a man has 12 fquare feet in his body and limbs, the preffure will be almoft equal to 135 tons 1716 pounds weight; which would crufh him to atoms, were it not for the equilibrium between the air within him and the furrounding atmofphere.

The air is a part of the compofition of all bodies; hence it unites and preferves their parts. It is neceffary for the prefervation of animal life, and the generation of flame, as I hinted before. Some animals cannot live without it; but toads, vipers, eels, fifhes, and all kinds of infects, will live in a receiver, when the air has been exhaufted by an air pump.

This element is a fluid, that cannot be converted into a folid by any method hitherto invented. Its particles are fo very fmall, that they cannot be difcovered through a microfcope, although they are larger than thofe of fire. Fire pervades glafs, oil, water, &c. and will pafs through many compact fubftances; whilft air is refifted by ftrong paper. The air is the objects of tafte and of the effluvia to the nofe: It is alfo the vehicle and conductor of found; for if there was no air, there would be no found at all.

Although, in reality, there is but one air; yet, by reafon of its being impregnated with different qualities, it is called by different names: as,

1. The atmofpheric air—This abounds with fulphur, and confifts of an acid phlogiftion.

2. A fixed

2. A fixed air, formerly called *gas;* but of late has been called artificial, factitious, and mephitic air.

3. An inflammable air—This confifts of an acid vapour and phlogiftion: it is ten times lighter than the common air, and will take fire like gunpowder, and caufe an explofion.

4. A nitrous air—This is generated by the pyrites and other metallics.

5. An acid air—This is obtained from metals with the fpirit of falt, or from this fpirit without metals.

6. An alkaline air—This is the vapour of volatile alkaline falt.

The common air is combined with all bodies in different proportions, and lies in a fixed ftate; but when it is let loofe by fermentation, putrefaction, or other caufes, it refumes its former elaftic powers.

The quantities of fixed air in the following bodies have been found as under: *viz.*

In yellow wax -	$\frac{1}{16}$	
coarfe fugar -	$\frac{1}{16}$	
oyfter fhells -	$\frac{1}{6}$	
muftard feed -	$\frac{1}{6}$	the part of its weight.
peafe - -	$\frac{1}{3}$	
tartar - -	$\frac{1}{2}$	
human blood -	$\frac{1}{43}$	

All kinds of air are capable of becoming fixed; becaufe they may be imbibed in fome fubftance or other, and fo become fixed in them.

A fixed

A fixed air is an antifeptic, which powerfully refifts putrefaction, and is one and an half heavier than the common air. Water imbibes more than its bulk of this air; flame is extinguifhed, animals are deftroyed, and even the vegetables fuffer by its influence.

A heavy air compreffes the cutaneous pores, dilates the lungs, and drives the blood to the head, which produces the vertigo, head-ach, pleurify, peripneumony, and quinfey.

Too light an air produces the gout, rheumatifm, fpitting of blood, hypochondriac and hyfteric complaints, nervous and intermitting diforders, by retarding the circulation of the blood, and diminifhing the external refiftance to the fluids contained in the pulmonary veffels.

A hot air quickens the circulation, promotes perfpiration, enlarges the humours, generates acrimony, and weakens the fibres. Hence, if the air fuddenly becomes cold, it produces bilious and other fevers.

A cold air conftringes the fibres, diftends the lungs, condenfes the humours, diminifhes the perfpiration, and caufes external inflammations, quinfies, pleurifies, and peripneumonies.

A dry air caufes fevers, by fhrinking the folids, and incraffating the fluids.

A moift air relaxes and weakens the conftitution, diminifhes the perfpiration, makes the blood watery, and produces the dropfy, cough, afthma, intermitting and nervous complaints.

3

A hot,

A hot, moift air, is very unwholefome; becaufe it relaxes and generates putrefaction: But
when it is infected with a malignant miafmata,
and other poifonous exhalations, it is very pernicious.

Let all thofe who may be heated by hot air,
be very careful of going into that which is cold,
becaufe it may produce dangerous diftempers.
The fumigations of tobacco and vinegar are very
excellent to keep off the noxious qualities of the
circumambient air.

III. *Of the Fire.*

FIRE is a pure element, and a part in the
compofition of all bodies. It may be called the
bafis of life and motion; for whenever the animal heat ceafes, the human body becomes cold,
and is a lifelefs lump. Hence, fire is the fubftance of all our motions and fenfes; for, without it, we cannot fee, hear, fmell, tafte, nor feel
any thing. It gives motion to the particles of the
air, fpring to their actions, and life and vigour
to the human frame.

Some fubftances attract and retain larger proportions of heat than others; and one part of a
body will attract and retain more of it than another: hence the red globules of the blood in the
human frame, attract and retain a greater degree
of heat than any other part.

Animal heat is produced, by the craffamentum
of the blood, which attracts and retains a part of
the fire which is difperfed through the terraqueous
globe.

globe. This fire being thus converged to the blood, makes the fibres become elaftic, diftends the cells and cellular membranes by rarefaction, begins and continues an action and re-action between the vital heat and the fibres, and caufes and fupports thofe motions on which life depends. But the nerves conduct the fire thus attracted to every part of the human frame, and from thence all our fluids become vehicles and conductors.

Hence the nervous fyftem muft be firft expanded by the heat, and afterwards the other veffels: But whatever increafes the craffamentum of the blood, increafes the vital heat. Hence animal food, and aromatics, will contribute towards the augmentation of this fire. Many difeafes have been called *ignis callidus*, hot fire; fuch as burning fevers, inflammations, &c.

The common heat in the human body, raifes the mercury in Fahrenheit's thermometer to 98 degrees, though fome people are healthy when it only rifes to 83; and this heat continues the fame, let the weather be hot or cold, unlefs fome difeafe is produced, which raifes or depreffes the animal heat; but this heat rarely rifes higher than 110 degrees, or falls lower than 94.

Fire, though it is a pure element, yet it may be impregnated with particles which confift of different qualities; or rather, the fumigations which arife from it, may be thus impregnated. Hence, when dog-wood or ivy is burnt in America, it will poifon thofe that ftand in the fmoke.

This element is of great fervice in chemiftry, cookery, and to keep us warm; and in a word,

it

it is a part of our bodies, without which we cannot exist one moment.

IV. *Of the Water.*

WATER, if not impregnated with other particles of matter, is a pure element. But I believe it is always impregnated in a greater or less degree, with particles of different kinds, imbibed from earths, minerals, falts, fulphur, &c. and that even when it comes from the clouds, becaufe fuch exhalations afcend into the air, and combine with the watery fluid.

The fluidity of water arifes from a certain degree of heat; for if the heat is two-thirds lefs than that of our blood, the water freezes; but if it is made about twice as hot, it boils, and cannot be made any hotter. But it will retain its qualities if it has been boiled or undergone the action of fermentation with other things, as that of brewing, &c.; but though it retains its qualities, it ought to be boiled before it is drank, to kill the animalculæ that may be therein.

This element is fubject to elafticity, expanfion, and compreffion; for the heat will expand and make it elaftic, and the cold will condenfe it into a fmaller compafs, and caufe it to become fixed or frozen.

River water is efteemed beft for fhort voyages, and fpring water for thofe that are long; becaufe the latter will not become putrid fo foon as the former.—Soft pure water, however, or that which falls from the clouds at a confiderable diftance

from

from great cities, is efteemed the moft healthy
and the beft for ufe. It is a great diluter and
promoter of digeftion.

Springs that proceed from a clean gravelly
earth on high land, alfo afford good water; and
water may be purified by diftillation, which makes
it the pureft of all kinds, and it is fuppofed to be
as good as the moft celebrated mineral waters.

Let people be careful of drinking water, or any
thing cold, when they are hot, left they die inftantaneoufly.

Stagnant waters are very prejudicial : they
abound with a falino-cauftic and volatile effluvia
which generates putrid and malignant difeafes.
Thefe waters ought not to be drank either by
man or beaft.

Water is of great fervice in navigation, chymiftry, cookery, &c. and if that which is good is
drank, quenches thirft, cools fevers, promotes
digeftion, perfpiration, urine, &c. and like the
other elements, it is a part of our bodies which
we cannot live without.

U CHAP.

CHAP. XXXVI.

*How to reſtore People to Life that have been drowned
—The* AUTHOR'S *Obervations—How he ſuffered
Shipwreck.*

IT is ſaid that ſome have been reſtored to life and
health, that have laid under water ſix hours.

Let us obſerve, 1. That when the body is taken
out of the water, it ſhould be put into a warm
bed, a warm bath, or expoſed to the heat of the
ſun. It ſhould not be rolled on the ground, nor
on a barrel, nor taken up by the heels; but removed gently to the bed, bath, or warm ſun.

2. Let it be rubbed with coarſe cloths, until a
glow is perceived in the ſkin.

3. Let the breath of a healthy ſtrong perſon be
blown into the mouth of the patient, to diſtend
the lungs.

4. Blow the ſmoke of tobacco in the mouth of
the patient.

5. If he was plethoric, bleed him in the jugular
vein, if he will not bleed at any other.

6. Tickle his throat with a feather, to excite
vomiting.

7. Force nothing down his throat; but apply volatiles, ſuch as ſpirits of hartſhorn, or of ſal-ammoni-
ac, to his noſe, and alſo ſnuff, to excite ſneezing:

8. Inject the fumes of tobacco into the inteſtines with a glyſter-pipe, fumigator, or a pair of
bellows if nothing elſe can be had.

9. When

9. When he can fwallow, give him a draught of warm water, with a table fpoonful of muftard mixed therein.

10. Apply bottles of warm water to his feet, joints and arm-pits, if he is not put into a warm bath; or it may be done after he is taken out; and warm bricks wrapped in cloths may be rubbed up and down his back, and over his body.

11. Wrap the body in a warm fkin, juft taken from a fheep; alfo, cloths dipped in brandy, rum, or gin, and the cheft, belly, back and arms rubbed with them, may be ferviceable; but fome rub the body with dry falt, fo as not to wear off the fkin.

Thefe frictions and other remedies fhould be repeated as occafion may require; it will perhaps be two hours before any figns of life may appear, and yet the patient may do well.

But a very fmall quantity of water is fwallowed by drowned perfons; for they do not attempt to breathe until they become infenfible. Hence it is needlefs to roll them on barrels, or to fet them on their heads.

I never had but one patient that was drowned; and after bleeding, rubbing, &c. when his life began to return, he fighed, gaped, twitched, and went into fuch violent convulfions that it took about four or five men to hold him. As foon as he could fwallow, I gave him (as I had nothing elfe with me) a large dofe of Bates's anodyne balfam in fome warm water, which allayed the fpafms, promoted a diaphorefis, and he foon recovered.

Another man was drowned at the same time; but he was not taken out of the water till it was too late to attempt to bring him to life.

This accident happened by the overſetting of a ſmall canoe; and I have often been ſurpriſed that the practice of making ſuch dangerous things, and the venturing of people's lives in them, has not been ſuppreſſed. I was very near loſing my life by being overſet in one of them, in the river St. Lawrence, in the province of Quebec.—I once alſo ſuffered ſhipwreck, in conſequence of the ill conduct of our Captain, who got drunk, and let the veſſel run too near the rocks. At laſt he fell over-board; and the ſailors, being ſurpriſed, left the helm in order to ſave his life. I ran out of the cabin, and ſeeing nobody at the helm, ſprang to it myſelf. In a moment, however, the ſtern of the veſſel ſtruck, and threw off the rudder; and the wind being violent, ſhe ſoon ſtruck again, and bulged, the Captain by this time having got into the veſſel. We all jumped overboard, and effected our eſcape to land. A woman with a child about a year old was with us: I carried the child aſhore myſelf.——Drunken Captains, and drunken ſailors, are by no means fit to have the care of veſſels.

People that have been hanged, and others that have died ſuddenly, may ſometimes be reſtored to life in the ſame manner that thoſe are who have been drowned.

CHAP.

CHAP. XXXVII.

Of the HOT SPRINGS *at* BATH—*Opinions concerning the Cause of their Heat—An Account of the Qualities and Operations of their Waters, with that of other Medicinal Waters in Europe—Of Artificial Baths, and the Mineral and other Waters in America—Poetical Prescriptions for Patients that may go to Saratoga, &c.*

THE moſt remarkable mineral ſprings that I have ſeen, are at the famous city of Bath, which is ſituated about 108 miles weſterly of London. This city is built of ſtone, and is the moſt beautiful place in the kingdom. Here the nobility and gentry flock in great multitudes, to drink the waters, and bathe themſelves. Here are alſo different baths that have different degrees of heat as from 94 to 116 degrees by Farenheit's mercurial thermometer. It is ſaid, that the hotteſt will boil an egg in four minutes: but there are ſuch conveniences, that the heat may be eaſily lowered to any degree for bathing, by the addition of cold water.

The time for bathing is from ſix to nine in the morning; afterwards the water is drawn off into the river Avon, and the baths are filled again with freſh water for uſe the next morning. The phyſicians order their patients to bathe in waters of ſuch degrees of heat as their circumſtances re-

U 3 quire.

quire. Thefe waters boil as they come out of the earth; and a great fteam arifes, which is faid to keep off infectious diftempers.

Various have been the opinions of Philofophers concerning the caufe of this heat.—Some have imputed it to fubterraneous fire in the bowels of the earth, whofe fumes find vent by throwing out the waters. Others have fuppofed that the heat proceeds from the waters running over beds of minerals, or being impregnated with the vapours of pyrites, or fire-ftones, which contain a large quantity of fulphureous and ferruginous matter.— The latter is probably the true caufe; for the mountains from whence the waters proceed, are full of fuch ftones; and if water is poured upon them, it will produce heat by fermentation. But hot fprings in general are produced no doubt from various caufes, as fubterraneous veins of liquid fires, beds of fulphur, and other minerals, which generate heat like the pyrites at Bath.

By analization it has been found, that a Winchefter gallon of Bath water contained,

	dwts.	grains
1. Of calcarious earth combined with a vitriolic acid, in the form of a felenite. - - - -	3	19 $\frac{2}{10}$
2. Of calcarious earth combined with an acidulous gas. - - -	0	22 $\frac{8}{10}$
3. Of marine falt of magnefia -	0	22 $\frac{2}{10}$
4. Of fea falt. - - - -	1	14 $\frac{4}{10}$
5. Of iron combined with acidulous gas	0	0 $\frac{5}{10}$

6. Of

6. Of afcidulous gas, twelve ounces by meafure.

7. Of atmofpheric air, two ounces.

From the combination of the ·fulphureous gas, feat falt, ferruginous and other qualities, it is that thefe waters are fo very ufeful in the cure of chronic and other diftempers.

Bath waters are attenuating, cleanfing, and ftrengthening. They are friendly to weak confti-tutions, and beneficial in gouty, fcorbutic, and · rheumatic complaints ; for wandering pains, pal-fies, convulfions, contractions, bilious cholic, ob-ftructions of the liver and fpleen, jaundice, hypo-condriac and hyfteric diforders, decayed appetite, leprofy, and all other cutaneous eruptions: they comfort the nerves, and warm the body.

They are hurtful in hæmorrhages, inflamma tions, and infractions of the lungs. When thefe waters are drank, high-feafoned meats and fauces, with fpiritous liquors, muft be avoided, becaufe they generate inflammatory diforders. Proper evacuations muft precede the ufe of thefe waters, and the patients muft drink and bathe fafting : not more than two pints ought to be drank in a day.

There·are three other hot fprings in England : *viz.* one at Buxton, one at Briftol, and another at Matlock—The firft raifes the *argentum vivum* in Farenheit's thermometer about 80 degrees ; the fecond, about 76 ; and the third, near 68.

Some impute the virtues of the mineral waters to a quantity of fixed air contained them.

U 4   Some

Thefe waters fhould be drank at the fountain, for their virtues will foon fly off through the niceft fealed cork. The Bath waters hold their heat longer than any other heated to the fame degree.

The Buxton waters operate as an alterative, and increafe the vital heat: They are efteemed to be ferviceable in the gout, rheumatifm, dry afthma, convulfions, indigeftion, lofs of appetite, contractions of the tendons, and catamenial defections.——Buxton is in Derbyfhire, about 159 miles from from London.

Briftol waters are impregnated with lime, and abound with a foft alkaline quality. They are a fpecific in coughs, confumptions, fpitting of blood, dyfentary, diabetes, inflammations, fcurvy, ulcerations, fpafms, and acrimonious humours.—Briftol is 120 miles wefterly from London.

Matlock waters are flightly impregnated with felenites, or fome other earthy falt; and have the fame virtues as the waters at Briftol.—Matlock is in Derbyfhire, 104 miles from London.

All mineral waters participate in a greater or lefs degree, of earthy, falineous, fulphureous, and other matters over which they run in their fubterraneous paffages. Hence their virtues are various, according to the different qualities of the matter with which they are impregnated.

There is a fpring near Wales in England, that throws matter out of it, which refembles tar—fuppofed to be occafioned by fubterraneous fires, and the confumption of coal-mines.

Befides

Befides the preceding fprings in Great-Britain, there are, 1. Alkaline waters at Upminfter, Brentwood, Weal, Selter, and Tilbury; the latter is the ftrongeft. It is good in acidities, crudities, alvine fluxes, and other diforders from a debility of the fibres. A quart may be drank in a day.

2. The bitter purging waters at Northaw, Brant, Alford, Colchefter, Lambeth, and Dulwich. A patient may drink from one to three pounds in a day as a purge; but it muft be taken in a lefs quantity as an alterative—a little brandy or aromatic tincture is recommended to prevent their griping. They may be mixed with milk, whey, wine, &c. and ufed as common drink in fuch quantities as to keep the body lax.

3. Steel waters are thofe of Pyrmont, Spa, Tunbridge, Hampftead, Iflington, Hartfell, &c. all of which are in England. The firft and the third are efteemed beft for medical ufe. They have the virtues of iron and fteel, which are alike. They open, corroborate, and aftringe: Hence, they are good for weak, lax, pale, leucophlegmatic habits. They encreafe the vital heat, raife the pulfe, ftrengthen the ftomach, and invigorate the whole fyftem. They promote deficient, and reftrain redundant difcharges. From one to three pints of this water may be drank in a day.

4. The principal hot waters in Europe, are, thofe of Bath, Aix-la-Chapelle, in France, and Bourbon in Germany. Germany is faid to contain more mineral waters than all Europe befides.

Some

Some of them are fo hot, that the patients let the waters cool ten or twelve hours before they are ufed. The bath and medicinal waters at Embs, Wifbaden, Schwalbach, Willdungen, and thofe in many other places, are faid to perform wonders in the cure of internal and external difeafes. Thofe of Dungen, are faid to intoxicate as much as wine; and for that reafon they are inclofed, fo that people cannot come at them without permiffion, otherwife they might drink too freely.

The waters at Aix-la-Chapelle are ftrongly impregnated with fulphur: they are very naufeous, and their purgative quality is fo great that but few can bear it.

There are other remarkable fprings in France; as,—1. One at Bareges, whofe waters are efteemed the beft in that kingdom for the cure of difeafes—

2. One at Sultzbach, whofe waters are good for the ftone, palfy, and a weaknefs of the nervous fyftem—3. Several at Bagueus, whofe waters are efteemed beneficial in the cure of difeafes—4. At the Forges, in Normandy, are celebrated mineral waters—5. One at St. Amand, whofe waters open obftructions, and cure the gravel——6. One at Aigne, whofe waters are fo poifonous, that they kills birds that drink of it inftantaneoufly.

5. It is faid, that the water of the River of Thames, which runs through London, will burn like fpirits after it has been at fea about 18 or 20 months, and that fome other waters will do the like; but how to account for this, I know not, unlefs it

abounds

abounds with an oil or fpirit that rifes on the top, and becomes inflammable by the motion of the fea in long voyages. Perhaps the conftant friction may caufe the water to imbibe fomething from the cafk, that may make it inflammable.

6. Sea water has different degrees of faltnefs: The proportion is from $\frac{1}{33}$ to $\frac{1}{28}$ of the weight of the water. This water is the falteft at the equinoctial, and frefheft towards the polar regions: Hence 20lb. of water in the torrid zone, will yield 1lb. of falt; and 50lb. in the frigid zones, will yield the fame quantity: and in the intermediate latitudes, the quantity increafes and decreafes in proportion as we advance towards, or go from the equator.

Sea-water is difcutient, corroborant, and antifceptic. It purges gently, promotes the fecretions, warms and ftrengthens the body, and is good in fwellings, carious bones, and as a vermifuge. It prevents the falling off of the hair after patients have been ill of fevers, if the head is bathed therewith.— It is alfo efteemed beneficial in the bite of a mad dog, if the patient is plunged often in it: it is alfo good for thofe that are melancholy, and affected with madnefs. But it is hurtful in inflammations.—The dofe is from half a pound, to one and an half, in the morning.

Befides the natural, perhaps it may not be amifs to fay fomething concerning the virtues of the artificial baths, which may be either cold or hot.— Thefe are performed at a bath, or in veffels made for that purpofe, fuch as bathing-tubs, &c. which
                                                        fhould

should be made so large that the patients may sit or stand in them, as their circumstances may require.

Of these baths there are three kinds; as,

1. The *pediluvia*, or bath for the feet:

2. The *semicupium*, or half-bath, which reaches no higher than the umbilical region.

3. *Balneum totum*, or total immersion.

The water used for warm artificial bathing should be of the softest kind; that of rain is the best; that of melted snow is the next for softness, and that of a river the next, &c.; but where soft water cannot be had, that which is hard may be softened with castile-soap, milk, wheat-bran, camomile flowers, marsh-mallows, or white lily-roots, as either of these will make it soft.

The *pediluvia callida*, or warm bathing of the feet, promotes the circulation of the fluids; makes a revulsion from the head and vital parts; raises the pulse, and creates a temporary fever. It is of great service in colds, spasms, head-achs, recent, obstructions, fixed and wandering pains, pleurisies, peripneumonies, convulsions, cholic, hæmorrhoids, hypochondriac and hysteric complaints, menstrual obstructions, gout, rheumatism, caridalgia, and an obstructed perspiration : it promotes a diaphoresis, rest, and sleep; the water should not be too warm, because it will make the patient faint, weak and thirsty, and pains will be excited in his head. The feet and legs may be immersed as high as the calves; and the patient should drink a warm infufion

fion of camomile-flowers, keep his feet in the water
about half an hour, and then go into a warm bed.

The *pediluvia* is hurtful in inveterate obftructions
and fchirrous tumours; and it is dangerous to
drink any thing cold whilft the feet are in, or foon
after they come out of the water.

The *pediluvia frigida,* or cold bathing of the
feet, raifes pleafing fenfations in the mind, and
affifts cathartics and diuretics in their operation :
Hence it is of great fervice in the iliac paffion, as
it tends to produce thofe evacuations which are
neceffary to eradicate the diforder.—The going
with one's feet wet and cold, will often occafion a
diarrhœa.

The *femicupium,* 'or warm bath, affifts other remedies in the cure of grievous complaints ; an !
fo does a total immerfion, though it i beft for
the patient to fit with his head above the water.
In moft diforders, however, I prefer the *femicupium*
and the *pediluvia* to that of a total immerfion.—
Warm bathing is excellent in venereal complaints,
and efpecially when the taint has become univerfal. · Patients afflicted with cancers, have found
great relief from it.

Cold bathing is the moft ufeful when a violent
fhock is required ; but proper evacuations ought
to precede the ufe of it. It contracts the folids,
condenfes the fluids, and accelerates their circulation. It is beneficial when the body requires
bracing. Sometimes it is of great fervice in the
rheumatifm, palfy, melancholy, and madnefs, and

for

for children who have the rickets ; but none ought to make ufe of it, without the advice of a fkilful phyfician.

The North American Indians make ufe of a vapour bath, by fhutting themfelves up in a fmall tight room, and by throwing hot ftones into a pail of water. When they have thus fweated for fome time, they plunge themfelves into cold water, and go immediately into the vapour bath again. This mode of practice is very beneficial in the cure of recent diftempers.

Both the warm and cold baths ought to be ufed upon an empty ftomach : but when the fibres are rigid, and the *vifcera* unfound, cold bathing is improper.

But let us return to the *mineral waters.*—There are a number of fuch fprings in America, whofe waters are impregnated with different qualities.

At Lancafter, in the county of Worcefter, in the commonwealth of Maffachufetts, there is a fpring whofe waters are beneficial in rheumatic complaints, as I have found by my own experience and obfervation. The patient may drink half a pint two or three times in a day, and plunge himfelf once when his ftomach is empty. He fhould come out of the water immediately, and keep himfelf warm after the immerfion.

At Stafford, in Connecticut, there is a mineral fpring whofe waters are faid to be beneficial in fcorbutic complaints, cutaneous eruptions, and other diforders :   And, at Guildford, in the fame
government

government, there is another fpring, whofe waters
will evaporate, even when tightly corked in a
bottle; but I know not their virtues.

In the eafterly part of the county of Albany, in
the State of New-York, there is a mineral-fpring
whofe waters are much applauded in the cure of
diftempers. But the moft remarkable fprings in
this State, are thofe of Saratoga, which are eight
or nine in number: They are fituated in the
margin of a marfh, and furrounded by rocks formed by the petrefaction of the waters. One of
them is about five or fix feet above the furface of
the earth, and is in the of a pyramid. In the
top of this rock there is a cylindrical aperture,
about nine inches in diameter, through which the
water iffues, being always greatly agitated as if
boiling in a pot, although it is very cold. The
water runs over the top of the rock in the beginning of the fummer, but at other feafons it rifes
not fo high by twelve inches. The rocks that en-
compafs the other fprings, are of different forms;
but the waters feem to boil, and they run continually.

It is fuppofed that all thefe fpings proceed from
one fountain, but feparate in different canals,
whereby fome have greater connections with metallic bodies than others.

They are impregnated, 1. With a foffile acid—
2. A faline fubftance—3. A chalybeate property—
4. A calcareous earth—and, 5. With a prodigious
quantity of air.

This

This air, ftriving for vent, produces fermentation; and it is fo penetrating, that it cannot be
confined in a tight veffel: Hence it muft be
drank at the fpring, or it will lofe its virtue.

The particles of diffolved earth fubfide as thefe
waters run off, and, combining with the falts and
fixed air, concrete, and form the rocks about the
fprings.

By obfervation it has been found, 1. That if a
young turkey is held within a few inches of the
furface of the water, at the lower fpring, it will
be thrown into convulfions in lefs than half a minute.

2. That the holding of it in fuch a fituation
one minute, will make it become motionlefs.

3. That it will throw a dog into convulfions in
lefs than a minute.

4. That if a trout is thrown into a veffel of
this water, when juft taken from the fpring, it will
go immediately into convulfions, and expire in a
few minutes.

5. That if a lighted candle is held near the furface
of this water, it will fuddenly go out, and the fire
in the wick will be extinguifhed inftantaneoufly.

6. That if a bottle filled with this water is clofe-
ly corked, and afterwards fhaken, the airy matter
will expand, force out the cork, or fplit the bottle.

7. That wheat-flour mixed with this water, and
kneaded into dough, and then baked, makes light
and fpongy bread, without the addition of yeaft
or leaven.

8. That

8. That when the air is gone off by evaporation, the water loſes its tranſparency, and lets fall a calcareous ſediment.

9. That if a piece of the rock that environs the ſpring is put into the fire, it will calcine into quick-lime, which may be ſlacked with cold water. —Hence we may conclude, that the waters are impregnated with lime-ſtone, and that the gas is an aërial acid, which makes the water capable of diſſolving and conveying the ſtones above the ſurface of the earth.

Theſe waters are emetic, cathartic, and diuretic in general; but they have different effects in different conſtitutions. They have an agreeable taſte whilſt the patient is drinking, but ſoon after they produce one that is diſagreeable.

A gentleman of the faculty who lived near theſe ſprings, informed me, that a patient may drink a gallon of the waters in a day, with ſafety; and that they are excellent in ſcrophulous, rheumatic, and other complaints.

In the upper part of Morris County, in the Jerſeys, there is a cold mineral ſpring, whoſe waters are uſed with ſucceſs in the cure of ſome diſeaſes.

On a ridge of hills in Hanover, in the ſame county, there are a number of wells; and although they are about forty miles from the ſea, they ebb and flow near ſix feet, twice every day, as regular as the ocean.

In the county of Cape May, there is a freſh ſpring that boils up through the bottom of a ſalt-water creek. The tide riſes about four feet above this ſpring; and if a bottle well corked is let down

X   through

through the falt-water into the fpring, and the cork pulled out with a cord prepared for that purpofe, the bottle may be drawn up full of fine frefh water. There are other fprings of the like kind in different parts of the State.—In the county of Hunterdon in the Jerfeys, there is a noted mineral fpring, whofe waters are efteemed excellent. They are of the chalybeate kind.—It is faid, that there is a river, called Mill-ftone, in the Jerfeys, whofe waters in fome places emit an inflammable vapour, that will take fire, and burn for a fhort time. This vapour is fuppofed to be produced by the diffolution of vegetable fubftances in the river.

At Augufta, in Virginia, there are two fprings, one of which is called the warm fpring, and the other the hot. The heat of the warm fpring rifes to 96 degrees by Farenheit's mercurial thermometer. This water is impregnated with fulphureous particles; it is very volatile, and efteemed good in rheumatic complaints and other diforders. —The hot fpring is about fix miles from the warm fpring. It raifes the mercury in the aforementioned thermometer to a fever heat, viz. 112 degrees. This water is efteemed good in many complaints, and frequently relieves when the water of the other fpring fails.

There are hot fprings at Kamfchatka, which raife the mercury to about 200 degrees, which is within 12 degrees of the boiling point. Thefe fprings are much ufed for medical-purpofes.

In Botetourt, there are fweet fprings, whofe waters are cold. They have granted relief when other mineral waters have failed.

In

In the county of Berkeley, there are mineral ſprings which are much uſed; but their waters are ſcarcely warm, and not very powerful.

In the county of Louiſa, there are medicinal ſprings; but their waters are not much uſed.

In Richmond there is a ſpring of the chalybeate kind, and ſome others in various parts of the county.

There is a ſulphureous ſpring at Howard's creek of green briar, and another at Bonſborough on Kentucky.

At Great Kanhaway, ſeven miles above the mouth of Elk river, and ſixty-ſeven above that of the Kanhaway itſelf, is a hole in the earth, from which iſſues a bituminous vapour, with ſuch rapidity that it makes the ſand move about its orifice like the ſand in a boiling ſpring. This vapour will take fire if a torch or lighted candle is put within eighteen inches of the hole, and flame up in a column of eighteen inches in diameter, and four or five feet high. Sometimes it goes out in about one-third of an hour; at other times, it will burn three or four days. The denſity of the flame is like that of burning ſpirits, and the ſmell like that of burning pit-coal. Sometimes cold water is collected in the mouth of this hole, and· is kept in ebullition by the force of the vapour which iſſues through it. If the vapour is fixed in that ſtate, the whole of the water is ſoon evaporated.—There is a ſimilar vapour on Sandy River.

There are five noted ſalt ſprings in Kentucky, whoſe waters are ſalter than that of the ocean. The people in that country have been ſupplied

X 2 with

with falt made from thofe waters, for three dollars and one-third *per* bufhel.

There is a mineral fpring in the county of Wilkes, in the State of Georgia, which iffues out of a hollow tree about four or five feet above the furface of the earth. The infide of the tree is lined with a coat of nitre about an inch thick; and the leaves above the fpring are incrufted with a nitrous coat, which is as white as fnow. This water is excellent in gouty and rheumatic complaints, and for fcrophulous and fcorbutic diforders; alfo in confumptions, and other maladies. The patient may drink from one to two quarts in a day.

A gentleman informed me, that he had feen a hot fpring in the Weft Indies, whofe waters iffued, boiling hot, out of a burning mountain; but he did not tell what their virtues are.

I fhall conclude this chapter with the following prefcriptions for patients going to the medicinal waters at Saratoga; and perhaps they may be beneficial to thofe who may be inclined to go to other cold fprings.

I.

IF, Sifter Spleen, you want a *cure*,
At Saratog' a place procure;
With a warm lodging, and a bed,
Where you in peace may reft your head.

2.

There eat and drink, difcourfe and play,
And drive all anxious thoughts away;
And frequently, when you've a chance
To hear good mufic, up and dance.

3. Go

3.

Go in the morning to the rock,
And there let nature have a ſhock,
By plunging whilſt the air is cool,
Into the wholeſome wat'ry pool.

4.

But at the fountain, mind, and think
Before you plunge, to take a drink:
Bathe not too long—but ſoon come out,
Put on your cloaths, and walk about.

5.

And when you thus have took the air,
Unto your houſe again repair;
Drink coffee, chocolate, or tea,
Or ſuch things as beſt ſuiteth thee.

6.

Uſe gentle exerciſe—peruſe
For a ſhort time the lateſt news; ·
Remark the things that you may find,
Exceeding pleaſing to your mind:

7.

Not caring who it is that rules,
Providing no rebellious tools
Deprive the country of its peace,
And make your own therein decreaſe.

8.

Then if the weather's warm and fair,
Before you dine, walk in the air;

X 3

Or

Or if you have a prudent guide,
Go to a coach, and take a ride.

9.

Or if a gentle horfe you chufe,
To ride him oft do not refufe;
Don't exercife beyond your pow'rs,
But eat and fleep at proper hours.

10.

Go fee your friends as you ride round,
Where peace, where mirth, and joy abound;
In good difcourfe divert your mind
With thofe who are polite and kind.

11.

In food that's nourifhing and light,
No doubt you'll take the moft delight;
And whilft you on the ftage remain,
From all intemp'rance pray refrain.

12.

High-feafon'd food you'll not digeft;
It will deprive you of your reft:
In wines and fauces don't exceed;
Excefs therein diftempers breed.

13.

Eat food, then, of the lighteft kind,
And undifturbed keep your mind:
Digeftion's work is eafieft wrought,
By chearful chat, and little thought.

14. To

2

14.

To church on Sunday go you may,
To hear the word, to fing and pray;
And when the exercife is o'er,
Return to where you lodg'd before.

15.

Refrefh yourfelf, and, when you pleafe,
Lie on the bed, and take your eafe:
If you be young, or if you're old,
Be careful that ye take no cold.

16.

At night before you go to bed,
If vapours do affect your head,
Go bathe your feet, it may be beft
In a warm bath—'twill make you reft.

17.

When men fkill'd in the medic art
Their good advice to you impart,
Then fee that ye do not neglect
To take the things which they direct.

18.

Go neatly drefs'd, but not too gay;
Drive reftlefs thoughts and cares away:
Purfue thefe rules—wait the event,
And with your ftation be content.

19.

Then I doubt not but foon you'll find
Relief according to your mind;

X 4

That

That you'll get rid of all your pain,
Your health and ftrength return again.

20.

I hope you will, with much delight,
Do ev'ry thing that's good and right;
That when you die, you *will be blefs'd*
With *glory, honour, peace, and reft.*

Compofed by the *Author,* at Kentifh-town,
    Feb. 26, 1790.

CHAP.

C H A P. XXXVIIL

*The Widow's Addreſs to the Gentlemen—The Author
fights with a Swarm of Fleas, who obtain a
Victory over him—How to keep a Houſe clear of
thoſe diſagreeable Animals.*

A LADY who had loſt her huſband, and had
refuſed to marry again, requeſted that I
would favour her with ſome of my Poetry. I
therefore compoſed the following:

1.

YE *Gentlemen*, pray now attend
　To one that's in diſtreſs:
To one who wants a loving friend,
　In this world's wilderneſs.

2.

My huſband died ſome time ago;
　His fortune was not ſmall:
I have been courted, but cry'd, *No!*
　I'll *marry* not *at all.*

3.

But now, behold! I've *chang'd* my mind,
　And *ſing* another *tone;*
Becauſe it is not *good,* I find,
　For me to *live alone.*

4.

A man that's very young, or old ;
  A gamefter, or a fot ;
A ftingy fool, or fretting fcold,
  I know, will fuit me not.

5.

I want a man replete with fenfe,
  Whofe manners are refin'd ;
Whofe temper's fweet as innocence,
  And all his actions kind.

6.

With fuch an one I'd live in peace,
  Make him a prudent wife ;
Until his time or mine fhall ceafe,
  We'd live a happy life.

7.

Let fuch a man upon the ftage,
  A vifit pay to me ;
And if he likes me, I'll engage
  That married we fhall be.

8.

Remember that I've *chang'd* my *mind,*
  And *fing* another *tone ;*
Becaufe it is not *good,* I find,
  For me to *live alone.*

Jan. 19, 1790.

When I was in the city of Quebec, a gentleman invited me to pay him a vifit, which I accordingly did. Juft after I had got to his houfe, his wife was violently feized with convulfions ; and at his requeft, I adminiftered remedies which granted
relief.

relief. I tarried with them near two days, and was very well entertained. At his requeſt, I viſited him again about two months after ; but a ſwarm of fleas had taken poſſeſſion of the houſe, which prevented my getting to ſleep till near day. I dreamed I was making poetical lines on the ſubject, and therefore wrote the following :

ONE evening fair I took a walk,
To hear ſome genteel people talk ;
Who in me had ſo much delight,
They made me tarry through the night.
As time roll'd off, we did converſe
On ſubjects I ſhall not rehearſe,
Until at length we laid our heads
To reſt upon the downy beds.
But, lo! an hungry ſwarm of fleas
Crawl'd on my legs, and on my knees;
Nay, ſome of them did ſoon ariſe
Moſt rapidly above my eyes :
So nimbly on me they did creep,
By no means cou'd I go to ſleep :
They crawl'd, they jump'd, and grew ſo bold,
That of my fleſh they did take hold ;
Which put me into ſuch a rage,
That I in war did ſoon engage.
I knock'd them all both to and fro,
But from me far they wou'd not go.
I found my ſtrokes upon the bed
By no means ſtruck the creatures dead.
Though I drove them from place to place,
They boldly jump'd into my face,
And bit me from my very noſe
Down to the ends of all my toes ;
Which conſtantly did make me ſtart,
Like one prick'd with a piercing dart.
Whilſt through the dark and ſilent night,
I was oblig'd to lie and fight ;

I kick'd,

I kick'd, I fcratch'd, I rolled round,
And often on my foes did pound.
My labour prov'd fo much in vain,
A vict'ry I could not obtain :
When it was day, I had to yield,
And wholly quit the irkfome field.
Though much fatigu'd, I look'd, and found
My flefh moft forely they did wound :
On me extended very wide,
Their venom was on ev'ry fide.

  When I was up, the Lady faid,
The fleas bit you, I am afraid !
They are fo thick, I'm almoft craz'd,
And honeftly like one amaz'd.
She faid, the lads, to keep from harm,
Had lodg'd that night within the barn.
By what I heard, I truly found
The fleas from them had took the ground.

  Is it not ftrange, a neft of fleas
Shou'd do fuch mighty things as thefe !
Make men of might in battle yield,
And wholly take from them the field !

  Now, to the world, I will point out
A method that, without all doubt,
Will make our foes fo much decreafe,
That we may live and fleep in peace ;
I therefore will proceed to fhew
How we may kill this dreadful crew :

  With boiling water fcald the floors ;
Keep clean the ground around the doors ;
And from the houfe the cats and dogs,
The goats and cattle, fheep and hogs :
Then the *tormenting jaws* of *fleas,*
Will not *prevent* our *fleep* and *eafe.*

Compofed at Quebec, in 1788.

Bed-bugs

Bed-bugs are another difagreeable vermin, which I cannot endure. They are very numerous and troublefome in fome old houfes in America, that are chiefly made of oak. Some fay, that they will not live in a bed-ftead that has been painted with verdigreafe, and that the fpirits or oil of turpentine will keep them off. And fome ufe the *ung. ceruel.* for the fame purpofe. Cold water, and falt and water, are alfo ufed to kill bugs.

Lice and crabs may be deftroyed as follows :—Go to the apothecary, and buy Aq. rofar. 4 oz.—Merc. crof. fublimat. 1 fcr. m. f. lotio.——Or, ung. fimp. 2 oz.—Merc. præcip. alb. 1 fcr. *mifce.*——But fome apply the ung. ceruel. mit.—Let a phyfician, or an apothecary, tell how much you ought to apply at one time.

It has been faid that boiling water will not kill lice; and that if a loufy garment is wet, and expofed to the froft, the lice will die.

The ftings and bites of hornets, wafps, bees, and bugs, may be cured with oil, honey, and vinegar, applied *pro re nata.*

In fome places, the flies, gnats, and mofchetoes are very troublefome. Some drive them out of their houfes by fumigations, and explofions of gunpowder. Emollient fomentations, and cataplafms with oil mixed with theriaca, are good in all bites and ftings. Milk and oil, both internally and externally, are excellent remedies in all poifons that produce inflammations.

CHAP.

CHAP. XXXIX.

Of a Battle between a Toad and a Spider—Of the Death of a Man bit by a Spider—Of a Patient who loſt his Senſes by ſwallowing a Spider—Of the Death of a Family by the Poiſon of a Lizard —Of Poiſon Fiſh—And how Two Women were burnt to Death in conſequence of their drinking to Exceſs.

A TOAD was ſeen to fight with a ſpider in Rhode-Iſland; and when the former was bit, it hopped to a plantain leaf, bit off a piece, and then engaged with the ſpider again. After this had been repeated ſundry times, a ſpectator pulled up the plantain, and put it out of the way. The toad, on being bit again, jumped to where the plantain had ſtood; and as it was not to be found, ſhe hopped round ſeveral times, turned over on her back, ſwelled up, and died immediately.— This is an evident demonſtration that the juice of plantain is an antidote againſt the bites of thoſe venomous inſects.

We have different kinds of ſpiders in America, all of which have a greater or leſs degree of poiſon, though ſome people have been otherwiſe minded. The largeſt ſort, which are of a greeniſh colour, are the moſt venomous.

At

At the high lands on Hudſon's river, in the State of New-York, in the year 1780, a Mr. Thomas Nelſon, who belonged to the Continental Army, was bit by a green ſpider, in a vein juſt above his fore-finger. The part firſt itched, then ſmarted, ached, and ſwelled to his arm-pit; from thence the ſwelling ran to the middle of his breaſt, and, in about twelve hours from the time he was bit, he expired. This I received from a Captain Hubbal, who commanded the company that Nelſon belonged to.

A learned phyſician in the Maſſachuſetts, with whom I was acquainted, viſited a patient who was violently ſeized with a delirium. An emetic was exhibited—a large ſpider was vomited up, and the patient's ſenſes were ſoon reſtored. He recollected, that as he was drinking ſome water in the dark, on the preceding evening, he ſwallowed ſomething, which he ſuppoſed to be the ſpider.

A cook-maid in Virginia, accidentally boiled a lizard in the head of a cabbage: the poiſon proved mortal, for it killed her, and all the reſt of the family.

Fiſh that live upon beds of copper-mines, are poiſonous. The way to know whether they are ſo or not, is to boil a ſilver ſpoon with them; and if it comes out bright, the fiſh is not poiſon; but if it is coloured, they are by no means fit to be eaten. In the year 1789, a man died at New-York, by eating a piece of a dolphin, ſaid to be impregnated with ſuch *virus*.

A woman who lived in the practice of drinking a quart or more of brandy in a day at New-York, became

became fo impregnated with that inflammable
fpirit, that fhe took fire when fhe was alone in
the night, and was found the next morning almoft
confumed.   It was fuppofed that the fire was communicated from a candle to her breath, and from
thence conveyed to her internal parts.   The room
was covered with a blackifh fmut; but the floor
on which fhe lay was not burnt.   It was fuggefted,
that the fat that ran from her body prevented the
floor from taking fire; but perhaps the tightnefs
of the room, and the feparation of the watery
particles from the inflammable, might be the
caufe thereof.

Another woman, who lived on Long-Ifland,
near New-York, followed the practice of drinking rum to excefs, till fhe took fire by the flame
of a candle, in the prefence of her friends.   They
foon extinguifhed the flame; but her infides were
fo much burnt, that fhe died in a fhort time.
This account was communicated to me by the
phyfician who was called in when the accident
happened.

CHAP.

C H A P. XL.

Of the Rattle-fnakes, Black Snakes, Vipers, and Mad Dogs—How to cure their Bites.

I. *Of the* RATTLE-SNAKE.

THESE reptiles have been very numerous in fome parts of America; but their number has greatly decreafed of late, by reafon of the rapid increafe of the Englifh and other fettlements. Their bites are very poifonous, and fometimes prove mortal; but their flefh is fuppofed to be good in confumptions, though I have not feen any good effects from its ufe. The oil is the moft penetrating and relaxing of all animal oils, and is efteemed excellent for quinfeys, ftiff joints, corns, &c.

The bite of a rattle-fnake may be cured by the juice of the roots and branches of plantain and horehound, forced down the patient's throat, if it cannot be taken otherwife. A large fpoonful is a dofe. If one dofe does not relieve the patient, in an hour, give another, and repeat it as occafion may require. If the herbs are dry, moiften them with a little water before they are bruifed in a mortar: a leaf of tobacco, fteeped in rum, may be applied to the wound.

Y   Seneka,

Seneka, or rattle-fnake root, is faid to be a fpecific againft the poifon of thefe reptiles.   The powder of the root, or the frefh root, may be applied
as a cataplafm to the wound; and the patient may
take from a fcruple to a drachm of the powder in
fubftance; or three ounces of the root may be
boiled in water enough to make a pint of decoction, of which the dofe is from two to four fpoonfuls, three or four times in a day.

A decoction and poultice of blood-root is alfo
beneficial in the bites of thefe ferpents; but the
plantain and horehound is fuppofed to be the beft
remedy.

A Captain Haftings informed me, that he pro-/
voked a rattle-fnake to bite a piece of elm-bark in
three different places.   From the firft place that
was bitten, the poifon extended itfelf about 18
inches each way, and was of a deep green colour:
from the fecond place, it ran about 9 inches; and
in the third, he could fcarcely difcern any colour
at all.   Hence he concluded, that the poifon of
the ferpent was almoft entirely exhaufted by the
two firft bites.

II. *Of the* BLACK SNAKE.

BESIDES the rattle-fnake, there is one of a
black kind in America; but I have not heard of
their biting any perfon.   But they are very
dangerous; for fometimes they get round people's
necks, and fometimes round their waifts, and draw
themfelves tighter and tighter 'till the people expire.   It has been faid, that an Indian woman,
who

who had killed fome young fnakes of this kind, loft her life in that manner by an old one.

A very remarkable inftance happened in the county of Worcefter, in the commonwealth of Maffachufetts, fince the commencement of the late war.—A boy dreamed feveral nights running, that he was killed as he was going after the cows, at a certain place, by a black fnake; and told his mafter and miftrefs of his dreams, and that he was afraid to go after the cattle. At laft he grew fo timorous, that he actually refufed to go at all unlefs he could have company; but his mafter flogged him, and fent him off. The next morning the poor boy was found dead at the place he had mentioned, with a large black fnake round his waift.

Thefe ferpents will climb trees, to get birds eggs; and both they and the rattle-fnake often charm birds into their mouths.

When a black fnake gets round a perfon, 'tis beft to cut it in two. Hence the neceffity of travelling with a pen-knife; for whether they are round a perfon's neck or waift, they draw themfelves tighter and tighter as he fetches his breath, and at laft put an end to life.

Cure for the BITE of a VIPER.

WARM common fallad-oil, and rub it well into the part that has been bitten. This is faid to complete the cure, if repeated *pro re nata.*

Names

Names of the different Snakes or Reptiles in the
United States of America.

1 The rattle-fnake	16 Green rattle-fnake
2 Small ditto	17 Wampam ditto
3 Yellow ditto	18 Glafs ditto
4 Copper-bellied fnake	19 Bead ditto
5 Bluifh green ditto	20 Striped or garter ditto
6 Black ditto	21 Water ditto
7 Ribbon ditto	22 Hiffing ditto
8 Spotted ribbon ditto	23 Thorn-tailed ditto
9 Chain ditto	24 Speckled ditto
10 Joint ditto	25 Ring ditto
11 Green fpotted ditto	26 Two-headed ditto
12 Coach-whip ditto	27 Wallor-houfe adder
13 Corn ditto	28 Water viper
14 Hog-nofe ditto	29 Black ditto
15 Houfe ditto	30 Brown ditto.

The toad is alfo called a reptile.

The thorn-tail fnake is of a middling fize, and very venemous. It has a thorn in its tail, with which it fometimes ftings thofe that come near it.

The fkin of the joint-fnake is as fmooth as glafs, and fo hard that it will break to pieces like the tube of a pipe. It has fo few joints, and is fo ftiff, that it cannot eafily bend itfelf into the form of a hoop.

Two-headed fnakes are very fcarce, and perhaps of a monftrous kind, though it has not as yet been determined whether they are fo or not.

There are more fnakes in the fouthern than in the northern governments, for they love hot climates beft.

The remedies I have prefcribed, are efteemed good for the bites of all fuch kinds of reptiles.

Of

Of the Signs of Madnefs in a Dog.

THE figns of madnefs in a dog, are,

1. A dull, heavy look;

2. His trying to hide himfelf;

3. His feldom or ever barking;

4. His being angry with, and fnarling at ftrangers;

5. His fawning and leaping at his owner;

6. His refufing to eat or drink;

7. His drooping, hanging down his head, ears, and tail;

8. His often lying down as if going to fleep— This is called the firft ftage of madnefs.

9. His breathing quick and heavy;

10. His running out his tongue, flavering and frothing at the mouth;

11. His appearing to be half-afleep;

12. His flying at the by-ftanders;

13. His running forward in a curved line;

14. His not knowing his mafter;

15. His eyes watering as they grow thick and dim;

16. His tongue being of a leaden colour;

17. His growing faint, weak, falling down, rifing up and attempting to fly at fomething— This is the laft ftage of madnefs, and the dog commonly dies in lefs than 30 hours.

18. The higher the madnefs is, the more dangerous are the bites.

19. When a dog is mad, all other dogs, upon fmelling him, run off with horror.

Y 3

Symptoms

Symptoms confequent on the Bite of a Mad Dog.

The fymptoms confequent upon the bite of a mad dog, are,

1. A pain in the part bitten;
2. The gradual approach of wandering pains;
3. An uneafinefs and heavinefs, with difturbed fleep and frightful dreams;
4. A tolling of the body, fudden ftartings, fpafms, &c.
5. A fighing, folitude, and anxiety;
6. Shooting pains from the wound to the throat;
7. A ftraitnefs, and fenfation of choaking;
8. A horror and dread at the fight of water and other liquors;
9. A trembling, and lofs of appetite;
10. A ftarting back when any fluid touches their lips, attended with great agony and fury;
11. A naufea, and vomiting of bilious matter;
12. A continual watching, drynefs and rough-nefs of the tongue, with a high fever;
13. A thirftinefs and hoarfenefs, with a lolling of the tongue out of the mouth;
14. An attempting to fpit at the by-ftanders, and to bite thofe they can come at;
15. A raging and foaming at the mouth;
16. An averfion to the fight of a dog, and to a perfon dreffed in fcarlet;
17. A barking like a dog, finking of the pulfe, failure of breathing, followed by cold clammy fweats, convulfions, and death.

A *Hydro-*

A *Hydrophobia* is a nervous diforder, attended with inflammatory fymptoms. There are two kinds, *viz.* a *hydrophobia rabiofa*, or a defire of biting; and a *hydrophobia fimplex*, or no defire of biting. Some patients grow dumb, others rave with madnefs; and fometimes the madnefs is periodical.

The fmalleft quantity of the *faliva* of a mad dog, either frefh or dry, may produce this diftemper. The poifon generally operates in three or four weeks; but fometimes it lies dormant many months. The infection is communicated to the human race by the *faliva* only; but dogs have received it by going into kennels where mad dogs have been before.

When a patient is bitten by a mad dog, let the wound be immediately dilated, or entirely cut out; and the poifon extracted by a cupping-glafs, with fcarifications, or by drawing cataplafms: perhaps a poultice of onions, often applied, might be of great utility, and alfo epifpaftics.

Some cauterize the wound, after it is fcarified: —but I cannot fee wherein that can be beneficial; for the parts being feared, muft become callous in fome degree, and obftruct a difcharge of the *virus.*

The frequent wafhing the wound with falt-water and vinegar, and keeping it open by efcharotics, has been recommended; but, do not thefe remedies contract the parts, and fhut in the poifon?

It is faid, that the Americans have poured cold frefh water from a tea-kettle upon the part bit

Y 4   by

by a mad dog, and continued it a long time, and
that it has been ferviceable in carrying off the poifon : but it is my opinion, that warm water would
do better ; becaufe the cold condenfes, and the
heat relaxes the parts, and may open a way for
the *virus* to make its efcape.

Hence may we not conclude, that the dilating
of the wound, wafhing frequently in warm water,
the application of a cupping-glafs with fcarifications, and of attra&ive fomentations and cataplafms, muft be of greater utility than thofe things
that cicatrize, contra&, and condenfe the parts,
and hinder the poifon from efcaping at the place
where it was imbibed ?

The frequent ufe of the cold bath is efteemed
advantageous in the canine madnefs.

When the poifon has extended itfelf through
the whole mafs of the fluids, the cure muft be attempted by fuch things as will prevent or deftroy
the nervous or fpafmodic irritation, or, by a fpecific property, deftroy the acrimony that generates
the diforder.

Hence, if there is an inflammation, or a *ple-*
thora, bleed, and give *Gm. Opii.* gr. j. *vel.* gr. jfs.
every three hours ; and alfo the following bolus,
once in fix or eight hours :—*Mofch. Optim.* gr,
xvj. — *Cinnab. fa&. lævigat.* 3fs.—*Pil. Sapon.* gr.
viij.—*Gum. Camph.* gr. vij. *Balf. Peruv.* q. f. f. *ut*
bolus.

The next morning take the following purge :—
Infuf. Sennæ, ʒiij.—*Tin&. Sennæ,* ʒfs.—*Sal. Cath.*
Glaub. ʒiij.—*Syr. Solutiv.* ʒij. mix. *

* ʒ Signifies a drachm.

The

The fame evening,* or the next day, put the patient into the cold bath; rub him dry, and put him to bed; and promote a diaphorefis, by repeating the opiates and mufk-bolus, and by half a pound of the infufion of Valerian and Saffafras, with as much white-wine whey as he can drink.

Let thefe remedies, with the bathing, be repeated for feven nights, if the dog was raving mad; and for three or four nights at the next full and change of the moon.

If the patient is feized with a *hydrophobia*, apply fponges dipped in hot vinegar, conftantly to his nofe and mouth; and a piece of thin flannel moiftened in the following liniment, to his throat, three or four times in a day:

Linimentum Thebaicum.

R. *Tinct. Theb.* ʒiij.—*Gum. Camph.* ʒj. m.

Mercurials are efteemed excellent in the bite of a mad dog, both before and after a *hydrophobia*. Some rub the *Ung. Cærul. Fort.* into the wound, and raife a falivation by mercurial unction externally applied. A ptyalifm fhould be continued three or four weeks. Calomel in fmall dofes is beneficial; and the following emetic is called a fpecific, and will help in bringing forward a falivation:

R. *Merc. Emet. Flav.*—*Gum. Camph.* āā gr. iij. *mifce bene;* and add *Conf. Cynofb.* q. f. ut f. bolus.

A falivation has fometimes worked a radical cure; and although the cold bath has been highly extolled, it is my opinion, that a warm one of frefh water would prove more effectual in expelling the *virus.*

Every

Every dog, on the leaft appearance of madnefs, ought to be immediately killed and buried. Is it not ftrange that fuch great numbers of thofe animals are fuffered to live, and efpecially in capital towns and cities, when they fo frequently run mad, and their bites are fo extremely dangerous? Would it not be better for the community, if nine-tenths of them were killed?

I have lately read a melancholy account of a man who loft his life a few months ago in the State of New-York, by fkinning a cow that died by the bite of a mad dog. The poifon was communicated to him that way, and he died of a *hydrophobia.*

Wolves, foxes, cats, cocks, hogs, cattle, &c. &c. alfo run mad, and their bites are dangerous. A gentleman died not long ago by being bit by a cat, in or near London; and a young lady was in the agonies of death at Briftol, in England, when I was in that city, in Jan. 1790, who had been bit by a cat: It was fuppofed that the cat was bit by a mad dog before it run mad.

People that have been bit by a mad dog, will bark like a dog; and thofe bit by a cat, will mew like one of thofe animals.

Let thofe who may be bit by any mad animal, fend immediately for a fkilful phyfician.

Thus have I mentioned the common methods of cure, with my own opinion upon the fubject. It is hoped that fome better antidotes will be difcovered in time, than thofe hitherto found out.

CHAP.

CHAP. XLI.

Of the Birds, Beasts, Fishes, Insects, and Amphibious Animals in North-America.

HAVING mentioned the names of the North-American reptiles in the preceding chapter; perhaps it may not be amifs to mention the names of the birds, beafts, fifhes, infects, and amphibious animals in that part of the world.

I fhall therefore proceed to mention, 1. The birds; 2. The beafts; 3. The fifhes; 4. The Infects; and, 5. The amphibious animals.

I. *Of the* BIRDS.

1	THE Black-bird	15	Bald-coot bird
2	Razor-bellied ditto	16	Cut-water
3	Baltimore	17	White curlew
4	Blue	18	Cat-bird
5	Buzzard	19	Cuckow
6	Blue jay	20	Crow
7	Blue grofbeak	21	Cowpen-bird
8	Brown bittern	22	Chattering plover, or kil-dee
9	Crefted bittern		
10	Small bittern	23	Crane, or blue heron
11	Booby	24	Yellow-breafted chat
12	Great booby	25	Cormorant
13	Blue peter	26	Hooping crane
14	Bull-finch	27	Pine-creeper

28 Yellow

28 Yellow-throated creeper
29 Dove
30 Ground dove
31 Duck
32 Ilathera duck
33 Round-crefted duck
34 Sheldrach or canvafs duck
35 Buffel's-head duck
36 Spoonbill duck
37 Summer duck
38 Black-headed duck
39 Blue-winged fhoveller
40 Little brown duck
41 Sprigtail
42 White-faced teal
43 Blue-winged teal
44 Pied-bill dobchick
45 Eagle
46 Bald eagle
47 Flamingo
48 Fieldfare of Calolia, or ro-
bin
49 Purple finch
50 Bahama finch
51 American gold-finch
52 Crefted fly-catcher
53 Black-cap ditto
54 Little brown ditto
55 Red-eyed ditto
56 Finch-creeper
57 Storm-finch
58 Goat-fucker of Carolina
59 Gull
60 Laughing gull
61 The góofe
62 Canada goofe
63 Hawk
64 Fifhing Hawk
65 Pigeon-hawk
66 Night-hawk

67 Swallow-tailed hawk
68 Hang-bird
69 Heron
70 Little white heron
71 Heath-cock
72 Humming bird
73 Purple jack-daw or crow
black-bird
74 King-bird
75 King-fifher
76 Loon
77 Lark
78 Large lark
79 Blue linnet
80 Mock bird
81 Mow bird
82 Purple martin
83 Nightingale
84 Noddy
85 The Nuthatch
86 Oyfter-catcher
87 Owl
88 Screech-owl
89 American partridge or quail
90 Pheafant or mountain partridge
91 Water-pheafant
92 Pelican
93 Water ditto
94 Pigeon of paffage
95 White-crowned pigeon
96 Parrot of Paradife
97 Paroquet of Carolina.
98 Raven
99 Rice-bird
100 Red bird
101 Summer ditto
102 Swan
103 Soree
104 Snipe

105 Red

105 Red ſtart
106 Red-winged ſtarling
107 Swallow
108 Chimney-ſwallow
109 Snow-bird
110 Little ſparrow
111 Bahama ditto
112 Stork
113 Turkey
114 Wild turkey
115 Tyrant
116 Creſted titmouſe
117 Yellow ditto
118 Bahama do.
119 Hooded do.
120 Yellow rump
121 Towhe bird
122 Red thruſh
123 Fox-coloured thruſh
124 Little thruſh
125 Tropic bird
126 Turtle of Carolina
127 Water-wag-tail
128 Water-hen
129 Water witch
130 Wakon bird
131 Whetſaw
132 Large white-bellied wood-pecker
133 Large red-creſted ditto
134 Gold-winged ditto
135 Red-bellied do.
136 Hairy do.
137 Red-headed do.
138 Yellow-bellied do.
139 Smalleſt ſpotted do.
140 Wren

Unto this catalogue ſhould be added the winter phebe, and the ſummer phebe; alſo the red mavis, whip-poor-will, and robin-red-breaſt.

The Americans raiſe great numbers of geeſe, turkies, peacocks, doves, ducks, dunghill fowls, Guinea hens, &c. ſo that poultry is very plenty and cheap. In ſome places, numerous flocks of pigeons come from diſtant countries, and are caught by the people in nets.

The ſwan is the biggeſt of all web-footed water-fowls.

The pelican is alſo a water-fowl. It lives at the River Miſſiſſippi. Its pouch, or crop, will hold eight quarts. They are about five feet from the end of their bills to that of their tails.

The humming bird is the ſmalleſt, and the lark aſcends the higheſt of all the winged tribe.

II. Of

II. *Of the* BEASTS.

1	Mammoth	25	Black fox
2	Buffalo	26	Red do.
3	Panther	27	Grey do.
4	Carcajou	28	Racoon
5	Wild cat	29	Wood-chuck
6	Bear	30	Skunk
7	Elk	31	Opoſſum
8	White bear	32	Polecat
9	Wolf	33	Weaſel
10	Mooſe deer	34	Martin
11	Stag	35	Minx
12	Carrabou	36	Beaver
13	Fallow deer	37	Muſquaſh
14	Greenland deer	38	Otter
15	Rabbit	39	Fiſher
16	Bahama coney	40	Water-rat
17	Monax	41	Muſk-rat
18	Grey ſquirrel	42	Houſe-mouſe
19	Grey fox ſquirrel	43	Field-mouſe
20	Black ſquirrel	44	Moles
21	Red ditto	45	Quick-hatch
22	Ground ditto	46	Morſe
23	Flying do.	47	Porcupine
24	Striped do.	48	Seal.

The mammoth is not to be found in the civilized parts of America. It is ſuppoſed he lives North of the Great Lakes. They are very large according to their ſkeletons, which have been found on the Ohio, and in New Jerſey.

The opoſſum is about the bigneſs of a common cat.

The buffalo is larger than an ox.

The tyger is a very fierce ravenous animal, and will ſpare neither man nor beaſt; but it is not apt to fly at mankind if it can get the flefh of other animals to live upon: its fhape is fomething like that of a lionefs.

The wild cat is much like a common cat, but a great deal larger: they are very fierce, but feldom attack people.

The elk refembles a deer, but is much larger than a horfe: they have very large horns, which they fhed every year, in February; and by Auguft, their horns almoft come to their full growth.

The moofe is about the bignefs of a deer: they have large horns, which they fhed annually.

The carrabou refembles a moofe, but is not fo large.

The carcajou is of a cat kind: I fuppofe they are what we call catemounts in New-England. They kill elks, carrabous, and other deer, by lying in ambufh on the limbs of trees, or in fome other place; and when an elk or deer draws near, he jumps upon its neck, feizes the jugular vein, and foon kills his prey; but if the elk can jump immediately into the water, he may fave his life, for the carcajou will lofe his prey rather than venture into that element.

The fkunk, called by the French, *Enfant du Diable*, the child of the devil, is fomething lefs than a polecat. When this animal is purfued, it fends forth, in its defence, a fmall ftream of water from a receptacle near its bladder, which has fuch a fubtile, powerful and penetrating fmell, that it will taint the air with a horrible ftench, to a furprizing diftance. Their fat is an emollient,

and

and very beneficial for ſtiff joints, and for gouty and rheumatic complaints.

The porcupine, or hedge-hog, is about the big-neſs of a middling dog. It is covered with quills near four inches long. They ſhoot their quills at their enemy; and 'if they enter the fleſh at all, they will work through, unleſs extracted by in-ciſion; for they cannot be extracted without, any more than a fiſh-hook.

The wood-chuck is about fifteen inches· in length; it digs holes ſeveral feet into the ground, in which it burrows.

The racoon is about the bigneſs of a fox, only it is not ſo thick; they climb trees. The firſt I ever ſaw, I ſhot from the top of a high tree, when I was young; and could not tell what it was, till an old hunter came along, and told me what I had killed.

The bears ſometimes do much damage, by kill-ing ſheep, deſtroying Indian corn, &c. And the wolves are great ſheep-killers; and ſometimes when they have been very hungry, they have killed people, and eat their fleſh: And the bears have alſo killed people, when they have come near their young cubs; but they do not often meddle with the human race, unleſs they have been wounded, or are afraid of loſing their young.— But the catemounts are the moſt to be dreaded of all the wild beaſts in America; for they are ſo very fierce, that it is dangerous coming near them.

The Americans raiſe great numbers of neat cattle, horſes, ſheep, ſwine, dogs and cats.

III. *Of*

III. *Of the* FISHES.

IN the rivers, brooks, ponds, and lakes, we have divers kinds of Fishes, as well as in the falt-waters adjoining the American Continent.

The American Fishes are,

1	The whale	18	Chivens
2	Shark	19	Froft fish
3	Dolphin	20	Eels
4	Flying fish	21	Pouts
5	Sword fish	22	Breams
6	Sturgeon	23	Shiners
7	Haddock	24	Shad
8	Salmon	25	Sheep's-head
9	Salmon-trout	26	Lobfters
10	Common trout	27	Clams
11	Flounders	28	Oyfters
12	Cod-fish	29	Succers
13	Pike	30	Black fish
14	Mackarel	31	Porpoife
15	Herring	32	Sea-tortoife
16	Sprats	33	River ditto.
17	Smelts		

The Sharks are very large, and fo very greedy that they will kill and fwallow a man inftantaneoufly.

IV. *Of* INSECTS.

1	The glow-worm	9	Wall-loufe or bug
2	Earth-worm	10	Sow-bug
3	Leg or Guinea worm	11	Horn-bug
4	Naked fnail	12	Bed-bug
5	Shell-fnail	13	Flea
6	Tobacco-worm	14	Gnat
7	Wood ditto	15	Sheep-tick
8	Silk do.	16	Wood-loufe

Z   17 Forty

17 Forty legs, or centipes
18 Caterpillar
19 Adder bolt
20 Cicadia, or locust
21 Man-gazer
22 Cock-roche
23 Cricket
24 Beetle
25 Fire-flying bug
26 Butterfly
27 Moth
28 Ant
29 Bee
30 Humble-bee
31 Black wasp
32 Yellow wasp
33 Hornet

34 Fly
35 Sand-fly
36 Black fly
37 Horse-fly
38 Musketo
39 Spider
40 Millar
41 Head-lice
42 Body-lice
43 Cattles lice
44 Hogs lice
45 Hessian fly
46 Dores
47 Maggots
48 Crabs
49 Ear-wigs.

V. *Of* AMPHIBIOUS ANIMALS.

THESE go sometimes on the land, and sometimes in the water.—The Alligators are often five yards long; they kill hogs, dogs, fish, &c. and live in South-Carolina. When winter draws near, they fill their bellies with pine-wood, and crawl into their dens in the bank of some creek or pond, and lie all winter without any other sustenance.

The guana, green lizard, blue-tailed lizard, and lion lizard, are found in the Southern States.

The beaver is an amphibious animal, about four or five feet in length, and fifteen inches in breadth. They cut down trees, make dams across small rivers and large brooks, and build cabins to live in.

The musquash is also amphibious, and so are frogs, otters, and minxes.

C H A P.

CHAP. XLII.

Of Burns, Scalds, and Freezes—Of the Growth of Hair, Baldness, &c.

I. *Of Burns and Scalds.*

DRAW the fire out immediately by the application of a poultice of raw onions beat fine in a mortar. Boiled or roafted onions may anfwer; but they are not fo drawing as when raw. Renew the cataplafm twice or thrice in a day; bleed the patient, if he is plethoric; and keep the body open with gentle cathartics:—this will prevent an inflammation.

When the fire is extracted, go to the apothecary, and buy *Ol. Lini.* 6oz. *Spir. Vin. Camph.* 2oz. *mix.* and apply it as occafion requires.—This is faid to prevent the rifing of blifters.

If blifters have rifen, open them, and drefs the parts with *ceratum album,* or *ceratum epuloticum,* or *ceratum faturninum.*

If there are figns of a mortification, apply antifeptics, both internally and externally.

Perfons burnt with lightning, fhould take cordials; and if the pain is great, anodynes are neceffary.

The oil of olives, and emollient fomentations and cataplafms, are good in burns and fcalds.

Z 2

II. *Of*

II. *Of Freezes.*

KEEP the parts in cold water 'till the froft is out. Then ufe emollient fomentations and cataplafms, with the other remedies ufed in burns.

When people are expofed to the froft, they ought to drink cold water, inftead of fpiritous liquors, as it will prevent freezing much longer than inflammable fpirits.

Copperas diffolved in warm water, and linen-rags dipped therein, and applied often to a freeze, is faid to be excellent.

III. *Of the Growth of Hair, the Caufe of Baldnefs, and how to prevent it.*

A HAIR hath a bulbous root, of an oval fhape, which is lodged in the fkin. The hair itfelf is hollow, and is furnifhed with veffels fomething like the quills of geefe, or feathers of birds. Hairs have joints and branches, like fome forts of grafs, and are apt to fplit at the ends, if worn long without moifture. They will grow as long as any moifture remains at their roots, in a body, even if it is dead and mouldered into duft.

Robuft perfons have generally ftrong hair; and thofe that are feeble, that which is weak.

Malignant and contagious difeafes, and the eating of mufhrooms, will fometimes deftroy the roots of hairs, and occafion baldnefs. Violent fevers, that dry up the moifture that nourifhes the hair, may alfo caufe it to fall off. The meeting

4

with trouble, great furprize, and bad humours, often makes the hair turn white or yellow, or caufes baldnefs, by deftroying the nutritious juices.

Hair-dreffers ought to be very gentle in the dreffing of hair, for pulling of it may weaken the roots, and make it fall off.

I have known baldnefs prevented by a frequent bathing in falt-water when the hair began to fall off. The falineous particles, and the coldnefs of the water, contracts, braces up, and ftrengthens the parts relaxed by fome diforder.

The following is efteemed beneficial in baldnefs:

1. Rub the parts with a frefh-cut onion, till they turn red; but if no rednefs appears, it is a bad fign.

2. Wafh the head every night, with a warm and very ftrong fomentation, made by boiling bruifed burdock-roots in white-wine.

3. Or, bruife the fmall fpiral branches of grape-vines, and mix them with honey, and apply the mixture twice in a day.

4. Or, R. *Ung. Simpl.* 3jv.—*Balf. Peru.* 3j— *Ol. Nuc. Mofch. Gutt.* x. *mix.* and apply it twice in a day.

Hair-powder and pomatums are nourifhing to the hair; but if they are too highly fcented with chymical oils, which are of a burning nature, they may prove injurious.

Some are fo fuperftitious, that they fuppofe it is unlawful to nourifh their hair by powder. I

Z 3   knew

knew a clergyman that·preached upon probation, and the people thought he was unfit for a Minifter of the Gofpel, becaufe he wore powder on his hair ; however, they fuppofed it was legal for other clergymen to wear powdered wigs. But we may judge it is lawful to powder our hair, in as much as we have had no command from Heaven that forbids that practice.

CHAP.

C H A P. XLIII.

Account of Prescriptions—How regular-bred Phy-
sicians are often treated—Physical Receipts for the
Cure of Agues, Asthmas, Bruises, Cancers,
Coughs, Cholics, Colds, Consumptions, Cramps, Con-
vulsions, Deafness, Diabetes, Diarrhœa, Dropsy,
Dysentery, Epilepsy, Fainting, Fevers, Gout, Gravel,
Gripes, Head-ach, Heart-burn, Hypochondriac
Distempers, Hysteric Complaints, Hoarseness, Hœ-
morrhoids, Jaundice, Inflammations, Indigestion,
Itch, King's Evil, Lethargy, Lowness of Spirits,
Madness, Measles, Mortification, Pains, Palsy;
Perspiration to check, or to promote; Phlegm,
Pleurisy, Quinsey, Rheumatism, Rickets, Rupture,
Scurvy, Shingles, Small-pox, Stitches in the Side,
Sprains, Sore Throat, Tetters, Thrush, Tumours,
Vertigo, Vomiting, Ulcers; Urine suppressed—Heat
of—Involuntary—Bloody; Worms, and Wounds;
with Directions for Nursing Children.

THE remedies mentioned in the subsequent
pages, if properly exhibited, are very efficacious in the cure of distempers; and I hope the
prescriptions will be of great utility to people in
general, and to those in particular who may be
settled in places where physicians cannot be had,
which is often the case in many parts of America.

I have

I have mentioned the dofes, and given directions concerning the ufe of the compofitions, in
order to prevent injury to thofe who may be under
the neceffity of taking medicine without the advice of a phyfician : but all the dofes, excepting
thofe prefcribed for children, are for perfons of
an adult age, and muft be enlarged, or diminifhed, according to the age and conftitution of
the patient.

As the fymptoms of difeafes are fometimes very
fubject to mutation, they require different modes
of treatment : Hence, the medicines fhould be
changed, or altered, according to the circumftances of thofe afflicted with bodily weaknefs and
indifpofition.

I have often obferved, that a medicine that will
cure a difeafe at one time, will not cure it at another. Hence alfo appears the neceffity of altering
our practice, by exhibiting fome other remedies
that will work a radical cure.

Thofe who attempt to practife phyfic, ought to
know,

1. What difeafe a patient is feized with ;

2. What his conftitution is, that is, whether
it is ftrong or weak ;

3. What remedies ought to be applied ; and,

4. What their ftrength is, and how they will
operate.

But it cannot be expected that thofe unacquainted with the noble art of phyfic can know all
thefe things ; and therefore, it will be moft prudent to fend for a fkilful Phyfician where one can
be had, and to be guided by his directions. The
                                                    fooner

fooner he is called, the better; becaufe a difeafe is much eafier cured when it firft begins, than after it is feated.

Some who have called themfelves Phyficians, have fuffered difeafes to gain ground, by neglecting to make proper evacuations. A patient who appeared to be almoft gone in a confumption, and had been given over by his phyficians as incurable, applied to me for advice.—Said I, what have your phyficians done for you?—Have they bled you? He anfwered, No.—Have they given you an emetic? No.—Have they given you a cathartic? No.—Have they given you any medicine? Yes: they have given me fimple fyrups and decoctions for more than fix months paft; but they would not bleed me, nor give me an emetic, becaufe they fuppofed I was fo weak that I could not bear either.—I bled him immediately, gave an emetic, ordered the bark, and fome other remedies. His cough, night-fweats, and other terrible fymptoms, left him, and he foon recovered his former health and ftrength. It is my opinion, that it is almoft as proper to throw medicines into the fire, as it is to give them to patients, without making thofe evacuations which are neceffary to expel the morbific matter.

Much damage has been done by ignorant women, who have rufhed into the practice of midwifery, without thofe qualifications which are requifite for this important bufinefs. I have frequently been called to affift them when there has not been the leaft difficulty, except that which

arofe

arose from their ignorance and misconduct. Sometimes I found they had poured down the decoctions of hot herbs, and had raised fevers, &c. Sometimes they had almost affrightened the women into convulsions, by telling frightful stories, and by talking about the doctrine of original sin, election, reprobation, the unpardonable sin, and the torments of hell.—But after I had administered proper remedies, and had, by encouraging them, brought them out of their despair, they have been safely carried through their perils and dangers without any uncommon difficulty. It is dangerous for women to venture their lives in the hands of those who know not the construction of the human frame, nor the nature and operations of medicines, and who, by scare-crows and bug-bears, bring them into a state of discouragement, to the great injury of the child and the mother.

It is thought, that no men are treated much worse than the Physicians have been in some parts of the world; for, let their skill be ever so great, they have frequently been interrupted in their practice, to the great injury of their patients: for, when they have laid a foundation for a cure, other medicastors have taken the work out of their hands, and hindered a regular course of physical operations; just as a Divine might be hindered from preaching a sermon, by being turned out of his pulpit, after he had named his text and the heads of his discourse, by some up-start not skilled in divinity.

I have often thought that this illegal practice has been the cause of the death of thousands; for

3   whilst

whilft the quack is adminiftering his *noftrums*, the difeafe gains ground, and an end is put to the life of the patient.

Regular-bred Phyficians are frequently impofed upon in this way, for many people are very fond of thofe who have raifed their fame by quackery: Hence they leave the man of fkill, and run after impoftors.

Sometimes when a fkilful Phyfician has prefcribed proper remedies for a patient, his orders are difobeyed by the nurfes; and whilft he is abfent, in comes Mother Midnight with her budget of herbs, and makes and adminifters decoctions deftructive to the relief of the diftreffed, 'till at length death clofes the fcene.

I have often wondered at the madnefs and folly of fome people, who will venture their lives in the hands of quacks, fooner than they will venture their eftates. When they go to law, they will be fure to employ a good lawyer, for fear of lofing their money; but when they are taken ill, and their lives are in imminent danger, they will pafs by a fkilful Phyfician, and employ an impoftor, and thus perhaps lofe their lives by their folly.

A Phyfician muft turn out at all times in the night, even in the moft violent ftorms, and take care of both the rich and the poor; and he muft wait a long time for his money, as the merchant, baker, butcher, brewer, &c. muft have their payment firft; and then, if he charges but a very moderate price for his fervices, he will be curfed, railed at, defamed, and at laft cenfured to the infernal regions, as an extortioner. I do not fay
that

that this is the practice in every place within the circle of my acquaintance; but it has been too much the practice in some places, and it is now high time there was a reformation.

I own that people have a right to employ what physicians they please, providing they are men of skill; but they have no right to commit self-murder, by employing quacks.—Let all, therefore, who may have any regard for their own lives, and the lives of those under their care,

1. Send for a man of skill—who is very temperate, humane and just; because a drunkard, unmerciful, or inhumane person, is by no means fit for the important work.

2. Be very strict in observing his directions.

3. Let him not be interrupted by impostors.

4. Let him visit the patient as often as may be necessary.

5. If other advice shall be thought needful, give him notice.

6. If another physician is called in, let him that has had the care of the patient first, tell the symptoms of the disease, what remedies have been applied, and how they have operated.

7. After they have prescribed remedies, still employ the first physician. Let the same directions be observed in regard to surgeons and midwives.

This is much safer than to change physicians, or employ quacks, and female impostors, who frequently impede the regular practice of well-bred physicians, and bring destruction on their patients.

Physicians

Phyficians ought to vifit their patients often when they are fmitten with dangerous diforders, and efpecially if the fymptoms vary, becaufe new remedies may be needful.

A conftant fire ought to be kept in a room where a patient is ill; and if the difeafe is of a putrid kind, the fumes of cyder-vinegar, burnt in a hot crucible, is an excellent antifeptic; it is not only good for the patient, but prevents the by-ftanders from taking the diftemper.

Thefe things being premifed, I proceed to the Phyfical Recipes, and fhall write in Englifh, for the benefit of thofe unacquainted with Latin.

Ague.—Boil four ounces of the beft Peruvian bark in a gallon of water, till half is confumed; and take two ounces of the decoction thrice in a day, after proper evacuations have been made.

Afthma.—Take twelve ounces of the milk of ammoniacum; of the fyrup of fquills, four ounces: mix, and take a fpoonful when the fhortnefs of breath is troublefome.

Bruifes internal.—Take of Lucatellus's balfam, one ounce; conferve of rofes, two ounces; fyrup of red poppies, a fufficient quantity: mix, and take a drachm three times in a day.

Bruifes external.—Take of the fpirits of rofe-mary, one pint; of hard Spanifh foap, three ounces; camphor, one ounce: digeft the foap in

the

the fpirit till it is diffolved, then add the camphor.
Rub fome of the compofition into the parts affected, and repeat it as occafion may require. It
may alfo be taken inwardly, from 30 to 50 drops
in a glafs of water.

Cancers.—Apply the extract of hemlock as a
plaifter, for a long time. Some have taken it inwardly, by beginning with two grains in the
morning, and as many in the evening; increafing
the dofe gradually to fifteen grains. But fometimes it will make the patient giddy-headed.

Cough.—Take of fpermaceti in powder, three
drachms; oil of olive, half an ounce; yolk of
egg, a fufficient quantity; of fpring-water, fix
ounces; of ftrong cinnamon-water, two ounces:
mix. The dofe is two fpoonfuls, to be taken when
the cough is troublefome.

Cholic.—Bleed; give an infufion of camomile-
flowers; inject anodyne clyfters; exhibit gentle
cathartics, &c. But fend for a Phyfician.

Colds.—Take of diftilled vinegar, two ounces;
drop into it, by degrees, the fpirits of fal-ammoniac, till the effervefcence entirely ceafes. The
dofe is half an ounce twice in a day, in an equal
quantity of the fyrup of marfh-mallows. It will
promote fweat.

Confumptions.—Take ground-ivy, colts-foot, and
liquorice-root, of each two ounces; elecampane,
one

one ounce: boil them in nine quarts of water to a gallon. A quarter of a pint may be drank at once, and taken as common drink, or three or four times in a day. It is good for spitting of blood, and inward bruises, as well as the consumption.

Cramp.—Drink a glass of tar-water night and morning. The taking hold of a roll of brimstone, which will soon break, gives relief. The same remedies that are prescribed for bruises, are also excellent.

Convulsions.—Take of native cinnabar, one scruple; of the conserve of red roses, four grains: mix, and form it into a pill. This quantity is to be taken every night and morning. A decoction of the powder of Valerian root may also be taken.

Deafness.—Take of the oil of bitter almonds, three drachms; spirit of sal-ammoniac, one drachm. Drop a few drops into the ear at bedtime, and stop it with black wool.

Diabetes.—Take of the powder of Peruvian bark, one ounce; mix it into an electuary, with simple syrup. Take the quantity of a nutmeg three or four times in a day. Simple syrup is made by dissolving in water, so much of double-refined sugar as will make a syrup.

Diarrhœa.—Take of rhubarb in powder, fifteen grains; scordium electuary, half a drachm; mix. This

This is for one dofe, and muft be repeated as occafion fhall require.

The patient muft abftain from malt-liquors, and
may take the following, viz. Take of burnt
hartfhorn, two ounces; gum-arabic, two drachms;
of water, three pints: boil till one-third is confumed. This is prefcribed for common drink.

Dropfy.—Take of the powder of jalap, half a
drachm; powder of ginger, fix grains; fyrup of
buckthorn, a fufficient quantity; mix. This may
be taken twice a week. Alfo,

Infufe a handful of camomile-flowers in a quart
of boiling water, and add a gill of melaffes fpirits.
Take a quarter of a pint twice in a day. Or,

Take of the roots of zedoary, two drachms;
dried fquills, rhubarb, and juniper-berries bruifed,
of each one drachm; the powder of cinnamon,
three drachms; falt of wormwood, one drachm
and an half: infufe in a pint and an half of old-
hock wine. Strain, and take a gill twice or
thrice in a day: It is a powerful diuretic.

Dyfentery.—Take of the jelly of ftarch, two
ounces; of ftyptic tincture, one ounce; extract
of opium, two grains: mix. For an enema.

Purges of rhubarb are excellent, alfo the common drink directed in the diarrhœa.

If the patient has a fever, let a drachm of nitre
be diffolved in the common drink: a quarter of a
pint may be drank four or five times in a day.

Epilepfy.

Epilepfy—Take two ounces of the powder of Valerian root; of fimple fyrup, fix ounces : mix ; and take a quarter of an ounce twice in a day.

Fainting.—Take of fimple alexiterial water, half a pint; of treacle water, two ounces; fyrup of red poppies, half an ounce ; mix. Two or three fpoonfuls may be taken at a time.—Or,

Take of wood-foot, two ounces ; of afafœtida, one ounce ; of proof fpirit, a quart : digeft and ftrain. Take two drachms twice in a day. All volatiles are good for fainting.

Fevers, inflammatory.—Take of the falt of tartar, one ounce and an half; of the juice of lemons, eighteen ounces ; of fpiritous alexiterial water, half a pint; of fpring water, a quart; of loaf fugar, three ounces : mix. Take three large fpoonfuls thrice in a day.—Or,

Take of fal-nitre, half an ounce ; of white fugar, two ounces ; cochineal, one fcruple ; of fpring water, two pounds and an half : boil to a quart, and pour off the decoction when it is fettled. The dofe is four ounces three times in a day.

Vomits and purges may alfo be needful.

When a fever is too high, it ought to be lowered by evacuations, coolers, &c. : and if it is too low, it ought to be raifed by cordials, bliflers, &c. I have made a practice of bleeding patients in inflammatory fevers in America, and never per-ceived that it hurt any perfon. Nay, I have had 185 patients under my care at one time, that were

A a   ill

ill with fevers; the greateſt part of whom I bled; and they all recovered excepting a woman, who was ſo far gone when I was called to her, that ſhe could not take any medicine.—My practice was,

1. To bleed, if the patient was plethoric, and the fever inflammatory.

2. To exhibit an emetic, when there was too great a quantity of bile.

3. To keep the body open with laxatives and gentle purges.

4. To lower the fever, if it was too high, by nitrous preparations, and an antiphlogiſtic regimen.

5. To raiſe it, if it was too low, by bliſters, cordials, &c.

6. To exhibit antiſeptics freely, when the patient could bear them.

I have found preparations of the gum myrrh very beneficial, when the bark could not be taken.

I frequently obſerved, that where phyſicians had neglected to bleed their patients, and to make other evacuations, that death commonly cloſed the ſcene.

I find that bleeding is very much exploded in London, although its effects have been ſo beneficial in America. But it appears to me, that there is a difference in the climates, which makes bleeding not ſo requiſite here, as it is in the weſtern parts of the world.

Bleeding in general has been neglected in America, in the putrid ſore throat; but I have often
thought,

thought, that in fome cafes it may be of great fervice, and efpecially when the patient is firft taken ill, and the fymptoms are inflammatory.

In the year 1783, I vifited a patient who had been ill with this diforder about feven days, and could neither fpeak nor fwallow any thing. I at a venture opened a vein, and it gave immediate relief. In lefs than an hour he could fpeak very well, and take medicine. He recovered in a few days.

Bleeding, in my opinion, is proper when there is too much *craffamentum* in the veffels, or when the veins and arteries are too much crouded. But the pulfe are the beft guide; for when they are full, ftrong, and tenfe, they indicate that phlebotomy is needful; and if it is neglected, the fluids may ftagnate, and bring on putrid diforders. Bleeding when a patient is plethoric, makes way for a free circulation; and thofe whofe blood circulates freely, can endure the cold much better than thofe whofe fanguinary veffels are crouded. But the pulfe may be raifed by rarefaction; and when that is the cafe, bleeding may be improper. It ought to be known, before an attempt is made to bleed a patient, whether it is a plethora, or a rarefaction, that raifes the pulfe.

The fevers are fo numerous, that I fhall not mention the whole of them in this Oracle; and therefore will conclude by obferving, that if they are intermitting, the bark is a fovereign remedy; if nervous, nervines, &c.

Gout.—Take half a dram of gum-guaicum in powder; of conferve of rofes, one fcruple; of

fimple

fimple fyrup, a fufficient quantity for a mixture. This is for one dofe, to be taken every morning. —Or,

Take of the fpirits of fal-ammoniac, and liquid laudanum, of each half an ounce; of the fpirits of wine camphorated, three ounces: mix. This is excellent for external ufe.

But about 12 drops of camphorated fpirits ought to be taken in a little water, to defend the ftomach when the external remedy is applied.

Gravel.—Take of the beft white foap, half a drachm; of the oil of juniper, five drops; of fimple fyrup, enough for a bolus. This quantity is to be taken twice in a day.—Or,

Take of hard foap, one ounce; oil of anife-feeds and carraway-feeds, of each half a drachm; of fimple fyrup, a fufficient quantity: mix. The dofe is a drachm thrice in a day.—Gentle purges and anodynes are fometimes needful.

Gripes.—See *Cholic.*

Head-ach.—Bleeding, emetics, cathartics, cephalics, &c. as *Rad. Valerian.* Let the caufe of the pain be enquired into before remedies are exhibited.

Heart-burn.—Take two or three drachms of *magnefia alba* every day.

Hypochondria—Take of Virginia fnake-root, and *hicra picra*, of each two drachms; extract of gentian,

tian, half an ounce : make them into pills with white fyrup. Take half a drachm night and morning.

Hyfterica.—Take of the milk of ammoniacum, one pint ; of the tincture of afafœtida, half an ounce ; mix.—The dofe is two fpoonfuls, as occafion may require.

Hoarfenefs.—Take of fpermaceti, two drachms ; diffolve it in the yolk of an egg : add of alexiterial water, fix ounces ; of nutmeg water, one ounce ; of white fugar, a drachm and an half ; mix.—This quantity may be drank, or taken at two or three times.

Hæmorrhoids—Take of lenitive electuary, and the flour of fulphur, of each equal parts ; of fimple fyrup, enough for an electuary. A drachm may be taken night and morning.

Jaundice.—Take of white foap, half a drachm ; oil of juniper, five drops ; of fimple fyrup, enough for a mixture. This quantity may be taken twice in a day.—Sometimes emetics and gentle purges are very beneficial.

Inflammations.—Bleeding, emetics, cathartics, nitrous preparations, ointment of marfh-mallows, anodynes, &c.

Indigeftion.—After the operation of an emetic, take of the powder of ginger, and long pepper, of each fifteen grains ; conferve of orange peel,

a fcruple ;

a fcruple; fimple fyrup, enough for a bolus: mix.
A bolus is only one dofe.

Itch.——Take of corrofive fublimate, half a
drachm; diffolve it in a pint of boiling water;
and at bed-time, wafh the parts affected. Be very
careful of the fublimate, for a few grains taken
inwardly before it is diffolved, will foon kill a patient. But the folution applied outwardly, with
prudence, will do no harm, and wholly cure the
itch. It may be proper to take the bolus prefcribed for the hæmorrhoids, feveral times, whilft
the folution is externally applied.

King's Evil.—Take one drachm twice in a day
of fea-oak calcined. This plant is alfo called
fea-wrack, and is common on rocks that are left
dry at ebb-tide. The leaves gathered in July,
beat in a mortar, and put into a glafs, with the
fame quantity of fea-water, will, after ftanding
ten or fifteen days, make an excellent liquor for
difcuffing of glandular fwellings: it penetrates
through the fkin, exciting a flight fenfe of pun-
gency. The parts fhould be rubbed two or three
times in a day with the ftrained liquor, and be
afterwards wafhed with clean water. Let the calcined powder be taken in the mean time.

Lethargy.—Take of the falt of hartfhorn, two
drachms; of fpring water, a pint; of fpiritous
alexiterial water, one ounce; of loaf fugar, half
an ounce: mix. Take four large fpoonfuls thrice
in a day.——Bleeding, emetics, blifters, ftimu-
lating enemas, volatiles, &c. are often beneficial.

Lowneſs

Lowness of Spirits. --- Take fimple alexiterial water, half a pint; of fpiritous alexiterial water, two ounces; of cordial confe&ion, two drachms; mix, and take three or four large fpoonfuls every fix hours.

Madnefs.---Bleed, vomit, purge, blifter, bathe in warm water; ufe gentle exercife, a flender diet, travelling, &c.; or ufe thofe remedies that your Phyfician's fhall think may be beft.

Meafles.---Bleed, if the patient is phlethoric; vomit, if there is too much bile; and purge, as occafion may require. Let not the patient be kept too warm; and let him have a plenty of boiled water, with a little nitre, if he is feverifh.

I had the meafles when I was young, and was almoft murdered by being kept in a hot bed for five days, without being fuffered to get up; by having inflammatory deco&ions poured down, and by being kept from drinking water. This raifed a high fever, and brought on a delirium; but an hemorrhage at my nofe fupervened, which gave fome relief. The nurfes informed me that I fainted away when I was permitted to fit up; but I was not fenfible of it. This evil pra&ice of keeping patients too hot, of not letting them have water, a proper air, &c. has been the death of thoufands who have had the fmall-pox and meafles; but modern pra&ice teaches better things.

Mortification.---Bleed, if it is needful, and exhibit antifeptics plentifully.

Pain.

Pain.---The brain is faid to be the feat of pain, becaufe it is the feat of fenfation ; but moft authors have imputed the caufe of pains to the ftretching of the nerves.

Pain may be caufed by a variety of difeafes, and by bruifes, wounds, diflocated joints, broken bones, &c.

Anodynes, gentle opiates, an infufion of ca-momile, &c. are proper remedies for patients af-flicted with pain.

Palfy.---Take two ounces of the powder of Vale-rian root, and of fimple fyrup fix ounces; mix, and take two drachms twice in a day.

Perfpiration to check.---Elixir vitriol, Peruvian bark, &c.

Perfpiration to promote. --- Take of alexiterial powder, twenty-four grains; of fimple fyrup, enough for a mixture. This quantity may be taken once every fix hours, and the patient may drink an infufion of camomile.

Phlegm.---Take of the milk of ammoniacum, twelve ounces ; of the fyrup of fquills, four ounces ; mix.   A large fpoonful is a dofe.

Pleurify.---Bleed, and make other evacuations ; take of barley, raifins ftoned, and figs, of each two ounces ; of liquorice root, half an ounce ; of water, two quarts.   Boil the barley firft, then add the raifins, and afterwards the figs and liquorice :
half

half of the water muſt be boiled away. This may be drank freely.

Quinſcy.---Bleed, give warm water-gruel, barley-water, and chicken-broth, as occaſion may require.

Take of ſenna, one ounce and a half; cryſtals of tartar, three drachms; of carraway-ſeeds, two drachms; of water, one pint. Boil the tartar till it is diſſolved, and whilſt it is boiling, pour it on the other ingredients, and ſtrain when it is cold.

To three ounces of this infuſion, add one ounce of the ſyrup of buckthorn, and half an ounce of carraway water. This may be taken two or three times in a week for a purge.

For a Gargle.—Take of the tinĉture of roſes, one pint; of the honey of roſes, two ounces. Mix.

Rheumatiſm.—There are different kinds of rheumatiſms, and hence there muſt be different modes of treatment.

When there is an inflammation, bleeding is proper, and alſo nitrous preparations.

Emetics, cathartics, anodynes, diaphoretics, &c. may all be requiſite in ſome caſes.

Sometimes, after evacuations, the cold bath has done great ſervice.

Rickets.—Magneſia alba may be taken, and a ſtrengthening plaiſter applied to the back. Some plunge their children into cold water, rub them

with

with a cloth, and afterwards make them fweat, between two blankets. The water ought not to be too cold, and the child fhould be dipped with its face downward, to prevent its being ftrangled.

Rupture.—The parts fhould be gently reduced to their former pofition, and then fomented with the following, *viz.* Take of oak-bark, an ounce and an half; of fmiths forge-water, three pints; boil to one quart, then add two drams of roche allum. A ftrengthening plaifter is alfo good, and corroborants taken inwardly.

Scurvy.—Abftain from liquors boiled in copper veffels; and take freely of the juice of lemons, and other acid vegetables.

Shingles.—Abftain from pork, malt liquors, and cheefe; gentle purges fhould be exhibited.

Take of gum guaicum, half a fcruple; Æthiop's mineral, half a drachm; fimple fyrup, enough for a bolus; mix, and take this quantity twice in a day.

Small-pox.—If the inflammation and pain is great, bleed; keep the patient cool, and let him exercife as much as his ftrength will admit. Nitrous de-coctions, and a plenty of diluting liquors may be drank cold: nothing ought to be taken that will inflame the blood. Sometimes emetics and ca-thartics are of fervice; and calomel is excellent in many cafes, and likewife the bark. I obferved when I practifed inoculation, that when proper

evacuations

evacuations were made in the beginning of the diftemper, the patients had it very light.

Stitches in the Side.—Take half a pint of neats-foot oil; of the fpirits of wine camphorated, and the fpirits of fal-ammoniac, of each two ounces; mix, and rub into the parts affected :---taking in the mean time, about twelve drops of camphorated fpirits, to defend the ftomach.

Sprains.—Apply opodeldock to the parts injured, and take in the mean time from thirty to fixty drops of the *balfamum traumaticum.*

Sore throat.—Take of Mindererus's fpirit, and the fyrup of marfh-mallows, of each an ounce; mix, and fweaten with honey. This quantity may be taken at bed-time, or as occafion may require.

Tetters.—Take of quick-filver, one ounce; of ftrong fpirits of nitre, two ounces; digeft in a fand-heat till the mercury is diffolved, and add, whilft it is hot, one pound of fweet oil: ftir the compofition till it is cold, then rub fome of it into the parts affected, and repeat it till a cure is completed.

Thrufh.—Take of the frefh inner bark of elm, four ounces; of water, three pints; boil till one-third is confumed; ftrain, and fweaten with honey. A gill or more may be taken at once; it may alfo be ufed warm as a gargle.

Tumurs.

Tumours.—If they muſt be brought to a ſuppu-
ration, take of white-lily roots, onions, and lint-
ſeed flour, of each one ounce: boil in a ſufficient
quantity of water, till they are ſoft, and add one
ounce of Burgundy pitch. Apply this as a poultice.

If they muſt be diſcuſſed, take of the grounds of
ſtale beer, a pint; of oat-meal, a ſufficient quantity:
boil to the conſiſtence of a poultice; and add, of
the oil of olives, ſix ounces: then apply it to the
parts affected.

Vertigo.—Bleed and purge, with the following,
viz. Take of the ſacred tincture, one ounce; of
the compound ſpirits of lavender, one drachm;
mix. The whole may be taken at once, and repeated as occaſion may require.

Vomiting.—Take of the dried leaves of ſpear-
mint, one ounce; then pour on a pint of boiling
ſimple mint water. Strain, when cold, and take
a large ſpoonful every hour.

Ulcers.—Take half a pound of yellow baſilicon;
of verdigreaſe prepared, one drachm; mix: and
apply ſome of it as a plaiſter.---It deterges, cleanſes,
and wears away fungous fleſh.

Urine ſuppreſſed, and heat of.—-Take of nitre,
half an ounce; white ſugar, two ounces; of cochineal, one ſcruple; of ſpring water, a quart
and half a pint; boil to a quart, and pour off the
decoction after it is ſettled.- The doſe is two or
three ounces, three or four times in a day.

Urine,

Urine, involuntary.---See *Diabetes.*

Urine, bloody.—Take of red rofe-buds, half an ounce; oil of vitriol, twenty drops; boiling water, two pints and an half; of loaf fugar, an ounce and an half; when it is cold, ftrain off the liquor. The dofe is three ounces thrice in a day.

Worms.—Take of prepared tin, one pound; conferve of wormwood, two ounces; of fimple fyrup, enough for an electuary; mix. Half an ounce is a dofe, to be taken every morning.

Wounds.—Drefs them with dry lint, general balfam, ointment of gum elemi, yellow bafilicum, &c.

If the wounds are internal, fee *Bruifes.*

Directions for Nurfing Children.

Infants fhould be kept clean, and their clothing ought to be loofe and cool; but not fo cool as to make them take cold. It was formerly the practice in America, to wrap a flannel fwathe, that was near two yards in length, tight round the waift of every new-born infant, to make it grow ftraight. This pernicious practice has undoubtedly been the caufe of the death of thoufands; for it obftructed the circulation of the fluids, hindered digeftion, generated crudities, and produced convulfions.— It was alfo the practice to keep three or four caps on their heads, and to fqueeze their heads together, when, according to the vulgar expreffion, they

appeared

appeared to be open. ' But this practice was also very hurtful; for it often injured the brain, and impaired the fenfes.—The head of the child, as well as the body, ought to be loofely clothed, and its formation left to the action of the *dura mater;* for the open or foft parts will naturally grow hard, without any manual operations.

From an infant's birth, till its mother's milk can be obtain.d, no other diet will be requifite but milk and water, which may be given luke-warm; fome add a little fugar to the compofition. Warm milk, however, juft taken from an animal, is the beft.

If the child is to be nurfed without the breaft, equal parts of milk and water will be fufficient at firft; and as ftrength increafes, a more folid diet will be required.

The milk of the mother may be injured by dif- eafes, frights, weak nerves, anxiety of the mind, &c. any of which may injure its quality, diminifh its quantity, or caufe it to be wholly dried up. In fuch cafes it is proper to wean the child; but if it will not feed with a fpoon, or if it is difordered in its ftomach and bowels, it may be proper to feek for another nurfe, taking care to procure one that is healthy. She ought to fee that the child is not infected with any dangerous complaint; be- caufe it may be communicated to her by fuckling the infant:—or a difeafe may be communicated from her to the infant, if fhe has any difagreeable infection, not only by her milk, but by fpoon- food, many having the nafty practice of firft put-
ing

ing the fpoon into their own mouth, and then into the child's.

Healthy women, who accuftom themfelves to exercife, bring forth children more robuft than thofe that are delicate. A child ought to be put to the breaft within ten or twelve hours after it is born ; this will excite the milk to flow fooner than could be expected, and tend to prevent a fever.

Wet nurfes ought to eat one meal of animal food in a day, with a proper quantity of vegetables ; broth, or milk, are proper for their fuppers and breakfafts : and they fhould abftain from acids, becaufe they will caufe their milk to curdle, and generate griping pains in the ftomach and bowels of infants. If a child is afflicted with acidities in the *prime vie*, let it take freely of *magnefia alba ;* about eight or ten grains may be given at a time, in a fpoonful of milk and water ; or, three or four drops of the fpirits of hartfhorn may be exhibited in the milk, &c. The child may alfo take frefh broth once in a day, without any fat.

When children are fed, to prevent ftrangulation, their heads and bodies ought to be raifed almoft erect, and not fuffered to lie in a horizontal pofture, as is too often the practice among ignorant nurfes.

Gentle exercife is very beneficial to infants ; it preferves and reftores their health, and makes them vigorous when they grow up.—But let us obferve,

1. That this exercife ought to be very gentle.

2. That the hoifting and toffing of an infant up and down with violence, hinders digeftion ; gene-

rates

rates acidities, gripings, convulfions, &c.; may break or bend its tender ribs, and expofe it to pain when the caufe is not thought of.

3. That children fhould not be kept too warm in bed, nor be nurfed in a fmall room, becaufe too fmall or crouded rooms caufe a relaxation, and fubject them to colds when expofed to the open air.

4. When they are dreffed and undreffed, their bodies fhould be gently rubbed before the fire, to promote a free circulation.

5. If an acid in the ftomach and inteftines produces fits, griping pains, naufeas, vomitings, &c. give from five to ten drops of antimonial wine. If it doth not operate in half an hour, repeat the dofe. It commonly proves emetic and cathartic, and does much good to the infant. After the operation, make free ufe of the *magnefia*.

6. That young children fhould not be fed after bed-time, nor forced to eat when they feem to have got enough.

7. Do not awake a child when it is afleep, becaufe it will make it fick and peevifh: but divert and keep it awake in the day-time, and then it will reft in the night.

8. When teeth begin to appear, give a child a piece of flefh to chew, every now and then; but fee that it does not choke itfelf.

9. Be careful of expofing an infant to the cold air: when it is carried abroad, let it be fufficiently clothed; and let not the nurfe fit ftill with it in the wind, but let it be kept in motion, to preferve it from taking cold.

CHAP.

C H A P.   XLIV.

Of P H Y S I O L O G Y.

A Definition of ANATOMY—*Of the Bones, Cartilages, Ligaments, Fibres, Membranes, Muscles, Glands, Tendons, Arteries, Veins, Nerves, Teguments, Teeth, and Nails, which belong to the Human Body.*

PHYSIOLOGY is the history of the human frame; and Anatomy confifts in an accurate diffection of all its parts, in order to make known their fituation, figure, connexion, ftructure, and mutual relation to each other, for the benefit of Philofophers, Phyficians, and Surgeons. I fhall therefore treat of the Solids and Fluids, with the vital, natural and animal functions of the body.

The firft anatomical production that was printed in Englifh, was publifhed by Mr. Thomas Vicary furgeon in London, about the year 1548; and fince his time, a number of ingenious Phyficians and Surgeons have made great difcoveries and improvements in the art, which have done honour to their profeffion.

I fhall, in this chapter, give a fhort defcription of the Solids in the human body, and of the Fluids in the next. And,

B b   I. *Of*

I. *Of* Osteology; *or, A Defcription of the Bones.*

A BONE is a web of folid fibres, which is compofed of three fubftances, called *compact, fpungeous,* and *reticula.* The fkin of a bone is called the *periofium,* and that of the fkull the *pericranium.*

The bones form and fupport the whole body; they are deftroyed in living animals, by the admiffion of the air, or by the lodging of blood upon them.

The difeafes of the bones are pains, caries, exoftofes, rickets, fractures, fiffures, *fpina ventofa,* and luxations; but fractures and luxations are produced by accidents.

There are 61 bones in the head, 64 in the trunk, 60 in the hands and arms, and 60 in the legs and feet—in the whole 245.—But fome Anatomifts reckon 248; and others, 249; befides the *offa fefamoidea,* which are very fmall bones that are found in the joints of the hands and feet, being in the form of fefamum feeds. They are 48 in number, according to fome Anatomifts; but others reckon not fo many.

The names of the Bones, with their number, are as follows, *viz.*

1. *The Bones of the Head.*

Latin Names.	English Names.	No.
Os Frontis,	The bone of the forehead,	1
—— *Occipitis,*	In the back of the head,	1
Offa Parietalia,	Two bones in the upper part of the head,　-	2
—— *Temporum,*	The temple bones,　-	2
Offcula Auditus,	Little bones of the ears,	8
Os Ethmoides,	Bone between the eyes,	1

4

Os

LATIN NAMES.	ENGLISH NAMES.	No.
Os Sphenoides,	It runs into the bafis of the fkull from one temple to the other	1
Offa Malæ,	The bones of the cheeks,	2
— *Maxillare,*	The jaw-bones, -	2
— *Unguis,*	The inner bones of the eyes,	2
— *Nafi,*	The bones of the nofe,	2
--- *Palati,*	The bones of the palate,	2
Vomer,	A bone juft above the palate,	1
Maxilla Inf.	The bone of the lower jaw,	1
Dentes Incifivi,	The upper and under fore-teeth	8
--- *Canini,*	The dog teeth, -	4
--- *Molares,*	The grinders, or large teeth,	20
Os Hyoides,	A bone between the root of the tongue and the top of the wind-pipe, -	1

Total 61.

2. *The Bones of the Trunk.*

Vertebræ Cervicis,	Bones of the neck,	7
——— *Dorfi,*	———of the back,	12
——— *Lumborum,*	———of the lines,	5
Offa Sacri,	The loweft bones in the back but three, -	6
— *Coccygis,*	The loweft bones in the back	3
--- *Scapulæ,*	The bones called the fhoulder-blades, -	2
--- *Claviculæ,*	The collar-bones,	2
--- *Coftæ,*	The ribs, -	24
Os Sternum,	The great bone in the fore-part of the breaft,	1
Offa Innominata,	Bones juft above the hips, called *Os Ilium,* -	2

Total 64.

The *Os Pubis* ought to have been added.

3. *The*

3. *The Bones of the Arms and Hands.*

LATIN NAMES.	ENGLISH NAMES.	No.
Os Humerus,	The upper bones of the arms, - -	2
—*Ulna,*	The great bones of the arms below the elbow, -	2
— *Radius,*	The fmaller bones of the arms below the elbow, -	2
— *Carpi,*	The bones of the wrifts,	16
— *Metacarpi,*	The bones between the wrifts and fingers, - -	8
— *Digitorum,*	The bones of the thumbs and fingers, -	30

Total 60.

4. *The Bones in the Legs and Feet.*

Offa Femoris,	The upper bones of the thighs,	2
Rotula, vel *Patella,*	The knee-pans, -	2
Tibia,	The largeft bones in the legs,	2
Fibula,	The fmalleft bones in the legs,	2
Offa Tarfi,	Bones between the ancles and thofe which join the toes,	14
— *Metatarfi,*	The bones of the feet which run to the toes, -	10
— *Digitorum,*	The bones of the toes,	28

Total 60.

As the *Os Pubis* contains two bones, our number is augmented to - -	247
Befides the *Sefamoidea,* which are -	48
Bones in the human body, -	295

Bones, like other things, often receive new names.

The

The teeth are bones, whofe ufe is to chew the food, and make it more nourifhing to the body.

Of the Nails.

The nails are whitifh, tranfparent bodies, much like horn. They are fuppofed to have their origin from the *papillæ* of the fkin, or a continuation of the *epidermis*. Their ufe is to corroborate and defend the ends of the fingers and toes.

Of the Hairs.

The hairs are fmall round long bodies, which arife from the fkin; their roots are hollow, like the roots of birds feathers. Their ufe is to cover and preferve certain parts from the cold. *See p.* 340.

Of the Skin.

The fkin is an outward covering, which confifts of four parts:—the firft is compofed of membranes and nervous fibres: the fecond is formed of the capillary threads of the nerves: the third is made of a mucous fubftance; and the fourth, or outermoft part, is compofed of a thin tranfparent fenfible membrane. The ufe of the fkin is to defend the nerves and other parts againft external injuries.

II. Of SARCOLOGY.

THIS treats of the foft parts of the human body, and is divided into *Myology*, *Splanchnology*, *Angeiology*, *Neurology*, and *Adenology*.

Myology,

Myology treats of the muscles.

Splanchnology, of the entrails.

Angeiology, of the veins, arteries, and other vessels.

Neurology, of the nerves. And,

Adenology, of the glands.

But before I proceed to describe those parts, I will just premise,

1. That a cartilage is a gristle, whose use is to cover the extremities of the bones, and unite them together at the joints.

2. That a ligament is a white fibrous substance, which is hard to break or extend. It serves to join and preserve the bones and other parts of the body from injuries. Those of the bones are void of sensation; but those of other parts are not.

3. That a fibre is a round oblong vessel, which is said to take its origin from the brain and spinal marrow. Its use is to convey the animal spirits to all parts of the body.

4. That a membrane is a nervous, fibrous, broad, white spreading substance; whose use is to line the principal cavities of the body, and make the veins and arteries.

5. That a tendon is the extremity of a muscle, where its fibres run into a springy strong cord. Their use is, *first*, to confine the flesh, and prevent its obstructing the motion of a limb near the joint—*secondly*, to prevent clumsiness in particular places — *thirdly*, to keep the fleshy part of a muscle near the centre of motion —*fourthly*, for the better admitting of that friction, which, in less

compact

compact parts, would have been very injurious, were not the flesh braced and strengthened by the tendons.

I. Of Myology; or, A Description of the Muscles.

A MUSCLE is a mass of fibres covered with a membrane, and being capable of contraction and extension, is the principal instrument of voluntary motion; such as, that of the heart, veins, arteries, nerves, stomach, intestines, bladder, &c.

A muscle has a head, belly, and tail.—The head is the tendinous part, which is fixed on the joint, and is called its *origin*. The belly is the middle, or fleshy part, whose fibres are truly muscular. The tail is the tendinous part inserted into the part which is to be moved by it, and is called the *insertion*.

Let us observe, 1. That the action of a muscle will make it grow harder and shorter, it being capable of contracting till it is shortened one-third.

2. That the diameter of a muscle in action is greatly increased.

3. That if the brain is injured to a certain degree, all the muscles subservient to the will become paralytic.

4. That if the *cerebellum* is injured, all the involuntary motions cease.

5. That if a nerve or an artery joining to a muscle is tied or destroyed, the muscle becomes paralytic.

6. That irritation upon the muscles will produce motion.

B b 4 7. That

7. That fome mufcles continue to act, after all communication with the nerves and blood-veffels is taken away.

8. That the action of the mufcles is inftantaneous; and, in moft parts of the body, fubfervient to the will.

This laft appearance is contrary to the opinion of fome men who have been famous in anatomy; as Keil, Boerhaave, &c.

Some Anatomifts make 529 mufcles; others, 446; and others, 435. The fubfequent Table agrees with the latter.

PARTS.	No.	PARTS.	No.
Forehead,	2	Elbows,	12
Occiput,	2	*Radii*,	8
Eye-lids,	6	*Carpi*,	12
Eyes,	12	Fingers,	48
Nofe,	7	Refpiration,	57
External ear,	8	Loins,	6
Internal ditto,	4	*Abdomen*,	10
Lips,	13	Tefticles,	2
Tongue,	8	Bladder,	1
Palate,	4	*Penis*,	4
Larynx,	14	*Anus*,	4
Pharynx,	7	Thighs,	30
Hyoides,	10	Legs,	22
Under-jaw,	12	Feet,	18
Head,	14	Toes,	44
Neck,	8		
The fhoulder-blades,	8	Total	435
Arms,	18		

The

The mufcles are fo numerous, that I have not room to give a complete table of their names in this book.

II. *Of* SPLANCHNOLOGY; *or, A Defcription of the Entrails.*

THERE are two kinds of Inteftines, *viz.* the *great* and the *fmall.* They are between feven and eight times as long as the whole body : thofe that are fmall, are about five-eighths of the length of the whole.

The fmall inteftines are called, 1. the *Duodenum;* 2. the *Jejunum;* and, 3. the *Ileum.*

Thofe that are large, are called, 1. the *Cæcum;* 2. the *Colon;* and 3. the *Rectum.*

The inteftines have four coats :—The *firft,* or outermoft, is a membrane called the *Peritoneum*— the *fecond,* is of a mufcular kind—the *third,* is nervous, or cellular---and the *fourth,* is the villous, or fhaggy. This laft is the inner coat, in which the arteries terminate, and the veins begin. The glands of the inteftines are fuppofed to be lodged in the third coat.

The ufe of the inteftines is to complete digeftion, to ftrain off the chyle, and carry off the fæces in a regular manner ; all of which are performed by the periftalic motion caufed by the mufcular coat.

The periftalic motion is not conftant ; but takes place when the bowels are ftimulated by their con- tents. The action of the lungs on the diaphragm, and that of the abdominal veffels, caufes the fto- mach and inteftines to difcharge their contents, by the affiftance of the chyle, bile, rarefied air, &c.

Anatomifts

Anatomiſts divide the body into three cavities, called bellies; as, 1. The head, or upper belly; 2. The breaſt, or middle belly; and, 3. The *abdomen*, or lower belly.

The belly is divided, on the outſide, into four regions; as,

1. The *epigaſtric*—This reaches from the pit of the ſtomach to the imaginary line above the navel.

2. The *umbelical*—This is the middle external region on the fore part, &c.

3. The *hypogaſtric*—This is the lower fore part of the belly.

4. The *Lumbaris*—This extends from the loweſt ribs on each ſide, to the laſt *vertebra* of the back.

The internal regions contain the thorax, wind-pipe, heart, liver, gall-bladder, diaphragm, ſpleen, veins, arteries, caul, inteſtines, kidneys, myſentery, pancreas, urinary bladder, ſeminal veſſels, &c.

III. *Of* ANGEIOLOGY; *or, A Deſcription of the Veins and Arteries.*

THERE are but two Arteries, *viz.* the *Pulmonic*, and *Aorta*, or *Arteria magna*. But from theſe a number of branches proceed, which have different names, according to their ſituations in the human frame. Their extremities are ſo very ſmall, that they cannot be diſcerned with the naked eye. Theſe extremities end in the veins and lymphatic veſſels.

The

The *aorta* proceeds, with a single trunk, from the left ventricle of the heart; and at its beginning, reflects back two branches called the *coronary arteries*, which are distributed into the substance of the heart and its auricles. The *aorta* thence runs a little obliquely to the right, then turns to the left, forming a semi-circle. From the upper part of this, which is called the *aorta ascendens*, arises three branches. The trunk continued from the *aorta*, is called the *aorta descendens*, and descends through the *thorax* and *abdomen*, towards the *os sacrum*.

The three branches of the great *aorta* are called, 1. The right subclavian;—2. Left ditto;—and, 3. The left, caroted.

The pulmonary artery arises from the left ventricle of the heart; divides into two branches, one on each lobe of the lungs; and being subdivided again and again into smaller branches, they are distributed into every part of the lungs.

Some say that the arteries have five coats; as, the *vasculous*, *cellulous*, *tendinous*, *musculous*, and *nervous*. Others suppose they have but three in a human body, though those of an ox actually have five. The names of the numerous branches I shall not mention.

These vessels are subject to inflammations, ulcers, polypuses, aneurisms, ossification, &c.

The use of the arteries is to convey the blood from the heart to all the extremities of the body. They have two motions: the one is called *diastole*, and the other *systole*, that is, a dilation and a contraction.

The

The veins are thin, ramifying, elaſtic tubes; which ariſe from the extremity of the body, and terminate in the heart or liver: They begin where the arteries end. Their coats are the ſame with thoſe of the arteries, only they are thinner.

There are three kinds of veins, *viz.* the *vena cava,* the *pulmonary* veins, and the *vena portæ.*

Their uſe is to return the blood from the arteries to the heart. In general, they are called by the ſame names as the arteries they accompany.

IV. *Of* NEUROLOGY; *or, a Deſcription of the Nerves.*

IN deſcribing the Nerves, I ſhall mention,

1. That they are round, white, ſmooth bodies, like a cord; being the productions of the brain, and the organs of ſenſe and motion.

2. That they are continuations of the medullary ſubſtance of the brain; and, like the ſame, have a great number of blood-veſſels diſperſed about them.

3. That they receive their ſtrength from the membranes, by which they are ſurrounded.

4. That they have two coats, one from the *pia mater,* and the other from the *dura mater.*

5. That from the head there proceeds 10 pair of nerves, and from the ſpinal marrow 24, making 68 in the whole. Some, however, ſay there are more; but be that as it may, they ſpread into branches, and are diſperſed over the whole body.

6. That

6. That thofe which fubferve the vital functions, arife from the *cerebellum ;*—thofe fubfervient to the fenfes, proceed chiefly from the bafis of the brain ;—and thofe which produce the voluntary motions, are principally from the fpinal marrow.

I faw *Dr. Monro* demonftrate in the College of Edinburgh, in Scotland, that when a nerve is cut, compreffed, or deftroyed, all motion, fenfation, and nutrition in the part where the nerve is fituated, is loft. However, if the principal nerves are not deftroyed, the parts will recover their health and vigour. But if the *cerebrum, cerebellum,* and *medulla fpinalis,* are either of them wounded, the patient dies inftantaneoufly. All nerves whofe pofition are below a wound in the *medulla fpinalis,* lofe their fenfe and motion.—A limb may lofe its motion, and yet retain its fenfation; or it may lofe its fenfation, and not its motion, for fenfation will remain fome time after a member has been amputated; and preffure will make a part palfaic.

The ufe of the nerves is to convey an exceeding fine fluid from the brain to all the extremities of the body. This fluid is called the Animal Spirits, and is the caufe of fenfe and motion.

V. Of Adenology; *or, A Defcription of the Glands.*

THERE are two kinds of Glands, *viz.* the *fimple* and the *compound.* The former is called *conglobate* or *lymphatic,* and the latter *conglomerate.*

The fimple confift of elaftic, circular fibres, which impel the lympha and chyle into their proper ducts. The compound have each of them a

leffer

leſſer canal, which being continued, forms a larger; and they have excretory veſſels, through which ſome particular fluid is to paſs. Thoſe fluids differ from each other, as they conſiſt of ſaliva, bile, the nervous fluid, urine, mucus, ſweat, milk, &c.

The glands have different names, according to their various ſituations in the body and limbs; which are as follows:

1. Of the Brain,   The pineal and the pituitary.
2. —— Mouth,   — parotid, maxillary, ſublingual, labial, buccal, palatine, amygdalæ; and externally, the epiglottis and pharynx.
3. —— Eyes,   — lachrymal.
4. —— Noſe,   — pituitary.
5. —— Ears,   — ceruminous.
6. —— *Thorax*,   — thymus, bronchial, tracheal, arytenoidal, and thyroidæal.
7. —— *Abdomen*, — pancreas, liver, kidneys, ſtomach, inteſtines, &c.
8. —— Secrets,   — uterine, febaceous, &c.
All theſe are *conglomerate* glands.

The *conglobate* are thoſe of the head, *thorax*, *abdomen*: thoſe of the latter are called gaſtric, hepatic, cyſtic, ſplenic, epiploic, lumbar, myſenteric, iliac, and ſacred.

The conglobate glands are alſo found in the extremities of the body; as the axillary, crural, &c. The uſe of the glands are to ſecrete and ſeparate the fluids, juſt as the kidneys ſeparate the urine
from

from the blood; they are of the conglomerate kind: and thofe of the arm-pits, groins, and myfentery, which perfect the *lympha*, are conglobate, &c.

VI. *Of the* LYMPHÆDUCTS *and* LACTEAL VESSELS.

THE Lymphatic Syftem confifts of the lacteals, lymphatic veffels, the conglobate glands, and the thoracic duct.

The Lymphæducts are flender pellucid tubes, which arife from all parts of the body, and permit a thin tranfparent liquor to pafs through them towards the heart, &c.; for the courfe of the lymph, and that of the chyle, is from the circumference of the body to the centre.

The Lymphatics are commonly fituated clofe to the large veins and arteries in the extremities of the human frame.

The Lacteals are flender pellucid veffels, difperfed in great numbers through the myfentery. They begin at the inteftinal tube; and all of them, with moft of the lymphatics, open into the thoracic duct, which lies upon the fpine, and runs up towards the neck, where it commonly opens into the angle between the jugular and the fubclavin veins of the left fide; and thus both the chyle and the lymph are mixed with the blood.

The Lacteals are the abforbents of the bowels, and the Lymphatics are abforbents in other parts. Hence, as both are abforbents, and terminate in

one

one duct, they are alike ; only they are differently
fituated.   The coats of thefe veffels are thin and
tranfparent, being much crouded with valves.

Any compreffion upon the thoracic duct, will
bring on an atrophy and death.

The *vafa chylifera* are called *venæ lactæ*, becaufe their valves are difpofed as thofe of the
blood-veins are, and becaufe, like them, they
convey their contents from the fmaller to the
larger tubes.

CHAP.

CHAP. XLV.

Of the FLUIDS *in the Human Body; viz. The Chyle, Blood, Bile, Saliva, Tears, Urine, Perspiration, Pancreatic Juice, Mucus, Milk, Sebaceous Humour, Cerum, Spiritus Animalis, Amygdalæ, Gastric Fluid, Lympha, Phlegm, &c. The Vital, Natural, and Animal Functions.*

I. *Of the* CHYLE.

THE chyle is a milky fluid, extracted from what we eat and drink by means of digestion. In general, it is a juice inspissated to a middle consistence between moist and dry. It seems to consist of oil, mucilage, water, a coagulated part, and fixed air.

When the aliment is converted into a fluid state, the oily part mixes with the *saliva,* and the juices in the stomach and *duodenum,* till it becomes like milk. This mixture is called chyle; and the bile mixing with it in the *duodenum,* assists in separating the nutritious chyle from the excrementitious part, and the former is conveyed by the lacteals into circulation, to be converted into blood, milk, &c.

When the chyle enters the blood, it does not immediately mix with it, but, in some intestines, passes in a separate state through the whole circu-

C c

lation.

lation. I have frequently feen it floating upon the furface of the blood, when I have bled a patient; and in the laft ftage of a *diabctcs*, the chyle may be feen in the urine.

II. *Of the* Blood.

IT has been demonftrated by a chymical analyfis, that human blood contains,

1. A fine chalky earth.
2. A portion of fixed air.
3. A quantity of elementary fire.
4. A quantity of water.
5. A quantity of fea-falt.
6. A quantity of acidous gas.
7. A number of volatile particles, like thofe of fal-ammoniac.
8. A fmall quantity of iron, which the loadftone will attraɛt.

Thefe earthy, airy, igneous, aqueous, falineous, acidous, volatile, and ferruginous particles, are derived from the four elements, and thofe things which nourifh and fupport the human frame. Dr. William Harvey, of Kent, in England, difcovered the circulation of this fluid, in 1657.

The blood is capable of imbibing the infeɛtions which float in the air, and alfo the poifons of minerals, vegetables and animals.

This fluid is contained in the veins and arteries; the arteries convey it from the heart to all the extremities of the body; and the veins convey it back again to the heart.—As mentioned before, it circulates,

circulates, at a medium, with a velocity equal to about fifty-two feet in a minute. ˙ But the circulation is quicker in young perfons, than in thofe that are old : hence fmall children will live longer in the cold, than the aged. The arteries have a pulfation, like the heart ; and when they are cut, the blood will fpirt out with a very unfteady motion ; but when a vein is opened, the blood will run with a fteady ftream : but it runs with a greater velocity in the arteries, than in the veins.

Two great arteries, called the *aorta* and the *pulmonic* artery, diftribute the blood to the extremities of the body. The firft arifes from the left ventricle of the heart, and extends itfelf in different branches to the moft diftant parts of the human frame. Thefe branches have divers names, as *aorta afcendens*, *aorta defcendens*, &c.

The *pulmonic* artery rifes from the left ventricle of the heart, runs upwards to the left *aorta*, and is divided into branches. The blood is returned back to the heart by three forts of veins, *viz.* the *vena cava*, the pulmonary veins, and the *vena portæ*. Vid. ANGEIOLOGY, p. 378.

When the blood is taken from a patient, the volatile particles fly off in the form of a fteam ; and what remains, congeals into a trembling mafs. The greateft part of this mafs is called *craffamentum*, which is red, and gives that colour to the other parts of the blood. If the *craffamentum* is feparated from the watery part, the remainder becomes inflammable.

The

The globules of the blood are elaftic, and they preferve the heat of the body: a redundancy of them creates acute fevers, inflammations, &c. and their deficiency generates chronic diforders.

The *ferum* of the blood is a cruft that rifes on its furface, after it is taken by phlebotomy, &c. The *ferum* generates nutrition; and the fecretions that flow from it, moiften the furface of the body, and preferve the flexibility of the folids.

The red colour of the blood is fuppofed to be produced by an acid it receives from the air, in the lungs; but Dr. Hunter imputed it chiefly to the degree of its condenfity.

Obftructions in the circulation of the blood, may be produced by a redundancy or a deficiency in that fluid. Cold water drank when people are hot, a too free ufe of acids and fpiritous liquors; fudden frights, grief, terror, fear; the apoplexy, epilepfy, fpafmodic afthma, pleurify, peripneumony, convulfions, hyfteric and hypochondriac complaints, with other acute diftempers, and feveral chronic diforders, will produce obftructions in the fanguinary veffels.

The blood is called the life of all animals; for when it is exhaufted, they die immediately. Coagulations and concretions of the blood fend off many ramifications to the neighbouring veffels, which lays a foundation for a number of diforders. It is dangerous to have too much blood, and alfo to have not enough. When the veins and arteries are too full, bleed; when too empty, live upon a nourifhing diet.

4

When

When the life of a patient is in danger, by a hemorrhage, from a wound or any other caufe, apply ftyptics immediately, and prefs the parts together with your hand. If it has not the defired effect, let a Surgeon take up the vein, or artery, with an arterial needle. A cooling balfamic regimen, and nitrous preparations, will be beneficial.

Some apply the following ftyptic to the part from whence the hemorrhage proceeds, *viz.* Take of the powder of burnt allum, half a drachm ; of the powder of dragons blood, one drachm ; mix : and apply it as occafion may require.

The *volatile flour alkali* has lately been difcovered at Naples, to be a fovereign *ftyptic.*

III. *Of the* BILE.

THE Bile is a thick, yellow, bitter liquor, compofed of aqueous, falineous, rofinous, and fulphurous parts, which are feparated from the venal blood by the liver ; it is brought thereto by the *vena porta,* from the fpleen, ftomach, inteftines, and epiploon. It is collected into the gall-bladder, and difcharged from thence into the lower end of the *duodenum.* Ten parts of the bile, out of twelve, has been found to be water.

It is the leaft putrefcent of any of the animal fluids, and is capable of diffolving almoft all kinds of animal and vegetable fubftances. Hence it mixes with the chyle, roufes the periftaltic motion of the inteftines, and completes digeftion. An exceffive ufe of acids will produce indigeftion, by overcoming the qualities of the bile.

The

The ſtones formed in the gall-bladder, are generated by the coagulation of the bile, and are of
an unctuous inflammable nature. They undoubtedly riſe from the too free uſe of acids; but the
vegetable acids, uſed with moderation, is a great
antidote againſt the putrefaction of the bilious fluid.

When the bile is vitiated, it produces crudities in
the *prime vie*, nauſeas, jaundice, flatulencies, coſtive-
neſs, cachexy, fevers, conſumptions, dropſies, &c.

The putreſcency of the bile increaſes fevers, and
makes them malignant and putrid. Hence it ought
to be evacuated by emetics; and antiſeptics ought
to be exhibited before it is too late, otherwiſe an
end will be put to the life of the patient.

The bilious ducts have different names; as,
Ductus Hepaticus, Ductus Cyſticus, &c.

IV. *Of the* SALIVA.

THIS is an aqueous, ſalineous, oily fluid,
which is ſeparated from the blood by the ſalival
glands ſituated in the mouth. This fluid is almoſt
without taſte or ſmell: It is thin and pellucid,
being incapable of being concreted by fire.

By chewing, it flows from the glands, mixes
with our food, and promotes digeſtion. In hungry
perſons it becomes acrid, penetrating, and reſolvent.
Too much ſpitting cauſes a thirſt, loſs of appetite,
bad digeſtion, and an atrophy.

V. *Of the* TEARS.

TEARS are an aqueous, ſubtile, limpid, ſalineous fluid, which is ſeparated from the arterial
blood

blood by the lachrymal glands; their ufe is to moiften and deterge the eyes.

VI. *Of the* URINE.

THIS is a fluid fecreted from the blood by the kidneys, is conveyed by the ureters to the bladder, and from thence difcharged from the body through the *urethra*. If it is retained too long in the bladder, it turns putrid, and endangers the life of the patient. Sometimes it has paffed off through the cutaneous pores, when it could not find vent the natural way.

A fuppreffion of urine often produces fpafms, pains, inflammations, jaundice, lofs of appetite, faintnefs, tremors, cold fweats, and putrid diforders.

A total fuppreffion is called an *Ifchuria.*

A partial, ——————— *Stranguria.*

If the latter is attended with great heat, *Dyfuria.*

When there is a total fuppreffion, it ought to be drawn off with a catheter, if the patient cannot be relieved by bleeding, fomentations, anodynes, diuretics, enemas, nitrous preparations, &c. Sometimes, after bleeding, I have obferved that emetics and gentle cathartics have been of great fervice.

Some have pretended, that they could tell, by feeing the urine of a patient, what diforder he was afflicted with, and that they could prefcribe proper remedies without any further knowledge; but this is judged by men of learning and fkill to be an impofition, becaufe the fame kind of urine is not always difcharged in the fame diforders.

C c 4   I have

I have been credibly informed, that a foreigner who practifed that way in America, had fome urine brought to him that had been taken from a fwine. After he had viewed it for fome time, he cried out, " By God, dis woman is with child !" This is an evident proof that he was an impoftor : and I believe it may not be improper to rank fuch practitioners with the conjurers and fortune-tellers; for, though they may guefs right fometimes, yet they may often be deceived, and prefcribe remedies that are very improper for thofe that need relief.

The urine contains,

1. A microcofmic falt, which is found in no other fluid.
2. A marine falt.
3. If diftilled, it yields only a volatile falt; and,
4. An empyreumatic oil ; and alfo,
5. A peculiar kind of phofphorus.
6. A quantity of water, &c.

VII. *Of the Perfpiration.*

PERSPIRATION is a fteaming, or fweating, through the cutaneous pores ; and the qualities of this fluid are analogous to thofe of the urine. Infenfible perfpiration is the greateft of all evacuations in hot weather ; but that of urine exceeds it in winter. The perfpiration cleanfes the blood, by carrying off its falineous particles, to fupple the fkin, and preferve the body from various maladies. An obftructed perfpiration produces fevers, pleurifies, peripneumonies, arthretic complaints, violent pains, difeafes of the head, breaft, &c. It increafes

4

the

the impure humours, and generates corruption and putrefaction.

VIII. *Of the* PANCREATIC JUICE.

This is an aqueous, limpid, viscous fluid, separated from the arterial blood by the pancreas, and conveyed by the pancreatic duct to the *duodenum*. It is discharged with the bile through the *ductus choledocus*. Its use is to moisten and dissolve the aliment, to mix with and soften the bile, and to render the chyle fit for its entrance into the lacteal veins.

IX. *Of the* MUCUS.

THIS is a mucilaginous fluid, separated from the blood by the glands that are seated in the pituitary membrane which covers the internal parts of the nose. Its use is to moisten and preserve the inward parts of the nostrils from being injured by the air.

Mucus is also a covering for the surface of all the membranes in the body, such as the skin, internal membrane of the mouth, lungs, intestines, urinary passages, &c. It is a compound of coagulable matter and water, which prevents the membranes from being stimulated by things which touch them.

X. *Of the* MILK.

THIS is a white fluid, separated from the blood by the glands of the breasts: it is nothing but the chyle more highly laboured.

By

By a chymical analyfis it has been demonftrated, that it contains the fame fubftances that are found in the vegetable kingdom. Its ufe is to nourifh infants, &c.

Milk differs in degrees of goodnefs, in the following order, *viz.* 1. Woman's is the beft — 2. Afs's the next beft — 3. Mare's — 4. Goat's — 5. Sheep's — 6. Cow's is the worft, becaufe it is the hardeft to digeft. The milk of animals which feed on green herbs, is more diluting than that of thofe which feed upon dry.

When milk becomes cold, it lofes its excellent qualities, like moft other animal fluids, and they cannot be reftored by heat. Boiled milk is improper for weakly perfons, and thofe who have weak ftomachs.

If milk difagrees with a patient, a tea-fpoonful of the fpirits of hartfhorn may be put into every pint, which will make it agreeable. Milk is not good in fevers, but it is an antidote againft poifons.

New milk whey is cooling, diluting, and aperient : it is good for coftive patients, and in acute rheumatifms, and for other diforders when the humours are impure, being a general promoter of the natural excretions.

XI. *Of the* SEBACEOUS HUMOUR.

THE Sebaceous Humour is an unctious, thick, vifcous matter, which is filtered by the febaceous glands, and depofited in fmall bags, where it appears in black fpots, and may be fqueezed out in

the

the fhape of little worms.—This humour forms the fmall fcales which appear upon the fkin.

Its ufe is to defend the fkin from being injured by the action of the falts, and to render it fmooth and polifhed.

XII. *Of the* CERUMEN AURIS.

THIS is called Ear Wax. It is feparated from the glands in the ear; is moift at firft, but grows harder by lying. It is bitter and vifcid, and has qualities much like thofe of the bile.

Sometimes it caufes deafnefs, by growing hard; but warm water will diffolve it, and often cure the diforder.—This has been found to be a better remedy than any hitherto difcovered.

The ear-wax prevents infects from hurting the *membrana tympani.*

XIII. *Of the* SPIRITUS ANIMALIS.

THE *Spiritus Animalis,* or Animal Spirits, have been fuppofed to confift of a very thin liquor, conveyed from the blood to the external or cortical part of the brain, where it is exalted into fpirit; and from thence conducted through the *medullar* fubftance of the brain, by the *corpus callofum,* and *medulla oblongata,* into the nerves, and in them performs all the actions of fenfe and motion. But the nerves are conductors which not only carry thefe fpirits from the head, but return them back again.

Any fine volatile fubftance which exhales from bodies by a given degree of heat, is called *fpirit:*

hence,

hence, by a fort of an imaginary analogy, the nervous fluid has been called Spirit, and is generally termed Animal Spirit.

The fpirit in the human body is fpoken of under different characters; as thofe of natural, vital, and animal.

The firft prefides over digeftion, the elaboration of the chyle, and all the natural actions—The fecond, over the motion of the heart and lungs, or the vital actions;—and the third, over the animal actions; as, fenfation, voluntary motion, &c.

XIV. *Of the* AMYGDALÆ.

THE *Amygdalæ*, or Almonds, are a glandulous fubftance, like two kernels, on each fide of the *uvula*, at the 'root of the tongue. They are called a thick humour, through which a juice is filtered that moiftens the infide of the *œfophagus*, and other parts, which facilitates fwallowing, creates an appetite, and promotes digeftion. This liquor is analogous to that of *faliva*.

XV. *Of the* GASTRIC FLUID.

THIS is the juice of the ftomach, being a thin pellucid liquor, which diftils from certain glands, for the dilution of food.

XVI. *Of the* LYMPHA.

THIS is a pellucid, infipid, pure liquor; the more fubtile parts of which afford the matter of the fluid of the brain, fpinal marrow, nerves, and alfo the feminal fluid.

The

The gelatinous parts of this fluid nourish all the
folids; and its finer aqueous parts are, through the
lymphatic veffels, by means of the valves and the
conglobate glands, again conveyed to the heart,
where being again united with the blood, it is
with it conveyed to all the parts of the body.
When eight ounces of blood have been diftilled
over a gentle heat, feven ounces of lymph have
arofe by the diftillation.

XVII. *Of the* PHLEGM.

PHLEGM is a flimy excrement of the blood,
often raifed by taking cold, or too much nitrous
air. It is alfo an inflammation.

XVIII. *Of* FAT, *or* ANIMAL OIL.

FAT is an animal oil: It is an unctuous fulphureous fluid, contained in that part of the cellular membrane called *membrana adipofa.* But how
it is feparated from the blood, is not certainly
known.

Fat is compofed of a little earth, elementary
fire, acid falt, volatile alkaline falt, and water.
In human fat, and the fuet of beafts that chew
the cud, there is a large quantity of inflammable
oil, and an acid empyreumatic liquor.

By profufe fweating, the fat is melted down,
and carried off through the cutaneous pores,
which greatly weakens the patient.

The human fat does not become fluid when
Farenheit's thermometer rifes to 96 degrees; but
when

when it begins to putrify, a small degree of warmth will make it run into oil.

The use of this fluid is, 1. to temperate the acrimony of the salts in the blood—2. to fill up the empty spaces between the muscles, which beautifies the formation of the body—3. to render the skin flexible, smooth and soft—4. to moisten and soften the fleshy tendinous parts—and, 5. to nourish the animal at certain times.

Fats and animal oils are good to relax the parts to which they are applied, and to stop perspiration. In the present practice in London, I understand that three kinds are chiefly used, *viz.* That of vipers, hogs-lard, and mutton suet.

Fats are of an emollient quality, and good in divers kinds of ointments, as the *unguentum cæruleum mitius, ung. cæruleum fortius, unguentum* vulgo, *inimentum arcæi. ung. nervinum,* &c.

Animal fats are not soluble in the spirits of wine rectified, nor in water. If they are scented with essential oils, the oils may be totally extracted by digestion in the rectified spirits of wine; and by the same means also, in a lesser degree, by water. By such operations, fats that are old may be freed from their ill smell, and made sweet.

The whale affords more oil than any creature belonging to the animal kingdom. It has been said, that some of them will yield 120 barrels.

Of

Of the Vital, Natural, and Animal Functions.

HAVING given a fhort defcription of the greateft part of the Solids and Fluids in the human body; I fhall now proceed to fay fomething further concerning their action and re-action on each other, or the vital, natural, and animal functions. Thefe I fhall defcribe in their order. And,

I. *Of the* VITAL FUNCTIONS.

THESE confift of the circulation of the blood, the action of the brain, and the refpiration.

On the action and re-action of the folids and fluids, the vital functions depend; for, the circulation of the blood from the heart, through the arteries, to the extremities of the body, and its return to the fame again by the veins, produces a motion which is caufed chiefly by the dilation and contraction of this organ; and whenever this motion totally ceafes, life is come to an end.

The action of the brain feparates a very fubtile fluid from the blood, called Animal Spirits, which are conveyed by the nerves into all parts of the body. They pafs in an inftant, at the command of the will, from the brain to the extremities of the body, and back again with the fame velocity. The brain is the refervoir of this fluid, by which the foul has a perception of objects, and performs all the bodily actions.

Refpiration

Refpiration is compofed of two motions, called, Infpiration, and Expiration: by the former, the air is received into the lungs; and by the latter, it is returned back again. The air is heated by entering the breaft; and if the weather is cold, it will be condenfed, and appear in the form of a vapour, as it returns into the furrounding atmofphere.

Refpiration is the caufe of fpeaking, laughing, fighing, coughing, fneezing, yawning, fucking, &c.

II. *Of the* NATURAL FUNCTIONS.

THE Natural Functions are, manducation, deglutition, digeftion, nutrition, growth, generation, fecretion, and evacuation.

Manducation, is the chewing of our food.

Deglutition, is the fwallowing of the fame.

Digeftion, is a change of the aliment into chyle, by its mixing with the bile and the pancreatic juice, and the action of the inteftines.

Nutrition, is the repairing of the continual lofs which the different parts of the body fuftain; for life is deftructive of itfelf, as its very offices caufe a conftant wafte. The motion of the parts of the human frame, the friction of thefe parts upon one another, and efpecially the action of the air, would deftroy the body entirely, if the lofs was not repaired by materials of the fame kind of thofe carried off by evacuations.

Growth, is an increafe of the body by the nutritious juices.

Generation,

Generation, is the production of any thing in a natural way, which was not in being before.

Secretion, called Excretion, is the feparation of fome fluid mixed with the blood, by means of the glands ; or, in other words, it may be called the feparation of one fluid from another.

Evacuation, is produced by the periftaltic motion of the bowels, emetics, cathartics, diuretics, diaphoretics, &c.

III. *Of the* ANIMAL FUNCTIONS.

THE Animal Functions are the mufcular motions and voluntary actions of the body : they conftitute the fenfes of feeling, tafting, fmelling, feeing, hearing, perceiving, reafoning, imagining, remembering, judging, with all the affections of the mind.

The mufcles are the organs of the voluntary motions : they act chiefly by contracting or fhortening the flefhy fibres.   This contraction, by drawing the tendons or tails of the mufcles, to which the moveable bones are connected, moves the folid parts ; and by leffening the cavities of certain hollow mufcles, fuch as the heart, inteftines, and other veffels, it caufes the motion of the fluids.

The inftruments of the involuntary motions, are the nervous and mufculous or fiefhy tunics, compofed of fibres : they confift of all kinds of veffels, through which the fluids circulate.

The involuntary motions are thofe which are produced without the confent of the mind ; fuch

as,

as, the beating of the heart, pulsation of the arteries, convulsions, &c.

Feeling is produced by the application of bodies to the nervous *papillulæ* of the skin; and from hence proceed the sensation of heat, cold, moisture, dryness, softness, hardness, roughness, tickling, pain, &c.

Tasting proceeds from the touching of things to the *papillulæ* of our tongues: hence we know whether a thing is bitter, sweet, salt, or sour, &c.

Smelling arises from the entrance of exhalations into our nostrils, and their striking a nervous membrane which covers the internal parts of the nose: hence we distinguish one thing from another by the smell.

Seeing is performed by the expanded membrane of the optic nerve, called the *retina*. The rays of light which proceed from all points of external objects, pass through the transparent part of the eye; and after having undergone various refractions in the *aqueous*, *vitrous* and *crystalline humours*, they fall upon the *retina*, which is the immediate organ of sight, and forms the image of the object.

Hearing proceeds from the different agitations of the air caused by sounding bodies. These agitations pass through the external part of the ear to the *tympanum* or drum, to the air contained in the turnings and windings of this organ, 'till it is communicated to the interior membrane of the auditory nerve.

Perceiving is a clear and distinct apprehension of objects: it is produced by the extension of the nervous membranes.

4

Reasoning

Reafoning is an arguing upon a fubject, in a juft, right, and rational manner: this is produced by a perfect underftanding arifing from the organs of the fenfes being in good repair.

Imagining is a faculty by which we picture bodily fubftances in our minds, as though we actually faw them with our eyes; being conceit, fancy, thought, &c. It may be fometimes true, and fometimes falfe.

Remembering is a calling to mind, or having in one's memory, fomething paft, prefent, or to come.

Judging is the trying of caufes, the making up of a judgment, and the determination of things in one's mind.

As to the *affections* of the mind, they have already been mentioned. Vid. p. 212.

Having thus defcribed the vital, natural, and animal functions, I will juft obferve, that Anatomifts do not agree in fome things, and therefore frequently contradict one another, owing no doubt to new difcoveries that have been made in thefe latter days. I have endeavoured to calculate the preceding account of the Solids and Fluids according to the lateft difcoveries; and hope that what I have written will prove profitable to thofe who may be inclined to obtain a general idea of the conftruction of the human frame, which, by the the *Divine Artificer*, is fearfully and wonderfully made!

CHAP.

C H A P.　XLVI.

Of AGRICULTURE—*Thoughts on Vegetation, and of the Rise of Sap in Trees, Plants, and Herbs —The Farmer and Gardener's Calendar.*

AGRICULTURE is the Art of Hufbandry, and confifts in the improving of lands in the beft manner, in order to make them produce large crops of grain, hay, &c.

GARDENING confifts in the dreffing of ground, and in the raifing of a variety of plants and flowers, &c.

The Art of Gardening, according to the Scriptures, is almoft as old as the creation; for the LORD GOD, having planted a garden eaftward of Eden, did put Adam into it, to drefs and keep it. *Vid.* Gen. ii. 8. 15. But, according to Chronology, this Art was invented by Queen Elizabeth, who reigned in England about the year 1559. —It alfo appears by the Scriptures, that Agriculture is nearly as old as Gardening; for Cain was a tiller of the ground, *Vid.* Gen. iv. 2. But Chronology tells us, that it was invented by Triptolemy, about 1600 years before Chrift.

Thefe excellent Arts are very beneficial to mankind, as a great part of our food and raiment is derived from them; and the King himfelf is ferved by the field. Were the farms and gardens to lie uncultivated, a great part of the people would perifh with famine. Hence nothing can be of

greater

greater importance as to our temporal felicity, than the cultivation and improvement of thefe ufeful Arts.

I fhall treat, in the *firft* place, of Vegetation; and *fecondly*, give fome important directions concerning the management of farms and gardens in the middle governments in North-America; which may be of great fervice in other States, providing a proper allowance fhall be made for the difference of climates. Hence, in thofe which are colder than the middle governments, directions for March, April, May, &c. muft be obferved later in the feafon, but earlier in thofe which are hotter.

I. *Of* VEGETATION.

VEGETABLES proceed from feeds of the fame fpecies; though fome have been otherwife minded, becaufe they have fuppofed that fome plants have no feed. It is true, indeed, that fome are male, and others female; as, *filix mas*, male fern; *filix fœmina*, female fern, &c. The female produces fruit and feeds, but not the male. Some plants bear flowers, which never bear any fruit; and others bear fruit, without flowers.

Plants are diftributed into 28 claffes, by Ray; as,

1. Fungufes, which feem to have neither flowers nor feed.
2. Submarine plants; as, fponges, &c.
3. Moffes.
4. Capillary herbs—Thefe have no main ftock or ftem, but their leaves arife immediately from their roots; as, harts tongue, &c.

5. Herbs

5. Herbs with an imperfect ftaminous flower; as, jointed glafs-wort, marfh-famphire, &c.

6. Herbs with a compound flower, full of a milky fubftance; fuch as, the different kinds of wild lettuce, &c.

7. Herbs not milky, with compound flowers, and a downy feed; as, colts-foot, &c.

8. Herbs with a compound difcoride flower, with feeds not downy; as, corn-marigold, common ox-eye, &c.

9. Herbs with a flower compounded of fiftular *flofculi*, or capitated herbs; as, *carduus*, different thiftles, baftard faffron, &c.

10. Herbs with a fimple perfect flower, with naked folitary feeds, or fingle feeds in fingle flowers; as, fmall and wild valerian, corn fallad, &c.

11. Umbelliferous herbs, whofe flowers grow on the top of their ftalks; after which, grows two naked feeds, which are joined together in each flower; as, cow parfnips, &c.

12. Stellated herbs, whofe leaves encircle their ftalks by intervals; as, crofs-wort, wild madder, &c.

13. Rough-leaved herbs—Thefe have their leaves fet upon the ftalks in no proper order; as, buglofs, cowflips, great hounds-tongue, &c.

14. *Suffrutices* and verticillated herbs—Thefe have two leaves on the ftalk, placed one againft the other, and every flower produces four feeds; as, the common mother thyme.

15. Polyfpermous herbs, with naked feeds—Thefe have more than four feeds in a flower; fuch as, the leffer celandine, &c.

16. Bacciferous herbs—Thefe are thofe whofe fruit,

fruit, when ripe, are clothed with a thin membrane, containing a foft moift pulp. Thefe fruits are called berries; as, cloud berries, bramble berries, &c.

17. Multifiliquous or corniculated herbs—Each flower of this kind produces two pods, fuch as periwinkles, houfe-leek, &c.

18. Herbs with a fingle dry fruit, and a monopetalous flower; as, common henbane, marfh gentian, &c.

19. Vafculiferous herbs, with a dipetalous and tritaplous flower; as, the enchanter's night-fhade, water-wort, or ftar, headed water chickweed, &c.

20. The fame as the former.

21. Terapetalous, filiquous, and filiculous herbs; as, the great fea ftock gilliflower, &c.

22. Vafculiferous herbs, anomalous, with a tetrapetalous flower; as, the wild poppy, red poppy or corn-rofe, &c.

23. Leguminous herbs, or with a papilionaceous flower—Thefe flowers refemble the expanded wings of a butterfly; fuch as, the different kinds of peafe, &c.

24. Pentapetalous vafculiferous herbs—Thefe have two leaves fet againft each other on the ftalk; as, maiden pinks, common pinks, Deptford pinks, &c.

25. Hexapetalous, and pentapetalous, vafculiferous herbs; as, the fmall hedge hyffop, water lily, &c.

26. Herbs with bulbous roots; as, different kinds of garlics, &c.

27. Culmiferous grafs-leaved herbs, with an imperfect flower; as, fpiked grafs, dog grafs, &c.

28. Grafs-leaved herbs, not culmiferous, with

an

an imperfect or ftaminous flower ; as, the great vernal cyprus grafs, &c.

Trees and Shrubs are alfo differently diftributed into claffes.

Thofe of an apetalous flower at a diftance from the fruit, are,

1. The nuciferous; as, the walnut-tree, &c.

2. The coniferous; the female or yew-leaved fir-tree.

3. The bacciferous; the juniper-tree, &c.

4. The lanigerous; as, the feveral kinds of poplar trees, &c.

5. The foliaceous veffels ; the horn-beam, &c.

Of Trees and Shrubs with the Fruit contiguous to the Petaloid Flower.

THOSE that have the flowers feated upon the top of the fruit, are fuch as pomiferous and bacciferous trees; as, the apple, pear, and crab trees, &c.; the apple-rofe, currants, &c.

Trees whofe flowers adhere to the bottom of the fruit, which is moift when ripe, is called *pruniferous.* Of this kind are the common, black, and wild cherry-trees, and the like.

Trees with the flowers growing at the bottom of the fruit, which is dry when ripe, are the bladder nut-tree, the common elm, wych, hazel, &c.

Having given the preceding fhort defcription of the different genus's of plants, &c. let us obferve,

1. That every vegetable muft fpring from feeds of the fame fpecies, though they may be very fmall.

2. That feeds may be carried to a great diftance from the places where they grew, by the wind,

and

and by the birds and beasts, and thus be planted in an uncultivated wilderness.

3. That some seeds · may lie 40 or 50 years in a dry place, and afterwards spring up, if moisture gets to them.

4. That the vegetable productions derive the greatest part of their weight from the moisture of the earth, and the circumambient air, is evident, because the growth of a willow in 200lb. of earth, gained, in five years, 164lb. 3 oz. and only imbibed two ounces of that element. Hence air, fire and water, must make the other part of the bulk.

5. That when a seed is sown, the parts thereof is in *embryo*. It begins to vegetate by the heat of the sun, and the surrounding moisture; every part swells, the external part unfolds and dilates, till at last sprouts come forth out of their native bed: one or more of these sprouts run downward, and are called roots; and one or more of them grow upward, and produce stalks, or a tree, according to the nature of the seed.

6. That the bark of the roots, being spungy, imbibes and sucks up moisture from the earth, which impregnates the vegetable with those principles on which its life and growth depends. This moisture abounds with oil, alkaline salts, alkaline earth, &c.

7. That this moisture is called sap; which being distributed through the roots, supplies their organical parts with those principles of nutrition which every one requires. Hence they grow larger, and more solid, as their age advances.

8. When the roots are thus formed, with their

organs

organs of vegetation, they draw from the earth, through their veffels, proper vegetable juices, which they communicate to the feed plant, and thereby caufe it to unfold all its blades, and fhoot forth branches, buds, leaves, flowers, and feeds, from the different parts of its ftalk or trunk.

9. The fap afcends the firft year of the growth of the plant, by the veffels of the pith ; after which the pith grows dry, and remains fo.   Afterwards the fap rifes in the wood ; and laftly, in the bark.

10. That the fap afcends, in the fpring, to all the extremities of a tree or plant, and defcends into the roots in the autumn.   Though fome will not allow that the fap hath any circulation at all ; but I am fure they are miftaken, becaufe I have often feen maple-trees tapped, which have yielded a barrel of juice ; and how could the juice run out if it had no circulation?

11. Some have fuppofed, that the fap rifes every month in the year ; and I have thought, that the moon may have fome influence on the vegetable fluids, at the time of the fpring tides, as well as upon the waters of the fea, and the atmofphere. But, in cold countries, where the trees are froze hard in the winter, it is not probable, that whilft they are in that condition, the fap can have much circulation when the fpring-tides happen.

12. The fap in fome vegetables has a flow cir-culation, which generates and makes it appear like milk, and is of an oily balfamic quality. But when the fap is ftrained more freely through each organical part, it appears like clear water.   All vegetables perfpire in a greater or leffer degree, in

warm weather; the heat and air within them tends to generate a kind of fermentation, which keeps the fluids in motion. Many vegetables emit an effluvia, called *odours*, which confifts of very fine invifible particles, that fly off in all directions, and being received into our noftrils, produce the fenfation of fmell.

Vegetables cannot exift without air and nourishment, any more than animals. Their greennefs is attributed to a portion of iron imbibed from the earth, &c.

The Farmer and Gardener's CALENDAR.

JANUARY.

1. CUT your wood in the firft quarter of the moon; improve the fledding, and get a plenty of fuel for the following year.

2. See that the vermin do not deftroy your grain and vegetables.

3. Cut timber for building, fencing, &c. in the laft quarter of the moon, to prevent its rotting.

4. Let not your horfes ftand in the cold, when they have been heated with exercife; and keep your cattle warm and clean, and fee that they have water in feafon.

5. Sweep your chimnies often, to prevent your houfes from taking fire.

6. Go to bed in feafon, and rife early: this will fave your candles and fire-wood.

FEBRUARY.

1. PRUNE your orchards and forefts.

2. Sow

2. Sow peafe, if the weather will permit.

3. Get your tools ready to do your fpring work.

4. Look over your garden-feeds, and fee that they are not injured by the moifture, or by the froft.

5. Cut timber for building in the old of the moon, if you did not cut enough laft month.

6. When the fnow is gone, put your fleighs and fleds, with their tackling, into a tight and dry place, to prevent their being damaged by the rain.

7. Take good care of your fheep and lambs.

8. Plow your grafs land, if the froft is out of the ground; the clods will rot fooner than at any other time in the year.

MARCH.

1. REPAIR your fences.

2. Graft or inoculate young trees, and fet them out for an orchard.

3. Sow tobacco, cabbage, parfnip, carrot, onion feeds, &c.

4. Plow your ground for your flax, wheat, rye, oats, and barley.

5. Plant potatoes, Indian corn, peafe, &c. with fuch other vegetables as may be wanted before fall, early in the fpring; thofe for winter may be planted later.

APRIL.

1. SOW your flax-feed, and fpring grain, as early as poffible.

2. Dung and plow your ground, for the planting of Indian corn, potatoes, beans, pumpkins, melons, cucumbers, &c.

3   3. Plant

3. Plant more Indian corn, potatoes, &c.

4. Look well to your garden, fow feeds, and tranfplant roots, &c.

MAY.

1. PLANT corn, potatoes, beans, peafe, lettice, rofemary, lavendar, thyme, with all kinds of feeds that were not planted or fowed in February, March, and April.

2. Weed your garden, hoe your corn, fet out your cabbage and tobacco plants, and water your new-grafted trees, if the weather is dry.

3. Wafh and fhear your fheep, hive your bees when they fwarm, and fee that your vegetables are not deftroyed by the cattle, or by infects.

4. Bleed the cattle you intend to fatten.

JUNE.

1. HOE Indian corn, weed your garden, and kill black flies, worms and fpiders, which devour your plants, by the fumes of tobacco, conducted to thofe vegetables through fome proper pipe, or tube.

2. Plant Indian corn, beans, peafe, melons, and cucumbers, for ufe in the fall.

3. Water your plants in the evening, or early in the morning, if the weather is dry. Watch your bees, left they fwarm, and fly away, for the want of a new hive.

4. Begin to mow grafs, as foon as it is ripe, or in the bloom; rake and cock your hay every evening before the dew falls, fpread it out the next morning, and cart it into your barn as foon as it is fit; but let it not be dried too much. Keep your barn-doors fhut tight, to prevent the ingrefs

of

of the air, for a free admiffion of that element will caufe the hay to generate heat by fermentation, and make it mufty, and fometimes caufe it to take fire; but if it is kept from the air, it will look green, and have an agreeable flavour the next year.

5. Plow the land you defign to fow with winter grain. The grafs fhould be plowed in; and the more there is of it, the more will the ground be enriched.

6. Gather cherries, currants, ftrawberries, goofeberries, &c.

JULY.

1. CONTINUE to get in your hay; let not your grain ftand too long, left it fhould wafte by the blaft, but get it into your barns in feafon.

2. Hill your Indian corn, and fow peafe and turnips for the fall and winter.

3. Turn bulls to ftore heifers; lay up herbs for winter, when they are in their bloom.

4. Deftroy the weeds in your gardens, and water thofe vegetables that have been tranfplanted.

5. Gather and lay up all kinds of feeds when they are ripe.

6. Suffer not yourfelf, or any man or beaft under your care, to drink cold liquor when you or they are hot, left death enfue.

AUGUST.

1. REAP or cradle your oats, get in your barley, and pull your flax.

2. Gather feeds as they ripen, and herbs for diftilling and drying.

3. Water your gardens in the evening, if the feafon is dry.

4. When

4. When the weather is cloudy, re-inoculate thofe trees, where the fcions are dead, that were inoculated in the fpring.

5. Make cyder when your apples are ripe, and mow your fecond crop of grafs as foon as it is fit.

6. Cut trees, bufhes, briars, and thiftles, when the moon is in Leo, or the fign is in the heart; it is faid, that it will kill their roots.

SEPTEMBER.

1. CUT the ftalks of your Indian corn; bind them in bundles when they are dry, and put them into the barn.

2. Make cyder, pickle cucumbers, gather early apples.

3. Shut up your fwine to fatten.

4. Deftroy drone bees.

5. Dig potatoes, and rot your flax, but fee that it is not rotted too much.

6. Sow winter rye and wheat in the new of the moon; gather your hops.

OCTOBER.

1. GATHER and hufk your Indian corn.

2. Prune and plant fruit and foreft-trees.

3. Clean out your ditches, drain off all ftagnant waters, and deftroy vegetable poifons, to prevent the generation of malignant diftempers.

4. Make your winter cyder, and gather winter apples in the old of the moon.

5. Stop the growth of weeds in the garden.

6. Threfh out your garden-feeds, and put them in bags, and where they will not be hurt by the froft.

7. Prune

7. Prune and tranfplant fruit trees.   The fetting out of young orchards is too much neglected where people fettle upon new lands.   It has been faid, that a young orchard will produce apples enough in feven years, if it is well pruned, for a family, both for cyder and other ufes.

8. Gather chefnuts, walnuts, hazel-nuts, &c.

NOVEMBER.

1. BLEED your horfes.

2. Houfe your cattle, as the cold weather ap-proaches.

3. Move your bees under a fhelter, or into a warm place.

4. Continue to plant timber and fruit-trees.

5. Take up your beets, carrots, parfnips, turnips, cabbages, &c.

6. Secure your cellars againft the froft, to pre-vent your potatoes, &c. from being deftroyed by freezing.

DECEMBER.

1. TAKE good care of your cattle.

2. Threfh out your grain.

3. Break and fwingle your flax.

4. Grind your tools, and keep them in good order for ufe.

5. Kill your hogs and fat cattle.

6. Take care of your geefe, turkies, and fowls.

7. Feed your bees, if they have not laid up honey enough to live upon.

8. In long evenings, read Theology, Geography, Hiftory, and the *American Oracle*, if you pleafe.— Farewel! May *peace* and *profperity* crown your *labours!*   Amen.

London, April 25, 1791.

CHAP.

CHAP. XLVII.

*Of the Revolution of the American Colonies; Declaration
of Independence.—Their Alliance with France.—Definitive Treaty of Peace with Great Britain.—Proclamation of Congress.—Treaty with Prussia.—Present Constitution, and Character of Gen. Washington.*

HIS Excellency *Benjamin Franklin, Esq.* L.L. D.
F. R. S. is said to be the prime conductor of the American Revolution; but be that as it
may, it appears that the Foreign Powers were
fearful that in process of time Great Britain would
be too powerful, if her Colonies remained under her
Government, and that from hence they aided and
assisted in dismembering those Governments from
the Mother Country.

I shall not attempt to give a long history of the
war; but only observe, that on the 4th of July,
1776; thirteen colonies, viz. New Hampshire, the
Massachusetts, Rhode-Island, Connecticut, New
York, New Jersey, Pennsylvania, Delaware, Maryland, Virginia, North Carolina, South Carolina,
and Georgia, were declared independent of the
English Crown, by a Congress of Delegates, con-

E e   vened

vened at Philadelphia, who had been fent there by the Legiflative Affemblies in the different Provinces. A terrible war enfued, not only between Great Britain and the Revolted Colonies; but between England, France, Spain, and Holland. It has been faid, that the Britifh loft upwards of 100,000 men, and that the National Debt was augmented more than 100 millions of pounds fterling, by the conteft; flaughter and defolation overfpread the land, in many parts of America; great numbers fell by the fword; many died of camp difeafes, and many towns and villages were laid wafte. How many of the Americans were loft by this war is unknown to me, but a clergyman, who was a travelling preacher, in the Southern Governments, whilft the war continued, and not a Loyalift, informed me, that the inhabitants of South Carolina were not fo numerous by 100,000 when the war ended, as they were when it began; but it is thought, that the greateft part of them died with ficknefs. A Britifh Major told me, that more than 50 died in a day, take one day with another, with illnefs, for a long time, at a place where he was ftationed in that Government. This war involved the Americans in debt, to the amount of 65 millions of dollars, according to a late publication which I have feen, as was before obferved. Gen. Wafhington was Commander in Chief of the American armies during the war, and conducted his military operations with fuch great fkill, that at laft a peace was eftablifhed, whereby the Revolted

Colonies

Colonies were not only declared independent by some Foreign Powers, but by Great Britain.

For the Benefit of my Readers, I shall conclude this chapter, by adding,

1.   The Declaration of the American Independence.

2.   The Alliance of the States with France.

3. Their Definitive Treaty of Peace with Great Britain.

4.   A Proclamation of Congress.

5.   Their Treaty with Prussia.

6.   Their present Constitution, and

7.   The character of General Washington.

1. IN CONGRESS, *July* 4, 1776.

A DECLARATION *by the Representatives of the United States of America, in General Congress assembled.*

WHEN, in the course of human events, it becomes necessary for a people to dissolve the political basis which have connected them with another, and to assume among the powers of the earth the separate and equal station, to which the laws of nature, and of Nature's God entitle them, a decent respect to the opinions of mankind requires that they should declare the causes which impel them to the separation.

We hold these truths to be self-evident—that all men are created equal ; that they are endowed by

their

their Creator with certain unalienable rights; that among these are life, liberty, and the pursuit of happiness. That to secure those rights governments are instituted among men, deriving their just powers from the consent of the governed; and whenever any form of government becomes destructive of these ends, it is the right of the people to alter and abolish it, and to institute a new government, laying its foundation on such principles, and organizing its powers in such form as to them shall seem most likely to effect their safety and happiness.—Prudence, indeed, will dictate that governments long established, should not be changed for light and transient causes, and accordingly all experience hath shewn, that mankind are more disposed to suffer, while evils are sufferable, than to right themselves, by abolishing the forms to which they are accustomed; but, when a long train of abuses and usurpations, pursuing invariably the same object, evinces the design to reduce them under absolute despotism, it is their right, it is their duty to throw off such government, and to provide new guards for their future security. Such has been the patient sufferance of these Colonies, and such is now the necessity which constrains them to alter their former systems of government. The history of the present ——— of ——— is a history of repeated injuries and usurpations, all having in direct object the establishment of an absolute tyranny over these states. To prove this, let facts be submitted to a candid world.

He

He has refuſed his aſſent to laws the moſt wholeſome and neceſſary for the public good.

He has forbidden his governors to paſs laws of immediate and preſſing importance, unleſs ſuſpended in their operation till his aſſent ſhould be obtained; and when ſo ſuſpended, he has utterly neglected to attend to them.

He has refuſed to paſs other laws for the accommodation of large diſtricts of people, unleſs thoſe people would relinquiſh the right of repreſentation in the legiſlature, a right ineſtimable to them, and formidable to Tyrants only.

He has called together legiſlative bodies at places unuſual, unconformable and diſtant from the depoſitory of the public records, for the ſole purpoſe of fatiguing them into compliance with his meaſures.

He has diſſolved repreſentative houſes repeatedly, for oppoſing, with manly firmneſs, his invaſions on the rights of the people.

He has refuſed a long time after ſuch diſſolution to cauſe others to be erected, whereby the legiſlative powers, incapable of annihilation, have returned to the people at large for their exerciſe, the ſtate remaining, in the mean time, expoſed to all the dangers of invaſion from without, and convulſions within.

He has endeavoured to prevent the population of theſe ſtates; for that purpoſe obſtructing the laws for naturalization of foreigners, refuſing to paſs others to encourage their migration hither,

and

and raifing the conditions of new appropriated lands.

He has obftructed the adminiftration of juftice, by refufing his affent to laws for eftablifhing judiciary powers.

He has made judges dependent on his will alone for the tenure of their offices, and the amount and payment of their falaries.

He has erected a multitude of new offices, and fent hither fwarms of officers to harrafs our people, and eat out their fubfiftence.

He has kept amongft us, in times of peace, ftanding armies, without the confent of our legiflature.

He has affected to render the military independent of, and fuperior to the civil power.

He has combined with others to fubject us to a jurifdiction foreign to our conftitution, and unacknowledged by our laws, giving his affent to their pretended acts of legiflation.

For quartering large bodies of armed troops amongft us.

For protecting them, by a mock trial, from punifhment for any murders which they fhould commit on the inhabitants of thefe ftates.

For cutting off our trade with all parts of the world.

For impofing taxes on us without our confent.

For depriving us, in many cafes, of the benefit of trial by jury.

For tranfporting us beyond feas to be tried for pretended offences.

For abolifhing the free fyftem of Englifh laws in a neighbouring Province, eftablifhing therein an arbitray government, and enlarging its boundaries, fo as to render it at once an example and a fit inftrument for introducing the fame abfolute rule into thefe Colonies.

For taking away our charters, abolifhing our moft valuable laws, and altering fundamentally the forms of our governments.

For fufpending our own legiflatures, and declaring themfelves invefted with power to legiflate for us in all cafes whatfoever.

He has abdicated government here, by declaring us out of his protection, and waging war againft us.

He has plundered our feas, ravaged our coafts, burnt our towns, and deftroyed the lives of our people.

He is at this time tranfporting large armies of foreign mercenaries to complete the works of death, defolation, and tyranny, already begun with circumftances of cruelty and perfidy fcarcely paralleled in the moft barbarous ages, and totally unworthy the head of a civilized nation.

He has conftrained our fellow citizens, taken captive on the high feas, to bear arms againft their country, to become executioners of their friends and brethren, or to fall themfelves by their hands.

He has excited domeftic infurrections amongft us, and has endeavoured to bring on the inhabitants of our frontiers, the mercilefs Indian favages,

E e 4   whofe

whofe known rule of warfare is an undiftinguifhed deftruction of all ages, fexes, and conditions.

In every ftage of thefe oppreffions we have petititioned for redrefs in the moft humble terms; our repeated petitions have been anfwered only by repeated injury. A prince whofe character is thus marked by every act which may define a tyrant, is unfit to be the ruler of a free people.

Nor have we been wanting in attention to our Britifh brethren; we have warned them, from time to time, of attempts by their legiflature to extend an unwarrantable jurifdiction over us; we have reminded them of the circumftances of our emigration and fettlement here; we have appealed to their native juftice and magnanimity, and we have conjured them by the ties of our common kindred, to difavow thefe ufurpations, which would inevitably interrupt our connections and correfpondence. They too have been deaf to the voice of juftice and confanguinity. We muft therefore acquiefce in the neceffity which denounces our feparation, and hold them as we hold the reft of mankind, enemies in war, in peace friends.

We, therefore, the reprefentatives of the United States of America, in General Congrefs affembled, appealing to the Supreme Juftice of the world for the rectitude of our intentions, do, in the name of, and by the authority of the good people of thefe Colonies, folemnly publifh, and declare, that thefe united Colonies are, and of right, ought to be, FREE and INDEPENDENT STATES, and that

they

they are abfolved from all allegiance to the Britifh Crown, and that all political connection between them and the ftate of Great Britain is, and ought to be, totally diffolved; and that as free and independent States, they have full power to levy war, conclude peace, contract alliances, eftablifh commerce, and to do all other acts and things, which Independent States may of right do. And for the fupport of this declaration, with a firm reliance on the protection of Divine Providence, we mutually pledge to each other our lives, our fortunes, and our facred honour.

(Signed by order, and in behalf of the Congrefs.)

JOHN HANCOCK, Prefident.

(Atteft) CHARLES THOMSON, Sec.

II. ALLIANCE WITH FRANCE.

A Treaty of Amity and Commerce between his MOST CHRISTIAN MAJESTY *and the* UNITED STATES *of* AMERICA.

WHEREAS his Moft Chriftian Majefty and the United States of North America, namely, New Hampfhire,

Hampſhire, &c. &c. having this day concluded a Treaty of Amity and Commerce, for the mutual advantage of their ſubjects, think it neceſſary to take under their moſt ſerious conſideration the means of eſtabliſhing thoſe engagements upon a ſolid baſis, and rendering them ſubſervient to the ſecurity and peace of both parties; eſpecially in caſe Great Britain, in deteſtation of ſuch good correſpondence, which is the object of the ſaid treaty, ſhould break with France, either by direct hoſtilities, or by annoying its commerce and navigation, contrary to the rights of the nations, and to the good underſtanding ſubſiſting between the two Crowns.

And whereas his Majeſty and the United States have come to a reſolution, in the aforeſaid caſe, to unite their Councils, and direct their joint efforts againſt the undertakings of the common enemy; the reſpective Plenipotentiaries, authoriſed to agree upon ſuch conditions moſt likely to anſwer their intentions, after the moſt mature deliberation ſtipulated and agreed upon the following articles:

Art. 1. In caſe war ſhould break out between France and Great Britain, during the preſent conteſt between the latter and the United States, his Moſt Chriſtian Majeſty and the ſaid States will join in one cauſe, and mutually aſſiſt each other with their reſpective good offices, councils, and forces, as circumſtances may require, and as becomes good and faithful Allies.

Art. 2.

Art. 2.   The direct and effential meaning of the prefent defenfive alliance is effectually to maintain the freedom, fovereignty, abfolute and unbounded independence of the United States both in matters of government and commerce.

Art. 3.   The contracting Powers fhall each on its part, and in fuch manner as may be deemed beft, direct all their efforts againft the common enemy, to the purpofe of fulfilling the prefent engagement.

Art. 4.   The contracting Powers covenant, that, in cafe either of them fhall undertake any thing in which the concurrence of the other fhall be deemed requifite, the latter fhall directly, and *bona fide*, join the former, in order to act in concert, as far as circumftances and fituations will permit; and, in fuch cafe, they fhall by private convention regulate the number and kind of forces to be found, as well as the time and manner of acting, and the advantages which may be granted as a compenfation.

Art. 5.   If the United States fhall think it convenient to attempt the reduction of the remaining Britannic poffeffions in the Northern parts of America, or in the Iflands of Bermuda; fuch countries in cafe of fuccefs, fhall be confederate with, or dependent on, the faid States.

Art. 6.   His Moft Chriftian Majefty, for ever, gives up all thoughts of poffeffing himfelf of the Iflands of Bermuda, or any part of the Continent in North-America, which, before the Treaty of

Paris

Paris, 1763, or by virtue thereof, have been acknowledged as belonging to the Crown of Great
Britain, or the United States, heretofore denominated Britiſh Colonies, or are at preſent, or hitherto have been, under the power of the King and
Crown of Great Britain.

Art. 7. In caſe his Moſt Chriſtian Majeſty
ſhould attack any of the iſlands ſituate in or near
the Gulf of Mexico, which are at preſent within
the dominions of Great Britain, and ſhould take
the ſame, they ſhall belong to the Crown of
France.

Art. 8. Neither of the contracting Powers
ſhall be at liberty to conclude peace or truce with
Great Britain, without the previous and formal
conſent of the other. And they do mutually engage not to lay down their arms before the independence of the United States ſhall have been
formally or implicitly ſecured by the treaty or
treaties, which ſhall terminate the war.

Art. 9. The contracting parties do declare,
that, being reſolved, each on its part, to fulfil the
articles and conditions of the preſent Treaty of
Alliance, according to their power and circumſtances, there will be no manner of compenſation
reſerved, neither on one part nor the other, whatever may be the iſſue of the war.

Art. 10. His Moſt Chriſtian Majeſty and the
United States do agree to invite or admit any
other Power as may have experienced any wrongs
from England to join with them, and accede to
the

the prefent alliance, under fuch conditions as may freely be agreed upon and regulated between all parties.

Art. 11. The two contracting parties guaranty each other, from this inftant, and for ever, againft all other Powers, viz. The United States to his Moft Chriftian Majefty all the American poffeffions now belonging to the Court of France, as well as thofe that may be made over to it by a future treaty of peace; and his Moft Chriftian Majefty guaranties on his part to the United States their freedom, fovereignty, and abfolute independence both in matters of goverment and commerce, as alfo their poffeffions and the increafe or conquefts, as may arife from their confederation during the war, over any of the domains now, or heretofore the property of Great Britain, in North-America, agreeable to the foregoing 5th and 6th Articles; fo that the poffeffion fhall be fixed and fecured to the faid States at the conclufion of their prefent war with England.

Art. 12. That the meaning of the foregoing Articles may be more precifely underftood, the contracting parties do declare, that, in cafe of a rupture between France and England, the guaranty aforefaid fhall be in full force, from the inftant the war fhall be declared; if the cafe fhould be otherwife, the mutual obligations of the faid guaranty fhall only take place from the time that a ceffation of hoftilities between England and the faid States fhall have afcertained the latter.

Art. 13.

Art. 13. The prefent Treaty fhall be ratified on both fides, and the ratification interchanged within the fpace of fix months, or fooner if poffible.

In witnefs whereof the refpective Plenipotentiaries, viz. on the part of his Moft Chriftian Majefty, the Sieur Conrad Alexandre Gerard, &c. &c. On the part of the States, the Sieur Benjamin Franklin, Deputy to Congrefs from Pennfylvania, and Prefident of the Convention to the faid States, Silas Deane, &c. and Arthur Lee, LL. D. who have hereunto fet their hands and feals; declaring meanwhile, that the prefent Treaty was compofed and concluded in the French language.

Done at Paris, Feb. 6, 1778.

(L. S.) C. A. GERARD.

(L. S.) BENJ. FRANKLIN.

(L. S.) SiLAS DEANE.

(L. S.) ARTHUR LEE.

The

III. *The* DEFINITIVE TREATY *between* GREAT-BRITAIN *and the* UNITED STATES OF AMERICA. *Signed at Paris, the 3d Day of September,* 1783.

In the Name of the Moſt Holy and Undivided Trinity.

IT having pleaſed the Divine Providence to diſpoſe the hearts of the Moſt Serene and Moſt Potent Prince George the Third, by the Grace of God King of Great Britain, France, and Ireland, Defender of the Faith, Duke of Brunſwick and Lunenburgh, Arch-Treaſurer and Prince Elector of the Holy Roman Empire, &c. and of the United States of America, to forget all paſt miſunderſtandings and differences that have unhappily interrupted the good correſpondence and friendſhip which they mutually wiſh to reſtore, and to eſtabliſh ſuch a beneficial and ſatisfactory intercourſe between the two countries, upon the ground of reciprocal advantages and mutual convenience, as may promote and ſecure to both perpetual peace and harmony; and having for this deſirable end already laid the foundation of peace and reconciliation, by the Proviſional Articles ſigned at Paris on the 30th of November, 1782, by the Commiſſioners empowered on each part, which Articles were agreed to be inſerted

in,

in, and to conftitute the Treaty of Peace propofed to be concluded between the Crown of
Great Britain and the faid United States, but
which Treaty was not to be concluded until terms
of Peace fhould be agreed upon between Great
Britain and France, and his Britannic Majefty
fhould be ready to conclude fuch Treaty accordingly; and the Treaty between Great Britain and
France, having fince been concluded, his Britannic Majefty and the United States of America,
in order to carry into full effect the Provifional
Articles above-mentioned, according to the tenor
thereof, have conftituted and appointed, that is
to fay, his Britannic Majefty on his part, David
Hartley, Efq. Member of the Parliament of Great
Britain, and the faid United States on their part,
John Adams, Efq. late a Commiffioner of the
United States of America at the Court of Ver-
failles, late Delegate in Congrefs from the State
of Maffachufetts, and Chief Juftice of the faid
State, and Minifter Plenipotentiary of the faid
United States to their High Mightineffes the
States-General of the United Netherlands; Ben-
jamin Franklin, Efq. late Delegate in Congrefs
from the State of Pennfylvania, Prefident of the
Convention of the faid State, and Minifter Plenipotentiary from the United States of America at
the Court of Verfailles; and John Jay, Efq. late
Prefident of Congrefs, and Chief Juftice of the
State of New-York, and Minifter Plenipotentiary
from the faid United States at the Court of Madrid,

drid, to be the Plenipotentiaries for the con-
cluding and figning the prefent Definitive Treaty;
who, after having reciprocally communicated
their refpective full powers, have agreed upon and
confirmed the following Articles:

ART. I. His Britannic Majefty acknowledges
the faid United States, viz. New-Hampfhire,
Maffachufetts-Bay, Rhode-Ifland and Providence
Plantations, Connecticut, New-York, New-Jerfey, Pennfylvania, Delaware, Maryland, Virginia,
North-Carolina, South-Carolina, and Georgia, to
be free, fovereign, and independent States; that
he treats with them as fuch, and for himfelf, his
heirs, and fucceffors, relinquifhes all claims to the
government, propriety, and territorial rights of
the fame, and every part thereof.

ART. II. And that all difputes which might
arife in future on the fubject of the boundaries of the faid United States may be prevented,
it is hereby agreed and declared, that the following
are and fhall be their boundaries, viz. From the
north-weft angle of Nova-Scotia, viz. That angle
which is formed by a line drawn due north from
the fource of St. Croix River to the Highlands,
along the faid Highlands, which divide thofe rivers that empty themfelves into the river St.
Lawrence, from thofe which fall into the Atlantic
Ocean to the North-wefternmoft head of Connec-
ticut-river; thence down along the middle of that
river to the forty-fifth degree of north-latitude;
from thence by a line due weft on faid latitude,

F f until

until it ftrikes the river Irriquois or Caatraquy; thence along the middle of the faid river into Lake Ontario; through the middle of faid lake, until it ftrikes the communication by water between that lake and Lake Erie; thence along the middle of faid communication into Lake Erie, through the middle of faid lake, until it arrives at the water communication between that lake and Lake Huron; thence through the middle of faid lake to the water communication between that lake and Lake Superior; thence through Lake Superior northward of the Ifles Royal and Phelipeaux to the Long Lake; thence through the middle of faid Long Lake and the water communication between it and the Lake of the Woods, to the faid Lake of the Woods; thence through the faid lake to the moft north-weftern point thereof, and from thence on a due weft courfe to the River Miffiffippi; thence by a line to be drawn along the middle of the faid River Miffiffippi; until it fhall interfect the northernmoft part of the thirty-firft degree of north latitude. South, by a line to be drawn due eaft from the determination of the line laft-mentioned in the latitude of thirty-one degrees north of the equator, to the middle of the River Apalachicola or Catahouche; thence along the middle thereof to its junction with the Flint-river; thence ftrait to the head of St. Mary's River; and thence down along the middle of St. Mary's River to the Atlantic Ocean; eaft, by a line to be drawn along the middle of the River

St.

St. Croix from its mouth in the Bay of Fundy to
its fource, and from its fource directly north to
the aforefaid Highlands, which divide the rivers
that fall into the Atlantic Ocean from thofe which
fall into the River St. Lawrence, comprehending
all Iflands within twenty leagues of any part of
the fhores of the United States, and lying between
lines to be drawn due eaft from the points where
the aforefaid boundaries between Nova-Scotia on
the one part, and Eaft-Florida on the other, fhall
refpectively touch the Bay of Fundy and the Atlantic Ocean, excepting fuch Iflands as now are or
heretofore have been within the limits of the.faid
province of Nova Scotia.

ART. III. It is agreed that the people of the
United States fhall continue to enjoy unmolefted
the right to take fifh of every kind on the Grand
Bank, and on all the other Banks of Newfoundland, alfo in the Gulph of St. Lawrence, and all
other places in the fea, where the inhabitants of
both countries ufed at any time heretofore to fifh.
And alfo that the inhabitants of the United States
fhall have liberty to take fifh of every kind on
fuch part of the coaft of Newfoundland as Britifh
fifhermen fhall ufe, (but not to dry or cure the
fame on that Ifland) and alfo on the coafts, bays
and creeks of all of his Britannic Majefty's dominions in America; and that the American fifhermen fhall have liberty to dry and cure fifh in any
of the unfettled bays, harbours and creeks of
Nova-Scotia, Magdalen Iflands and Labrador, fo

F f 2   long

long as the fame fhall remain unfettled; but fo
foon as the fame or either of them fhall be fettled,
it fhall not be lawful for the faid fifhermen to dry
or cure fifh at fuch fettlement, without a previous
agreement for that purpofe with the inhabitants,
proprietors or poffeffors of the ground.

ART. IV. It is agreed that the creditors on
either fide fhall meet with no lawful impediment
to the recovery of the full value, in fterling money, of all *bona fide* debts heretofore contracted.

ART. V. It is agreed that Congrefs fhall earneftly
recommend to the Legiflatures of the refpective
States, to provide for the reftitution of all eftates,
rights, and properties, which have been confifcated, belonging to real Britifh fubjects; and alfo
of the eftates, rights, and properties of perfons refident in diftricts in the poffeffion of his Majefty's
arms, and who have not borne arms againft the
faid United States; and that perfons of any other
defcription fhall have free liberty to go to any
part or parts of any of the Thirteen United States,
and therein to remain twelve months unmolefted
in their endeavours to obtain the reftitution of
fuch of their eftates, rights, and properties, as
may have been confifcated; and that Congrefs
fhall alfo earneftly recommend to the feveral States
a re-confideration and revifion of all Acts or Laws
regarding the premifes, fo as to render the faid
Laws or Acts perfectly confiftent not only with
juftice and equity, but with that fpirit of concilia-
tion, which, on the return of the bleffings of

peace,

peace, fhould univerfally prevail; and that Con¦grefs fhall alfo earneftly recommend to the feveral States, that the eftates, rights, and properties of fuch laft-mentioned perfons fhall be reftored to them, they refunding to any perfons who may be now in poffeffion the *bona fide* price (where any has been given) which fuch perfons may have paid on purchafing any of the faid lands, rights, or properties fince the confifcation.

And it is agreed, that all perfons who have any intereft in confifcated lands, either by debts, marriage fettlements, or otherwife, fhall meet with no lawful impediment in the profecution of their juft rights.

ART. VI. That there fhall be no future confif-cations made, nor any profecutions commenced againft any perfon ór perfons for, or by reafon of the part which he or they may have taken in the prefent war; and that no perfon fhall, on that ac-count, fuffer any future lofs or damage, either in his perfon, liberty, or property; and that thofe who may be in confinement on fuch charges, at the time of the ratification of the Treaty in America, fhall be immediately fet at liberty, and the profe-cutions fo commenced be difcontinued.

ART. VII. There fhall be a firm and perpetual peace between his Britannic Majefty and the faid States, and between the fubjects of the one, and the citizens of the other; wherefore all hoftilities both by fea and land fhall, from henceforth, ceafe; all prifoners on both fides fhall be fet at

F f 3   liberty,

liberty, and his Britannic Majesty shall, with all convenient speed, and without causing any destruction, or carrying away any negroes, or other property of the American inhabitants, withdraw all his armies, garrisons, and fleets from the said United States, and from every post, place, and harbour within the same, leaving in all fortifications the American artillery that may be therein; and shall also order and cause all archives, records, deeds, and papers belonging to any of the said States, or their citizens, which in the course of the war may have fallen into the hands of his officers, to be forthwith restored, and delivered to the proper States and persons to whom they belong.

ART. VIII. The navigation of the River Mississippi, from its source to the ocean, shall for ever remain free and open to the subjects of Great Britain, and the citizens of the United States.

ART. IX. In case it should so happen that any place or territory belonging to Great Britain, or to the United States, should have been conquered by the arms of either from the other, before the arrival of the said Provisional Articles in America, it is agreed that the same shall be restored without difficulty, and without requiring any compensation.

ART. X. The solemn ratifications of the present Treaty, expedited in good and due form, shall be exchanged between the the Contracting Parties in the space of six months, or sooner, if possible,

poffible, to be computed from the day of the fig-
nature of the prefent Treaty. In witnefs whereof
we the underfigned, their Minifters Plenipotentiary, have in their name, and in virtue of our full
powers, figned with our hands the prefent Definitive Treaty, and caufed the Seals of our Arms to
be affixed thereto.

Done at Paris, this 3d day of September, in
the year of our Lord one thoufand feven hundred
and eighty-three.

    (L. S.) JOHN ADAMS.
(L. S.) DAVID HARTLEY.
    (L. S.) B. FRANKLIN.
    (L. S.) JOHN JAY.

GEORGE R.

George the Third, by the Grace of God, King
of Great Britain, France and Ireland, Defender of
the Faith, Duke of Brunfwick and Lunenburgh,
Arch-Treafurer and Prince Elector of the Holy
Roman Empire, &c. To all to whom thefe Prefents fhall come, Greeting:

Whereas, for the perfecting and eftablifhing the
peace, friendfhip, and good underftanding, fo
happily commenced by the Provifional Articles
figned at Paris the thirtieth day of November laft,
by the Commiffioners of us and our good friends
the United States of America, viz. New-Hampfhire, Maffachufetts-Bay, Rhode-Ifland, Connecticut, New-York, New-Jerfey, Pennfylvania, the
three Lower Counties on Delaware, Maryland,

Virginia, North-Carolina, South-Carolina and Georgia, in North-America, and for opening, promoting and rendering perpetual the mutual intercourse of trade and commerce between our kingdoms and the dominions of the said United States, we have thought proper to invest some fit person with full powers on our part to meet and confer with the Ministers of the said United States, now residing at Paris, duly authorized for the accomplishing of such laudable and salutary purposes. Now know ye that we, reposing special trust and confidence in the wisdom, loyalty, diligence, and circumspection of our trusty and well-beloved David Hartley, Esq. (on whom we have therefore conferred the rank of our Minister Plenipotentiary) have nominated, constituted, and appointed, and by these presents do nominate, constitute and appoint him our true, certain, and undoubted Commissioner, Procurator, and Plenipotentiary, giving and granting to him all and all manner of faculty, power, and authority, together with general as well as special order (so as the general do not derogate from the special, nor on the contrary) for us and in our name, to meet, confer, treat and conclude with the Minister or Ministers furnished with sufficient powers on the part of our said good friends the United States of America, of and concerning all such matters and things as may be requisite and necessary for accomplishing and completing the several ends and purposes herein before-mentioned ; and also for

us

us and in our name to fign fuch Treaty or Treaties, Convention or Conventions, or other inftruments whatfoever, as may be agreed upon in the premifes; and mutually to deliver and receive the fame in exchange, and to do and perform all fuch other acts, matters, and things as may be any ways proper and conducive to the purpofes above-mentioned, in as full and ample form and manner, and with the like validity and effect, as we ourfelf, if we were prefent, could do and perform the fame ; engaging and promifing on our Royal word, that we will accept, ratify, and confirm, in the moft effectual manner, all fuch acts, matters, and things, as fhall be fo tranfacted and concluded by our aforefaid Commiffioner, Procurator, and Plenipotentiary, and that we will never fuffer any perfon to violate the fame in the whole or in part, or to act contrary thereto. In teftimony and confirmation of all which, we have caufed our Great Seal of Great Britain to be affixed to thefe prefents, figned with our Royal hand.

Given at our Palace at St. James's, the fourteenth day of May, in the year of our Lord one thoufand feven hundred and eighty-three, and in the twenty-third year of our reign.

I David Hartley, the Minifter above-named, certify the foregoing to be a true Copy from my original Commiffion, delivered to the American Minifters this 19th day of May, 1783.

(Signed)   DAVID HARTLEY.

The

The UNITED STATES of AMERICA in CONGRESS affembled,

To all to whom thefe Prefents fhall come, fend Greeting.

WHEREAS thefe United States, from a fin-cere defire of putting an end to the hoftilities be-tween his Moft Chriftian Majefty and thefe United States on the one part, and his Britannic Majefty on the other and of terminating the fame by a peace founded on fuch folid and equitable prin-ciples as reafonably to promife a permanency of the bleffings of tranquillity, did heretofore ap-point the Hon. John Adams, late a Commiffioner of the United States of America at the Court of Verfailles, late Delegate in Congrefs from the State of Maffachufetts, and Chief Juftice of the faid State, their Minifter Plenipotentiary, with full powers general and fpecial to act in that qua-lity, to confer, treat, agree, and conclude with the Ambaffadors or Plenipotentiaries of his Moft Chriftian Majefty, and of his Britannic Majefty, and thofe of any other Princes or States whom it might concern, relating to the re-eftablifhment of peace and friendfhip; and whereas the flames of war have fince that time been extended, and other Nations and States are involved therein: Now know ye, that we ftill continuing earneftly de-firous, as far as depends upon us, to put a ftop to the effufion of blood, and to convince the Powers

of

of Europe, that we wifh for nothing more ardent-
ly than to terminate the war by a fafe and honourable peace, have thought proper to renew the
powers formerly given to the faid John Adams,
and to join four other perfons in commiffion with
him; and having full confidence in the integrity,
prudence, and ability of the Honourable Benjamin Franklin, our Minifter Plenipotentiary at the
Court of Verfailles, and the Honourable John
Jay, late Prefident of Congrefs and Chief-Juftice
of the State of New-York, and our Minifter Plenipotentiary at the Court of Madrid, and the Hon.
Henry Laurens, formerly Prefident of Congrefs,
and commiffionated and fent as our Agent to the
United Provinces of the Low Countries, and the
Hon. Thomas Jefferfon, Governor of the Common-wealth of Virginia, have nominated, conftituted, and appointed, and by thefe prefents do
nominate, conftitute, and appoint the faid Benjamin Franklin, John Jay, Henry Laurens, and
Thomas Jefferfon, in addition to the faid John
Adams, giving and granting to them, the faid
John Adams, Benjamin Franklin, John Jay,
Henry Laurens, and Thomas Jefferfon, or the
majority of them, or of fuch of them as may affemble, or, in cafe of the death, abfence, indifpofition, or other impediment of the others, to any
one of them, full power and authority, general and
fpecial, conjunctly and feparately, and fpecial command to repair to fuch place as may be fixed upon
for opening negociations for peace, and there, for

us

and in our name, to confer, treat, agree, and conclude with our Ambaffadors, Commiffioners Plenipotentiaries of the Princes and States whom it
may concern, vefted with equal powers relating to
the eftablifhment of.Peace; and whatfoever fhall
be agreed and concluded for us and in our name
to fign; and thereupon make a Treaty or Treaties
and to tranfact every thing that may be neceffary
for compleating, fecuring, and ftrengthening the
great work of pacification, in as ample form, and
with the fame effect, as if we were perfonally prefent and acted therein, hereby promifing in good
faith that we will accept, ratify, fulfil, and execute
whatever fhall be agreed, concluded, and figned
by our faid Minifters Plenipotentiary, or a majority of them, or of fuch of them as may affemble,
or in cafe of the death, abfence, indifpofition,
or other impediment of the others, by any one of
them; and that we will never act nor fuffer any
perfon to act contrary to the fame in whole or in
any part. In witnefs whereof we have caufed thefe
prefents to be figned by our Prefident, and fcaled
with his Seal.

Done at Philadelphia, the fifteenth day of June,
in the year of our Lord one thoufand feven hundred and eighty-one, and in the fifth year of our
Independence. By the United States in Congrefs
fembled.

(Signed)   SAM. HUNTINGTON, Prefident.
CHARLES THOMSON, Sec.

We

We certify the foregoing copies of the refpective full powers to be authentic.   Paris, Sept. 3, 1783.

(Signed) GEORGE HAMMOND Secretary to the Britifh Commiffion.

W. T. FRANKLIN, Secretary to the American Commiffion.

RATIFICATION *of* PEACE *by the* AMERICAN CONGRESS.

By the UNITED STATES, in CONGRESS affembled.

A   PROCLAMATION.

WHEREAS definitive articles of peace and friendfhip, between the United States of America and his Britannic Majefty, were concluded and figned at Paris, on the 3d day of September, 1783, by the Plenipotentiaries of the faid United States and of his Britannic Majefty, duly and refpectively authorifed for that purpofe ; which definitive articles are in the words following :

And we the United States in Congrefs affembled, having feen and duly confidered the definitive articles aforefaid, did by a certain act under the feal of the United States, bearing date this 14th

2   day

day of Jan. 1784, approve, ratify and confirm the same, and every part and claufe thereof, engaging and promifing that we would fincerely and faithfully perform and obferve the fame, and never fuffer them to be violated by any one, or tranfgreffed in any manner as far as fhould be in our power; and being fincerely difpofed to carry the faid articles into execution truly, honeftly, and with good faith, according to the intent and meaning thereof, we have thought proper by thefe prefents, to notify the premifes to all good citizens of the United States, hereby requiring and enjoining all bodies of magiftracy, legiflative, executive and judiciary, all perfons bearing office, civil or military, of whatfoever rank, degree, powers, and all others the good citizens of thefe States of every vocation and condition, that the reverencing thofe ftipulations entered into on their behalf, under the authority of the federal bond by which their exiftence as an independent people is bound up together, and is known and acknowledged by the nations of the world, and with that good faith which is every man's fureft guide within their feveral offices, jurifdictions, and vocations, they carry into effect the faid definitive articles, and every claufe and fentiment thereof, fincerely, ftrictly and completely.

Given under the Seal of the United States. Witnefs his Excellency THOMAS MIFFLIN, Prefident, at Annapolis, this 14th day of January, in the year of our Lord one thoufand

1   feven

feven hundred and eighty-four, and of the fovereignty and independence of the United
States of America the eighth.

CHARLES THOMSON, Sec.

A TREATY *of* AMITY *and* COMMERCE *between his*
Majefty the King of PRUSSIA, *and the United*
States of AMERICA.

HIS.Majefty the King of Pruffia, and the United States of America, defiring to fix in a permanent and equitable manner, the rules to be obferved in the intercourfe and commerce they defire to eftablifh between their refpective countries,
have judged, that the faid end cannot be better
obtained than by taking the moft perfect equali-
ty and reciprocity for the bafis of their agreement.

With this view, his Majefty the King of Pruffia has nominated and conftituted, as his Plenipotentiary, the Baron Frederic William de Thulemeyer, Envoy Extraordinary with their High
Mightineffes the States General of the United Netherlands; and the United States have, on their
part, given full powers to John Adams, Efq. now
Minifter Plenipotentiary of the United States with
his Britannic Majefty: Dr. Benjamin Franklin,
and Thomas Jefferfon, refpective Plenipotentiaries

ries, have concluded articles, of which the following is an abftract, fo far as concerns the States of America.

The fubjects of his Majefty the King of Pruffia may frequent all the coafts and countries of the United States of America, and refide and trade there in all forts of produce, manufactures, and merchandize, and fhall pay within the faid United States no other or greater duties, charges, or fees whatfoever, than the moft favoured nations are or fhall be obliged to pay; and they fhall enjoy all the rights, privileges, and exemptions, in navigation and commerce, which the moft favoured nation does or fhall enjoy; fubmitting themfelves to the laws and ufages there eftablifhed.

In like manner, the citizens of the United States of America may frequent all the coafts and countries of his Majefty the King of Pruffia, and refide and trade there in all forts of produce, manufactures, and merchandize, and fhall pay in the dominions of his faid Majefty, no other greater duties, charges, or fees whatfoever, than the moft favoured nation is or fhall be obliged to pay; and they fhall enjoy all the rights, privileges and exemptions, in navigation and commerce, which the moft favoured nation does or fhall enjoy; fubmitting themfelves as aforefaid.

Each party fhall have a right to carry their own produce, manufactures and merchandize, in their own or any other veffels, to any parts of the dominions

minions of the other, where it fhall be lawful for all the fubjects or citizens of that other freely to purchafe them; and thence to take the produce, manufactures and merchandize of the other, which all the faid citizens or fubjects fhall in like manner be free to fell them, paying in both cafes fuch duties, charges, and fees only, as are or fhall be paid by the moft favoured nation.

Each party fhall endeavour to protect and defend all veffels, and other effects, belonging to the citizens or fubjects of the other, which fhall be within the extent of their jurifdiction by fea or land; and fhall ufe all their efforts to recover, and caufe to be reftored to their right owners, their veffels and effects which fhall be taken from them within the extent of their faid jurifdiction.

If one of the contracting parties fhould be engaged in war with other powers, the free intercourfe and commerce of the fubjects or citizens of the party remaining neuter with the belligerent powers, fhall not be interrupted. On the contrary, in that cafe, as in full peace, the veffels of the neutral party may navigate freely to and from the ports, and on the coafts of the belligerent parties, free veffels making free goods, infomuch, that all things fhall be adjudged free which fhall be on board any veffel belonging to the neutral party, although fuch things belong to an enemy of the other; and the fame freedom fhall be extend-

G g   ed

ed to perfons who fhall be on board a free veffel, although they fhould be enemies to the other party, unlefs they be foldiers in actual fervice of fuch enemy.

In the fame cafe of one of the contracting parties being engaged in war with any other power—to prevent all the difficulties and mifunderftandings which ufually arife refpecting the merchandize heretofore called contraband, fuch as arms, ammunition and military ftores of every kind—no fuch articles carried in the veffels, or by the fubjects or citizens of one of the parties to the enemies of the other, fhall be deemed contraband, fo as to induce confifcation or condemnation, and a lofs of property to individuals. But in the cafe fuppofed—of a veffel ftopped for the articles heretofore deemed contraband, if the mafter of the veffel ftopped will deliver out the goods fuppofed to be of contraband nature, he fhall be admitted to do it, and the veffel fhall not in that cafe be carried into any port, nor further detained, but fhall be allowed to proceed on her voyage.

If the contracting parties fhall be engaged in war againft a common enemy, the following points fhall be obferved between them.

1ft, If a veffel of one of the parties, re-taken by a privateer of the other, fhall not have been in poffeffion of the enemy more than 24 hours, fhe fhall be reftored to the firft owner for one third of the value of the veffel and cargo; but if fhe fhall

2   have

have been more than 24 hours in poffeffion of the enemy, fhe fhall belong wholly to the re-captor. 2d, If in the fame cafe the re-capture were by a public veffel of war of the one party, reftitution fhall be made to the owner of one thirtieth part of the veffel and cargo, if fhe fhall not have been in the poffeffion of the enemy more than 24 hours; and one tenth of the faid value where fhe fhall have been longer; which fums fhall be deftributed in gratuities to the re-captors. 3d, The reftitution in the cafes aforefaid fhall be after due proof of property, and furety given for the part to which the re-captors are entitled. 4th, The veffels of war, public and private, of the two parties, fhall be reciprocally admitted with their prizes into the refpective ports of each; but the faid prizes fhall not be difcharged nor fold there, until their legality fhall have been decided according to the laws and regulations of the ftate to which the captors belong, but by the judicators of the place into which the prize fhall have been conducted. 5th, It fhall be free to each party to make fuch regulations as they fhall judge neceffary for the conduct of the refpective veffels of war, public or private, relative to the veffels which they fhall take and carry into the ports of the two parties.

Where the parties fhall have a common enemy, or fhall both be neutral, the veffels of. war of each fhall upon all occafions take under

G g 2 their

their protection the veffels of the other going the fame courfe, and fhall defend fuch veffels as long as they hold the fame courfe, againft all force and violence, in the fame manner as they ought to protect and defend veffels belonging to the party of which they are.

If war fhould arife between the two contracting parties, the merchants of either country, then refiding in the other, fhall be allowed to remain nine months to collect their debts and fettle their affairs, and may depart freely, carrying off all their effects, without moleftation or hinderance.

This treaty fhall be in force during the term of ten years from the exchange of ratifications;

(Signed)

F. G. de THULEMEYER, *à la Haye, le* 10 *Septembre* 1785.

THO. JEFFERSON, *Paris, July* 28, 1785,

B. FRANKLIN, *Paffy, July,* 9, 1785.

JOHN ADAMS, *London, Aug.* 5, 1785.

NOW KNOW YE, That we the faid United States in Congrefs affembled, having confidered and approved do hereby ratify and confirm the faid Treaty. Witnefs the Hon. Nathaniel Gotham, our Chairman, in the abfence of his Excellency John Hancock, our Prefident, the 7th day of May, in the year of our Lord 1786, and of our Independence and Sovereignty the tenth.

The

The new Plan of the Conſtitution of the UNITED STATES *of* AMERICA, *upon which the Convention of all the moſt diſtinguiſhed Men in the States have been deliberating for ſeveral Months.*

New-York, Sept. 21.

In Convention, Sept. 17, 1787.

SIR,

WE have now the honour to ſubmit to the conſideration of the United States, in Congreſs aſſembled, that Conſtitution which has appeared to us the moſt adviſeable.

The friends of our country have long ſeen and deſired, that the power of making war, peace, and treaties, that of levying money, and regulating commerce, and the correſpondent executive and judicial authorities, ſhould be fully and effectually veſted in the general government of the Union: but the impropriety of delegating ſuch extenſive truſt to one body of men is evident. Hence reſults the neceſſity of a different organization.

It is obviouſly impracticable, in the fœderal government of theſe States, to ſecure all rights of independent ſovereignty to each, and yet provide for the intereſt and ſafety of all. Individuals, entering into a ſociety, muſt give up a ſhare of liberty to preſerve the reſt. The magnitude of the ſacrifice muſt depend as well on ſituation and circumſtance, as on the object to be obtained. It is

G g 3 at

at all times difficult to draw with precifion the line between thofe rights which muſt be furrendered, and thofe which may be referved; and, on the prefent occafion, this difficulty was encreafed by a difference among the feveral States, as to their fituation, extent, habits, and particular interefts.

In all our deliberations on this fubject, we kept fteadily in our view, that which appears to us the greateft intereft of every true American—the confolidation of our Union, in which is involved our profperity, felicity, fafety, perhaps our national exiftence. This important confideration, ferioufly and deeply impreffed on our minds, led each State in the Convention to be lefs rigid on points of inferior magnitude than might have been otherwife expected; and thus the Conftitution, which we now prefent, is the refult of a fpirit of amity, and that mutual deference and conceffion which the peculiarity of our political fituation rendered indifpenfible.

That it will meet the full and entire approbation of every State is not perhaps to be expected; but each will doubtlefs confider, that had her interefts been alone confulted the confequences might have been particularly difagreeable or injurious to others; that it is liable to as few exceptions as could reafonably have been expected, we hope and believe; that it may promote the lafting welfare of that country fo dear to us all, and fecure her freedom and happinefs, is our moft ardent wifh.

With

With great refpect, we have the honour to be, Sir, your Excellency's moft obedient and humble fervants,

GEORGE WASHINGTON, Prefident.

By unanimous order of the Convention.

His Excellency the Prefident of Congrefs.

WE, the people of the United States, in order to form a more perfect union, eftablifh juftice, infure domeftic tranquility, provide for the common defence, promote the general welfare, and fecure the bleffings of liberty to ourfelves and our pofterity, do ordain and eftablifh this conftitution for the United States of America.

ARTICLE I.

1. All legiflative powers herein granted fhall be vefted in a Congrefs of the United States, which fhall confift of a Senate and Houfe of Reprefentatives.

2. The Houfe of Reprefentatives fhall be compofed of Members chofen every fecond year by the people of the feveral States, and the electors in each State fhall have the qualifications requifite of electors of the moft numerous branch of the State Legiflature.

No perfon fhall be a Reprefentative, who fhall not have attained to the age of 25 years, and been feven years a citizen of the United States, and who fhall not when elected be an inhabitant of that State in which he fhall be chofen.

Reprefentatives

Reprefentatives and direct taxes fhall be ap-
portioned among the feveral States which may be
included within this union, according to their
refpective numbers, which fhall be determined by
adding to the whole number of free perfons, including thofe bound to fervice for a term of years,
and excluding Indians not taxed, three-fifths of all
other perfons. The actual enumeration fhall be
made within three years after the firft meeting of
the Congrefs of the United States, and within every
fubfequent term of ten years, in fuch manner as
they fhall by law direct. The number of Reprefentatives fhall not exceed one for every thirty
thoufand; but each State fhall have at leaft one
Reprefentative; and until fuch enumeration fhall
be made, the State of New Hampfhire fhall be
entitled to chufe three, Maffachufetts eight,
Rhode Ifland and Providence Plantations one,
Connecticut five, New York fix, New Jerfey four
Pennfylvania eight, Delaware one, Maryland fix,
Virginia ten, North Carolina five, South Carolina
five, and Georgia three.

When vacancies happen to the Reprefentation
from any State, the executive authority thereof fhall iffue writs of election to fill fuch vacancies.

The Houfe of Reprefentatives fhall chufe their
Speaker and other officers; and fhall have the
fole power of impeachment.

3. The

3. The Senate of the United States ſhall be compoſed of two Senators from each State, choſen by the Legiſlature thereof for ſix years; and each Senator ſhall have one vote.

Immediately after they ſhall be aſſembled in conſequence of the firſt election, they ſhall be divided, as nearly as may be, into three claſſes. The ſeats of the Senators of the firſt claſs ſhall be vacated at the expiration of the ſecond year ; of the ſecond claſs at the expiration of the fourth year; and of the third claſs at the expiration of the ſixth year, ſo that one-third may be choſen every ſecond year; and if vacancies happen by reſignation, or otherwiſe, during the receſs of the Legiſlature of any State, the executive authority thereof may make temporary appointments until the next meeting of the Legiſlature which ſhall then fill ſuch vacancies.

No perſon ſhall be a Senator who ſhall not have attained to the age of 30 years, and been nine years a citizen of the United States, and who ſhall not, when elected, be an inhabitant of that State for which he ſhall be choſen.

The Vice Preſident of the United States ſhall be Preſident of the Senate, but ſhall have no vote unleſs they be equally divided.

The Senate ſhall chooſe their other officers, and alſo a Preſident *pro tempore,* in the abſence of the Vice Preſident, or when he ſhall exerciſe the office of Preſident of the United States.

The

The Senate fhall have the fole power to try all im-
peachments.   When fitting for that purpofe, they
fhall be on oath or affirmation.   When the Prefident of the United States is tried, the Chief Juftice
fhall prefide; and no perfon fhall be convicted
without the concurrence of two-thirds of the
Members prefent.

Judgment in cafes of impeachment fhall not extend farther than removal from office, and difqua-
lification to hold and enjoy any office of honour,
truft or profit, under the United States; but the
party convicted fhall neverthelefs be liable and
fubject to indictment, trial, judgment, and punifhment according to law.

4.   The times, places, and manner of holding
elections for Senators and Reprefentatives, fhall
be prefcribed in each State by the Legiflature
thereof; but the Congrefs may at any time by law
make or alter fuch regulations, except as to the
places of chufing Senators.

The Congrefs fhall affemble at leaft once in
every year, and fuch meeting fhall be on the firft
Monday in December, unlefs they fhall by law
appoint a different day.

4.   Each Houfe fhall be the judge of the elections, returns, and qualifications of its own Members, and a majority of each fhall conftitute a quorum to do bufinefs; but a fmaller number may adjourn from day to day, and may be authorifed to
compel the attendance of abfent Members, in fuch

manner,

manner, and under fuch penalties, as each houfe may provide.

Each Houfe may determine the rules of its proceedings, punifh its Members for diforderly behaviour, and, with the concurrence of two-thirds, expel a Member.

Each Houfe fhall keep a journal of its proceedings, and from time to time publifh the fame, excepting fuch parts as may in their judgment require fecrecy; and the yeas and nays of the Members of either Houfe on any queftion fhall, at the defire of one-fifth of thofe prefent, be entered on the journal.

Neither Houfe, during the feffion of Congrefs, fhall, without the confent of the other, adjourn for more than three days, nor to any other place than that in which the two Houfes fhall be fitting.

6. The Senators and Reprefentatives fhall receive a compenfation for their fervices, to be afcertained by law, and paid out of the Treafury of the United States. They fhall in all cafes, except treafon, felony, and breach of the peace, be privileged from arreft during their attendance at the feffion of their refpective Houfes, and in going to and returning from the fame; and for any fpeech or debate in either Houfe, they fhall not be queftioned in any other place.

No Senator or Reprefentative fhall, during the time for which he was elected, be appointed to any civil office under the authority of the United

State,

States, which fhall have been created, or the emolument whereof fhall have been encreafed, during
fuch time, and no perfon holding any office under
the United States fhall be a Member of either
Houfe during his continuance in office.

7. All bills for raifing revenue fhall originate in
the Houfe of Reprefentatives; but the Senate
may propofe or concur with amendments as on
other bills.

Every bill, which fhall have paffed the Houfe
of Reprefentatives and the Senate, fhall, before it
become a law, be prefented to the Prefident of
the United States; if he approve, he fhall fign it,
but if not, he fhall return it with his objections
to that Houfe in which it fhall have originated,
who fhall enter the objections at large on their
journal, and proceed to reconfider it. If, after
fuch reconfideration, two-thirds of that Houfe
fhall agree to pafs the bill, it fhall be fent, together with the objections, to the other Houfe, by
which it fhall likewife be re-confidered, and if approved by two-thirds of that Houfe, it fhall become a law. But in all fuch cafes the votes of
both Houfes fhall be determined by yeas and
nays, and the names of the perfons voting for
and againft the bill fhall be entered on the journal
of each Houfe refpectively. If any bill fhall not
be returned by the Prefident within ten days (Sun-
days excepted) after it fhall have been prefented
to him, the fame fhall be a law, in like manner as

I   if

if he had figned it, unlefs the Congrefs by their adjournment prevent its return, in which cafe it fhall not be a law.

Every order, refolution, or vote, to which the concurrence of the Senate and Houfe of Reprefentatives may be neceffary (except on a queftion of adjournment) fhall be prefented to the Prefident of the United States ; and, before the fame fhall take effect, fhall be approved by him, or, being difapproved by him, fhall be repaffed by two-thirds of the Senate and Houfe of Reprefentatives, according to the rules and limitations prefcribed in the cafe of a bill.

8. The Congrefs fhall have power to lay and collect taxes, duties, impofts and excifes, to pay the debts and provide for the common defence and general welfare of the United States; but all duties, impofts, and excifes, fhall be uniform throughout the United States.

To borrow money on the credit of the United States.

To regulate commerce with foreign nations, and among the feveral States, and with the Indian tribes.

To eftablifh an uniform rule of naturalization, and uniform laws on the fubject of bankruptcies throughout the United States.

To coin money, regulate the value thereof and of foreign coin, and fix the ftandards of weights and meafures.

To

To provide for the punifhment of counterfeiting the fecurities and current coin of the United States.

To eftablifh poft-offices and poft-roads.

To promote the progrefs of fcience and ufeful arts, by fecuring for limited times to authors and inventors the exclufive right to their refpective writings and difcoveries.

To conftitute tribunals inferior to the Supreme Court.

To define and punifh piracies and felonies committed on the high feas, and offences againft the law of nations.

To declare war, grant letters of marque and reprifal, and make rules concerning captures on land and water.

To raife and fupport armies, but no appropriation of money to that ufe fhall be for a longer term than two years.

To provide and maintain a navy.

To make rules for the government and regulation of the land and naval forces.

To provide for calling forth the militia, to execute the laws of the Union, fupprefs infurrections, and repel invafions.

To provide for organizing, arming, and difciplining the militia, and for governing fuch part of them as may be employed in the fervice of the United States, referving to the States refpectively the appointment of the officers, and the authority

of

of training the militia, according to the difcipline prefcribed by Congrefs.

To exercife exclufive legiflation in all cafes whatfoever over fuch diftrict (not exceeding ten miles fquare) as may, by ceffion of particular States, and the acceptance of Congrefs, become the feat of the government of the United States, and to exercife like authority over all places pur-chafed by the confent of the Legiflature of the State, in which the fame fhall be, for the erection of forts, magazines, arfenals, dock-yards, and other needful buildings. And

To make all laws which fhall be neceffary and proper for carrying into execution the foregoing powers vefted by this Conftitution in the Govern-ment of the United States, or in any department or office thereof.

9. The migration or importation of fuch per-fons as any of the States now exifting fhall think proper to admit, fhall not be prohibited by the Congrefs, prior to the year of one thoufand eight hundred and eight; but a tax or duty may be impofed on fuch importation, not exceeding ten dollars for each perfon.

The privilege of the writ of *habeas corpus* fhall not be fufpended, unlefs when in cafes of rebellion or invafion, the Public fafety may require it.

No bill of attainder, or *ex poft facto* law fhall be paffed.

No

No capitation, or other direct tax, fhall be laid, unlefs in proportion to the cenfus or enumeration herein before directed to be taken.

No tax or duty fhall be laid on articles exported from any State. No preference fhall be given, by any regulation of commerce or revenue, to the ports of one State over thofe of another : nor fhall veffels bound to or from one State be obliged to enter, clear, or pay duties in another.

No money fhall be drawn from the Treafury, but in confequence of appropriations made by law ; and a regular ftatement and account of the receipts and expenditures of all public money fhall be publifhed from time to time.

No title of nobility fhall be granted by the United States ; and no perfon holding any office of profit or truft under them fhall, without the confent of the Congrefs, accept of any prefent, emolument, office, or title, of any kind whatever, from any King, Prince, or foreign State.

10. No State fhall enter into any treaty, alliance, or confederation ; grant letters of marque and reprifal ; coin money ; emit bills of credit ; make any thing but gold and filver coin a tender in payment of debts ; pafs any bill of attainder, *ex poft facto* law, or law impairing the obligation of contracts, or grant any title of nobility.

No State fhall, without the confent of the Congrefs, lay impofts or duties on imports or exports, except what may be abfolutely neceffary
for

for executing, its infpection laws; and the net produce of all duties and imposts, laid by any State on imports or exports, shall be for the use of the Treasury of the United States; and all such laws shall be subject to the revision and controul of the Congress. No State shall, without the consent of Congress, lay any duty of tonnage, keep troops or ships of war in time of peace, enter into any agreement or compact with another State, or with a foreign power, or engage in war, unless actually invaded, or in such imminent danger, as will not admit of delay.

ARTICLE II.

1. The executive power shall be vested in a President of the United States of America. He shall hold his office during the term of four years; and together with the Vice-President, chofen for the fame term, be elected as follows:

Each State shall appoint, in fuch manner as the Legislature thereof may direct, a number of electors, equal to the whole number of Senators and Reprefentatives to which the State may be entitled in the Congress; but no Senator or Representative, or perfon holding an office of truft or profit under the United States, shall be appointed an Elector.

The Electors shall meet in their refpective States, and vote by ballot for two perfons, of whom one at leaft shall not be an inhabitant of

H h the

the fame State with themfelves. And they fhall
make a lift of all the perfons voted for, and of the
number of votes for each, which lift they fhall
fign and certify, and tranfmit, fealed, to the feat
of the government of the United States, directed
to the Prefident of the Senate. The Prefident of
the Senate fhall, in the prefence of the Senate and
Houfe of Reprefentatives, open all the certificates,
and the votes fhall then be counted. The perfon
having the greateft number of votes fhall be the
Prefident, if fuch number be a majority of the
whole number of electors appointed ; and if there
be more than one who have fuch majority, and
have an equal number of votes, then the Houfe of
Reprefentatives fhall immediately choofe by ballot
one of them for Prefident, and if no perfon have
a majority, then from the five higheft on the lift
the faid Houfe fhall in like manner choofe the
Prefident. But in choofing the Prefident, the
votes fhall be taken by States, the reprefentation
from each State having one vote ; a quorum for
this purpofe fhall confift of a Member or Members
from two-thirds of the States, and a majority of all
the States fhall be neceffary to a choice. In every
cafe, after the choice of the Prefident, the perfon
having the greateft number of voters of the electors fhall be the Vice-Prefident. But if there
fhould remain two or more who have equal votes,
the Senate fhall choofe from them by ballot the
Vice-Prefident.

The

The Congrefs may determine the time of choofing the electors, and the day on which they fhall give their votes; which day fhall be the fame throughout the United States.

No perfon, except a natural born citizen, or a citizen of the United States, at the time of the adoption of this Conftitution, fhall be eligible to the office of Prefident; neither fhall any perfon be eligible to that office, who fhall not have attained to the age of 35 years, and been 14 years a refident within the United States.

In cafe of the removal of Prefident from office, or of his death, refignation, or inability to difcharge the powers and duties of the faid office, the fame fhall devolve on the Vice-Prefident, and the Congrefs may by law provide for the cafe of removal, death, refignation, or inability, both of the Prefident and Vice-Prefident, declaring what officer fhall then act as Prefident, and fuch officer fhall act accordingly, until the difability be removed, or a Prefident fhall be elected.

The Prefident fhall, at ftated times, receive for his fervices a compenfation, which fhall neither be encreafed or diminifhed during the period for which he fhall have been elected, and he fhall not receive within that period any other emolument from the United States, or any of them.

Before he enter on the execution of his office, he fhall take the following oath or affirmation:

H h 2   " I do

" I do folemnly fwear (or affirm) that I will faithfully execute the office of Prefident of the United States, and will to the beft of my ability preferve, protect, and defend, the Conftitution of the United States."

2. The Prefident fhall be Commander in Chief of the army and navy of the United States, and of the militia of the feveral States, when called into the actual fervice of the United States; he may require the opinion, in writing, of the principal officer in each of the executive departments, upon any fubject relating to the duties of their refpective offices, and he fhall have power to grant reprieves and pardons for offences againft the United States, except in cafes of impeachment.

He fhall have power, by and with the advice and confent of the Senate, to make treaties, provided two-thirds of the Senators prefent concur; and he fhall nominate, and, by and with the advice and confent of the Senate, fhall appoint Ambaffadors, other public Minifters and Confuls, Judges of the Supreme Court, and all other officers of the United States, whofe appointments are not herein otherwife provided for, and which fhall be eftablifhed by law. But the Congrefs may by law veft the appointment of fuch inferior officers as they may think proper, in the Prefident alone, in the courts of law, or in the heads of departments.

The

The Prefident fhall have power to fill up all vacancies that may happen during the recefs of the
Senate, by granting commiffions which fhall expire at the end of their next feffion.

3. He fhall from time to time give to the Congrefs information of the ftate of their Union, and
recommend to their confideration fuch meafures
as he fhall judge neceffary and expedient : He
may, on extraordinary occafions, convene both
houfes, or either of them, and in cafe of difagree-
ment between them, with refpect to the time of
adjournment, he may adjourn them to fuch time
as he fhall think proper; he fhall receive Ambaffadors and other public Minifters; he fhall take
care that the laws be faithfully executed, and
fhall commiffion all the officers of the United
States.

4. The Prefident, Vice-Prefident, and all civil
offices of the United States, fhall be removed
from office on impeachment for, and conviction
of, treafon, bribery, or other high crimes and
mifdemeanors.

ARTICLE III.

1. The judicial power of the United States
fhall be vefted in one Supreme Court, and in
fuch inferior Courts as the Congrefs may from
time to time ordain and eftablifh. The Judges,
both of the Supreme and Inferior Courts, fhall
hold their offices during good behaviour, and

H h 3 fhall,

shall, at stated times, receive for their services a compensation, which shall not be diminished during continuance in office.

2. The judicial power shall extend to all cases in law and equity, arising under this Constitution, the laws of the United States, and treaties made, or which shall be made, under their authority; to all cases affecting Ambassadors, other public Ministers and Consuls ; to all cases of Admiralty and maritime jurisdiction; to controversies to which the United States shall be a party; to controversies between two or more States, between a State and citizens of another State, between citizens of different States, between citizens of the same State claiming lands under grants of different States, and between a State, or the citizens thereof, and foreign States, citizens or subjects.

In all cases affecting Ambassadors, other public Ministers, and Consuls, and those in which a State shall be party, the Supreme Court shall have original jurisdiction, in all the other cases beforementioned the Supreme Court shall have appellate jurisdiction, both as to law and fact, with such exceptions, and under such regulations as the Congress shall make.

The trial of all crimes, except in cases of impeachment, shall be by Jury; and such trial shall be held in the State where the said crimes shall have been committed ; but when not committed within any State, the trial shall be at such place

or

or places as the Congrefs may by law have directed.

3. Treafon againft the United States fhall confift only in levying war againft them, or in adhering to their enemies, giving them aid and comfort. No perfon fhall be convicted of treafon unlefs on the teftimony of two witneffes to the fame overt act, or on confeffion in open court.

The Congrefs fhall have power to declare the punifhment of treafon, but no attainder of treafon fhall work corruption of blood or forfeiture, except during the life of the perfon attainted.

Article IV.

1. Full faith and credit fhall be given in each State to the public acts, records, and judicial proceedings of every other State. And the Congrefs may by general laws prefcribe the manner in which fuch acts, records and proceedings fhall be proved, and the effect thereof.

2. The citizens of each State fhall be entitled to all privileges and immunities of citizens in the feveral States.

A perfon charged in any State with treafon, felony, or other crime, who fhall flee from juftice, and be found in another State, fhall, on demand of the executive authority of the State from which he fled, be delivered up, to be removed to the State having jurifdiction of the crime.

No perſon held to ſervice or labour in one State, under the laws thereof, eſcaping into any other, ſhall, in conſequence of any law or regulation therein, be diſcharged from ſuch ſervice or labour, but ſhall be delivered up on claim of the party to whom ſuch ſervice or labour may be due.

3. New States may be admitted by the Congreſs into this Union; but no new State ſhall be formed or erected within the juriſdiction of any other State; nor any State be formed by the junction of two or more States, or parts of States, without the conſent of the Legiſlatures of the States concerned, as well as of the Congreſs.

The Congreſs ſhall have power to diſpoſe of and make all needful rules and regulations reſpecting the territory or other property belonging to the United States; and nothing in this Conſtitution ſhall be ſo conſtrued as to prejudice any claims of the United States, or of any particular State.

4. The United States ſhall guarantee to every State in this Union a Republican form of government, and ſhall protect each of them againſt invaſion; and on application of the Legiſlature, or of the executive (when the Legiſlature cannot be convened) againſt domeſtic violence,

ARTICLE V.

The Congreſs, whenever two-thirds of both Houſes ſhall deem it neceſſary, ſhall propoſe
amendments

amendments to this Conftitution, or, on the application of the Legiflatures of two-thirds of the feveral States, fhall call a Convention for propofing amendments, which, in either cafe fhall be valid to all intents and purpofes, as part of this Conftitution, when ratified by the Legiflatures of three-fourths of the feveral States, or by Conventions in three-fourths thereof, as the one or the other mode of ratification may be propofed by the Congrefs : provided that no amendment which may be made prior to the year one thoufand eight hundred and eight, fhall in any manner affect the firft and fourth claufes in the ninth fection of the firft Article ; and that no State, without its confent, fhall be deprived of its equal fuffrage in the Senate.

ARTICLE VI.

All debts contracted, and engagements entered into, before the adoption of this Conftitution, fhall be as valid againft the United States under this Conftitution, as under the Confederation.

This Conftitution, and the laws of the United States which fhall be made in purfuance thereof; and all treaties made, or which fhall be made, under the authority of the United States, fhall be the fupreme law of the land; and the Judges in every State fhall be bound thereby, any thing in the

the Conftitution or laws of any State to the contrary notwithftanding.

The Senators and Reprefentatives before mentioned, and the Members of the feveral State Legiflatures, and all executive and judicial officers, both of the United States and of the feveral States, fhould be bound by oath or affirmation to fupport this Conftitution; but no religious teft fhall ever be required as a qualification to any office or public truft under the United States.

Article VII.

The ratifications of the Conventions of nine States fhould be fufficient for the eftablifhment of this Conftitution between the States fo ratifying the fame.

Done in Convention, by the unanimous confent of the States prefent, the feventeenth day of September, in the year of our Lord one thoufand feven hundred and eighty-feven, and of the Independence of the United States of America the twelfth. In witnefs whereof we have hereunto fubfcribed our names.

GEORGE WASHINGTON, Prefident,
And Deputy from Virginia.

John Langdon, Nicholas Gilman—*New Hampfhire.*

Nathaniel Goreham, Rufus King—*Maffachufetts.*

William

William Samuel Johnſon, Roger Sherman—*Connecticut.*

Alexander Hamilton—*New York.*

William Livingſton, David Brearley, William Paterſon, Jonathan Dayton—*New Jerſey.*

Benjamin Franklin, Thomas Mifflin, Robert Morris, George Clymer, Thomas Fitzſimons, Jared Ingerſol, James Wilſon, Gouverneur Morris —*Pennſylvania.*

George Read, Gunning Bedford, jun. John Dickinſon, Richard Baſſett, Jacob Broom, *Delaware.*

James M'Henry, Daniel of St. Thomas Jenifer, Daniel Carroll—*Maryland.*

John Blair, James Madiſon, jun.—*Virginia.*

William Blount, Richard Dobbs Spaight, Hugh Williamſon—*North Carolina.*

John Rutledge, Charles Coteſworth Pinckney, Charles Pinckney, Pierce Butler—*South Carolina.*

William Few, Abraham Baldwin—*Georgia.*

Atteſt. William Jackſon, Secretary.

In CONVENTION, Monday, Sept. 17, 1787.
P R E S E N T,
The States of New Hampſhire, Maſſachuſetts, Connecticut, Mr. Hamilton from New York, New Jerſey, Pennſylvania, Delaware, Maryland, Virginia, North Carolina, South Carolina, and Georgia :

Reſolved

Refolved,

THAT the preceding Conftitution be laid before the United States in Congrefs affembled, and that it is the opinion of this Convention, that it fhould afterwards be fubmitted to a Convention of Delegates, chofen in each State by the people thereof, under the recommendation of its Legiflature, for their affent and ratification; and that each Convention affenting to, and ratifying the fame, fhould give notice thereof to the United States in Congrefs affembled.

Refolved,

That it is the opinion of this Convention, that as foon as the Conventions of nine States fhall have ratified this Conftitution, the United States in Congrefs affembled fhould fix a day on which Electors fhould be appointed by the States which fhall have ratified the fame, and a day on which the Electors fhould affemble to vote for the Prefident, and the time and place for commencing proceedings under this Conftitution. That after fuch publication the Electors fhould be appointed, and the Senators and Reprefentatives elected: That the Electors fhould meet on the day fixed for the Election of the Prefident, and fhould tranfmit their votes certified, figned, fealed, and directed, as the Conftitution requires, to the Secretary of the United States in Congrefs affembled, that the Senators and Reprefentatives fhould convene at

the

the time and place affigned; that the Senators fhould appoint a Prefident of the Senate, for the fole purpofe of receiving, opening, and counting the votes for Prefident; and that, after he fhall be chofen, the Congrefs, together with the Prefident, fhould, without delay, proceed to execute this Conftitution.

By the unanimous Order of the Convention,

GEORGE WASHINGTON, Prefident.
WILLIAM JACKSON, Secretary.

THE CHARACTER OF

GENERAL WASHINGTON.

GENERAL WASHINGTON was born February 11, O. S. 1732, in the parifh of Wafhington, in Weftmoreland County, in Virginia: His anceftors were from England as long ago as 1657: He had his education principally from a private tutor; learnt fome Latin, and the art of furveying. When he was fifteen years of age, he entered as a midfhipman on board a Britifh veffel of war, that was ftationed on the coaft of Virginia; but the plan was abandoned, on account of the reluctance his mother had againft it.

He was appointed a Major of a regiment before he was twenty years old; and as the French had

I   made

made encroachments on the Englifh fettlements, he was fent in 1753, by Lieutenant-Governor Dinwiddie, then Commander of the Province, to treat with the French and Indians, and to warn them againft making encroachments, &c. He performed the duties of his miffion with fidelity.

In 1754 the colony of Virginia raifed a regiment for its defence, which was put under the command of Colonel Fry, and Major Wafhington was appointed Lieutenant-Colonel of the fame; but the Colonel died that Summer, without joining the regiment, and the command fell to the Lieutenant-Colonel.

After forming his regiment, eftablifhing magazines, opening roads, and fundry marches, he built a temporary ftockade, at a place called the Great Meadows; and though his forces did not amount to four hundred effective men, he fallied out, and defeated a number of the enemy, who were coming to reconnoitre his poft; but on his return was attacked by an army about 1500 ftrong; and after a gallant defence, in which more than one third of his men were killed and wounded, he was obliged to capitulate. The garrifon marched out with the honours of war, but were plundered by the Indians, in violation of the articles of the capitulation. After this the remains of his regiment returned to Alexandria, in Virginia, to be recruited, &c.

In

In 1755, " As no officer who did not imme-
" diately derive his commiffion from the King
" could command one who did," Colonel Wafhington relinquifhed his regiment, and went as an
extra Aid-de-Camp into the family of *General Braddock,* who was fent to drive the French, &c. from
the borders of the Englifh fettlements.

The General was afterwards killed at the battle
of Monongahela, and his army defeated, where
Colonel Wafhington difplayed his abilities, in
covering a retreat, and faving the remains of the
army.

Afterwards the fupreme authority of Virginia
gave him a new and extenfive commiffion, whereby he was appointed Commander of all the troops
raifed, and to be raifed, in that Colony.

He conducted as a good officer in defending
the frontiers againft the enemy, and in 1758 he
commanded the *van brigade* of General *Forbes*'s
army, in the capture of Fort du Quefne ; and by
his prudent conduct, the tranquillity of the frontiers of the middle Colonies was reftored. But he
refigned his military appointment in 1759, by
reafon of his being ill of a pulmonic comp'aint.

As his health was afterwards gradually reftored,
he married a Mrs. Cuftis, who was born the fame
year that he was : She was a handfome and an
amiable young widow, poffeffed of an ample
jointure, and he fettled as a planter and a farmer
on the eftate where he now refides, in Fairfax

2   county.

county. After some years, he gave up planting tobacco, and went altogether into the farming business. He has raised 7000 bushels of wheat and 10,000 of Indian corn in one year. His domestic plantation contains about 9,000 acres, and he possesses large quantities of excellent lands in several other counties.

He thus spent his time in cultivating the arts of peace, but was constantly a Member of the Assembly, a Magistrate of his county, and a Judge of the Court. In 1774, he was elected a Delegate to the first Congress, and was chosen again in 1775; the same year he was appointed by Congress Commander in Chief of the Forces of the United Colonies.

His conduct as a General is so well known, that it is needless for me to say much upon the subject. He went through many hardships, perils, and dangers, and conducted his military operations with such great skill, that at last a peace commenced in 1783, whereby thirteen of the American Colonies were established as Sovereign and Independent States.

Afterwards he resigned his commission to Congress, and retired to his plantation in Virginia.

Some time after the peace commenced, he received a *diploma* from the University at Cambridge, in the Commonwealth of Massachusetts, constituting him a *Doctor of Laws*.

He

He is very regular, temperate, and induftrious; rifes in Winter and Summer at the dawn of the day; generally reads or writes fome time before breaftfaft; breakfafts about feven o'clock on three fmall Indian hoe cakes and as many difhes of tea, and often rides immediately to his different farms, and remains with his labourers till a little after two o'clock, then returns and dreffes. At three he dines, commonly on a fingle difh, and drinks from half a pint to a pint of Madeira wine. This, with one fmall glafs of punch, a draught of beer, and two difhes of tea (which he takes half an hour before the fetting of the Sun) conftitutes his whole fuftenance until the next day. But his table is always furnifhed with elegance and exuberance; and whether he has company or not, he remains at the table an hour in familiar converfation, then every one prefent is called upon to give fome abfent friend as a toaft.

His temper is of a ferious caft, and his countenance carries the impreffion of thoughtfulnefs; yet he perfectly relifhes a pleafant ftory, an unaffected fally of wit, or a burlefque defcription, which furprizes by its fuddennefs and incongruity, with the ordinary appearance of the object defcribed. After he has dined he applies himfelf to bufinefs, and about nine retires to reft; but when he has company, he attends politely upon them till they wifh to withdraw.

I i

His

His family confifts of eight perfons, but he has no children : He keeps a pack of hounds, and in feafon goes a hunting once in a week, in company with fome of the gentlemen of Alexandria.

Agriculture is his favourite employment : He makes obfervations concerning the produce of his lands, and endeavours to throw light upon the farmer's bufinefs.

Linen and woollen cloths are manufactured under his roof, and order and œconomy are eftablifhed in all his departments, both within and without doors.

In 1787, he was chofen Prefident of the Federal Convention that met at Philadelphia, and framed the new Conftitution; and fince that time, he has been chofen Prefident of Congrefs, and has a falary of twenty-five thoufand dollars *per annum*.

Some have pretended that he is a native of England; but I underftand that he never was in Europe.

CHAP.

CHAP. XLVIII.

How Provinces, Counties, Townships, and High-
ways, ought to be laid out. The Lengths and
Breadths of the American Governments. The Lon-
gitudes, Latitudes, Bearings, and Distances of the
principal Towns from Philadelphia.

I Have obferved, that fome of the American
Governments are too large, and that others
are too fmall; for the Province of Quebec is 800
miles in length, and 200 in breadth; Virginia is
758 miles long, and 224 broad; Rhode-Ifland
is 68 miles in length, and 40 in breadth; and
Delaware is 92 miles long, and but 16 broad, according to accounts given of their limits.

Where they are too large, fome of the Legiflatures muft be at a great diftance from the feat of
Government. Hence, thofe who live in the wefterly parts of Canada muft be four or five hundred
miles from Quebec, where the Legiflators convene, which is very inconvenient, as the fatigue
and expence of travelling is very great. Some
of the other Governments are alfo too large, and
others too fmall.

I fhould admire at the Provinces being laid out
in fuch forms, were it not for the newnefs of the

country,

country, and the various grants of lands that have from time to time been given by former Kings to emigrants who received charters, fpecifying different limits, and fettled in America.

Some counties are alfo too long, fome are too narrow, fome too large, and others too fmall; and the fame may be faid of townfhips and parifhes.

Would it not be more convenient, if the Provinces were about 100 miles fquare, the counties 25, and the townfhips fix and a quarter?—A State of this magnitude, divifions, and fub-divifions, would contain 16 counties, and each county 16 townfhips, making 256 townfhips in the whole; and if every townfhip was allowed to fend a Reprefentative to a General Affembly, there would be 256 Legiflators, befides the Governors and Councillors, which would be an Affembly large enough for a Province or State.

It may be moft convenient for Legiflators to meet in the center of a province, the Judges in the center of a county, and people in the center of a town or parifh, for the tranfaction of bufinefs, and the performance of religious worfhip.

I have obferved, that where churches have been built remote from the centers of towns and parifhes, it has been the caufe of much difturbance amongft the inhabitants, becaufe fome have had to travel a great way to get to church.

The

The highways in America ought to be at leaſt an hundred feet wide, and eſpecially where the ſnow falls deep; for where they are too narrow, they will be often filled to the tops of the fences when the ſnow is not more than eight inches deep upon a level; for the ſnow that is carried over one fence by the wind lodges againſt the other till the road is full, which endangers the lives of travellers, and proves a great hindrance to the tranſaction of buſineſs. Some are ſo ſtingy, that they will not allow a highway to be fenced wide enough, becauſe they ſuppoſe that they ſhall loſe the profits of their lands; but this is a miſtake, for the land in a highway will ſerve for a paſture for cattle, ſheep, &c. whilſt the people are freed from the labour and expence of fencing it.

I do not pretend to ſay, that every government, county, and townſhip, can be laid out exactly in the form that I have mentioned: I know that ſome places are almoſt ſurrounded by the ſea, as the peninſula on which the town of Boſton, in the Maſſachuſetts, is built, and many other places, where there is not room for a town of the bigneſs I have recommended; but where there is room, it will be beſt to lay them out in a regular form, &c.

But the globular form of the globe may, in ſome meaſure, interrupt my plan of laying out all the provinces, on a great continent, exactly ſquare; for ſome allowance ought to be made,

I i 3   for

for the variation of the degrees of longitude in the different parallels of latitude.

Hence, if on the lat. of 40 degrees north, we should meafure 100 miles fouth on the meridian of Philadelphia, and fet up a boundary for the fouth-eafterly corner of a province, and fhould meafure 100 miles weft to the fouth-weft corner, then exactly north 100 miles, and from thence to where we began, we fhould find that the north line would not be fo long as the fouth by about $\frac{9\,5}{100}$ of a mile, for the degrees of longitude are fhorter in the northern than in fouthern parallels of latitude. Vid. Tab. p. 75.

The kingdom of France is about **662** miles in length, from north to fouth, and 620 in breadth, from eaft to weft; and fince the late Revolution, the National Affembly have divided it into 80 grand divifions, or counties, of 18 leagues in length, and as many in breadth; and each grand divifion into 9 commonalties, which are 6 leagues fquare; and alfo each commonalty into 9 cantons, of 2 leagues in length and 2 in breadth.

Hence there are 80 grand divifions; 720 commonalties, and 6480 cantons. Each commonalty fends one Reprefentative to the National Affembly. Hence alfo, as a French league is longer than an Englifh, the cantons are about the bignefs of the townfhips which I have recommended.

The following Table exhibits the different forms, &c. of the North-American Governments.

DIVISION

DIVISIONS OF NORTH-AMERICA.

Names of States and Colonies.	Length. Miles.	Breadth. Miles.	Chief Towns.	Latitude. Deg.	Min.	Longitude from Philadelphia. Deg.	Min.	Distance from Philadelphia. Miles.	and bearing Points.
New Hampshire	180	60	Portsmouth.	43	5	3	54 E.	408	N. E.
Massachusetts	450	164	Boston.	42	25	3	39 E.	343	N. E.
Rhode-Island	68	40	Newport.	41	30	3	24 E.	280	E. N. E.
Connecticut	81	57	Newhaven.	41	19	1	56 E.	181	N. E.
New-York	350	300	New-York.	40	40	1	5 E.	95	E. N. E.
New-Jersey	160	52	Trenton,	40	15	0	23 E.	30	N. E.
Pennsylvania	288	156	Philadelphia.	39	56	0	0	0	
Delaware	92	16	Dover.	39	10	0	25 W.	72	S. S. W.
Maryland	134	110	Annapolis.	39	2	1	37 W.	132	S. W.
Virginia	758	224	Richmond.	37	40	2	42 W.	276	S. W.
North-Carolina	758	110	Edenton.	36	4	1	25 W.	442	S. S. W.
South-Carolina	200	125	Charlestown.	32	35	3	0 W.	814	S. S. W.
Georgia	600	250	Augusta.	33	39	7	0 W.	934	W. S. W.
Vermont	155	60	Bennington.	42	42	1	44 E.	299	N. by E.
Western Territory	1000	450	Adelphi.	39	34	6	30 W.	492	W.
Kentucky	including Virginia		Lexington.	38	25	10	0 W.	947	by Water W.
Province of Quebec	800	200	Quebec.	46	55	4	56 E.	690	N. N. E.
Nova Scotia	300	250	Halifax.	44	56	14	29 E.	925	N. E.
East and West Floridas	600	130	St. Augustine.	29	51	6	30 W.	1146	S. S. W.
Louisiana	indefinite		New Orleans.	29	57	14	40 W.	1646	S. W.
New Mexico	indefinite		St. Fee.	36	45	3	32 W.	2190	W.
California	765	212	St. Juan.	26	5	39	0 W.	3396	W. S. W.
Old Mexico	2700	250	Mexico.	20	0	26	0 W.	3021	S. W.

The distances of the capital towns from Philadelphia are reckoned as the roads run, and not according to the circles of Latitude and Longitude.

C H A P. XLIX.

Of Architecture.—How Cities, Churches, Houses, &c. ought to be built.—Magnificent Edifices, the Seven Wonders of the World.—The Danger of living in open Houses, and of Sleeping in New Plaistered Rooms.—Of the Vanity of Destroying Wood too fast.—Directions concerning the Preservation of Trees, and the Planting of Forests and Orchards.— How Prisons should be Constructed, and Prisoners managed, to prevent the Generation of Malignant Distempers.

ARCHITECTURE was first carried to a tolerable high pitch by the Tyrians, the Greeks took it from them, the Romans from the Greeks, and the English from the Romans. The Romans first introduced the building with brick, and that of stone was brought into England A. D. 670. In 886, the English began to build with brick, but it did not become general in Great Britain till 1600, when the Earl of Arundel promoted it. This art, in many places, is brought to a high degree of perfection in the present age; though in others, the mysteries of it are much hidden

hidden in many respects, and buildings are frequently erected to disadvantage, and the materials
almost spoiled. I have observed in the great cities
of London, Westminster, Bath, Bristol, Edinburgh, Glasgow, Dublin, Paris, Philadelphia,
and other cities in England, Scotland, Ireland,
France, and America, that a great number
of the houses are almost ruined by reason of
their being wrongly constructed. Rooms are frequently made so small that they are very inconvenient, and numbers of the streets are built so narrow, that it is dangerous passing, and especially
among teams, coaches, &c. Many of those houses
ought to be taken down and rebuilt, with streets
100 feet in breadth, laid out in a regular manner;
but the fashion of making such narrow streets
seems to be wearing away in *Great Britain*, and
elsewhere; for many houses and other buildings
have been taken down of late, the streets made
wider, and the buildings rebuilt in a more com-
modious form, which does honour to the Archi-
tects and others concerned in the work.

The wharfs in sea ports, ought to be made
wide; hence the buildings should be erected at
a distance, to leave room for the laying of lumber
and other commodities.

When a city is built, the streets ought to run
straight and at right angles with each other, and
to be 100 feet wide; the squares betwixt them
should be about 40 rods each way: The houses
should

should be built of brick or stone, and be four stories high, covered with flate, tyle, or lead, to secure them from the fire; and conductors ought to be erected to preserve the buildings from being injured by the lightening. A dwelling house ought to be about 46 feet in length, and 38 in breadth, with a paffage through the middle about 10 feet broad.   The rooms ought to be at leaft 18 feet long, 16 broad, and 9 or 10 feet high.   The doors and windows, ought to be of a fuitable length and breadth, and the chimneys should be fet againft the middle of the rooms, and be drawn in, till the draught againft the mantle piece, is very fmall.   If it should be faid that a fmall paffage would obftruct the ingrefs of the chimney fweepers; I anfwer, that a back made of sheet, or caft iron, might be conftructed and placed in fuch a manner, as to anfwer all the intentions of one made of brick; and it might eafily be taken out and replaced again, as occafion may require. Then the draught ought to be made larger and larger, which will prevent the fmoke from puffing out into the rooms; the force of the fire fending it through a narrow paffage will prevent its returning by the preffure of the atmofphere above; but remember, that the top of a chimney muft be built upon a perpendicular over the fire-place, otherwife the fmoke will defcend into the room; for if it is obftructed by turnings and windings, it

will

will fly the wrong way, as it is as natural for
fmoke to fly upwards as it is for a ftone to fall
downwards; hence chimneys fhould ftand erect.
Cities ought to be kept clean, and proper canals
of water turned under them, to carry off the
filth, and prevent the generation of difeafes.
Churches, palaces, and other buildings, ought to
be proportioned in fuch a manner as to make them
convenient, a large room ought not to be fquare,
but in the form of an oblong.

An Architect ought to be well fkilled both in
the theoretical and practical parts of the bufinefs.
The theory demonftrates how to plan out the work
in proportions requifite to form the fabric, and
the practical, how to execute the bufinefs in the
moft expeditious and advantageous manner.

Architecture confifts of three different claffes, as:

1. Civil; or the building of houfes, churches,
colleges, temples, palaces, halls, bridges, porti-
cos, &c. for the ufes of civil life.

2. Military; as fortifications, ramparts, &c. for
defence againft an enemy.

3. Naval; as the building of docks, and all kinds
of veffels to float on the water, with the works
belonging to them.

The laws of nature taught the ancients to build
houfes to fcreen themfelves and families from the
inclemency of the weather. It is faid, that before
the Romans invaded England, the natives had no
better lodgings than thickets, dens, and caves.

I   Some

Some of thofe caves were for winter habitations, and places of retreat in time of war. The Savages in America have followed much the fame example, having lodged in dens and caves, among the rocks and mountains, like the wild beafts, for the want of knowledge in Architecture.

We have an account in hiftory, of many wonderful fuperftructures, as: 1. The tower of Babel, which was 40 years in building. 2. The walls of Babylon, which were 60 miles in circumference, 587 feet thick, and 1350 feet high; through the walls were 100 gates.

3. The Pyramids of Egypt, the largeft of which covers 11 acres and a quarter of land, and is near 500 feet high.—4. Soloman's temple, which was adorned with gold and many fplendid ornaments.

5. The wall of China, which is 1500 miles in length, and 30 feet high; and of many other noble ftructures, edifices, and temples, which denote that Architecture fhone forth with great lufture and perfection among the ancients, though perhaps, not with that fplendor it does in the prefent age.

Authors difagree fo much in the accounts of the meafures of antiquity, that it is difficult to determine what the dimenfions of fome ancient buildings were, as fome have taken one meafure and fome another, without telling us what meafure they meant, whether it was Englifh, Romifh, &c. The following table fhews the different feet that

have

have been made ufe of among the nations, equi-
valent to 12 inches, Englifh meafure, being divided into 1000 equal parts.

Englifh — ——	1000
Romifh — —	967
French — ——	1068
Spanifh — —	920
Venetian — ——	1032
Rhinland — —	1033
Florentine — ——	1913
Naples — —	2190
Cairo — ——	1824
Turkifh — —	2200

Hence it appears that a Turkifh foot, is more
than as long again as an Englifh, and that the Romifh and Spanifh feet are fhorter; but would it
not be beft to have the meafures and weights alike
through the world, if the nations would agree to
it, as was before obferved.

Every part of a building made of timber ought
to be painted to prevent it from rotting, and to
keep the doors and windows from fwelling in wet
weather. Wooden houfes well painted once in
three years, will laft a long time; but if they ftand
without paint, they will foon rot, and wafte away.

Some are at a great expence in adorning their
buildings with fplendid ornaments, fuch as blank
doors and windows, tablets, medallions, with bas

and

and alto relievos, ftatues, bufts, niches, vafes, enriched ceilings, mouldings, foliage, ruftics, pilaf-
ters, columns, arches, intercoluminations, baluf-
trades, &c.

It is very dangerous to live in open houfes, or
to fleep in new plaiftered rooms, for our bodies
require a fufficient degree of heat to keep their
fluids in circulation. I was taught when I was
young, that open rooms are the moft healthy; but
I found by my own obfervation, that that opinion
is abfurd; for I have frequently obferved, that
where people have been obliged as it were to roaft
one fide, whilft the other was almoft freezing, that
they were often afflicted with colds, coughs, ca-
tarrhs, confumptions, quinfies, pleurifies peripp-
neumonies, and other diforders, whilft others, who
had lived in warm rooms, have been free from
thofe complaints.

Many of the houfes in Canada are built of
ftone: their walls are about two feet thick; the
rooms are large and are kept warm in winter with
ftoves, fituated in fuch a manner, as to warm every
part of the rooms, and make the people comfortable in the remoteft corner; but a fmall quantity
of fuel is expended, and the people were fo remarkably healthy, that I could fcarcely hear a perfon
cough in a large congregation, whilft the ftoves
were kept up; but when they were taken down,
which happened in May or June, the rooms grew
too damp and cold, and the inhabitants were

afflicted

afflicted with colds, coughs, and other diforders of the lungs. Some who have ventured to fleep in new plaiftered rooms, have been found dead the next morning, owing to the coldnefs and dampnefs of the walls.

It is dangerous to ftand ftill, fit, or fleep, with the doors, or windows open ; or where there are holes that let in the air, becaufe it will make people take cold; where they follow this practice in the fhops and public houfes in London, I have heard the inhabitants complain of head aches, coughs, &c. whereas, if they would only keep their rooms tight and warm, they might be freed of thofe complaints. But fome have imbibed an opinion, that they draw more cuftomers by keeping open doors, &c.

Some people have ftoops or piazzas by the fides of their houfes, where they frequently fit in the open air and take cold, by having their perfpiration obftructed by the cool breezes of the wind; but I difapprove of this practice, unlefs the weather is very warm, calm, and pleafant.

There are feveral orders of Architecture, all of which have their proportions as :

I. The Tufcan, which is void of ornaments, and the moft folid, and capable of bearing the heavieft burthen.

II. The Doric, the next in ftrength to the Tufcan, which is the moft ancient order in the world.

III. The

III. The Ionic; this is more fplendid than the Doric, and has but few ornaments.

IV. The Corinthian, this has elegant proportions, adorned with fplendid ornaments.

V. The Compofite; this is only a fpecies of the Corinthian order.

As it is not my defign to be prolix upon any fubject in the *American Oracle*, I fhall not branch out largely upon Architecture, but conclude by obferving, that an Architect ought to have fo much geometrical and philofophical knowledge; as to know how to choofe the beft materials, and conftruct a building in the beft manner. He fhould fee that the foundation he builds upon is good, the materials he builds with are found, and that the work is carried on with regularity in the building of towers, caftles, houfes, temples, palaces, markets, theatres, amphitheatres, villages, towns, cities, ftreets, wharfs, lanes, courts, &c.

The wars that have frequently broke out amongft the nations, have been a great hindrance to the flourifhing of Architecture, as well as to that of other arts and fciences. Hence men of great learning and ingenuity have been flain, famous libraries burnt, elegant towns and cities laid wafte, and fome arts wholly loft; amongft others, that of making cement, which is faid to be ftronger than brick or ftone. Had there not been any bloodfhed and devaftation, and had the nations been

K k   united

united in doing one another good inftead of evil; and had the armies been employed in cultivating the land, in digging down mountains, filling up vallies, the building of bridges, towns, cities, &c. would it not have been much better for the inhabitants of the world? Would not the arts and fciences have been brought to a higher degree of perfection, and the globe adorned and beautified with much more riches, fplendor, and magnificence, collected and depofited for the promotion of the happinefs of mankind, than at the prefent day?

I will juft mention the feven wonders of the world, but had there been no wars, it is probable there would have been more than a thoufand wonders before this time. I will fet them in their proper order, though fome of them are already mentioned in this chapter.

1. The Pyramids of Egypt.

2. The Maufoleum, or tomb built for Maufolus, King of Caria, by Artemifia his Queen.

3. The temple of Diana at Ephefus.

4. The walls and hanging gardens of Babylon.

5. The brazen image of the fun at Rhodes, called the Coloffus. It ftood with one foot on one ifland, and the other on another, fo high that a fhip with its mafts and fails up could fail between its legs. It was fhaken down by an earthquake 224 years before Chrift.

6. The rich ftatue of Jupiter Olympius.

7. The

7. The watch tower, built by Ptolemy Philadelphus, King of Egypt.

It is too much the practice in New England, and in some other places in America, to build houses, barns, &c. of timber; but it would be much better to build with brick or stone, and to cover them with slate or tile, instead of shingles, as they would be warmer, more durable, and more secure from taking fire, which, though commonly a good servant, is sometimes a bad master.

A room may be kept too warm, but this I also disapprove, because it may make people sweat, melt the fluids, relax the solids, and lay a foundation for some dangerous malady. Those who have sat in a warm room ought to put on a cloak or great coat when they go into the open air, and especially if the weather is very cold, or stormy.

There is a vanity which prevails in many parts of America that will make the future generations groan :—It is the rapid destruction of the wood, which is almost totally cut off in some new places, as well as in those which have been settled a long time. In some places which have not been settled more then twenty or thirty years, scarce any thing is left either for fuel or timber. Hence future generations will be greatly pinched with the cold, and especially in towns remote from pits of coal, which are very scarce in this part of the world, as

none have been difcovered, excepting in Newfoundland, Louifbourg, Nova Scotia, or New
Brunfwick, and North Carolina, if I miftake not.
How diftreffing then muft the condition of thofe be
who may live two or three hundred miles from any
fea port, or place where coal can be procured,
when the trees are cut off and nothing can be had
for fuel, or timber? they muft of courfe be pinch-
with the cold, and put to great difficulty in carrying on their cookery, &c.

People have been fo greatly diftreffed already
in fome places in America, that they have been
obliged to burn their barns, fences, and even
their houfhold furniture, to keep from perifhing
with the cold; and wood has been fometimes fo
very fcarce and dear at New-York, that it has
been fold for forty dollars, or nine pounds fterling, per cord.

Therefore, for the prevention of fuch calamities as much as poffible, I will recommend,

1. The building of warm, tight houfes, with
brick or ftone.

2. The ufe of ftoves, and the confumption of
a fmall quantity of fuel.

3. The prefervation of trees already grown.

4. The planting and pruning of forefts in
places where they are wanted.

5. The raifing of orchards, confifting of apple
trees, pear-trees, peach-trees, plumb-trees, cherry
trees, &c. which are beneficial both for fruit and
fuel.

fuel. But perhaps large quantities of coal mines may be difcovered in fome future time in places where fuel may be wanted. Coals are very cheap and plenty in Scotland, and I believe it is as cheap keeping a fire there, as it is in America, where wood is plenty. They are alfo very plenty in London, but they are dear by reafon of a duty which is laid upon them.

Farmers ought to have wood lots near their houfes, to keep their fuel houfed, and a good ftock by them; and efpecially in the Northern climates, where the fnow fometimes falls fo deep, that the teams cannot travel to the forefts.

Different kinds of ftoves have been ufed in America. They are chiefly tight in the Northern Governments, that is, the fire is fhut up fo that it cannot be feen, unlefs a door is opened; they are chiefly made of fheet or caft iron. But I have feen an open kind of ftoves at Philadelphia, which were invented by fome body about fixty miles wefterly of that city. They have been called Franklin's ftoves, becaufe Dr. Franklin wrote upon their utility.

It has been faid, that one cord of wood will do as much good, and go as far in a ftove, as four would in a chimney. Hence, ftoves muft be of great fervice where ever they are ufed.

When the furrounding atmofphere is colder than the rarified air in a room, it will rufh in if the doors or windows are opened, and continue

K k 3   fo

fo to do until an equilibrium is reftored, and chill thofe who have been warmed by the heat of a fire. But if the air in a room is colder than the atmofphere, and the doors, &c. are opened, the cold air will expand itfelf into the warm until an equilibrium is reftored that way.

I fhall conclude this chapter by making fome obfervations on Prifons, and the management of prifoners.

Prifons ought to be fituated in places where the air is good ; and ftreams of water ought to be conveyed under them to keep them clean.

Various plans have lately been invented for the conftruction of prifons, but it is not much matter how they are built, provided the apartments are convenient. The rooms ought to be large, and thofe confined ought not to be too much crowded, becaufe it may breed diftempers, which may cut down not only the prifoners, but fpread to a great diftance and almoft depopulate the country. By chronology we are informed, that 300 perfons, at the affizes at Oxford, caught a gaol diftemper, and died in 1577, and that many took the fame diftemper at the Old Bailey, in London, and died in 1750, &c.

Now we may reafonably fuppofe, that this diftemper was generated by the want of a proper air, a proper regimen, cloathing, and exercife, and by the prifoners being too much crowded, and that by their being thus infected by a contagion, it

was

was communicated to others when the prisoners were brought to trial before the the Courts of Justice.

The treatment that prisoners have met with in many parts of Christendom in time past would disgrace the most barbarous nations. Some have perished by being kept in pits and dungeons, some have lost their lives by being pent up in narrow places, where they could not lie down, and by being crowded to death by the company. Some have been smothered till they have lost their lives for the want of air, and some have perished with the cold, hunger, nakedness, and the like. Prisons about 100 feet in length, 50 in breadth, and three or four stories high, with entries, or passages about 10 feet wide, through the middle of each story from end to end, would be very convenient, in my opinion. The apartments might then be made large, and the Prison-keeper might easily convey to a considerable number of prisoners, those things they daily need for their sustenance. If a prisoner is taken ill, he ought to be kept in some apartment by himself to prevent the spreading of malignant disorders; they ought to be kept clean and warm, and to use gentle exercise, and also to have a good and wholesome diet.

Let men, or women, who may be confin'd,
Unto their mortal bodies be so kind,
As to take care that they *shun* ev'ry thing
Which may amongst them bad *disorders* bring

If they defire in good health to abide,
Whilft they're oblig'd in prifon to refide,
Let this thing always in their mind remain,
That from intemp'rance they muft all refrain:
Abftain from drunk'nefs, anger, rage and ftrife,
And aim to live an upright, fteady life.
Read and difcourfe with pleafure and delight,
Both in the day, and in the filent night.
Go to bed early, fee that ye arife
Nigh to the time the fun does in the fkies;
Wafh clean your face, comb out your matted hair,
And if need be, fee that your nails ye pare:
Keep up your fpirits, often talk and laugh,
And walk around, with, or without a ftaff:
Tell pleafant ftories, make the air to ring,
With a loud voice, when ye attempt to fing;
And often times, if you can get a chance,
Divert yourfelves with mufic, and a dance.
If you wou'd reft and not live in a teafe,
Deftroy the bed bugs, kill off all the fleas;
From other vermin always mind and fee
That ye at all times keep exceeding free.
Sweep oft your room, don't fpit upon the floor,
And keep no dirt within the prifon door.
From all bad fcents pray keep exceeding clear,
Left fome deftructive thing fhou'd foon appear.
When noxious vapours float within the air,
And bad diftempers fpread both here and there,
Amongft you let tobacco fumes arife,
Whofe virtues are extoll'd unto the fkies:

And

And vinegar burnt often in the day,
Is good to drive all noxious things away.
By what I've feen, I'm fure I can refift,
That putrefaction it will much refift.
Another thing I alfo do defire,
That in your room you'll keep a conftant fire;
For it is good, *Philofophers* declare,
To cleanfe and purify the ftagnant air.
Of wholefome things let all your food be made,
Go cleanly dreffed, and mind what I have faid;
Left whilft in prifon ye have to remain,
Defeafes fpread 'till you by them are *flain*.
My beft advice I freely thus do give,
And wifh mankind in happinefs may live;
That honeft prifoners always may be free
From illnefs, and be fet at liberty:
And that at laft they may come to the *fhore*
Where *loathfome Prifons* fhall *afflict* no more.

LONDON, *May* 14, 1791.

CHAP.

CHAP. L. •

A short History of the RISE, SUFFERINGS, DOC-
TRINES, *and* DISCIPLINE *of the* FRIENDS,
commonly called QUAKERS.

IN the beginning of the 17th century there
were great diffensions in Great Britain refpecting Religion ; many who had been diffatisfied
with the fettlement of the Church of England in
the reign of Queen Elizabeth, diffented, and
formed themfelves into various focieties, fome of
whom evinced their fincerity by grievous fufferings, under the intolerance of thofe who governed
church affairs.

In thofe times George Fox began to travel,
and to preach the principles and doctrines which
the Friends adhere to ; as he travelled he met with
divers who readily received his teftimony, and
feveral of them became preachers of the fame doctrine ; multitudes were afterwards converted, and
many meetings were fettled.

But many of thefe people were perfecuted on
account of their religious fentiments, by ftripes,
imprifonments, and other inhumanities.

George

George Fox, was one of the firſt of the Friends who was impriſoned. He was confined at Nottingham, in the year 1649. The next year he was brought before two Magiſtrates in Derbyſhire, where one of them ſcoffing at George Fox, for having bidden him and thoſe about him to *tremble at the word of the Lord,* gave thoſe people the name of *Quakers,* which appellation is retained to this day : But they have always called themſelves *Friends.*

The Friends ſuffered perſecution in England, in the days of Oliver Cromwell, and in the reign of King Charles II. but it does not appear that either Cromwell, or the King, was very ſevere againſt them. The perſecution was chiefly carried on by the Magiſtrates, and other barbarous and inhuman perſons of an inferior rank.

The firſt Friends that went to Boſton, in New-England, were women ; at that place they were impriſoned and cruelly treated, this happened in 1656. The following year the ſcourge was employed, and a law was made for cutting off their ears, which was executed. They were afterwards ſubjected to baniſhment on pain of death, and three men and one woman were actually hanged. The Friends were alſo perſecuted in ſome of the other American Governments, but I believe not with ſuch ſeverity.

In 1661 Samuel Shattock, a baniſhed *Friend* from Boſton, obtained a mandamus from the King to return

return to Boſton as a Deputy, and put a ſtop to the ſeverities in New-England, which was accordingly done.

In 1664 ſixty of the Friends were tranſported from England to America, by an order of Council.

In 1672 King Charles II. releaſed about four hundred of the Friends from confinement. But after his death, as they were not protected by law, about fifteen hundred were impriſoned, by reaſon of the implacable malice of their old perſecutors.

About the year 1675 Bobert Barclay wrote an apology in vindication of the principles and doctrines of the Friends, and preſented it to King Charles II.

In the reign of King James II. the operation of the penal laws againſt Diſſenters were ſuſpended, and the Friends were ſharers in the benefit. But it was not until the reign of King William that they obtained ſome degree of legal protection. In the reign of William and Mary, about the year 1696, an act was paſſed, which with a few exceptions, allowed to their affirmation the legal force of an oath, and provided a leſs oppreſſive mode of recovering tythes, under a certain amount : Thoſe proviſions were made perpetual in the reign of George I. and thus the Friends, in common with other Diſſenters, received the advantage of the act of toleration which had been paſſed in the year 1689. The Friends in Ireland alſo ſuffered perſecution, as

well

well as thofe in England, but when the act of toleration took place, they were relieved by law.

But though the friends have thus in a great
meafure been freed from perfecution, yet it is
faid, that it is not wholly removed in Great Britain and Ireland, for they are ftill liable to fuffer
in the Exchequer, and in the Ecclefiaftical Court,
in confequence of their being required to help
fupport the national miniftry. But the Friends
in America are free from that burthen, as the people at prefent are not bound to fupport fuch a
miniftry. It appears by hiftory, that the Friends
were often greatly perfecuted, becaufe it was
againft their confciences to kill their fellow mortals, and to take oaths before a magiftrate, and
that fome of the priefts have been very bufy in
carrying on thofe perfecutions.

About the year 1682, Pennfylvania was fold by
the Duke of York to the Penn family, and William Penn obtained a charter from the King for
the fettlement of that Government, into which
many of the Friends were induced to remove.
It foon became, and ftill continues to be, the
largeft fettlement of Friends in America; but
many fettled in other provinces and colonies.

In 1731, whilft Jonathan Belcher, Efq. was
Governor of the Maffachufetts, an act of the Affembly was paffed, which exempted the Friends
in that province from contributing to the fupport
of the public miniftry; and they enjoyed a great

2   fhare

ſhare of tranquillity in this and the other Governments, until the war commenced, which terminated in the ſeparation of the United States from the dominion of Great-Britain.

During thoſe commotions, they were involved in great trouble, by refuſing to join in the military ſervices which were required of them; many were impriſoned in divers Governments, and ſeveral ſuffered death at Philadelphia by reaſon of the war. Great numbers were reduced from circumſtances of eaſe, if not of affluence, to the verge of want, by the exceſſive ſeizures which were frequently made of their property, to recover the fines impoſed on them, for refuſing to ſerve perſonally, or to ſubſtitute others, to join the continental armies.

I have extracted the greateſt part of this ſhort account from various authors, but principally from a pamphlet lately publiſhed in London. I have, however, added a few things that I knew myſelf, and ſeveral which I received from perſons of good repute. Thoſe who may be deſirous of further information, are directed to read Sewell's Hiſtory, Edmondſon's Journal, and Rutty's Hiſtory, concerning the perſecutions the Friends have endured by reaſon of their religious ſentiments.

DOCTRINE.

DOCTRINE.

The Friends believe in one eternal God, the Creator, and Preferver of the Univerfe : and in Jefus Chrift, his Son, the Meffiah, and Mediator of the New Covenant. Vid. Heb. xii. 24.

When they fpeak of the gracious difplay of the love of God to mankind, in the miraculous conception, birth, life, miracles, death, refurrection, and afcenfion of Chrift, they prefer the ufe of fuch terms as they find in the Scriptures, and are contented with that knowledge which Divine wifdom hath feen meet to reveal ; and though they do not attempt to explain thofe myftcries which remain under the VEIL ; yet they acknowledge and affert the divinity of Chrift, who is the wifdom and power of God unto falvation. Vid. 1 Cor. i. 24.

To Chrift alone they give the title of the word of God. Vid. John i. 1. and not to the Scriptures, although they highly efteem thofe Sacred Writings, in fubordination to the Spirit. 2 Pet. i. 21. from which they were given forth ; and they hold with the Apoftle Paul, that they are able to make wife unto falvation, through faith, which is in Chrift Jefus. Vid. 2 Tim. iii. 15.

They reverence thofe moft excellent precepts which are recorded in Scripture, and believe they were delivered by our Great Lord ; that they are practicable, and binding on every Chriftian ; and

I that

that in the life to come, every man will be rewarded according to his works. Vid. Matt.
xvi. 27.

Of Univerſal and Saving Light.

That in order to enable mankind to put in
practice thoſe ſacred precepts, many of which are
contradictory to the unregenerate will of man,
Vid. John i. 9, Every man coming into the world is
endued with a meaſure of the light, and grace, or
good ſpirit of Chriſt; by which he is enabled to
diſtinguiſh good from evil, and to correct the diſ-
orderly paſſions and corrupt propenſities of his nature, which mere reaſon is altogether inſufficient to
overcome. For all that belongs to man is fallible
and within the reach of temptation; but this divine
grace, which comes by him who hath overcome the
world, John xvi. 33, is, to thoſe who humbly and
ſincerely ſeek it, an all ſufficient and preſent help in
time of need. By this the ſnares of the enemy are
detected, his allurements avoided, and deliverance
is experienced though faith in its effectual operation, whereby the ſoul is tranſlated out of the
kingdom of darkneſs, and from under the power
of Satan, into the marvellous light and kingdom
of the ſon of God.

Of

Of Worſhip.

The Friends being thus perſuaded that man, without the ſpirit of Chriſt inwardly revealed, can do nothing to the glory of God, or to effect his own ſalvation, they think this influence eſpecially neceſſary to the performance of the higheſt act of which the human mind is capable, even the worſhip of the Father of lights and of ſpirits, in ſpirit and in truth; therefore, they conſider as obſtructions to the pure worſhip, all forms which divert the attention of the mind from the ſecret influence of this unction from the Holy One. Vid. 1 John ii. 20, 22. Yet, although the true worſhip is not confined to time and place, they think it incumbent on Chriſtians to meet often together, (vid. Heb. x. 25,) in teſtimony of their dependence on the Heavenly Father, and for a renewal of their ſpiritual ſtrength; nevertheleſs, in the performance of worſhip, they dare not depend, for their acceptance with him, on a formal repetition of words and experiences of others; but they believe it to be their duty to ceaſe from the activity of the imagination, and to wait in ſilence, to have a true ſight of their condition beſtowed upon them; believing even a ſingle ſigh, (vid. Rom. viii.) 26, ariſing from ſuch a ſenſe of their infirmities, and of the need they have of Divine help, to be more acceptable

L l

to

to God, than any performances, however specious, which originated in the will of man.

Of the Ministry.

From the opinion the Friends are of concerning worship, it follows, that the ministry which they approve must have its origin from the same source; for that which is needful for a man's own direction, and for his acceptance with God, (vid. Jer. xxiii, 30, to 32,) must be eminently so to enable him to be helpful to others. Accordingly they believe the renewed assistance of the light and power of Christ, to be indispensably necessary for all true ministry; and that their holy influence is not at their command, or to be procured by study, but is the free gift of God to his chosen and devoted servants. From hence arises their testimony against preaching for hire, and in contradiction to Christ's positive command, "Freely ye have received, freely give." Vid. Matt. x. 8, And hence also arises their conscientious refusal of supporting such a ministry by tithes, &c.

Of the Preaching of Women.

As the Friends dare not encourage any ministry, but that which they believe to spring from the influence of the Holy Spirit, so neither dare they attempt to restrain this influence to persons of any condition

condition in life, or to the male sex alone; but, as the male and female are one in Christ, they allow such of the female sex as they believe to be endued with a right qualification for the ministry, to exercise their gifts for the general edification of the church; and this liberty they esteem to be a peculiar mark of the Gospel dispensation, as foretold by the Prophet Joel. Vid. Joel ii. 28, 29, and noticed by the Apostle Peter. Acts ii. 16, 17.

Of Baptism and the Supper.

There are two ceremonies in use amongst most professors of the Christian name, viz. water Baptism, and what is termed the Lord's Supper; the first of these being generally esteemed the essential means of an initiation into the church of Christ; and the latter of maintaining communion with him. But as the Friends have been convinced, that nothing short of his redeeming power, inwardly revealed, can set the soul free from the thraldom of sin, it is by this power alone that they believe salvation can be effected. And they hold that as there is one Lord and one Faith, (vid. Eph. iv. 5,) so Baptism is one in nature and operation; that nothing short of it can make us living members of his mystical body; and that the Baptism with water, administered by his forerunner John, belonged, as the latter confessed, to

L l 2   an

an inferior and decreasing difpenfation. Vid. John iii. 30.

With refpect to the other rite, they believe that communion between Chrift and his church is not maintained by that, nor any other external performance, but only by a real participation of his Divine nature through faith, vid. 2. Pet. i. 4; that this fupper is alluded to in Revelation. Vid. Rev. iii. 20. " Behold I ftand at the door and knock, " if any man hear my voice, and open the door, " I will come in to him, and will fup with him, " and he with me." And that where the fubftance is obtained, it is unneceffary to attend to the fha- dow, which doth not confer grace, concerning which different opinions and violent animofities have arifen amongft other profeffors of the Chrif- tian religion.

Of Univerfal Grace and Perfection.

As they thus believe that the grace of God, which comes by Jefus Chrift, is alone fufficient for falvation, they can neither admit that it is conferred on a few only, whilft others are left without it; nor, thus afferting its univerfality, can they limit its operation to a partial cleanfing of the foul from fin, even in this life. They enter- tain worthier notions both of the power and good- nefs of our Heavenly Father, and believe that he doth

2

doth vouchfafe to affift the obedient to experience a total furrender of the natural will to the guid- ance of his pure unerring fpirit, through whofe re- newed affiftance they are enabled to bring forth fruits unto holinefs, and to ftand perfect in their prefent rank. Vid. Matt. v. 48. Eph. iv. 13. Col. iv. 12.

Of Oaths and War.

There are not many of their tenets more gene- rally known than their teftimony againft oaths and war. With refpect to the former of thefe, they abide literally by Chrift's pofitive injunction, delivered in his fermon on the Mount, viz. " Swear not at all." Vid. Matt. v. 34. From the fame facred collection of the moft excellent precepts of moral and religious duty from the ex- ample of our Lord himfelf, (Matt. xxxix. 44, &c. Chap. xxvi. 52, 53. Luke xxii. 51. John xviii. 11.) and from the correfpondent conviction of his fpi- rit in their hearts, they are confirmed in the be- lief that wars and fightings are, in their origin and effects, utterly repugnant to the Gofpel, which ftill breathes peace and good will to men. They are alfo clearly of the judgment, that if the bene- volence of the Gofpel was generally prevalent in the minds of men, it would effectually prevent them from oppreffing, much more from enflaving, their brethren, (of whatfoever colour or com-

L l 3

plexion)

plexion) for whom as for themfelves, Chrift died;
and would even influence their conduct in their
treatment of the brute creation, which would no
longer groan the victims of their avarice, and of
their falfe ideas of pleafure.

Of Government.

Some of the tenets which the Friends profeffed,
fubjected their friends in former times to much
fuffering from Government, though as to the falutary purpofes of Government, their principles are
a fecurity. They inculcate fubmiffion to the laws
in all cafes where in confcience is not violated; but
they hold that as Chrift's kingdom is not of this
world, it is not the bufinefs of the Civil Magiftrate
to interfere in matters of religion, but to maintain
the external peace and good order of the community. They therefore think perfecution even in the
fmalleft degree, unwarrantable. Hence they are
careful in requiring their members not to be concerned in illicit trade, nor in any manner to de-
fraud the revenue.

Of their Deportment.

Their fociety from their firft appearance has dif-
ufed thofe names of the months and days, which
having been given in honour of the heroes or falfe
gods of the Heathens, originated in their flattery
and

and fuperftition; and the cuftom of fpeaking to a
fingle perfon in the plural number, as having
arifen alfo from motives of adulation. Compli-
ments, fuperfluity of apparel and furniture, outward fhews of rejoicing and mourning, and obfervation of days and times, they efteem to be in-
compatible with the fimplicity and fincerity of a
Chriftian life; and public diverfions, gaming,
and other vain amufements of the world, they cannot but condemn; they are a wafte of that time
which is given to us for nobler purpofes, and divert the attention of the mind from the fober duties of life, and from the reproofs of inftruction,
by which we are guided to an everlafting inherit-
ance.

Thus have I given a general defcription of the
tenets which the Friends adhere to. They believe
however that a true and living faith is not produced in the mind of man by his own effort, but that
it is the free gift of God, (vid. Eph. ii. 8.) in
Chrift Jefus, nourifhed and increafed by the pro-
greffive operation of the Holy Spirit in his heart,
and his proportionate obedience. Vid. John vii. 17.
Therefore, although, for the prefervation of the teftimonies given them to bear, and for the peace and
good order of their fociety, they deem it neceffary
that thofe who are admitted into memberfhip with
them, fhould be previoufly convinced of thofe
doctrines which are efteemed effential; but they
require no formal fubfcription to any articles,

L l 4 either

either as a condition of memberſhip, or as a qualification for the ſervice of their church.— They prefer the judging of men by their fruits, in a dependance on the aid of him who, by his Prophet, hath promiſed to be " a ſpirit of judgment to him that ſitteth in judgment." Vid. Iſai. xxviii. 6 ; that without this, there is danger of receiving numbers into the outward communion, without any addition to the ſpiritual ſheepfold, whereof Chriſt declared himſelf · to be both the door and ſhepherd. Vid. John x. 7, 11. that is, ſuch as know his voice, and follow him in the paths of obedience.

Of their Diſcipline.

Their diſcipline conſiſts chiefly in relieving the poor, the maintenance of good order, the ſupport of the teſtimonies which they believe is their duty to bear to the world, and the help and recovery of ſuch as are overtaken in faults.

In the practice of their diſcipline, they think it is indiſpenſibly neceſſary that the order recommended by Chriſt himſelf be invariably obſerved : Vid. Matt. xviii. 15, 17. " If thy brother ſhall " treſpaſs againſt thee, go and tell him his fault be- " tween thee and him alone : if he ſhall hear thee, " thou haſt gained thy brother; but if he will not " hear thee, then take with thee one or two more, " that in the mouth of two or three witneſſes, every " word

" word may be eftablifhed ; and if he fhall negleft
" to hear them, tell it unto the church."

Of their Meetings for Difcipline.

To effeft the falutary purpofes of difcipline,
meetings were appointed at an early period of the
fociety, which from the times of their being held
were called quarterly meetings.   It was afterwards
found expedient to divide the diftricts of thofe
meetings, and to meet more often ; from hence
arofe their monthly meetings, fubordinate to thofe
held quarterly.   At length, in 1669, a yearly
meeting was eftablifhed, to fuperintend, affift, and
provide rules for the whole ; previous to which,
generally meetings had been occafionally held.

Of their Monthly Meetings, Poor, convinced Per-
fons, Certificates of Removal, Overfeers, and Mode
of dealing with Offenders.

A monthly meeting is commonly compofed of
feveral particular congregations, fituated within a
convenient diftance of each other, and where this
is the cafe, it is ufual for the members of each congregation to form what is called a preparative
meeting, becaufe its bufinefs is to prepare whatever
may occur among themfelves to be laid before
the monthly meeting.   Their bufinefs at the
monthly meeting is to provide for the fubfiftence
of the poor, and for the education of their children ; to judge of the fincerity and fitnefs of perfons

fons appearing to be convinced of the truth of the
religious principles of the fociety, and defiring
to be admitted into memberfhip; to excite due
attention to the difcharge of religious and moral
duties, and to deal with diforderly members.

When any have made application to become
members of the fociety; a fmall committee is appointed to vifit the party, and make a report to
the monthly meeting; which is directed not to
admit any into memberfhip, without allowing a
feafonable time to confider of their conduct.

At the monthly meetings the Friends alfo grant
to fuch of their members as remove into other
monthly meetings, certificates of their memberfhip
and conduct, without which they cannot gain
memberfhip in fuch meetings.

Each monthly meeting is required to appoint
certain perfons, under the name of *Overfeers*, who
are to take care that the rules of their difcipline
is put in practice; and when any account of diforderly conduct comes to their knowledge, they
are to fee that private admonition, agreeable to
the Gofpel rule before-mentioned, is given, previ-
vioufly to its being laid before the monthly meeting.

When a cafe is introduced, it is ufual for a
fmall committee to be appointed to vifit the of-
fender, in order to endeavour to convince him of
his error, and induce him to forfake and condemn
it if they fucceed, the tranfgreffor generally figns
                                         a written

a written acknowledgment, and he is by a minute
declared to have made fatisfaction for the offence;
if not, he is difowned as a member of the fociety.
This is done by what is termed a teftimony of de-
nial, which is a paper reciting the offence, and
fometimes the fteps which have led to it; next,
the means unavailingly ufed to reclaim the of-
fender; after that, a claufe difowning him; to
which is ufually added, an expreffion of defire for
his repentance, and for his being reftored to
memberfhip.

It has long been the decided judgment of the
fociety that its members fhall not fue each other at
law; hence whence difputes arife between individuals, they are fettled by arbitrators; and if any
refufe to adopt this mode, or, having adopted it,
to fubmit to the award, it is the direction at the
yearly meeting, that fuch fhall be difowned.

Of Marriages, Births and Burials.

The allowance of marriages alfo belongs to the
Friends monthly meetings; for their fociety has
always fcrupled to acknowledge the excluſive
authority of the priefts in the folemnization of
marriage. Thofe who intend to marry appear together, and propofe their intention to the monthly
meeting, and if not attended by their parents or
guardians, produce a written certificate of their
confent, figned in the prefence of witneffes. The
meeting

meeting then appoints a committee to inquire whether they are clear of other engagements respecting marriage; and if at a subsequent meeting, to which the parties also come and declare the continuance of their intention, and no objections are reported, they have the meeting's consent to solemnize their intended marriage. This is done in a public meeting for worship, towards the close whereof the parties stand up, and solemnly take each other for husband and wife. I was once present at one of their weddings, in America, where the man took the woman by her right hand, and uttered the following words before the meeting, as near as I can remember.

· " *Friends, bear witness ; I Thomas H———d, take this my friend, Nancy R———d, to be my kind and loving wife; and I promise, through the assistance of Divine Grace, to conduct towards her like a kind and loving husband, till by death we are separated.*"

She then took him by the right hand, and cried, " Friends, bear witness, I Nancy R———d, do take this my friend Thomas H———d, to be my kind and loving husband, and I promise, through the assistance of Divine Grace, to conduct towards him, like a kind and loving wife, till by death we are separated."

A certificate of the proceedings was then publicly read by the clerk of the meeting, and signed by the parties, and afterwards by the relations, and others as witnesses. Of such certificates the monthly meeting keeps a record; as also of the

births

births and burials of its members. A certificate of the date, of the name of an infant, and of its parents, figned by thofe prefent at the birth, is the fubject of one of thefe laft mentioned records; and an order for interment, counterfigned by the grave-maker, of the other. The naming of children is without ceremony. Burials are alfo conducted in a fimple manner. The body, followed by the relations and friends, is fometimes previous to interment carried to a meeting, and at the grave, a paufe is generally made; on both which occafions it frequently falls out, that one or more of the Friends prefent have fomewhat to exprefs for the edification of thofe who attend: but no religious rite is confidered as an effential of a burial.

Of Quarterly Meetings, Queries, and Appeals.

Several monthly meetings compofe a quarterly meeting. At the latter are produced written anfwers from the monthly meetings, to certain queries concerning the conduct of their members, and the meeting's care over them. The accounts thus received, are digefted into one, which is fent alfo in the form of anfwers to queries, by reprefentatives, to the yearly meeting.—Appeals from the judgment of monthly meetings are brought to the quarterly meetings; whofe bufinefs alfo it is to affift in any difficult cafe, or where remiffnefs

appears

appears in the care of the monthly meetings over
the individuals who compofe them.

Of Yearly Meetings.

The annual meeting has a general fuperintend-
ance of the fociety in the country in which it is
eftablifhed; and therefore as the accounts which
it receives difcover the ftate of inferior meetings,
as particular exigencies require, or as the meeting is impreffed with a fenfe of duty, it gives
forth its advice, makes fuch regulations as appear
to be requifite, or excites to the obfervance of
thofe already made; and fometimes appoints committees to vifit thofe quarterly meetings which appear to be in need of immediate help. Appeals
from the judgment of the quarterly meetings are
here finally determined; and brotherly correfpondence, by epiftles, is maintained with other quarterly meetings.

According to an account I have lately received
in London, there are feven yearly meetings, which
are held at the following places, viz.

1. London.
2. New England.
3. New York.
4. New Jerfey, and Pennfylvania.
5. Maryland.
6. Virginia.
7. The Carolinas, and Georgia.

I   Hence

Hence, according to this account, the four
New England governments compofe one meeting; New York another; New Jerfey, and Pennfylvania another, &c.

The annual meeting is held at London, in the
fifth month of this prefent year, 1791. To this
meeting reprefentatives come from Ireland, and
from other parts of the world. Annual meetings
have been held in almoft every government of
the United States of America, but as the times of
their fitting are often altered, I fhall not fay any
thing further on the fubject.

Of Women's Meeting.

As the Friends believe that women may be
rightly called to the work of the miniftry, they
alfo think, that to them belongs a fhare in the
fupport of their Chriftian difcipline; and that fome
parts of it, wherein their own fex is concerned,
devolve on them with peculiar propriety. Accordingly they have monthly, quarterly, and
yearly meetings of their own fex, held at the fame
time and in the fame place with thofe of the men;
but feparately, and without the power of making
rules: and it may be remarked, that during the
perfecutions, which in the laft century occafioned
the imprifonment of fo many of the men, the care
of the poor often fell on the women, and relief was
by them fatisfactorily adminiftered.

Of

Of the Meeting of Ministers and Elders.

Those who believe themselves required to speak
in the meetings for worship, are not immediately
acknowledged as ministers by their monthly meetings; but time is taken for judgment, that the
meeting may be satisfied of their call and qualifications. It will also sometimes happen, that such
as are not approved, will obtrude themselves as
ministers to the grief of their brethren; but
much forbearance is used towards these, before
the disapprobation of the meeting is publicly tes-
tified. But in order that those who are in the
situation of approved ministers, may have the tender sympathy and counsel of either sex, who by
their experience in the work of religion, are qua-
lified for that service, the monthly meetings are
advised to select such, under the denomination of
elders. These, and ministers approved by their
monthly meeting, have meetings peculiar to
themselves, called meetings of ministers and
elders, in which they have an opportunity of
exciting each other to a discharge of their several
duties; of extending their advice to those who
may appear weak, without any needless exposure.
These meetings are generally held in the compass
of each monthly, quarterly, and yearly meeting.
They are conducted by rules prescribed by the
yearly meeting, and have no authority to make

any

any alteration or addition to them. Thefe members unite with their brethren in the meetings for difcipline, and are accountable to the latter for their conduct.

Of the Second Day, Morning Meeting.

It is to a meeting of this kind held in London, that the revifal of manufcripts intended for publication concerning their principles, is intrufted by the yearly meeting held in the fame place, and alfo the granting, on the intervals of the yearly meeting, certificates of approbation to fuch minifters as are inclined to travel in the work of the miniftry in foreign parts. When a vifit of this kind does not extend beyond Great Britain, a certificate from the monthly meeting, of which the minifter is a member is fufficient; if to Ireland, the concurrence of the quarterly meeting is alfo required. Regulations of a fimilar tendency obtain in other yearly meetings.

Meetings for Sufferings.

The yearly meeting held in London, in the year 1675, appointed a meeting to be held in that city, for the purpofe of advifing and affifting, in cafes of fuffering for confcience fake, which hath continued with great ufe to the fociety to this day. It is compofed of Friends, under the name of correfpondents, respondents, chosen by the several quarterly meetings, and who reside in, or near the city. The same meetings also appoint members of their own in the country as correspondents, who are to join their brethren in London on emergency. The names of some of the correspondents, previous to their being recorded as such, are submitted to the approbation of the yearly meeting. Those of the men, who are approved ministers, are also members of this meeting, which is called the meeting for sufferings; a name arising from its original purpose, which is not yet become entirely obsolete.

The yearly meeting has intrusted the meeting for sufferings with the care of printing and the distribution of books, and with the management of its stock, which is collected by an occasional voluntary contribution, and expended in printing books, house-rent for a clerk, and his wages for keeping records, the passage of ministers who visit their brethren beyond the sea, and some small incidental charges.

The Committee that has the care of this stock, &c. is considered as a standing Committee for the yearly meeting; and hath a general care of whatever may arise, during the intervals of that meeting, which affect the society, and require immediate attention; particularly of those circumstances which may occasion an application to government.

2   There

There is not any Prefident in any of their meet.
ings, as they believe that Divine wifdom alone
ought to prefide ; nor has any member a right to
claim pre-eminence over the reft. The office of
Clerk, with a few exceptions, is undertaken voluntarily by fome member, as is alfo the keeping
of records. Where thefe are very voluminous,
and require a houfe for their depofit, (as is the
cafe in London, where the general records of the
fociety in Great Britain are kept) a clerk is hired
to have the care of them; but except a few clerks
of this kind, and perfons who have had the care
of meeting houfes, none receive any ftipend or
gratuity for their fervices in a religious fociety.

Conclusion.

Thus have I given a fhort account of the rife,
fufferings, doctrines, and difcipline of the Friends,
the greateft part of which I have extracted from
their own publications. They are a very civil,
induftrious, and honeft people; and as they do
not harrafs one another with law fuits, are very
temperate, avoid fuperfluities, and thofe vanities
and follies, which are too much followed by many
others who are called Chriftians, they commonly
grow rich, or, at leaft, get a comfortable fubfiftence. They are hofpitable to ftrangers, kind to
the poor, promoters of brotherly love, and of the
M m 2 public

public tranquillity; and they augment the national revenue, as they pay their taxes, and refuse to run goods, or to buy any that have been run. Would not the world be almoſt a *paradiſe*, if all the people would follow the example of the Friends, in walking *honeſtly*, and in living *peaceably?*

CHAP.

CHAP. LI.

An Account of the Moravians.

THE Moravians are a fect of Proteſtants called *Unitas Fratrum*; or the United Brethren. They appeared in Bohemia, in the year
1457; and have been ſettled a long time at Hern-
huth, in Germany. In 1737, there were ſome
in England, but of late years they have ſpread
themſelves over many parts of America. They
poſſeſs the utmoſt veneration for our Bleſſed Sa-
viour, whom they conſider as their immediate
head and director; they alſo enjoin the moſt im-
plicit obedience to the rules of their church, and
are ſaid to practiſe much brotherly love amongſt
one another. The ſubſtance of the conſtitution of
their church, dated in the year 1733, at Hern-
huth, in Upper Saxony, in Germany, is as follows,
viz.

1. They have a *Senior*, or *Eldeſt*, who is to
aſſiſt the church by his counſel and prayers, and
to determine what ſhall be done in matters of importance. Of him is required, that he be well
experienced in the things of God, and witneſſed
by all for holineſs of converſation.

2. They

2. They have *Deacons*, or *Helpers*, who are in private affemblies to inftruct : To take care that outward things are done decently and in order : and to fee that every member of the church grows in grace, and walks fuitable to his holy calling.

3. The *Paftor*, or *Teacher*, is to be an overfeer of the whole flock, and every perfon therein ; to baptize the children ; diligently to form their minds, and bring them up *in the nurture and ad-monition of the Lord:* When he finds in them a fincere love of the crofs, then to receive them into the church : to adminifter the fupper of the Lord : To join in marriage thofe who are already married to Chrift : To reprove, admonifh, quicken, and comfort, as need requires : To declare the whole counfel of God : Taking heed at all times to fpeak as the oracles of God, and agreeably to the analogy of faith : To bury thofe who have died in the Lord, and to keep that fafe which is committed to his charge, even the pure doctrine and apoftolical difcipline which they have receiv-ed from their forefathers.

4. They have alfo another fort of *Deacons* who take care that nothing be wanting to the *orphan-houfe*, to the poor, the fick, and the ftrangers. Others again there are, who are peculiarly to take care of the fick ; and others, of the poor. And two of thefe are intrufted with the public ftock, and keep accounts of all that is received or expended.

5. There

5. There are women who perform each of the above-mentioned offices, among thofe of their own fex: For none of the men converfe with them, befide the eldeft, the teacher, and one, or fometimes two of the Deacons.

6. Towards magiftrates, whether of a fuperior or inferior rank, they bear the greateft reverence, and chearfully fubmit to their laws; and even when many of them have been fpoiled of their goods, driven out of their houfes, and every way oppreft by them, yet they refifted them not, neither opened their mouths, nor lifted up a hand againft them. In all things which do not immediately concern the inward fpiritual kingdom of Chrift, they fimply, and without contradicting, obey the higher powers. But with regard to confcience, the liberty of this they cannot fuffer to be any way limited or infringed. And to this head they refer whatever directly and in itfelf tends to hinder the falvation of fouls: Or, whatfoever things Chrift and his holy apoftles (who meddled not with outward worldly things) took charge of, and performed, as neceffary for the conftituting and well-ordering of his church. In thefe things they acknowledge no head but Chrift; and are determined, God being their helper, to give up not only their goods but life itfelf, rather than the liberty which God hath given them.

7. As it behoves Chriftians not to be *flothful in bufinefs*, but diligently to attend to the works of

M m 4   their

their calling, there are perfons chofen by the church, to fuperintend all thofe who are employed in outward bufinefs. And by this means alfo, many things are prevented which might otherwife be an occafion of offence.

8. They have alfo *Cenfors* and *Monitors*; of thofe experience and perfpicacity, wifdom and modefty are chiefly required. The *Cenfors* fignify what they obferve (and they obferve the fmalleft things) either to the *Deacons* or *Monitors*. Some *Monitors* there are, whom all know to be fuch; others who are fecretly appointed; and who, if need require may freely admonifh in the love of Chrift, even the rulers of the church.

9. The church is fo divided, that firft the hufbands, then the wives, then the widows, then the maids, then the young men, then the boys, then the girls, and laftly the little children, are in fo many diftinct claffes: each of which is daily vifited, the married men by a married man, the wives by a wife, and fo of the reft.* The larger are alfo divided into fmaller claffes, or bands, over each of which one prefides who is of the greateft experience. All thefe leaders meet the fenior every week, and lay open to him and to the Lord, whatfoever hinders or furthers the work of God, in the fouls committed to their charge.

* This work all the married brethren and fifters, as well as all the unmarried, perform in their turns.

10. In

10. In the year 1727, four and twenty men and as many women agreed, that each of them would fpend an hour in every day, in praying to God for his bleffing on his people; and for this purpofe both the men and women chofe a place, where any of their own fex who were in diftrefs, might be prefent with them. The fame number of unmarried women, of unmarried men, of boys, and of girls, were afterwards, at their defire, added to them, who pour out their fouls before God, not only for their own brethren, but alfo for other churches and perfons, that have defired to be mentioned in their prayers. And this perpetual interceffion has never ceafed, day or night, fince its firft beginning.

11. And as the members of the church are divided, according to their refpective ftates and fexes : fo they are alfo, with regard to their proficiency in the knowledge of God. Some are dead, fome are quickened by the fpirit of God: Of thefe, fome again are untractable, fome diligent, fome zealous, burning with their firft love; fome babes, and fome young men. Thofe who are ftill dead, are vifited every day. And of the babes in Chrift efpecial care is taken alfo, that they may be daily infpected and affifted to grow in grace, and in the knowledge of our Lord Jefus.

12. In the *orphan-houfe*, a number of children are brought up, feparate according to their fex. Befide which, feveral experienced perfons, ap-

pointed

pointed to confult with the parents, touching the education of the other children. In teaching them Chriftianity, they make ufe of Luther's Catechifm, and ftudy the amending of their wills as weil as their underftanding; finding by experience, that when their will is moved, they often learn more in a few hours, than otherwife in many months. Their little children they inftruct chiefly by hymns; whereby they find the moft important truths moft fuccefsfully infinuated into their minds.

13. They highly reverence marriage, as greatly conducive to the kingdom of Chrift. But neither their young men nor women enter into it till they affuredly know, they are married to Chrift. When any know it is the will of God, that they fhould change their ftate, both the man and woman are placed for a time, with fome married perfons, who inftruct them how to behave, fo that their married life may be pleafing to God. Then their defigns are laid before the whole church, and after about fourteen days, they are folemnly joined, tho' not otherwife habited, than they are at other times. If they make any entertainment (which is not always) they invite only a few intimate friends, by whofe faithful admonitions they may be the better prepared to bear their crofs, and fight the good fight of faith. If any woman is with child, mention is made of her condition in the public prayers, and fhe is alfo exhorted in private, wholly to give herfelf up into the hands of her

faithful

faithful Creator. As foon as a child is born, prayer is made for it, and if it may be, it is baptifed in the prefence of the whole church. Before it is weaned, it is brought into the affembly on the Lord's Day.

14. Whoever either of the male or female children feek God with their whole heart, know their fins are forgiven, and obey the truth, are not ufed to be much incited to come to the Lord's fupper; neither are they forbidden fo to do, if they defire it. They think it enough to teach their children juft conceptions of it, and the difference between this food of the foul, and that milk which they every day receive of Chrift. They then publicly declare the fentiments of their hearts concerning it. They are afterwards examined both in private by the paftor, and alfo in public: And then after an exhortation by the *Senior,* are by him, thro' laying on of hands, added to the church and *confirmed.* The fame method is ufed with thofe who renounce the Papal fuperftitions, or who are turned from the fervice of Satan to God; and that, if they defire it, altho' they are not young; yea, though they are well ftricken in years.

15. Once or twice in a month all the church receives the Lord's Supper, and the power of God being prefent amongft them, a general confeffion of fins is made by one of the brethren in the name of all. Then a few folid queftions are afked; which when they have anfwered, the abfo-

lution

lution or remission of sins is either pronounced to all in general, or confirmed to every particular person, by the laying on of hands. The Seniors first receive ; then the rest in order, without any regard had to worldly dignity, in this, any more than in any other of the solemn offices of religion. After receiving, all the men (and so the women) meet together, to renew their covenant with God, to seek his face, and to exhort one another to the patience of hope and the labour of love.

16. They have a peculiar esteem for lots, and accordingly use them both in public and private, to decide points of importance, when the reasons brought, on each side appear to be of equal weight. And they believe this to be then the only way of wholly setting aside their own will, of acquitting themselves of all blame, and clearly knowing what is the will of God.

17. At eight in the morning, and in the evening, they meet to pray and to praise God, and to read and hear the Holy Scriptures : The time they usually spend in sleep, is from eleven at night till four in the morning. So that allowing three hours in a day for taking the food both of their bodies and souls, there remains sixteen for work. And this space those who are in health spend with all diligence and faithfulness.

18. Two men keep watch every night in the streets, as do two women, in the women's apartment : They may pour out their souls for those

that

that sleep; and by their hymns raise the hearts of any who are awake to God.

19. For the further stirring up of the gift which is in them, sometimes they have public, and sometimes private Love-feasts: At which they take a moderate refreshment, with gladness and singleness of heart, and the voice of praise and thankfgiving.

20. If any man amongst them having been often admonished, and long forborn, persists in walking unworthy of his holy calling, he is no longer admitted to the Lord's Supper. If he still continues in his fault, hating to be reformed, the last step is, publicly, and often in the midst of many prayers and tears, to cast him out of their congregation. But great is their joy, if he then sees the error of his ways, so that they may receive him amongst them again.

21. Most of their brethren and sisters have, in some part of their life, experienced holy mourning and sorrow of heart; and have afterwards been assured, that *there* was *no* more *condemnation for them, being passed from death unto life.* They are therefore far from fearing to die, or desiring to live on earth; knowing that to them *to die is gain*, and being confident that they are the care of him, whose are the *issues of life and death.* Wherefore they depart as out of one chamber into another, and after the soul has left its habitation, the remains are deposited in the earth, appointed for

that

that purpofe, and the furvivors are greatly com-
forted, and rejoice over them, with a *joy the world
knoweth not of.*

It appears from hiftory, that the Moravians fuffered a moft horrible perfecution in Moravia
and Bohemia, about the year 1458: for the King
having promifed by his coronation oath, to extir-
pate the Heretics, was under a neceffity to perfecute the United Brethren: Hence they were declared unworthy of the common rights of fubjects,
and in the depth of Winter, turned out of the
cities and villages, with the forfeiture of all their
effects. The fick were caft out in the open fields,
where many perifhed with hunger and cold; and
having been accufed by the Romifh priefts, and
fome others, of being fecret fowers of fedition,
many were thrown into prifons, with a view of ex-
torting from them by hunger, cold, racks, and
other tortures, a confeffion of having been guilty
of feditious defigns; but as they were innocent,
nothing could be extorted from them that way.
Hence numbers were inhumanly dragged at the
tails of horfes, or carts, and quartered, or burnt
alive. Many died in the prifons, and fuch as fur-
vived were, at laft, when no crime could be proved againft them, difcharged in a moft pitiful condition.

It alfo appears, that the various perfecutions
that thefe people met with from time to time,
was the caufe of their emigrating from their own
country,

country, and fettling in different parts of the world.

Thus have I related the fubftance of their conftitution as it ftood in 1733; and whether they have added any thing to it, or diminifhed any thing from it fince that time, I have not learnt. I was once at their meeting in London, where they read the fervice and made ufe of both vocal and inftrumental mufic, but their prayers are different from thofe of the church of England.

CHAP.

CHAP. LII.

An account of the METHODISTS.

METHODISM took its rife in 1734; the Rev. George Whitfield, B. A. a Divine of the Church of England, who was born, 1714, and died 1770, and the Rev. John Wefley, M. A. a minifter of the fame church, who was born 1703, and died, 1791, are faid to be the founders of this inftitution. But Mr. Whitefield's followers and Mr. Wefley's difagree in fentiment, in that the former believe that falvation is obtained by faith alone in Chrift Jefus, and that the love of God to his elect cannot be broken off; the latter believe that men are juftified by works and grace, and that it is poffible for them to go on in degrees of holinefs, till they arrive at laft even to a ftate of perfection in this life. Mr. Wefley's converts are fo very numerous, that one of his preachers informed me there are about 70,000 in Great Britain, and Ireland; and, according to a publication which I have lately feen, there are upwards of 43,000 in America. Some of Mr. White-

I

field's

field's followers are said to be rigid obfervers of the 39 articles of the Church of England, whilft others call themfelves Calvinifts.

The places appointed for affembling together are called Tabernacles by Mr. Whitefield's people, and preaching houfes by Mr. Wefley's adherents. Both fometimes pray according to the forms in the Common Prayer book, and fometimes extempore. They are very ferious in their devotions, obferve the Eucharift, water baptifm, and a love feaft, the latter being only bread and water. When people enter into their church, they confefs their fins, tell what experiences they have had of the new birth, own a covenant, and receive a ticket, denoting that they belong to the Methodiftical fociety, and are entitled to all the privileges of the fame. Thefe tickets are exchanged once in fix months for new ones. But if any brother or fifter has walked diforderly, they are excommunicated, by being debarred from the benefit of receiving a new ticket, unlefs repentance and reformation takes place.

Many of thofe people within the circle of my acquaintance have pretended to very remarkable convictions and converfions; that their minds have been inftantaneoufly illuminated by the rays of Divine grace; that they have thus been turned from darknefs to light, and enabled to walk in newnefs of life; and fome have pretended that they have feen vifions, &c. Thefe things have been imput-

N n ed

ed to the powers of imagination only. by some people, and others have imputed them to a supernatural power, but let them be as they may, I have seen a visible change in some who have pretended they have been thus converted; as they have appeared to be more honest in their dealings and more exemplary in their lives and conversations than they were before.

Mr. Whitefield travelled through and preached in many parts of America; and Mr. Wesley, was about a year and nine months in Georgia and South Carolina: he also travelled and preached in Great Britain and Ireland, and has been several times in Holland and Germany. Mr. Whitefield was also a great traveller and preacher in England; and both of these Ministers often preached in the fields, to ten, fifteen and sometimes to twenty thousand people.

It appears that these preachers have done much good, by uniting the people, and by promoting brotherly love, acts of kindness, charity and humanity amongst mankind; for their followers are very kind to the poor, to strangers, &c. as I have found by my own experience and observations.

Mr. Whitefield, died in New-England, in America, in the year 1770, and Mr. Wesley at London, March the 2d, 1791.

I shall conclude this chapter by adding the following, which I composed and published just after his death, viz.

An

AN ELEGY

On the Death of the late Reverend JOHN WES-
LEY, A. M.

GREAT *Wesley's* gone, he's landed on the shore,
Where grief and trouble shall afflict no more;
A pious life he liv'd upon the stage,
Until he was nigh eighty-eight of age.
In Lincolnshire it truly has been found
This man was born, upon Great-Britain's ground.
When he was young, it often has been said,
His father's house was all in ashes laid:
The room in flames! behold, the child did wake,
Sprang to the window, which he up did take;
There, all alone, he loudly rais'd his cry
Unto some neighbours, that were drawing nigh
To him they ran, on hearing the loud call,
And took him out just as the house did fall:
Thus they the *lad* from *burning flames* did *pluck*,
And thank'd the *Lord* that they had such good *luck*.
His mind on learning very much was bent,
Hence to a college he in time was sent;
Studies profound the *pupil* follow'd till
He was a man of scientific skill.
As time roll'd on, with pleasure and with ease,
He did receive the requisite degrees;
After his learning he had thus obtain'd,
To preach the word, he truly was ordain'd:
From place to place, as godly teachers shou'd,
He often went, and daily did do good.

N n 2

I understand

I underſtand that he, in former times,
Did croſs the ocean to the Weſtern climes :
He preached at Georgia, as ſome people ſay,
But left the place, and came again this way.
Has ſpent much time upon Old England's ground,
In writing books, and preaching all around.
Sometimes he landed on the Iriſh ſhore,
And many people preached the word before :
To Scotland too he frequently did go,
'And twice to Holland, with his friends alſo ;
A famous man he was to preach and pray,
When he was old, and in his younger day.
Both great and good, we truly may relate ;
Exceeding uſeful both in church and ſtate ;
Kind to the poor ; he often gave relief
To men and women overwhelmed with grief ;
Who taught the people always to ſuppreſs
Thoſe things, indeed, which lead to wickedneſs.
He loyal was, impreſs'd the bleſſed thing
Of fearing God, and honouring the King ;
Exhorted men to let contention ceaſe,
To live in love, in harmony, and peace.
But he's been ſtruck a *fatal ſtroke* by *death* ;
His body *fell*, and off did fly his *breath*.
The ſprightly *actions*, which he once poſſeſt,
Are wholly gone, and all is ſtill at *reſt* :
Can't ſee, nor hear, nor any way converſe,
Nor move one finger in the univerſe.
This is the *fate*, I plainly do relate,
Of ev'ry creature in this mortal *ſtate* !

The

The high, the low, the rich, the poor, the fmall,
By the great *King* of *Terrors* down muft fall.
Though fome live long when they pafs through
  this world,
Yet fome by death foon from the ftage are hurl'd :
The tender infants in their lovely bloom
Are often hurried to the filent tomb.
Adults grown up, nay, fome of ev'ry age,
By cruel Death are taken from the ftage.

 When *Wefley* died, his fpirit then did fly
To him that rais'd the arches of the fky ;
To realms above, where Saints and Angels fing,
Loud Hallelujahs to their Heav'nly King.
Thus whilft his body ftays behind at reft,
His pious foul with happinefs is bleft.

 O, happy ftate, in which this man is caft !
His pains are gone, and all his trouble's paft !
Needs no phyfician to give him relief,
Is free from pain, from forrow, and from grief ;
And from the rage of all the fons of ftrife,
And the vexations of a mortal life.
The fland'ring tongue, and the backbiting knave
Can't hurt him now, he's in the filent grave :
Neither the thief that robs both night and day,
Nor any murd'rer who kills on the way ;
By no means can the tyrant him opprefs,
Nor wicked mortals lead him to diftrefs.

 When roaring winds bring up the thicken'd
  cloud,
When the grum thunder rumbles out aloud,

      When

When the earth quakes, when lofty mountains fall,
When cities fink, and can't be found at all ;
When inundations o'er the land arife ;
When burning mountains burft towards the fkies:
When famine and the peftilence doth rage ;
When wicked nations in a war engage ;
When blood and carnage greatly do expand,
When defolation overfpreads the land ;
And boift'rous tempefts rage upon the fea,
Great Wefley then from danger muft be free :
Can't be afraid of being hurt or flain,
Like wretched mortals who alive remain.
Let not his *bearers* then at death repine;
Since it was made by God an *aƐt divine,*
To raife the *Juft,* the *Hufband, Child,* and *Wife,*
From fcenes of trouble to a better *life.*

But let them all whilft in the prefent ftate,
His good *example* mind to *imitate;*
That when they *die,* like *him,* they may be *bleft*
With *glory, honour, happinefs,* and *reft,*

London, March 7, 1791.

CHAP.

CHAP. LIII.

An Account of the Swedenborghers, called the New Church.

THE Hon. Emanuel Swedenborg, fon of Jafper Swedborg, a Swedifh Bifhop, was born at Stockholm, in Upland, in Sweden, January 29, 1688, is faid to be the founder of this New Church. He was related to fome illuftrious families in that kingdom, and when young, made a great progrefs in the mathematics, natural hiftory, phyfic, chymiftry, anatomy, &c. which foon recommended him to the patronage of Charles XII, who made him Extraordinary Affeffor to the Royal College of the Mines, which office he quitted, that he might apply himfelf to the new function to which he had been called : but he retained his falary, though he declined accepting a place of higher dignity in the State, left it fhould be a fnare to him.

He was ennobled by Queen Ulrica Eleonora, and named Swedenborg (his name before was

N n 4   Swedborg)

Swedborg) and took a feat with the Nobles of the Equeftrian Order, in the triennial affemblies of the States, and was chofen a Fellow of the Royal Academy of Sciences at Stockholm.

He pretended that he belonged to a fociety of angels, in which things fpiritual and heavenly were the only fubjects of difcourfe and entertainment; that he converfed frequently with them, and the fouls of thofe who had departed this life, and that he had a call to teach the doctrines o f the *New Church*. That in 1743, the Lord appeared to him perfonally, and opened in him a fight of the fpiritual world, and enabled him to converfe with fpirits and angels.

He publifhed a number of books in the Latin language, containing an account of the things he had feen, and thofe revealed, concerning Heaven and Hell; the ftate of men after death, the worfhip of God, the fpiritual fenfe of the Scriptures, and many other important truths, tending to falvation and true wifdom.

After he had made eight voyages to England, he fettled in the ftudy of theology, was much efteemed by the bifhops and nobles of his own country, and correfponded with many diftinguifhed characters in various parts of Europe; he died at the houfe where he refided when in London, in Cold-bath-ftreet, Cold-bath-Fields, March 29, 1772, aged 84 years. Some of his works have been tranflated and printed in Englifh.

The

The principles and doctrines of his followers, as communicated to me by a *Divine* of the Church of England, as are follow :

1. That there is a Divine Trinity in the perfon of Jefus Chrift, confifting of Father, Son, and Holy Ghoft, juft like the human trinity in every individual man, of foul, body, and operation; and that as the latter trinity conftitutes one man, fo the former trinity conftitutes one Jehovah God, who is at once the Creator, Redeemer, and Regenerator.

2. That Jehovah God himfelf came down from Heaven, and affumed human nature for the purpofe of removing Hell from man, of reftoring the Heavens to order, and of preparing the way for a *New Church* upon earth ; and that herein confifts the true nature of redemption, which was effected folely by the omnipotence of the Lord's divine humanity.

3. That the notion of obtaining pardon by a vicarious facrifice, or atonement, is a fundamental and fatal error. But that repentance is the foundation of the *Church* in man, and confifts in his abftaining from all evils, becaufe they are fins againft God, &c. That it is productive of regeneration, which is not an inftantaneous, but a gradual work, effected by the Lord alone, through charity and faith, during man's co-operation.

4. That

4. That man has free-will in fpiritual things, whereby he may join himfelf by reciprocation with the Lord.

5. That the imputation of the merits and righte-oufnefs of Chrift is a thing as abfurd and impof-fible, as it would be to impute to any man the work of creation; for the merits and righteouf-nefs of Chrift confift in redemption, which is as much the work of a Divine and Omnipotent Being as creation itfelf. That the imputation which really takes place, is an imputation of good and evil, and that this is according to a man's life.

6. That the doctrine of predeftination and jufti-fication by faith alone, is a mere human inven-tion, and not to be found in the word of God.

7. That the two Sacraments of Baptifm and the Holy Supper are effential inftitutions in the *New Church*, the genuine and rational ufes of which are now difcovered, together with the fpi-ritual fenfe of the Holy Word.

8. That there is not a fingle genuine truth re-maining in the *Old Church* but what is falfified, and therefore the *Old* and the *New Church* cannot poffibly be reconciled together.

9. That the Holy Word, or Sacred Scripture, contains a threefold fenfe; namely, celeftial, fpi-ritual, and natural, which are united by corre-fpondencies; and that in each fenfe it is Divine truth, accommodated refpectively to the angels of the three Heavens, and alfo to men on earth.

10. That

10. That the books of the word (or Scriptures) are thofe which have the internal fenfe, and are the five books of Mofes, and thofe of Jofhua, Judges, Samuel, Kings, the Pfalms, and all the Prophets; alfo, the four Evangelifts, and the Revelation; and that the books of Ruth, Chronicles, Ezra, Nehemiah, Efther, Job, Proverbs, Ecclefiaftes, Song of Solomon, the Acts and Epiftles of the Apoftles, not having the internal fenfe, are not the word, or Divine Revelation.

11. That in the fpiritual world there is a Sun diftinct from that of the natural world, the effence of which is the pure love of Jehovah God, who is in the midft thereof; that the heat alfo proceeding from that of that Sun is in its effence love, and the light thence proceeding is in its effence wifdom; and by the inftrumentability of that Sun all things were created, and continue to fubfift, both in the fpiritual and in the natural world.

12. That there is not in the univerfal Heaven, a fingle angel that was created fo at firft, nor a fingle devil in the infernal regions, that ever was created an angel of light, and was afterwards caft out of Heaven; but that all, both in Heaven and Hell, are of the human race; that thofe in Heaven are fuch as had lived in heavenly love and faith in this world; and thofe in Hell are fuch as had lived in hellifh love and faith on earth.

13. That

s

13. That the material body never rifes again; but that man, immediately on his departure from this life, rifes again, as to his fpiritual and fubftantial body, (which was inclofed in his material body, and formed from his predominant love, whether it be good or evil) wherein he continues to live as a man, in a perfect human form, in all refpects as before, fave only the grofs material body, which he puts off by death, and which is of no further ufe.

14. That the ftate and condition of man after death is according to his paft life in this world; and that the predominant love which he takes with him into the fpiritual world, continues with him for ever, and can never be changed to all eternity; and, confequently, if it be good, he abides in Heaven to all eternity; but if evil, he abides in Hell to all eternity.

15. That true conjugal love, which can only fubfift between one hufband and one wife, is a primary characteriftic of the *New Church*, being grounded in the marriage of goodnefs and truth, and correfponding with the marriage of the Lord and his *Church*; and therefore it is more celeftial, fpiritual, holy, pure, and clean, than any other love in angels, or men.

16. That the fcience of correfpondencies (which has been loft for fome thoufands of years, but is now revived in the theological works of the Hon. Emanuel Swedenborg) is the only key to
the

the fpiritual and internal fenfe of the Holy Word, every page of which is written by correfpondencies, that is, by fuch things, in the natural world, as correfpond unto, and fignify things in the fpiritual world.

17. That all thofe paffages in the Scripture, generally fuppofed to fignify the deftruction of the world by fire, &c. commonly called the laft judgment, muft be underftood, according to the above fcience, which teaches, that by the end of the world, or confummation of the age, is not fignified the deftruction of the world, but the deftruction or end of the prefent Chriftian Church, both among Roman Catholics and Proteftants of every defcription; and that this laft judgment actually took place in the fpiritual world in the year 1757.

18. That the fecond Advent of the Lord, which is a coming not in perfon, but in the fpiritual or internal fenfe of his Holy Word, has already commenced; that it is effected by means of his fervant Emanuel Swedenborg, before whom he hath manifefted himfelf in perfon, and whom he hath filled with his fpirit, to teach the doctrines of the *New Church* by the word from him; and that this is what is meant in the Revelation by the New Heaven and the New Earth, and the New Jerufalem thence defcending.

Thefe people hold to the *Doctrine* or *Science* of *Correfpondencies*, which Mr. Swedenborg fets forth

to

to be the moft exalted of all fciences, and as the fountain from whence the ancients derived all their underftanding and wifdom, being the only key whereby the Holy Scriptures can be properly underftood.

This fcience confifts in a correfpondence between the natural and fpiritual world, and feems to include every thing that hath an exiftence, becaufe this globe, with all its furniture, exifts and fubfifts from the fpiritual world, and both from the Almighty ; and were the correfpondence to ceafe, every thing in the natural world would perifh and be annihilated. For further information concerning this fcience, I refer the Reader to Mr. Swedenborg's publications. A confiderable number of people have embraced thefe principles in England ; there is a fociety in London, and one in Birmingham ; and I underftand that a Society has lately fprung up in New-York, and another in Virginia, in America.

Such are the general outlines of the doctrines of the *New Church*, which I have taken fome pains to collect from the beft authority, and on the merits of which I fhall leave to the judgment of my Readers to decide.

CHAP.

CHAP. LIV.

Of the MOSAIC, EVANGELIC, *and* CIVIL LAWS. *What Punishments have been ordered to be inflicted on Criminals.*

THE Mosaical laws are those contained in the five books of Moses, viz. Genesis, Exodus, Leviticus, Numbers, and Deuteronomy; they were given by the Almighty to Moses, and were by him communicated to the children of Israel.

Those guilty of idolatry, blasphemy, murder, adultery, sodomy, beastiality, rape, man-stealing, house-breaking, cursing or smiting of parents, witchcraft, &c. were to suffer death. Those who were guilty of fornication were to pay a fine; and those who had stolen any thing were to restore four-fold. Those who perjured themselves were to be punished with death, if the judges thought they deserved it, but the punishment by scourging was not to exceed forty stripes.

The Evangelical laws are those contained in the Gospels of Matthew, Mark, Luke, and John; and also in the Writings and Epistles of the Apostles, who were sent by Christ to preach the glad tidings of peace and salvation to the inhabitants

of

of the world; and, in a word, thefe laws contain a complete fyftem of the principles and doctrines of the Chriftian Religion.

No punifhments are ordered to be inflicted under the Gofpel difpenfation, only an excommunication from the church. Hence it is faid, if any man love not the Lord Jefus Chrift, let him be *Anathema Maran-atha*. (Vid. 1 Cor. xvi. 22.) But the workers of iniquity who die in their fins, are to be punifhed in the world to come. Hence, indignation and wrath, tribulation and anguifh, upon every foul of man that doth evil, &c. Vid. Rom. ii. 8, 9.

The civil laws are thofe compofed out of the beft of the Roman and Grecian laws. They were obferved throughout the Roman dominions for more than twelve hundred years. They are alfo thofe laws which have been made by other legiflators, for the government of empires, kingdoms, ftates, provinces, counties, and cities.

Different kinds of punifhments have been ordered to be inflicted on criminals in different kingdoms and countries.

In Great Britain it is death, by the laws, to commit murder, highway robbery, theft, burglary, forgery, to coin money, become a traitor, commit a rape, fodomy, &c. Thofe found guilty of blafphemy are to have their tongues bored through with a hot iron, and various fines are impofed for offences lefs capital. Not more than forty

forty ftripes can be put upon a criminal for one offence according to the Civil law.

The Martial laws are very fevere, not lefs than a thoufand ftripes may be inflicted on a criminal in an army at one time, if the officers fee fit, as I have been informed; but only forty can be inflicted in a navy. It is death to defert from an army, and I believe it is fometimes to defert from a fleet.

Various punifhments have been inflicted among different nations, fuch as fines, imprifonments, confifcation of property, banifhment, fcourging, ftanding in the pillory, cutting off of the ears, lying in the ftocks, burning, hanging, drawing in quarters, racking on a wheel, cutting to pieces by inches, fawing afunder, drowning, the dafhing of criminals to atoms by throwing them down from high places upon rocks, ftoning to death, &c. and many have loft their lives by hunger, cold and nakednefs, in dungeons, and prifons, and by being driven from their habitations into the open fields. Some have fuppofed that no punifhments ought to be inflicted but fuch as are mentioned in the law of Mofes.

I have often thought that children ought to be taught the laws of their country when they are young, as well as the Mofaical and Evangelical laws, for it might tend to deter them from committing crimes they may commit, if they are trained up in ignorance.

O o   CHAP.

CHAP. LV.

Of the Laws of Nature, Motion, and Rest. Attrac-
tion, Repulsion, and Compression. The Velocity of
the Rays of Light, and different Colours in the
Universe. The Cause of Sound, and the Rapidity
of its Motion.

THE laws of Nature are those by which natural bodies are governed in all their actions
upon one another.

Laws of motion are a continual and succeffive
mutation of place, or a moving from one place to
another.

Laws of rest are those which cause bodies to remain in their different positions without motion.

Attraction is a drawing unto, or the tendency
which bodies have towards one another.

Repulfion is a beating or driving back, and
where attraction ends repulfion begins. But there
are no bodies which repel only at certain diftances. Hence a loadstone will not repel a needle
only at a certain distance.

Compreffion is a fqueezing or preffing together, by the weight of the atmofphere, or any
other thing.

There

There are certain laws by which the motions of all natural bodies are conftantly governed, and rules by which every thing relating to motion may be explained.

Sir Ifaac Newton defcribed three kinds of the laws of Nature, viz.

1. That all bodies continue in their ftate of reft, or motion, uniformly in a right line, ex-cepting they are obliged to change that ftate by forces impreffed.

Hence all bodies are incapable of moving themfelves, and, unlefs moved by fome external or internal agent, muft remain at reft.

A rock will therefore lie ftill, unlefs it is moved by an outward or an inward force. The former may be produced various ways, and the latter by an explofion of gun-powder, after the powder has been put into its center, by means of a drill, &c. and other bodies may be moved in like manner, or from fome other caufe.

When a rock is put in motion, it will con-tinue to move in a right-lined direction, until the refiftance of the air, the power of its own gravity, or fome other external caufe, turns it from that direction, diminifhes its velocity, and brings it at laft to a ftate of reft.

But the regions through which the planets and comets move make but a fmall refiftance to their bodies, which are vaftly large : hence their mo-tions are continued the longer. If it was other-

wife,

wife, they would foon fall into the Sun, and be at reft.

2. That all change of motion is proportional to the power of the generating force, and is always made according to a right line in which that force is impreffed. Hence, if we ftrike a mufket-ball in a horizontal direction, with hammer, or any other thing, it will fly off with a velocity in proportion to the violence of the blow, and in the fame direction ; hence alfo there can be no perpetual motion, becaufe all motion produced by any means is always in proportion to the generation force.

3. That repulfion, or re-action, is always equal, and in a contrary direction, to impulfe, or action, that is, the actions of two bodies upon each other, are always equal, and in contrary directions.

Hence if we prefs a ftone with our fingers downward, the ftone equally preffes them again upwards. An anvil ftrikes a hammer with the fame force that the hammer ftrikes the anvil. If a mill-ftone fhould be caft from the top of a fteeple to the ground, the ground would ftrike the ftone with the fame velocity that the ftone would ftrike the earth. If a horfe draws a cart, the cart draws the horfe with the fame force, for the harnefs is equally diftended both ways. When a boat is pulled to the fhore by a rope, the fhore pulls the boat as much as the boatfinan pulls the fhore, &c. &c.

Of

1. If one body ſtrikes againſt another at reſt, they will both move in the ſame direction of the firſt motion, providing the latter was moveable.

2. If one body ſtrikes another moving the ſame way, but ſlower, they will both continue their motion in the ſame direction as before ; and the quantity of motion in both will ſtill be the ſame.

3. When two bodies with equal quantities of motion tend both directly towards, and ſtrike each other, the whole motion will be deſtroyed by their meeting, and both will fall to the ground, and be at reſt.

4. Two bodies moving directly towards each other with different velocities, will, after the ſtroke, both continue their motion in the direction of that motion which had the greateſt velocity ; and the quantity of motion after the ſtroke will be equal to the difference of their motions before it.

Of the Striking of Bodies which are Elaſtic.

Suppoſe two ſuch bodies as A and B; A has three parts of matter and eight degrees of velo-city, and B has nine parts of matter and two de-grees of velocity ; then the quantity of motion in A will be 24, and that of B 18. Now, ſuppoſing theſe bodies to impinge on each other, the velo-

city

city of each after impact, and the direction of their motions may be known as follows :

1. Let the body of A impinge on B at reſt; then from A take B, and multiply the remainder by the velocity of A; divide this product by the ſum of the bodies A and B, the quotient will ex-preſs the velocity of A after the ſtroke. As the body A is lefs, equal to, or greater than B, ſo it will be retrogade, or direct in motion after im-pact. Thus in the preſent caſe the difference of A and B is 6, which multiply by A's velocity 8, the product is 48; this divided by the ſum of the bodies 12, quotes 4, the degrees of velocity with which A will return back after impact.

2. Again, divide twice A's motion by the ſum of the bodies, the quotient will be the velocity of B after impact; thus 48 divided by 12, quotes 4, the velocity of B after the ſtroke; ſo that though the velocity be the ſame, the motion in both bo-dies is double to what it was at firſt in A.

3. Let the bodies both tend one way, and A follow B; then to the motion of A add twice the motion of B; from that ſum ſubtract the product of A's velocity multiplied into the matter in B; di-vide the remainder by the ſum of the bodies, the quotient will be the velocity of A after the im-pact. As the product is leſſer, equal to, or greater than the ſum above-mentioned, ſo the motion of A will be direct, none at all, or backward, after the ſtroke.

4. Again,

4. Again, to twice the motion of A add the motion of B, from that fum fubtract the product of B's velocity into, A; divide the remainder by the fum of the bodies, the quotient will be the volicity of B after the impact.

5. An example of each, in our prefent cafe, is as follows: To 24 add 36, the fum is 60, which I take from 72, (as being the greateft) the remainder is 12, which divided by 12, the quotient is 1; fo that A returns back with one degree of velocity, having loft *feven*.

6. Again, to 48 add 18, the fum is 66, from which I take 6, and the remainder 60 I divide by 12; the quotient is 5 for the velocity of B's motion.

7. If the bodies tend the contrary way, or meet, then from the fum of twice B's motion, and the product of A's velocity into B, take the motion of A, and divide the remainder by the fum of the bodies, the quotient is A's velocity after meeting; and as the fum is greater, equal to, or lefs than the faid motion of A, the motion of A will be backward, none at all, or forward.

8. Again, to the difference of B's motion and twice A's add the product of B's velocity into A, divide the fum by the fum of the bodies, the quotient will be the velocity of B after reflection.

9. To illuftrate both of thefe cafes by our prefent example. The fum 72 and 36 is 108, from which I take 24, the remainder 84 I divide by

O o 4

12, which quotes 7 for A's velocity backward. Again, to the difference of 48 and 18, which is 30, add 6, and divide the fum 36 by 12, the quotient is 3 for B's velocity the contrary way.

These rules are applicable to all bodies and celerities, as may be eafily demonftrated by a great variety of examples.

Thus much for the laws of nature, motion, and reft. It may be proper, however, to add, that reft is produced either by the weight of bodies and the attraction of the earth beneath, or by their weight and the preffure of the atmofphere above.

All bodies thrown into the air defcend in right lines towards the earth's center, unlefs they are turned out of that courfe by the force of fome agent; but whether they defcend in a right, or an oblique courfe, they draw towards the center, when they come to reft. But the queftion is, what makes them draw towards the center, is it attraction, or compreffion?

Many of the philofophers have imputed it to the former, and they have fuppofed that the earth has fuch an attraction, that fhe fometimes draws the moon towards her center, as well as other bodies; that each globe attracts in proportion to its magnitude; hence the moon attracts the earth, but with a lefs power, then the earth attracts the moon, and that this is the cafe with all other primary and fecondary planets.

This

This attracting power is called attraction by philosophers; and the motion of bodies towards the earth's center, &c. is called gravitation. By this power the earth is formed into a denfe ball, and things animate and inanimate are confined to its furface. A body left to the power of this agent falls about a rood in the firft fecond of time, three roods in the fecond fecond, five in the third, feven in the fourth, &c. agreeable to the following odd numbers, 1, 3, 5, 7, 9, 11, 13, &c. for the *vis inertiæ* of the falling body, added to the power of gravity, accelerates its motion, and the nearer it approaches to the earth, the fwifter will its motion be till it comes to reft.

Hence we may conclude, that if it is the power of the attraction of the earth that draws this body to it, the attraction is greater near the earth's fur- face, than it is at a diftance, becaufe the rapidity of the motion of the falling body increafes as it draws nearer and nearer to the earth; but if it is the compreffion of the atmofphere on the body that drives it towards the earth's center, may we not conclude, that the air is heavier at, and near the circumference of the globe than it is in the upper regions, and that from hence the weight becomes greater and greater as the body fubfides which accelerates its motion. But perhaps attrac- tion and compreffion may both operate together.

A Mr. Pope, whom I mentioned page 45, has imputed the caufe of gravity, to the preffure of

the

the atmofphere above, and not to the attraction of the earth beneath; and whether he is right or wrong, I will not undertake to determine at prefent, but it feems as probable to me that it is from compreffion, as attraction, for we are told by philofophers, that the air which encompaffes the globe hath weight or gravity. That the atmofphere compreffeth the earth, with a force nearly equal to that of five thoufand millions of tuns. That this preffure on every fuperficial fquare foot, is more than 2000 pound weight, that the air is heavier on the furface of the globe than it is at a diftance. Now if the earth and waters are compreffed with fuch an amazing weight, will it not tend to drive things towards the center of the globe? Vid. page 283.

Of the Velocity of the Rays of Light.

Light is fuppofed to arife from a very fine ætherial matter, that is vaftly finer than the air, which is the medium by which the rays of thofe luminous particles are tranfmitted to our eyes from the fun, moon, ftars, and other refulgent bodies.

The rays of light are faid to fly 180,000 miles in a fecond of time; which is one million five hundred and thirty thoufand times fafter than the motion of a cannon ball, which flies a mile in about eight feconds and a half, hence fuch a ball would

would be about $32\frac{1}{2}$ years, in flying to the fun. But rays of light are fuppofed to be $7\frac{1}{2}$ minutes in defcending from the fun t⟩ this globe.

Of the different Colours in the Univerfe.

The colours are feven in number, viz. 1. Red, 2. Orange. 3. Yellow. 4. Green. 5. Blue. 6. Indigo. 7. Violet. (vid. page 166.) But black and white are not reckoned among the primary colours of light, for white is only a mixture of the feven original colours, and black only a hue of thofe bodies which abforb all the rays of light; and therefore as it abforbeth all the rays, and reflects none back it is properly no colour at all. Hence black clothes attract more heat than thofe which are white, becaufe they abforb it; but the white reflects it back. Hence alfo if we put a white glove on one hand, and a black one on the other, and hold them at an equal diftance from the fire, the black glove will abforb the heat, and the white will reflect it back, and the difference of the degrees of heat, will be fenfibly felt.

Of the Caufe of Sound, and the Rapidity of its Motion.

Sound is produced by a ftroke, explofion, and fome other caufes which puts the air in motion like the waves of the fea; which pulfations, ftriking on the *tympanum*, or drum of our

ears,

ears, convey by the nerves the fenfation of hearing to our minds.

Some founds have been heard to a great diftance. It has been faid, that the explofions of great guns, have been heard 200 miles, but fome can hear, as well as fee, much further than others.

As to the rapidity of the motion of found, it depends very much upon the denfity of the air, or the rarifaction of the fame, for the latter weakens, but the former operates *vice verfa*. The velocity of found at a medium, is about 1142 feet in a fecond of time. Hence by this rule we may tell nearly, how far an enemy is from us, fuppofing it is 10 feconds after we fee the flafh of a cannon, before we hear the report, we may conclude that it is ten times 1142 feet from us, which is equal to 11420 feet; hence alfo by the fame rule we may know the diftance of thunder and lightning.

CHAP.

C H A P. LVI.

How to raise Grapes, Silk, Hemp, and Flax.

IT is said that the art of making wine was discovered by Noah; that it was brought into India by Bacchus, and that none was produced in France in the time of the Romans. It was sold by the apothecaries as a cordial in England, in 1300; and licences were established for vending of it in 1661. But grapes were introduced in England in 1550, and cherries and pears the same year.

I have drank very good wine made of grapes that were raised on Long-Island, in the State of New-York, in America, and have also seen a silk gown that was raised and manufactured in the same Government. As to hemp and flax, a plenty of both is raised in many places on the American continent.

Many excellent wines are produced in France, as the Champagne, Burgundy, Bourdeaux, Gascony, Hermitage, Frontiniac, and Pontacke; and I have often thought that America may produce as good wine, if vines were properly cultivated.

vated. Such a cultivation, as well as that of raising silk, would be a great saving to the community.

We do not want either for heat or cold in America, for both are very extreme in some parts at particular seasons. Hence if cold climates were the most agreeable for the raising of grapes and silk, Canada, Nova-Scotia, and New-England, would be suitable; or if hot climates are the best, then the Carolinas and Georgia may be most convenient. I understand that grapes have thrived very well in South-Carolina, where attempts have been made to cultivate them; and although Paris, the capital of France, is situated in the latitude of 48 degrees and 50 minutes north, which is more than eight degrees further to the northward than Philadelphia; yet they raise a plenty of grapes. It is true, indeed, that the cold is not so extreme there, as it is in the same parallel of latitude in America; but it is much colder in Winter at Paris than it is in England, because it is situated on a continent.

I had the pleasure of viewing the vineyards in France when I was there in 1790. The vines were planted near two feet apart, and were hoed much like the Indian corn in America; they ran upon poles that were about four or five feet high; the grapes hung in clusters almost from the tops to the bottoms of the vines. The time for gathering and making wine is in the Fall. Towards Winter the vines are cut down close to

the

the ground, and from their roots another set arise, which bear grapes the next year.

If the tree or vine is wounded in the Spring, it yields a clear, limpid, watery juice, which has been esteemed good for sore eyes, malignant fevers, and a suppression of urine. The flowers have a pleasant smell, and, being distilled in water, yield an essential oil, possessing the fragrance of the flowers. The unripe fruit is very harsh, rough, and sour. The expressed juice, called verjuice, is said to be cooling and astringent; the ripe fruit dried are the raisins and currants of the shops. The juice affords, by fermentation, wine, vinegar, and tartar.

There are about twenty species of vines, accroding to accounts given by botanical writers; and as to wines, there are a great variety; but those used in the shops of London for medical purposes are the following, viz.

1. *Vinum album Hispanicum*—Spanish white wine, or mountain.

2. *Vinum album Gallicum*—French white wine.

3. *Vinum Canarium*—Canary, or sack.

4. *Vinum Rhenanum*—Rhenish.

5. *Vinum rubrum*—Red Port.

Good wine, drank with moderation, cheers the spirits, warms the habits, promotes perspiration, renders the vessels full and turgid, raises the pulse, and quickens the circulation; it helps digestion, and strengthens the solids. But if it is

drank

drank to excefs it hardens the fibres, affects the nerves, diminifhes the fecretions, deftroys the appetite, and generates chronic diftempers.

Many of the wines, as well as other liquors, are adulterated, which makes them very prejudicial to health.

, Sweet wines abound with a glutinous nutritious fubftance; they heat the conftitution more, and are not fo diuretic as other wines. Red wines have an aftringent quality; hence they ftrengthen the tone of the ftomach and inteftines, and reftrain immoderate fecretions. Thofe that are acid are faid to loofen the belly and promote urine; but they occafion gouty and calculous complaints, which is the effect of all new wines.

Of the Raifing of Silk.

According to chronology, raw filk was made in China 150 years before Chrift, and was firft brought from India, A. D. 274; filk worms eggs brought into Europe 527; the manufactory of it was introduced in Europe 551, firft worn in drefs 1455; firft manufactured in France 1521, firft worn by the Clergy in England 1534, broad filk manufactured from raw filk in England 1620, brought to perfection by the French refugees in London 1687, a filk throwing mill invented at Derby 1719. Vid. p. 11.

Silk

Silk is produced by a curious infect, called a filk-worm, which multiply very faft, as a female will fometimes lay 500 eggs. When a worm is firft hatched, it is about the bignefs of the head of a common pin. It feeds upon mulberry leaves, and grows to the fize of a caterpillar; after which it no longer eats, but prepares for its diffolution. It wraps itfelf in a kind of filken ball, fpun from its own bowels, its head feparates from its body, and in every refpect changes from its original form, and appears to be deftitute of life and motion. However, after it has remained in this condition fome time, it awakes, and becomes another kind of infect, refembling a large moth or butterfly. In this laft ftage the female lays a prodigious number of eggs, after which fhe dies.

Thefe infects are at firft black, then of an afh grey, afterwards they fhed their coats, and grow whitifh, or rather of a' bluifh caft; they again fhed their fkins, and in a few days become yellow, feed a little longer, and wrap themfelves in their filken balls, and go through the changes already mentioned.

On the day they begin their balls, they make a kind of flue or down; the next day they begin to form the out-fides in the midft of the loofe filk made the day before; on the third day it is entirely obfcured, and in a week the buildings are compleated. They are of a conic figure, like the eggs of pigeons.

P p

The

The Chinese have two methods of bringing up their silk-works; they either let them range on the mulberry-trees, or keep them in rooms; the latter produce the finest silk; but if they are not suffered to go abroad, they must be fed with mulberry leaves.

As to the manufacturing of silk, I am not acquainted with the different modes. There are nankins, damasks, sattins, tafseties, brocades, gauzes, &c. which I believe are manufactured different ways. What I have attempted to exhibit is how it may be raised.

Of the Raising of Hemp.

The ground ought to be well manured, and ploughed and harrowed several times. Moist land is esteemed the best, and ashes are the best manure; the seed should be sown early in the Spring, and harrowed in. When the hemp is ripe, it must be pulled; and when dry, the seed may be threshed out. Afterwards the stalk may be rotted in the water, or by being spread on the ground. When it is rotten enough, let it be dried, and put into a barn. In Winter let it be braked and swingled. Hemp is of great utility in the rigging of vessels, and in many other branches of business.

Of

Of the Raising of Flax.

The ground may be cultivated and manured in the fame manner as that for hemp, only fome have fuppofed that it is beft to draw a heavy roller over it, to beat it down, after the feed is fown; it may perhaps kill the infects; in other refpects it may be managed like hemp.

Linen was firft made in England in 1253, by Flemifh weavers; till then woollen fhirts were worn. The linen trade began in Ireland in 1634; and fine linen was made in that kingdom from nettles, in 1755.

CHAP.

CHAP. LVII.

Of Green, Bohea, Congo, Souchong, Singlo, Bloom, Imperial, Hyson, and Gunpowder Teas; and also the Rad. Ginfeng.

TEA was firft brought into Europe by the Dutch Eaft-India Company in the beginning of the feventeenth century. In 1666 a quantity of it was brought from Holland to England, and fince that time the ufe of it has become univerfal.

It grows on a *fhrub* in China and Japan, called the *Tea Plant*. It principally grows between the latitudes of 24 and 28. The beft teas are to be had at Nankin, in China.

There are feveral kinds of teas; fome finer, fmoother, and more fragrant than others, according to the foil they grow in; that called finglo is efteemed the moft elegant, and ufed by the more opulent.

Some teas are denominated for their particular colours and qualities. The bohea is much efteemed in China, on account of its flavour and medical qualities. It is from the fame plant with the

green,

green, and only differs from it by being gathered
fix or feven weeks fooner, that is in March, when
in its full bloom, and the leaves are full of juice;
whereas the other, by being left fo much longer
on the tree, lofes a part of its juice, and contracts
a different colour, tafte, and virtue, being more
rough to the palate and racking to the ftomach.
The bohea is gathered in March, the imperial in
April, and the finglo in May or June; fo that
the general divifion of teas is into two forts, viz.
the green and bohea, which both proceed from
the fame kind of plant, as already obferved; and
as to the appellations given to the other teas, they
arife from the time of gathering, the province
where produced, or the method of curing.

The method of curing is to infufe the leaves
in water for a certain time, by which the re-
finous particles are diffipated, and rendered palateable; for without this operation they would be
fo bitter, that fcarce any quantity of fugar would
be fufficient to correct the tafte. After this infufion, the bohea is expofed to the heat of the fun,
or dried by the fire, till it is crifped, or contracted
into the fmall compafs in which we fee it.

But the green having been affiduoufly turned
and ftirred about the whole time, is ftrewed upon
fheets of copper, (which are gently warmed by
embers beneath them) and rolled up and down by
perfons, whofe hands are defended by thick leather gloves from the effluvia, which, without fuch

P p 3 precaution

precaution, would prove of the moft pernicious confequence.

Though the green tea confeffedly derives the principal part of its tincture and flavour from the baneful vapours that exhale from the heated copper, thefe very circumftances, inftead of rendering it obnoxious, are the principal recommendations of it, not only to the Europeans and Americans, but to the Afiatics; for fuch is the infatuation of mankind, that they would rather pleafe the eye and gratify the tafte, than attend to the conftitution of their bodies, though effential to the prefervation of life.

The Chinefe make ufe of a weak infufion of bohea as their common drink : they do not drink it ftrong, nor ufe it in the manner we do. It corrects the unwholefome brackifhnefs of their waters, which in fome places would breed diftempers.

It is deemed by them a great diluter; they drink great quantities of it in fevers, colics, and other acute difeafes, and in chronic complaints. They call it a cephalic and diuretic, and good for the head-ache, and to promote urine, digeftion, perfpiration, and other fecretions, and alfo as a great ftrengthener of the brain and ftomach.

Various opinions have arifen amongft gentlemen of the *faculty* concerning the virtues of tea, both in Europe and America; but fome of the moft celebrated phyficians of the prefent age

efteem

efteem it as a diluter, agreeable to the palate and
ftomach. It operates as a cephalic, for it eafes
pains in the head, and prevents ftupidity, or
fleepinefs. It ought not to be drank too hot nor
too ftrong. A ftrong decoction of green tea will
excite vomiting, owing, it is faid, to its aftrin-
gency; but, perhaps, it is from the pernicious
qualities imbibed from the copper-plates. It is
high time that fuch an unjuftifiable practice was
fuppreffed.

The bohea tea, if not adulterated, is the moft
wholefome, in my opinion, both for food and medical ufes, and may be drank freely, without in-
juring a perfon, both in ficknefs and health.
Milk and fugar make tea very palateable.

Perhaps tea may be cultivated in America at
fome future time.

The *Radix Ginfeng* was formerly imported from
China, and fold at Bofton, in New-England, for a
guinea an ounce; but of late great quantities of
it have been found in Canada, Vermont, and
Pennfylvania, and vaft quantities have been exported to the Eaft-Indies. This root ought to be
cultivated in thofe countries, and enough exported
to balance the teas imported from the Eaft-Indies.

The Chinefe efteem this root as a general re-
ftorative and corroborant, and excellent in all decays of age, intemperance, or difeafe. It is a
mucilage, fweet to the tafte, with a flight degree
of bitternefs, and an aromatic warmth. I have

frequently ufed it for coughs and other diforders
of the lungs with fuccefs. A drachm, in flices or
powder, may be boiled in a gill of water, and the
decoction fweetened with fugar, and drank as
foon as it is cool enough. This is for one dofe;
it fhould be repeated night and morning.

CHAP.

C H A P. LVIII.

How to manage Bees.

OF bees there are two kinds, the male and female. The former are called drones, the latter, honey, or working bees. The drones are about half as big again as the females. The voice of the drone is much louder and more dreadful than that of the honey bee, and they often excite a caufelefs fear, for they have no ftings, and can hurt no creature, being under the dominion of the females. The bees have alfo a leader, called the Queen Bee ; her body is much bigger and larger than that of a honey bee ; her hinder parts are black, and fhe prefides over the reft.

The honey bees have ftings in their tails, and when they fting one another, it generally proves mortal both to thofe who fting and to thofe that are wounded.

They fuck their honey from flowers. It enters into a bottle, or bag, fituated in their hinder parts ; when it is full, they return home, and empty it into the honey-comb ; they alfo bring home water in the fame manner, to mix the bee-bread with, for feeding their young.

Bees

Bees proceed from fmall white eggs; they are maggots when they are firft hatched.

The tongues of the drones are fo much fhorter than thofe of the females, that they cannot reach the honey in the focketed flowers. Hence they cannot work if they would; their bufinefs is to ftay at home, and fit upon the eggs, which are hatched by their warmth, whilft the female follows the delightful vocation of gathering and bringing home the honey and water.

At about one or two o'clock the work of the day is chiefly over with the females; and on their return home to take care of their young, the drones are fuffered to go abroad, to recreate and empty themfelves; afterwards they return again to their beloved honey, and are kindly received by their imperious dames.

The females are very careful to work in warm weather, and lay up a ftock of honey to prevent their dying in the Winter. In wet Summers and bad weather, they are fometimes hindered from laying up a fufficient ftore, hence they die, unlefs they are fed. Some feed them with molaffes and gingerbread.

Bees commonly fwarm in May and June in America, and have often two or three broods in a feafon; and if a hive is not prepared for their reception, they are led off by the Queen Bee to a hollow tree, where they enter into a new habitation. Trees have been felled that have had more

than

than a barrel of honey in them. But there would
be no need of their fwarming at all, were their
hives large enough to hold the new generation.

The bees often rob each other of their honey.
Hence great battles enfue. But if the plundered
party have loft their Queen, they will join with
the robbers, and fuffer all the honey to be carried
out of the hive, and when they feek new quarters
amongft other bees, defperate wars commence.

Mice, moths, ear-wigs, hornets, wafps, fwal-
lows, and fparrows, are enemies to bees. The
mice will fometimes make the bees wholly leave
their hive.

When the bees bury their dead, they fly off
with them, and drop their bodies at fome diftance
from the hive. They do not live much more than
a year, as fome fay.

When people take up their bees, they dig a
hole in the ground, and at evening put a lighted
match of brimftone into it, and place the hive
thereon, which is immediately furrounded with
earth, to keep in the fumigation, and prevent the
bees from making their efcape. They fall to the
ground, and die in a few minutes, for the want of
air. Afterwards the honey is taken for ufe. Sometimes 120 pound has been taken out of a hive,
which has commonly been fold for fixpence fterling per pound, and the wax for a fhilling.
Hence the keeping of bees muft be very profitable.

Honey,

Honey, as a medicine, is aperient and detergent; it powerfully diſſolves viſcid juices, promotes the expectoration of tough phlegm, helps a ſore throat, coughs, aſthmas, and other diſorders of the lungs, heals and cleanſes the kidnies and urinary paſſages, and is good for wounds and ulcers; but it is hurtful to bilious, hypochondriac, hyſteric, and melancholic habits; for it generates bile, and ſometimes pain, if eaten when new; this may, however, be prevented by the boiling of it before it is eaten. The doſe alone is from one ounce to two.

CHAP.

CHAP. LIX.

Of the Raifing of Horfes, Cattle, Sheep, and Swine.
Obfervations on the Eating of Swine's Flefh.

THE barns in America ought to be built of brick or ftone, that the horfes, cattle, and fheep, may be kept warm; for they will eat lefs, and thrive better, if they are kept fo, than when they are pinched with the cold. But fheep ought not to be kept too warm, for it will caufe a relaxation of their cutaneous pores, and make them lofe their wool.

All thefe animals ought to be fed often, kept clean, and to have water in feafon; and if they are remote from the fea, or live on frefh grafs, or hay, they fhould have falt three or four times in a week, if not oftener, for it will make them eat, drink, and thrive much better than they will if they live without. Some fprinkle a weak brine on their hay, which will make them eat it, if it is not good.

Horfes and cattle fhould be curried with a curry-comb twice or thrice a day, for it promotes the circulation of the fluids, and makes them thrive.

All

All thefe animals are very profitable when they do well, and thofe that raife them commonly grow rich, if they are prudent, and have good farms. We have had fome cows in America, that have given about 20 quarts of milk in a day. But all thefe kinds of cattle are not very large in Canada, by reafon of the extremity of the Winters; however, the horfes, cattle, and fheep, are very good in New-England, New-York, &c. Sheep produce both meat and clothing. Great care ought to be taken of the lambs when they are young, to prevent their being devoured by wild beafts, dogs, and fwine. About half a pint of Indian corn given to a fheep every day is faid to be very good juft before and after fhe has brought a lamb.

Swine ought to be kept warm and clean, and to be fed often; but they are very unruly, and efpecially if they are fuffered to run at large, for they will be rooting up the ground and getting into mifchief, if they are not yoked and ringed. They are an unprofitable animal, for, like the *mifer*, they do no good until they are dead.

Some people have fuppofed that their flefh is not fit to be eaten; I fhall therefore adduce fome reafons on their fide of the queftion.

We find that nothing is more ftrictly forbidden in the *Law* of *Mofes*. For the commandment of the Almighty runs thus:

"Of their flefh ye fhall not eat, and their carcafe
" fhall

" fhall ye not touch : they are unclean to you."
Vid. Levit. xi. 8. And it feems that Chrift himfelf was no great friend to the fwine, otherwife he
would not have fuffered the devils to have entered
into them, nor have fuffered their owners to be
deprived of their property, by letting their fwine
run violently down a fteep place into the fea, and
perifh in the water. Vid. Matt. viii. 31, 32.

Now, if the fwine were unclean to the Jews,
how comes it to pafs that they are not fo to other
nations?—In the London Practice of Phyfic,
page 5 of the introduction, we are told, " that
" pork fed in London is far from being whole-
" fome diet." If that is true, then furely it ought
not to be eaten. I never eat much pork myfelf ;
but fometimes when I have been upon a journey,
or have fell into company, I have eat fome of it,
and if it was frefh, it has produced a naufea,
griping pains, and a diarrhœa, both in Great-
Britain and America, but it does not have fuch an
effect upon every conftitution.

According to the accounts mentioned by fome
phyfical authors, fwine's flefh generates the leprofy, and other cutaneous eruptions, in divers
countries, and efpecially in hot climates.

The Jews obey the commandment of the Lord
to this day ; for they abftain from the eating of
fwine's flefh, and other unclean things forbidden
in the Mofaical law. I once afked a Jew, why he
did not eat fwine's flefh, and he faid, it was becaufe

it

it is unwholefome. I was afterwards credibly informed, that feveral of his young children went to
a neighbour's houfe, where they eat fome pork,
but foon returned home, and told what they had
been eating; the father gave them an *emetic,*
which foon made their ftomachs difcharge their
contents.

According to the Law of Mofes, all kinds of
beafts are unclean but thofe that divide the hoof
and chew the cud; and all kinds of fifhes, excepting thofe that have fins and fcales. There
are alfo clean and unclean fowls.

Many befides the Jews adhere to the Mofaical
law, in regard to animal food.

The inhabitants of Abyffinia abftain from
blood, things ftrangled, and thofe unclean birds,
beafts, and fifhes, mentioned by Mofes. This is
a great country, for it is about 1300 miles long,
and 1100 broad.

The Perfians eat no pork, nor any thing forbidden in the Mofaical Law; their country is
alfo large, being about 1200 miles fquare.

The Empire of the Great Mogul is about
1700 miles in length and 1300 in breadth. The
inhabitants do not eat fwine's flefh.

Thefe things being premifed, I fhall proceed
to make fome philofophical obfervations.

The flefh of all animals is impregnated by the
nourifhment they fubfift upon. Hence thofe birds,
beafts, and fifhes, that feed upon poifonous and
filthy

filthy things, muft be unclean, and of courfe unwholefome to the human race. .

Fifh that live upon beds of copper mines
are poifon, becaufe their bodies are impregnated
with the qualities of that mineral.

That the fwine will feed upon the worft of car-
rion, and other filthy things, is evident to every
one that is acquainted with thofe animals. And
if their flefh is unclean to the Jews, and to the inhabitants of thofe great countries which I have
mentioned, how comes it to pafs that it is not
fo to other nations? If the learned and ingenious
phyficians have difcovered, that pork fed in London is far from being a wholefome diet, fhould
not the raifing of it be fuppreffed? Why fhould
the people be fuffered to raife and eat things prejudicial to their health?

But if any fhould objeft, and fay, that the
fwine may be fhut up, and kept from eating unclean things, and that their flefh may thereby be
made wholefome, I anfwer, that although that
may tend to make their flefh more wholefome
than it might be if they fed altogether upon poifonous things, yet fome animals are unclean and
unwholefome in themfelves by Nature.

Surely the Great Governor of the Univerfe
knew what was fo and what was not. The commandment I have mentioned came from him, for
the chapter (viz. Levit. xi.) begins thus—" And
" the Lord fpake unto Mofes, and to Aaron,

Q q   " faying,

" faying unto them, Speak unto the children of
" Ifrael, &c." and nothing is more ftrictly forbidden, not even murder and theft, than the
touching and eating of *fwine's flefh.*

But, perhaps, fome may fay, that this command
was ceremonial, and is abolifhed. .

I anfwer, that we have no account of its being
abolifhed, neither in the Old nor in the New
Teftament ; and that by the fame rule they may
fay, that the command againft murder is alfo
abolifhed.

But fome have pretended, that all thofe unclean
animals were changed, or made clean, at the
time that Peter went into a trance, and faw Heaven opened, and a certain veffel defcending unto
him, which contained all manner of four-footed
beafts of the earth, and wild beafts, and creeping
things, and fowls of the air, when a voice faid,
" Rife, Peter, kill, and eat. But he faid, Not fo,
" Lord; for I have never eaten any thing that is
" common or unclean. And the voice fpake unto
" him again, faying the fecond time, What God
" hath cleanfed, that call not thou common."
This was done *thrice*, and the veffel was received
up again into Heaven.

By this text it appears, 1. That Peter, who
had been one of Chrift's difciples, and was in-
ftructed by him in the principles and doctrines of
the Chriftian religion, had always adhered to the
law of Mofes, by abftaining from the eating of
fwine's flefh, and other unclean animals.

2. That although all kinds of beasts, creeping things, and fowls, were presented before him, he was not commanded to kill, or eat, those that were unclean.

3. That we have no account of any fishes being in the vessel. Hence if the birds and beasts were all made clean, it seems that nothing was done for the fishes, and that those that have not fins or scales still continue to be unclean.

4. That this vision had no reference to the changing and purifying of the natures of the swine and other unclean animals, but to the cleansing of the nations; for after Peter had doubted for some time concerning the meaning of the vision, and had fell in company with Cornelius, who was one of another nation, and with whom Peter had supposed it was unlawful to keep company, he said, " But God hath shewed me, that I " should not call any man common or unclean." And after further consideration, he said, " Of a " truth I perceive, that God is no respecter of " persons: but in every nation he that feareth " him, and worketh righteousness, is accepted." That as he was preaching, the *Holy Ghost* fell on all them which heard the word, and caused an astonishment amongst those of the circumcision, &c. that believed, because that on the Gentiles also was poured out the gift of the *Holy Ghost*, which purges, purifies, and cleanses the nations from inward filth and pollution; so that the vi-

sion

fion could have no reference to the cleanſing of the unclean birds, beaſts, and fiſhes, but to the cleanſing of the Gentile nations only. Vid. Acts x. 9, &c.

If any ſhould ſay, that liberty was given for the eating of unclean things, becauſe it ſeemed good to the *Holy Ghoſt*, and to the *Apoſtles*, to lay no other burthen upon the Gentiles than the abſtaining from meats offered to idols, from blood, things ſtrangled, and from fornication. Vid. Acts xv. 28, 29.

I would anſwer,

1. That this was a determination of the Apoſtles at a time when they were aſſembled at Jeruſalem, to conſult about circumciſion. For it appears that certain men had taught, that except the Gentiles were circumciſed, they could not be ſaved; and as the law of Moſes, which ſtrictly forbids the eating of unclean things was read in the ſynagogues every Sabbath-Day, the *Holy Ghoſt*, nor the *Apoſtles*, did not incline to lay on the new converts amongſt the Gentiles any other burthen, but the abſtaining from meats offered to idols, from blood, things ſtrangled, and from fornication.

But we muſt not ſuppoſe, that either the *Holy Ghoſt*, or the *Apoſtles*, gave liberty to commit murder, theft, adultery, and other atrocious crimes, becauſe they did not ſee fit to lay any other burthen upon the Gentiles, but the four things already

ready mentioned; for no other part of the Mofaical law was abolifhed by the difpenfation of the
Gofpel, but the ceremonial, which ftood only in
meats and drinks, and divers wafhings, and carnal ordinances, which impofed upon the Jews,
until the time of the reformation, (vid. Heb.
ix. 10.) until the New Covenant, or Difpenfation
of the Gofpel fhould be eftablifhed, the laws put
in the minds, and written in the hearts of believers. Vid. Heb. viii. 10. fo that the moral part
of the law of Mofes remains in full force to this
time, and ought to be obferved by all nations;
for it correfponds exactly with the principles and
doctrines of the Chriftian religion. Does the
Gofpel forbid murder? Yes, and fo does this
law. Does the Gofpel forbid theft? Yes, and fo
does this law alfo; fo that they both correfpond
in pointing out the principles of morality. As to
the meats, drinks, wafhings, and carnal ordinances, which belonged to the Old Covenant;
they confifted in thofe bulls, goats, and other animals, that were offered as a facrifice under the
Mofaical law, and the drinks and purifications
ufed in thofe times.

The eating of fwine's flefh is a practice that
was undoubtedly derived from the Pagans, and
took its rife before the Mofaical law was given;
and this practice has been handed down to us by
tradition; for as our fathers did fo do we; and

Q q 3   becaufe

becaufe it is cuftomary we continue the practice; for,

Cuftom is a living law, whofe fway
Men more than all the written laws obey.

Had our teachers taught us when we were young, that fwine's flefh is unwholefome and unclean, and that it is a tranfgreffion of the law of God to eat, or even to touch it; we fhould have efteemed our practice to be a great fin.

But though my doctrine may fuit the Jews and other nations who obferve the laws of the Lord, yet I do not expect it will pleafe all the raifers and venders of fwine, nor all the lovers of pork; and, perhaps, fome of them, may burn my book, becaufe I have laid down thefe principles; but by the fame rule they may burn their Bibles, for the very fame doctrine is mentioned there that I hold up, and it proceeded from the *Almighty himfelf.*

Some of the favage Nations eat human flefh; and if I fhould go and tell them that it is unwholefome and illegal, it is probable they would not believe me, and that I fhould make myfelf very unpopular amongft them, by preaching fuch a doctrine. The fame may be faid of the Turks; fhould I go amongft them and preach againft the eating of camel's flefh.

But why do not the Chriftians eat human flefh like the Savages?—Why, becaufe it is not the cuftom.—

tom.—Why do they not eat camel's flesh like the Turks?—Why because it is not the fashion?—Why do they not eat horses, dogs, cats, rats, and mice? Why because they have not been brought up to it?—Why do they not wear a cap of cow-dung, soot and grease, and choose to live upon the entrails of animals, instead of their flesh, like the Hottentots?—Why because they have not been accustomed to it—But why do they eat swine's flesh when it is forbidden by the law of Moses, and found to be unwholesome by the Physicians?—Why because they have imbibed the practice from their cradles.

But perhaps some may say, that the people would starve, if there were no swine.

I answer, that the expence of raising swine is very great; and that if the clean things which they eat, were to be given to the cattle and sheep, it would do more good, more meat would be raised, and with less expence: it would be more wholesome, and better for the community; and this is not only my opinion, but the opinion of many of the American farmers. But some have pretended, that all unclean animals are cleansed under the Gospel, because Christ said, "not that which goeth into the mouth, but that which cometh out defileth the man." But the question is, what the man was that Christ meant? Divines have frequently mentioned an inward and an outward man in America; hence they have prayed, just before they were about to deliver a sermon, "that

Qq 4 "they

" they might be ftrengthened both in the inward
" and in the outward man."* Now if Chrift meant
that the outward man could not be defiled by
things that goeth into the mouth, then of courfe
we may eat all kinds of filth and poifonous things,
without being defiled ; but our fenfes tell us better, for we know that if we fhould voluntarily eat
fuch things, they will defile our bodies, and foon
put an end to our exiftence; and that we fhould
be guilty of felf-murder by fo doing. But it is
evident that Chrift did not mean the prefent
earthly tabernacle, or outward man ; but the inward man, for when he came to tell what it was
that defiled the man, he had alluded to; he faid ;
" But thofe things which proceed out of the
" mouth, come forth from the heart, &c. That out
" of the heart proceed evil *thoughts, murders, adul-*
" *teries, fornications, thefts, falfe witnefs, and blaf-*
" *phemies.*" Vid. Matt. xv. 10, 11.—19, 20.

That thofe were the things which defiled the
man. But if he had meant that the poifonous natures of unclean animals were changed, he would
undoubtedly have told his difciples; and Peter
would not have thought that fome of thofe animals which he faw in his vifion were unclean.

But I have another objection to anfwer, before
I quit the field, which is, that all unclean animals
have been cleanfed and made fit for human food,
according to the direction of the Apoftle Paul
given to Timothy. The words run thus : " Now
" the fpirit fpeaketh expreffly, that in the latter

* Eph. iii. 16.

" times fome fhall depart from the faith, giving
" heed to feducing fpirits, and doctrines of devils.
" Speaking lies in hyprocrify, having their confci-
" ence feared with a hot iron ; forbidding to marry,
" and commanding to abftain from meats, which
" God hath created to be received with thankfgiv-
" ing of them which believe and know the truth.
" For every creature of God is good, and nothing
" to be refufed, if it be received with thankfgiv-
" ing : For it is fanctified by the word of God and
" prayer." Vid. 1. Tim. iv. 1, 2, 3, 4, 5.

Now the queftion. is, what were thofe meats
which God had created to be received with thankfgiving? were they only fome of the flefh of thofe
clean beafts, &c. that are mentioned in the Mofaical law? or do they include all kinds of mad-
dogs, ferpents, and other poifonous animals?
Have we any account that informs us, that the
Apoftle ever eat any fwine's flefh, mad-dogs, or
ferpents? or that he ever received any fuch animal
food with thankfgiving, or that it was ever fanctified to him by the word of God and prayer? If
all thofe poifonous things were included, why did
he not tell us plainly that they had been unclean
under the law of Mofes, but were changed under
the Gofpel, and that himfelf and his converts made
ufe of fwine, ferpents and toads in their diet?—
At another time he faid, " For I have not fhun-
" ned to declare unto you all the counfel of God."
Vid. Acts, xx. 27. Now if any fuch thing had

taken

taken place at the changing of the natures of poisonous animals, or if that had been the counsel of
God, it seems that the Apostle knew nothing of it,
or if he did, he uttered a falshood by saying, he
had declared all the counsel of God, when he had
kept a matter of such great importance behind the
curtain, without revealing it to the world.

But it is said, that every creature of God is
good, and nothing to be refused, if it be received
with thankfgiving, for it is sanctified by the word
of God and prayer.

These creatures of God unless we explain the
Scripture in a spiritual sense cannot, in my opinion,
be any thing but those made and chosen for the food
of the human race, clean animals that he had
which are made holy by those who use them with
moderation, and receive them with thankfgiving ;
and though every thing is good in itself, as a part
of the creation, yet we cannot suppose that every
thing is fit to be eaten. It is said, that when the
Almighty viewed every thing that he had made,
behold *it was very good.* Vid. Gen. i. 31. and although Adam and Eve were placed in a pleasant
garden, yet there was a *forbidden fruit* in it ; and
we find that there is still a *forbidden fruit* to the
posterity of Adam, which consists in those unclean
birds, beasts and fishes, that are poison to our
bodies, and destructive to our constitutions. A
catalogue of these animals may be seen in the
eleventh chapter of Leviticus.

Having

Having thus explained the words of the Apostle in a literal sense; let us in the next place attempt to do it in one that is spiritual. Were not those *meats* God had created to be received with thanksgiving, by them which believed and knew the truth, *spiritual meats?* Christ told the Jews to labour not for the meat which perisheth, but for that *meat* which endureth for ever. Vid. John vi. 27. And the apostle Paul in his Epistle to the Corinthians, speaking of the Israelites passing through the sea, mentions a *spiritual meat*, saying, " And " did all eat the same *spiritual meat*." Vid. 1. Cor. x. 3. Now this *spiritual meat* is nothing but the *bread* of *life* that cometh down from Heaven, and giveth life to the world. Vid. John vi. 50. It is the *hidden manna*, the *tree of life*, and the inward and *spiritual supper of the Lord*. Vid. Rev. ii. 7— 17. Chap. iii. 20. Now the Israelites that passed through the sea did all eat of this *heavenly meat*, and so did those Christian converts to whom the Apostle wrote his epistles. Hence all true believers, or all holy and upright persons, are partakers of this *heavenly food*. It is the *Holy Ghost* descending from Heaven and dwelling in the righteous. Hence they become the *sons of God*. Vid. Rom. viii. 14. And their *bodies* are the *temples* of the *Holy Ghost*. 1. Cor. vi. 19. Which they are commanded not to *defile*. 1 Cor. iii. 17. Hence also the Almighty *dwells* in his *saints*, *walks* in *them*, and *strengthens* and *enables them* both to *will* and to

do

do of his own good *pleasure:* they who are thus made to partake of this spiritual meat, do taste of the heavenly gift, are made partakers of the *Holy Ghost*, have tasted the good word of God, and the *powers* of the *world to come.* Vid. Heb. vi. 4, 5. They are thereby *married*, or *joined* to the *Lord*; and being thus *joined* unto him, become *one spirit.* Vid. 1 Cor. vi. 17.

The ministry of the Apostles under the dispensation of the Gospel, was *spiritual*, and not carnal; hence it was said, that God had made them able ministers of the New Testament; not of the letter but of the *spirit.* Vid. 2 Cor. iii. 6. This ministry did not consist in meats, and drinks, and divers washings, and carnal ordinances, like the ministry of the types and shadows under the Mosaical law : but in the glorious ministration of the spirit. Vid. 2 Cor. iii. 8.

Hence it appears that the *meat* that the Apostle mentioned to his son Timothy, was not carnal but *spiritual.* Hence also it could not be the flesh of bulls, goats, calves, lambs or swine; but that *spiritual meat* which giveth *life* to the world, of which all good people are made partakers.

So that the *marriage* alluded to might be *spiritual*; and also the *meats*, which God had created to be received with thanksgiving by them which believed, &c. and every creature of God that was thus married, and fed by this spiritual meat was good; being sanctifyed by the *word of God* (Vid. John,
i. 1.

i. 1.) and prayer, and therefore ought not to be refufed, or denied an admiffion into the outward and vifible church.

That this miniftry was fpiritual, is evident by the directions that Paul gave Timothy, in the 14th verfe of the fame chapter. "Neglect not "the gift that is in thee," which was a fpiritual gift.

Thus have I endeavoured to explain this text in a fpiritual fenfe, which wholly excludes animal food, or any purgation of the brute creation.

Let us obferve, that if we take the text in a literal fenfe, the moft filthy and poifonous animals are good, and are not be refufed in our diet, becaufe they may be fanctified by the *word of God* and *prayer*. How abfurd and ridiculous muft fuch a way of reafoning be? Can all the Clergy, and all the good men in the world, by praying over the carcafe of a mad dog that is full of the moft deadly poifon, change its nature, and make it a clean beaft?—No, no fuch thing can be expected.

The things that I attempt to hold up and plead for are,

1. That if fwine, and fome other animals, were unclean under the Mofaical law, they continue to be fo under the Gofpel; that their natures have not been changed, and therefore they muft ftill be unwholefome to the human race.

2. That

2. That the flesh of all animals fed upon filthy and poisonous things, is not fit to be eaten.

3. That as the swine naturally feed upon such things, they always were, and still continue to be unclean.

4. That the *Great Governor* of the *Universe,* knowing they were unclean and unwholesome, was pleased, in his infinite wisdom to make it known to the sons of men, and to forbid their eating or touching their flesh.

5. That that law still remains in force, and ought to be observed by all nations.

6. That the practice of eating swine's flesh commenced in Christendom in the times of Paganism, and has been handed down to the present generation by custom and tradition.

7. That it is our duty to abstain from every thing that may defile our bodies, or prejudice our health and constitutions.

8. That if we live altogether, or in part upon swine's flesh, the whole of our bodies, or a part, will be swine, though in a different form, and perhaps have a swinish temper and disposition.

9. That the Jews, Persians, Abyssinians, and habitants of the empire of the Great Mogul, do their duty in obeying the commandment of the Lord, in abstaining from those unclean things mentioned in the law of Moses.

10. That the learned and ingenious physicians of the kingdom of Great-Britain ought to be applauded

plauded for their obfervations upon the operation of fwine's flefh in the human body; and for making known to the world, that it is by no *means a wholefome diet.*

11. That it is our duty to make further obfervations, and to expunge out of our diet, and out of the practice of phyfic, every thing that hath already been, or may hereafter be, found prejudicial to our conftitutions.

12. That we ought not to eat any thing offered to idols, nor any animal that dies of itfelf, nor things ftrangled, nor any blood, or unclean thing, and to remember, that he that faid, " Thou " fhalt not kill," faid alfo, concerning the eating of fwine's flefh, " *Of their flefh ye fhall not eat, and their carcafe fhall ye not touch.*" Levit. xi. 8, 44.— Ifai. lxv. 4.

Although I have raifed the argument to its prefent heighth, perhaps fome may fay, that fwine's flefh is wholefome, and that it is lawful to eat it, though it is forbidden in the law of the Lord, becaufe they have been accuftomed to it, and it agrees with their conftitutions.

I anfwer, that though it may feem to agree with a few conftitutions for a time, yet it may produce ill effects afterwards. The favages may fay, that human flefh agrees with them, and yet it may be very prejudicial to their health, operate in an invifible manner, like flow poifon, and prove fatal at laft.

Thofe

Thofe who have perverted the Scriptures, by pretending that the natures of unclean animals were changed, and that they were cleared of their poifon under the difpenfation of the Gofpel, muft prove, before they can make me believe it, that Chrift and his difciples eat fwine's flefh, mad dogs, toads, and ferpents. But as no fuch thing is mentioned in the New Teftament, we muft conclude, that they fubfifted upon a wholefome diet, walked honeftly, and lived peaceably, without fetting any bad example for their followers to practife.

But what inhuman, difgraceful, and abominable conduct has there been in the different centuries that have rolled off fince Chrift was upon earth, amongft the inhabitants of Chriftendom, who have pretended to be his difciples. How have they violated the laws, by following the example of the heathen, in defiling themfelves with unclean things? How have they wrangled, quarelled, and murdered one another; burnt great cities, and laid countries wafte? Now had they followed the example of the Prince of Peace, all thofe murders and devaftations would have been avoided.

I have often thought, whether an improper regimen does not have an effect upon the tempers and difpofitions of men. Who knows but that many have had fwinifh tempers and difpofitions, by reafon of their living upon fwine's flefh.

Brandy and gunpowder, or rum and gunpowder, drank juft before men rufh into battle,

will

will make them fear no danger; and the saliva of mad animals will produce madness; and why may not the flesh of those that are naturally unruly, filthy, and unclean, affect our constitutions, tempers, and dispositions, in a greater or lesser degree? Surely, we ought not to defile ourselves with such abominable things, but to make a difference between those' animals that may be eaten and those that may not, for the former are clean, but the latter are *vice versa*, (vid. Levit. xi. 44, 47.) this will tend to preserve our health and happiness, a thing is required of us by HIM, whose *laws* and *commands* are *holy*, *just*, and *good*. Vid. Rom. vii. 12.

R r   CHAP.

C H A P. LX.

*Sundry Obfervations of the Multiplicity and Longe-
vity of Animals. Cautions concerning unruly Creatures.*

IN the preceding Chapter I have treated upon
a fubject that may pleafe fome people and dif-
pleafe others. For the lovers of fwine's flefh,
and thofe who get money by the raifing and felling
of it, would not be willing to forfake a thing
they fo much admire, even if there was a law
made againft it. However, as it is the duty of
every perfon to difclofe to the Public, whatever
appears to be prejudicial to the community, I
hope I fhall be excufed for the method I have
taken. They that lay down a doctrine according
to the *law* of the *Lord*, and the principles of natural philofophy, have a much better foundation
to work upon than thofe who have nothing but
tradition, and the example of the Heathen. Vid.
Ifai. lxv. 4.

We laugh at other nations on account of fome
of their ill cuftoms and manners, and it is probable they laugh at us for fome of ours. But I
hope there may be a general reformation in procefs of time, that as the knowledge of philofophy

advances,

advances, every thing that is prejudicial to our health and happinefs will be removed out of the way.

Thofe who may be pleafed to forfake the practice of raifing fwine, may raife cattle and fheep with lefs trouble and expence, have more meat, and that which is much more healthy and fuitable for their conftitutions.

Thefe things being premifed, I fhall, in the next place, fay fomething concerning the multiplication and longevity of animals.

*

Multiplication.

			Young brought at once.
Mare goes with young	11 months,	from 1 to 2
Cow	9 ditto,	1 — 3
Ewe	20 weeks,	1 — 3
Goat	20 ditto,	1 — 3
Sow	16 ditto,	4 - 16
Bitch	9 ditto,	3 — 4
Cat	9 ditto,	2 — 4
Fox	9 ditto,	1 — 4
Elephant	3 years,	0 — 1
Bear	40 days,	1 — 2

The

The Longevity, &c.

		Years.
Horfe has been known to live		40
Ox		16
Bull		16
Cow		16
Sheep		10
Goat		10
Swine		20
Dog		20
Cat		10
Fox		15
Camel		100
Dromedary		60
Elephant		200

Fowls.

Swan		300
Goofe		300
Dunghill cock		10
Pelican		60

But a few of thefe animals arrive to the age I have mentioned. The age of the goofe is doubtful.

Cattle that are apt to pufh with their horns, or run at people, ought to be kept in clofe confinement, or killed immediately. I have been knocked down twice by fuch kinds of mad animals. And I was acquainted with a gentleman who was killed by a ram that was wont to pufh with his horns.

CHAP.

CHAP. LXI.

*Obſervations on the Freedom of Speech, and the Liberty
of the Preſs.*

I HAVE already mentioned, page 123, " That
the *freedom* of *ſpeech*, and the *liberty* of the *preſs*,
are the natural rights of every man, providing he
doth not *injure himſelf* nor *others* by his *converſation*
or *publications*." But people have ſometimes been
debarred from the *liberty* of theſe *natural rights* by
tyrants and *rebels*. The innocent have been confined in priſons, upon falſe accuſations, and not
allowed the privilege of defending themſelves,
either by the freedom of ſpeech, or the liberty of
the preſs, whilſt to deſtroy their reputation,
ſlander and defamation has been ſpread abroad by
lying tongues, licentious preſſes, and pulpit ora-
tory.

When rebels can obtain the command of theſe
powerful engines, viz. the lying tongue, licentious preſs, and the clergy, ſedition may be eaſily
ſown, treaſon and rebellion excited, the government ſubverted, and anarchy and confuſion let

looſe

loofe, to the deftruction of the lives, *liberty* and *happinefs* of the people. And if any peaceable and quiet perfon refufes for confcience fake, to follow the multitude to do evil; or if he endeavours to convince the mifguided of their error, or if he even lies ftill, and attempts to be *neuter,* and the flandering tongue is let loofe againft him, he muft be dragged off to *prifon,* confined in a *dungeon,* and not allowed the *liberty* of *fpeaking, writing,* or *printing* any thing in his own *defence.*

But although the freedom of fpeech, and the liberty of the prefs, fhould not be denied to any perfon, yet thefe liberties ought not to be converted to licentious practices, for they tend to deftroy the public tranquillity and make mankind unhappy.

I fhall conclude this chapter with the following lines :

THE FREEDOM OF THE PRESS.

Though men and women have a *right,*
   With pleafure and with eafe,
To *fpeak* and *print* as they *delight,*
   Whenever they may pleafe.

Yet, they've no *right* for to expand,
   (Contention to encreafe,)
Sedition through the *peaceful land,*
   To interrupt the *peace.*

Hence

Hence the vile wretch, that wou'd *suppress*,
  The *grand important thing*,
The *freedom* of the *printing-press*,
  Moſt *ſurely* ought to *ſwing*.

And *he* that doth *ſedition ſow*,
  With his *tongue*, or the *preſs*,
Unto the *gallows* ought to *go*,
  For ſuch *baſe wickedneſs* :

Becauſe it may make *wars ariſe*,
  Deſtruction too *expand* :
The *people looſe* their *precious lives*,
  And *deſolate* the *land*.

Let *all* therefore who do *regard*,
  Their *good* the world around :
Stand conſtantly upon their *guard*,
  That *peace* may ſtill *abound*.

Suppreſs *ſedition*, *wrath*, and *ſtrife*,
  Make *wickedneſs decreaſe*,
And truly live a pious life,
  In harmony and peaee.

That when they *die* they may *ariſe*,
  Where *peaceful ones* are *bleſt*,
In *realms of joy* above the *ſkies*,
  With *happineſs* and *reſt*.   .

Compoſed at London, May 29, 1791.

CHAP.

CHAP. LXII.

Magnetical Communications.

IT was not my defign to have faid any more upon *Animal Magnetifm* in the *American Oracle,* inafmuch as I have already treated of it in the 23d chapter; where, after a deep contemplation on the fubject, I attempted to render a *philofophical reafon* for the *wonderful operations* of the *magnetical effluvia* upon the *human frame*: But as I have received further information; and have an inclination to promote the *progrefs of fcience,* by difclofing every thing that may induce mankind to make further difcoveries and improvements in things that may be beneficial to the human race; I fhall juft mention in this chapter, fome of the benefits which have already refulted from magnetical operations, as communicated to me, by Mr. *John Cue,* of the City of London, a very *worthy gentleman,* who, not for worldly gain, but for the fake of *relieving* the *diftreffed,* and making *difcoveries* and *improvements* in the fcience, has been a conftant *practitioner* in *Animal Magnetifm,* ever fince

fince the 3d of November, 1789; and although, he has often had more than one hundred patients in a day, and has wrought many *cures*, yet he has not charged one *farthing* for his *fervices*; and I underftand that he intends to *practife gratis* for the future; from hence we may conclude, that he has no inclination to impofe upon the public, either by continuing the practice of the fcience, or by any account he has communicated concerning the benefit of his magnetical operations.

I have received a great number of *certificates*, which give an account of fome of the remarkable *cures* which this gentleman has wrought by this new *remedy*; but, for the want of room, I fhall mention but a few of them, which are as follows, viz.

I, *Jane Caftle*, of No. 14, Crifpin-ftreet, Spital-fields, do declare, that I have been afflicted with a fevere rheumatifm in the whole habit, but efpecially in my head, ftomach, arms, hands, loins, fide, legs and feet, attended with fuch excrutiating pains, as led me to apprehend every paroxifm would terminate in my death; befides which I had a continual fwimming in my head, and a great fwelling in my legs. In this unhappy ftate I continued for the fpace of 25 years, though under the care of feveral eminent phyficians, but without fuccefs. On my firft application to the faculty, they ordered me an iffue in each leg but without the leaft relief. I was alfo fubject to fuch

cold

cold fenfations, that I could never go to reft without hot flat irons bound in flannels being applied
to my ftomach, when at the fame time my feet
were by an intermitting fever, in fuch violent heat
as to oblige me always to lay them out of bed.
My difordered ftate of body continued to grow
worfe, fo that at laft I was afflicted with epileptic
fits.   In this unhappy fituation I applied to Mr.
Cue, to be treated by the remedy commonly called *Animal Magnetifm*; when, to my great *furprize*,
I had no fooner fat down, than my whole frame
was put into the moft violent *conflict* and *perturba-
tion*:   I began to lofe my recollection, and imagined myfelf in bed, and felt as it were the flannels with the hot irons dropping from me : at the
fame time I had a fenfation of fomething like an
electric fhock, piercing me *through* and *through*, and
from that time my fits left me, with all my other
diforders.   My iffues dried up, although I ufed
every method to keep them open, yet received
no *injury* therefrom ; and though I was 70 years of
age, when I applied to Mr. *Cue*, yet *thanks* be to
God, I obtained a perfect *cure*, and now enjoy a
good ftate of health, though my firft application
to him was in January 1789.

May 3, 1791.   JANE CASTLE.

John Dorking, of Weftham, in Effex, breeches-
maker, affirms, that he was afflicted with a fevere
rheumatifm in the whole habit, but efpecially of
the right arm and head, for the fpace of eight
years :

years; during which time, a great variety of medicines were tried without effect—till fortunately hearing of the *cures* performed by Mr. *Cue*, he applied to that *gentleman*, who generously undertook, and in a short time *restored* me to the use of my *arm*, removed the *pain* and *giddiness* of my *head*, and I am at this time in perfect health. Witness my hand, this 28th of July, 1790.

JOHN DORKING.

Witness Thomas Marsh, M. D. of Highworth.

I, *Mary Gill*, daughter to Mr. Richard Gill, shoe-maker, No. 9, Great East-Cheap, aged 25, have been unhappily afflicted with the disorder called the epilepsy, or falling sickness, from the time, I was 13 years of age; and at the age of 16, I grew much worse, my fits came on every fortnight, and often continued eleven hours. But, by the blessing of God, to all human appearance, I have met with a complete cure, by the treatment called *Animal Magnetism*, without any other *remedy* whatsoever, having been recommended to Mr. *Cue*, for that purpose, and now am to be heard of at Messrs. Simpson's and Robinson's, Hoxton,

MARY GILL.

N. B. For the above disorder I was a patient in Guy's-hospital, but discharged as incurable, March 19, 1791.

I was present and saw the wonderful operations of the magnetical effluvia upon this patient; when

when she went in a crisis, she commonly sprang up from her chair, took hold of something, and afterwards had much such agitations and convulsive motions as described, page 208.

I shall conclude this chapter by just mentioning a few of the other remarkable cures performed by Mr. *Cue's* magnetical operations, without extracting the whole of the certificates; but it appears that the greatest part of his patients had been given over as incurable by the physicians.

Mrs Lucius Philips, No. 5, Paddington-green, after labouring under a grievous nervous complaint for near six years, received a *perfect cure*, only by one *magnetical operation*.

Mrs. Mary Stears, having been afflicted eleven years with the sick head ach, vomitings, numbness, pain, and hardness in her side, swelling in her legs, cold sensations, &c. received a complete cure by Animal Magnetism; and for a sprain in her knee received afterwards, was *cured* by the same *remedy*.

Mrs. Charlotte Rotelage, No. 20, Providence-row, after having the sick head ache, and a pain in her side for two years, received a perfect *cure*, by the *magnetical effluvia*.

A child, aged five years, belonging to Mrs. Elizabeth Cleveland, Paddington-green, after being afflicted with blindness seven months was cured in three weeks, by being treated twice in a week.

A child

A child aged three years, belonging to Mrs. Martha Allen, No. 9, Motley-court, Holywell Mount, after being treated twice, voided 20 knots of worms, and was reſtored to health.

A boy who had a decline, belongingto Mr. Travers Arundell, Keat-ſtreet, Spital-fields, was completely cured.

Mrs. Mary Swan, No. 23, St. John's-ſquare, Clerkenwell, having been deaf eleven years, was cured of the diſorder.

Mrs. Mary Bay, No. 10, Slaughter-ſtreet, Bethnal-Green, having been afflicted five years with a fever, and a pain in her ſide, was reſtored to perfect health.

Mrs. Margaret Tyſon Surry, ſide of Blackfriar's-road, after labouring under a rheumatic complaint, attended with great pain for three years, was reſtored to *health*.

A child aged 13 months, belonging to Mr. John Johnſon, Motley-court, Holywell-Mount; was *cured* of an inflammation in the ſtomach and bowels, attended with a hard ſwelling and convulſions.

Mrs. Mercy Benſon, having been afflicted five years, with epileptic fits, attended with a delirium, was reſtored to her health and ſenſes.

Mrs. Jane Allen, No. 146, White Croſs-ſtreet, was *cured* of various diſorders of 12 years ſtanding, occaſioned by her drinking cold water, when ſhe was very hot.

Mr.

Mr. Steven Holden, No. 167, White-Crofs-ftreet, having been afflicted ten years with lame-nefs, a lofs of appetite, memory and eye-fight, oc-cafioned by lying in a damp bed, was reftored to *perfect health.*

Mrs. Elizabeth Hathaway, Houndfditch, was afflicted about three years with a violent pain in her face, caufed by a cold, which terminated in a locked jaw, and rendered her fituation fo dread-ful, that fhe almoft perifhed with hunger; but to her unfpeakable furprife and joy, was fo far reliev-ed in 20 minutes, after Mr. *Cue* began to treat her, that fhe could take a table fpoon into her mouth, and at laft received a perfect *cure.*

Befides thefe remarkable cures, the certificates mention others performed on patients, fome of which were afflicted with blindnefs, fome with deafnefs, lofs of fpeech, fevers, violent pains, lame-nefs, ulcers, flatulencies, palpitation of the heart, obftructions, nervous, bilious, hyfterical, fcrophu-lous and afthmatical complaints. Such have al-ready been the wonderful operations and good effects of the magnetical effluvia in the cure of diftempers. Let the fcience therefore be ftill cultivated and improved in the beft manner.

CHAP.

CHAP. LXIII.

Modern Discoveries, Inventions, and Opinions.

ELECTRICITY, by *Mr. Ottoguericke, Mr. Cuneus*, Dr. *Franklin*, and Dr. *Priestly.*

Mr. Harrison's time-piece, in England,

Hadley's Quadrant, by an American.

Mr. *Rittenhouse's* Orrery, at Philadelphia.

Dr. Herschel's Astronomical Discoveries, viz. Georgium Sidus, with its two Satellites. Two moons of Saturn, the rotation of his ring, and spots in his body. Also the mountains in our moon, which are two miles high according to his *telescope* which magnifies 6500 times.

Air Balloons invented in France.

Dr. Priestly's Discoveries in the qualities of the air—in England.

The Hon. Baron Swedenborg's Theology.— Great-Britain.

The strange mode of worship adopted by the *Shaking Quakers,* in America.

A remarkable *Iron Bridge,* built over the river Severn, at Colebrooke-Dale, in the County of Salop, near Wales, in England : It contains about

500

500 tons of iron. The arch is 100 feet within, and 45 above the water the infide, but 55 the outfide.

Animal Magnetifm.

The American Conftitution, framed by the Federal Convention, at Philadelphia.

The Albion Grift-mills, with 20 pair of ftones, carried by a fteam of fire, near Black Friar's-bridge, London. They have lately been burnt.

The *Radix Ginfeng*, in Canada, Vermont, and Pennfylvania.

The Author's *Hypothefis* upon the caufe of the *Aurora Borealis*, at Vermont.

Many iflands, &c. difcovered in the Southern Hemifphere, and other parts of the world, by *Capt. Cook*, and other Navigators.

Some remarkable *Springs*, and *Pits of Coal*, difcovered in America.

A *Tide-table* invented by the *Author*, for the Sea Ports of the North American Continent.

The Conftitution of France, framed by the National Affembly.

Needlefs compofitions expunged out of the London and Edinburgh Pharmacopœias.

The Great Conftitution of *Liberty* framed by the *Author*, at London.

Mr. Pope's remarkable *Orrery*, and alfo his Hypothefis upon the caufe of the *Gravitation* of *Bodies*.

Mr. Walker's, Tranfparent Orrery. Weftminfter, London.

A new

A new *washing-mill*, London.

A curious iron bridge, to be placed over the Schuylkil, near Philadelphia, invented by *Mr. Thomas Paine*, in England.

A new *carriage*, with eight wheels, drawn by three horses, that will carry 14 people, he inside, Westminster, London.

The *Author's Hypothesis*, upon the cause of the wonderful *operation* of the *Magnetical Effluvia* in the *human frame*, &c.   Let us endeavour to make further discoveries.

CHAP.

C H A P. LXIV.

How to preserve our Health when it is present and Re-
store it when it is absent, and make ourselves happy
in this World, and the next.

I COME now to the grand and important things,
which I have proposed, viz. How to preserve our health when it is present, and restore it
when it is absent, and also how to make ourselves
happy in this world, and the next.

I shall therefore recommend 1. A good house,
situated in an agreeable neighbourhood, where
there is a wholesome air, and good water.

2. Good cloathing, and a suitable diet, free from
all kinds of filthy and poisonous things.

3. Industry, gentle exercise, and temperance.

4. When our health is impaired let us employ
the best physicians, and take the best remedies.

5. A contentment with the allotments of Providence, through all the various changing scenes
of life.

6. A strict observation of the *things* contained
in the *American Oracle,* and especially those mentioned

tioned in the *Epiſtle* of the *Author* to all *People*, *Nations* and *Languages*.

Finally, let us worſhip the *Creator*, live *peaceably*, and walk *honeſtly*, for it comprehends all the duties that are required of rational creatures. *Farewell.*

.

F I N I S.

I N D E X.

A.

Animals,

Coaches

Day,

Hail

Island

Philosophers

Servants

Streets

Tumours